FAUSTUS

The Tales of
Dr. Faustus, Sorcerer

The Tales of
Dr. Faustus, Sorcerer

Including

The Tragical History of Dr. Faustus
by
Christopher Marlowe

And

Faust
by
Johann Wolfgang von Goethe

And

The Faust Book
the
Wolfenbüttel Manuscript

The Tragical History of Dr. Faustus

Christopher Marlowe

The Tragical History of
Dr. Faustus

For Dr. Faustus (1480-1510)

The name 'Faust' has become deeply rooted in European mythology as the name of a man who sold his soul to the devil in return for earthly power and material wealth. The Faust legend has been embellished upon and retold in many formats but its origin appears to be centered around a man who called himself Dr. Johann Faust, who lived in Heidelberg during the early sixteenth century.

DRAMATIS PERSONAE

Chorus
Faustus
Wagner
Good Angel
Evil Angel
Valdes
Cornelius
First Scholar
Second Scholar
Mephistophilis
Robin, a Clown
Lucifer
Beelzebub
Sins
Pride
Covetousness
Wrath
Gluttony
Envy
Sloth

Lechery
The Pope
The Cardinal of Lorraine
a Friar
Ralph, a clown
a Vintner
The Emperor
a Knight
Alexander
his Paramour
a Horse-courser
The Duke of Vanholt
Duchess
Third Scholar
Helen (of Greece)
an Old Man
Devils
Friars
Attendants

INTRODUCTION

Enter CHORUS

CHORUS

NOT marching now in fields of Trasimene, Where Mars did mate [1] the Carthaginians; Nor sporting in the dalliance of love, In courts of kings where state is overturned'd; Nor in the pomp of proud audacious deeds, Intends our Muse to vaunt his heavenly verse: Only this, gentlemen,—we must perform The form of Faustus' fortunes, good or bad. To patient judgments we appeal our plaud, [2]And speak for Faustus in his infancy. Now is he born, his parents base of stock, In Germany, within a town call'd Rhodes;[3] Of riper years to Wittenberg he went, Whereas his kinsmen chiefly brought him up. So soon he profits in divinity, The fruitful plot of scholarism grac'd, [4]That shortly he was grac'd with doctor's name, Excelling all those sweet delight disputes In heavenly matters of theology; Till swollen with cunning, [5]of a self-conceit, His waxen wings[6] did mount above his reach, And, melting, Heavens conspir'd his overthrow; For, falling to a devilish exercise, And glutted [now] with learning's golden gifts, He surfeits upon cursed necromancy. Nothing so sweet as magic is to him, Which he prefers before his chiefest bliss. And this the man that in his study sits! [Exit.]

---

[1] Confound. But Hannibal was victorious at Lake Trasimenus, B. C. 217.

[2] For applause.

[3] Roda, in the Duchy of Saxe-Altenburg, near Jena.

[4] The garden of scholarship being adorned by him.

[5] Knowledge.

[6] An allusion to the myth of Icarus, who flew too near the sun.

SCENE I

FAUSTUS [discovered] in his Study

FAUSTUS

Settle my studies, Faustus, and begin To sound the depth of that thou wilt profess; [7]Having commenc'd, be a divine in show, Yet level [8]and at the end of every art, And live and die in Aristotle's works. Sweet Analytics, [9]'tis thou hast ravish'd me, Bene disserere est finis logices. [10]Is to dispute well logic's chiefest end? Affords this art no greater miracle? Then read no more, thou hast attain'd the end; A greater subject fitteth Faustus' wit. Bid [Greek][11] farewell; Galen come, Seeing Ubi desinit Philosophus ibi incipit Medicus; [12]Be a physician, Faustus, heap up gold, And be eternis'd for some wondrous cure. Summum bonum medicinæ sanitas, [13]"The end of physic is our body's health" Why, Faustus, hast thou not attain'd that end! Is not thy common talk sound Aphorisms? [14]Are not thy bills [15] hung up as monuments, Whereby whole cities have escap'd the plague, And thousand desperate maladies been eas'd? Yet art thou still but Faustus and a man. Couldst thou make men to live eternally, Or, being dead, raise them to life again, Then this profession were to be esteem'd. Physic, farewell.—Where is Justinian? [Reads.] Si una eademque res legatur duobus, alter rem, alter valorem rei, &c. [16]A pretty case of paltry legacies! [Reads.] Ex hæreditare filium non potest pater nisi, &c. [17]Such is the subject of the Institute [18]And universal Body of the Law. [19]His [20] study fits a mercenary drudge, Who aims at nothing but external trash; Too servile and illiberal for me. When all is done, divinity is best; Jerome's Bible,[21] Faustus, view it well.[Reads.] Stipendium peccati mors est. Ha! Stipendium, &c. "The reward of sin is death." That's hard. [Reads.] Si peccasse negamus fallimur et nulla est in nobis veritas. "If we say that we have no sin we deceive ourselves,

---

[7] Teach publicly.

[8] Aim.

[9] Logic.

[10] "To argue well is the end of logic."

[11] This is Mr. Bullen's emendation of QI., Oncaymæon, a corruption of the Aristotelian phrase for "being and not being."

[12] "Where the philosopher leaves off, there the physician begins."

[13] This and the previous quotation are from Aristotle.

[14] Medical maxims.

[15] Announcements.

[16] "If one and the same thing is bequeathed to two person, one gets the thing and the other the value of the thing."

[17] "A father cannot disinherit the son except," etc.

[18] Of Justinian, under whom the Roman law was codified.

[19] QI., Church.

[20] Its.

[21] The Vulgate.

and there's no truth in us." Why then, belike we must sin and so consequently die. Ay, we must die an everlasting death. What doctrine call you this, Che sera sera, "What will be shall be?" Divinity, adieu These metaphysics of magicians And necromantic books are heavenly; Lines, circles, scenes, letters, and characters, Ay, these are those that Faustus most desires. O what a world of profit and delight, Of power, of honour, of omnipotence Is promised to the studious artisan! All things that move between the quiet poles Shall be at my command. Emperor and kings Are but obeyed in their several provinces, Nor can they raise the wind or rend the clouds; But his dominion that exceeds[22] in this Stretcheth as far as doth the mind of man. A sound magician is a mighty god

Here, Faustus, try thy [23] brains to gain a deity. Wagner!

Enter WAGNER

Commend me to my dearest friends, The German Valdes and Cornelius; Request them earnestly to visit me.

WAGNER
I will, sir. Exit.

FAUSTUS
Their conference will be a greater help to me Than all my labours, plod I ne'er so fast.

Enter GOOD ANGEL and EVIL ANGEL

GOOD ANGEL
O Faustus! lay that damned book aside, And gaze not upon it lest it tempt thy soul, And heap God's heavy wrath upon thy head. Read, read the Scriptures
that is blasphemy.

EVIL ANGEL
Go forward, Faustus, in that famous art, Wherein all Nature's treasure is contain'd
Be thou on earth as Jove is in the sky, Lord and commander of these elements.
[Exeunt Angels.]

FAUSTUS

---

[22] Excels.
[23] Q3., tire my.

How am I glutted with conceit [24] of this! Shall I make spirits fetch me what I please, Resolve me of all ambiguities, Perform what desperate enterprise I will? I'll have them fly to India for gold, Ransack the ocean for orient pearl, And search all corners of the new-found world For pleasant fruits and princely delicates; I'll have them read me strange philosophy And tell the secrets of all foreign kings; I'll have them wall all Germany with brass, And make swift Rhine circle fair Wittenberg; I'll have them fill the public schools with silk, [25]Wherewith the students shall be bravely clad; I'll levy soldiers with the coin they bring, And chase the Prince of Parma from our land, [26]And reign sole king of all the provinces; Yea, stranger engines for the brunt of war Than was the fiery keel [27] at Antwerp's bridge, I'll make my servile spirits to invent.

Enter VALDES and CORNELIUS[28]

Come, German Valdes and Cornelius, And make me blest with your sage conference. Valdes, sweet Valdes, and Cornelius, Know that your words have won me at the last To practise magic and concealed arts
Yet not your words only, but mine own fantasy. That will receive no object, for my head But ruminates on necromantic skill. Philosophy is odius and obscure, Both law and physic are for petty wits; Divinity is basest of the three, Unpleasant, harsh, contemptible, and vile
'Tis magic, magic, that hath ravish'd me. Then, gentle friends, aid me in this attempt; And I that have with concise syllogisms Gravell'd the pastors of the German church, And made the flowering pride of Wittenberg Swarm to my problems, as the infernal spirits On sweet Musaeigus,[29] when he came to hell, Will be as cunning as Agrippa was, Whose shadows made all Europe honour him.

VALDES
Faustus, these books, thy wit, and our experience Shall make all nations to canònise us. As Indian Moors [30] obey their Spanish lords, So shall the subjects [31] of every element Be always serviceable to us three; Like lions shall they guard us when we please; Like Almain rutters [32]with their horsemen's staves Or Lapland giants, trotting by our sides; Sometimes like women or unwedded

---

[24] Idea.
[25] Qq., skill.
[26] The Netherlands, over which Parma re-established the Spanish dominions.
[27] A ship filled with explosives used to blow up a bridge built by Parma in 1585 at the siege of Antwerp.
[28] The famous Cornelius Agrippa. German Valdes is not known.
[29] Cf. Virgil, Æn. vi. 667; Dryden's trans. vi. 905 ff.
[30] American Indians.
[31] Q3., spirits.
[32] Troopers, Germ. Reiters.

maids, Shadowing more beauty in their airy brows Than have the white breasts of the queen of love

From Venice shall they drag huge argosies, And from America the golden fleece That yearly stuffs old Philip's treasury; If learned Faustus will be resolute.

FAUSTUS

Valdes, as resolute am I in this As thou to live; therefore object is not.

CORNELIUS

The miracles that magic will perform Will make thee vow to study nothing else. He that is grounded in astrology, Enrich'd with tongues, as well seen [33] in minerals, Hath all the principles magic doth require. Then doubt not, Faustus, but to be renown'd, And more frequented for this mystery. Than heretofore the Delphian Oracle. The spirits tell me they can dry the sea, And fetch the treasure of all foreign wrecks, Ay, all the wealth that our forefathers hid Within the massy entrails of the earth; Then tell me, Faustus, what shall we three want?

FAUSTUS

Nothing, Cornelius! O this cheers my soul! Come show me some demonstrations magical, That I may conjure in some lusty grove, And have these joys in full possession.

VALDES

Then haste thee to some solitary grove, And bear wise Bacon's [34] and Albanus' [35] works, The Hebrew Psalter and New Testament; And whatsoever else is requisite We will inform thee ere our conference cease.

CORNELIUS

Valdes, first let him know the words of art; And then, all other ceremonies learn'd, Faustus may try his cunning by himself.

VALDES

First I'll instruct thee in the rudiments, And then wilt thou be perfecter than I.

FAUSTUS

---

[33] Versed.
[34] Roger Bacon.
[35] Perhaps Pietro d'Abano, a medieval alchemist; perhaps a misprint for Albertus (Magnus), the great schoolman.

Then come and dine with me, and after meat, We'll canvass every quiddity thereof; For ere I sleep I'll try what I can do
This night I'll conjure though I die therefore. [Exeunt]

SCENE II

[Before FAUSTUS'S House]

Enter two SCHOLARS

IST SCHOLAR
I wonder what's become of Faustus that was wont to make our schools ring with sic probo?[36]

2ND SCHOLAR
That shall we know, for see here comes his boy.

Enter WAGNER

IST SCHOLAR
How now, sirrah! Where's thy master?

WAGNER
God in heaven knows!

2ND SCHOLAR
Why, dost not thou know?

WAGNER
Yes, I know. But that follows not.

IST SCHOLAR
Go to, sirrah! Leave your jesting, and tell us where he is.

WAGNER
That follows not necessary by force of argument, that you, being licentiate, should stand upon't
therefore, acknowledge your error and be attentive.

2ND SCHOLAR
Why, didst thou not say thou knew'st?

WAGNER
Have you any witness on't?

IST SCHOLAR

---

[36] "Thus I prove"—a common formula in scholastic discussions.

Yes, sirrah, I heard you.

WAGNER
Ask my fellow if I be a thief.

2ND SCHOLAR
Well, you will not tell us?

WAGNER
Yes, sir, I will tell you; yet if you were not dunces, you would never ask me such a question; for is not he corpus naturale? [37] and is not that mobile? Then wherefore should you ask me such a question? But that I am by nature phlegmatic, slow to wrath, and prone to lechery (to love, I would say), it were not for you to come within forty feet of the place of execution, although I do not doubt to see you both hang'd the next sessions. Thus having triumph'd over you, I will set my countenance like a precisian, [38] and begin to speak thus —Truly, my dear brethren, my master is within at dinner, with Valdes and Cornelius, as this wine, if it could speak, would inform your worships; and so the Lord bless you, preserve you, and keep you, my dear brethren, my dear brethren.

IST SCHOLAR
Nay, then, I fear he has fallen into that damned Art, for which they two are infamous through the world.

2ND SCHOLAR
Were he a stranger, and not allied to me, yet should I grieve for him. But come, let us go and inform the Rector, and see if he by his grave counsel can reclaim him.

IST SCHOLAR
O, but I fear me nothing can reclaim him.

2ND SCHOLAR
Yet let us try what we can do. [Exeunt]

---

[37] "'Corpus naturale seu mobile' is the current scholastic expression for the subject-matter of physics."—Ward.
[38] Puritan.

SCENE III

[A Grove.]

Enter FAUSTUS to conjure

FAUSTUS

Now that the gloomy shadow of the earth Longing to view Orion's drizzling look, Leaps from the antarctic world unto the sky, And dims the welkin with her pitchy breath, Faustus, begin thine incantations, And try if devils will obey thy hest, Seeing thou hast pray'd and sacrific'd to them. Within this circle is Jehovah's name, Forward and backward anagrammatis'd, The breviated names of holy saints, Figures of every adjunct to the Heavens, And characters of signs and erring [39] stars, By which the spirits are enforc'd to rise

Then fear not, Faustus, but be resolute, And try the uttermost magic can perform. Sint mihi Dei Acherontis propitii! Valeat numen triplex Jehovae! Ignei, aerii, aquatani spiritus, salvete! Orientis princeps Belzebub, inferni ardentis monarcha, et Demogorgon, propitiamus vos, ut appareat et surgat Mephistophilis. Quid tu moraris? per Jehovam, Gehennam et consecratum aquam quam nunc spargo, signumque crucis quod nunc facio, et per vota nostra, ipse nunc surgat nobis dicatus Mephistophilis! [40]

Enter [MEPHISTOPHILIS] a DEVIL

I charge thee to return and change thy shape; Thou art too ugly to attend on me. Go, and return an old Franciscan friar; That holy shape becomes a devil best. [Exit DEVIL] I see there's virtue in my heavenly words; Who would not be proficient in this art? How pliant is this Mephistophilis, Full of obedience and humility! Such is the force of magic and my spells. [Now,] Faustus, thou art conjuror laureat, Thou canst command great Mephistophilis
Quin regis Mephistophilis fratris imagine. [41]

Re-enter MEPHISTOPHILIS [like a Franciscan Friar]

MEPHISTOPHILIS

Now, Faustus, what would'st thou have me to do?

---

[39] Wandering.

[40] "Be propitious to me, gods of Acheron! May the triple deity of Jehovah prevail! Spirits of fire, air, water, hail! Belzebub, Prince of the East, monarch of burning hell, and Demogorgon, we propitiate ye, that Mephistophilis may appear and rise. Why dost thou delay? By Jehovah, Gehenna, and the holy water which now I sprinkle, and the sign of the cross which now I make, and by our prayer, may Mephistophilis now summoned by us arise!"

[41] "For indeed thou hast power in the image of thy brother Mephistophilis."

FAUSTUS

I charge thee wait upon me whilst I live, To do whatever Faustus shall command, Be it to make the moon drop from her sphere, Or the ocean to overwhelm the world.

MEPHISTOPHILIS

I am a servant to great Lucifer, And may not follow thee without his leave No more than he commands must we perform.

FAUSTUS

Did not he charge thee to appear to me?

MEPHISTOPHILIS

No, I came hither of mine own accord.

FAUSTUS

Did not my conjuring speeches raise thee? Speak.

MEPHISTOPHILIS

That was the cause, but yet per accidens; For when we hear one rack [42] the name of God, Abjure the Scriptures and his Saviour Christ, We fly in hope to get his glorious soul; Nor will we come, unless he use such means Whereby he is in danger to be damn'd
Therefore the shortest cut for conjuring Is stoutly to abjure the Trinity, And pray devoutly to the Prince of Hell.

FAUSTUS

So Faustus hath Already done; and holds this principle, There is no chief but only Belzebub, To whom Faustus doth dedicate himself. This word "damnation" terrifies not him, For he confounds hell in Elysium; [43]His ghost be with the old philosophers! But, leaving these vain trifles of men's souls, Tell me what is that Lucifer thy lord?

MEPHISTOPHILIS

Arch-regent and commander of all spirits.

FAUSTUS

Was not that Lucifer an angel once?

MEPHISTOPHILIS

---

[42] Twist in anagrams.
[43] Heaven and hell are indifferent to him.

24

Yes, Faustus, and most dearly lov'd of God.

FAUSTUS

How comes it then that he is Prince of devils?

MEPHISTOPHILIS

O, by aspiring pride and insolence; For which God threw him from the face of Heaven.

FAUSTUS

And what are you that you live with Lucifer?

MEPHISTOPHILIS

Unhappy spirits that fell with Lucifer, Conspir'd against our God with Lucifer, And are for ever damn'd with Lucifer.

FAUSTUS

Where are you damn'd?

MEPHISTOPHILIS

In hell.

FAUSTUS

How comes it then that thou art out of hell?

MEPHISTOPHILIS

Why this is hell, nor am I out of it. Think'st thou that I who saw the face of God, And tasted the eternal joys of Heaven, Am not tormented with ten thousand hells, In being depriv'd of everlasting bliss? O Faustus! leave these frivolous demands, Which strike a terror to my fainting soul.

FAUSTUS

What, is great Mephistophilis so passionate For being depriv'd of the joys of Heaven? Learn thou of Faustus manly fortitude, And scorn those joys thou never shalt possess. Go bear these tidings to great Lucifer
Seeing Faustus hath incurr'd eternal death By desperate thoughts against Jove's deity, Say he surrenders up to him his soul, So he will spare him four and twenty years, Letting him live in all voluptuousness; Having thee ever to attend on me; To give me whatsoever I shall ask, To tell me whatsoever I demand, To slay mine enemies, and aid my friends, And always be obedient to my will. Go and return to mighty Lucifer, And meet me in my study at midnight, And then resolve [44] me of thy master's mind.

---

[44] Inform.

MEPHISTOPHILIS

I will, Faustus. [Exit]

FAUSTUS

Had I as many souls as there be stars, I'd give them all for Mephistophilis. By him I'll be great Emperor of the world, And make a bridge through the moving air, To pass the ocean with a band of men
I'll join the hills that bind the Afric shore, And make that [country] continent to Spain, And both contributory to my crown. The Emperor shall not live but by my leave, Nor any potentate of Germany. Now that I have obtain'd what I desire, I'll live in speculation [45] of this art Till Mephistophilis return again. [Exit]

---

[45] Study.

SCENE IV

[A Street.]

Enter WAGNER and CLOWN

WAGNER
Sirrah, boy, come hither.

CLOWN
How, boy! Swowns, [46]boy! I hope you have seen many boys with such pickadevaunts [47] as I have. Boy, quotha!

WAGNER
Tell me, sirrah, hast thou any comings in?

CLOWN
Ay, and goings out too. You may see else.

WAGNER
Alas, poor slave! See how poverty jesteth in his nakedness! The villain is bare and out of service, and so hungry that I know he would give his soul to the devil for a shoulder of mutton, though it were blood-raw.

CLOWN
How? My soul to the Devil for a shoulder of mutton, though 'twere blood-raw! Not so, good friend. By'r Lady, I had need have it well roasted and good sauce to it, if I pay so dear.

WAGNER
Well, wilt thou serve me, and I'll make thee go like Qui mihi discipulus? [48]

CLOWN
How, in verse?

WAGNER
No, sirrah; in beaten silk and stavesacre.[49]

CLOWN

---

[46] Zounds, i. e., God's wounds.
[47] Beards cut to a sharp point (Fr. pic-à-devant).
[48] Dyce points out that these are the first words of W. Lily's "Ad discipulos carmen de moribus."
[49] A kind of larkspur, used for destroying lice.

27

How, how, Knave's acre![50] Ay, I thought that was all the land his father left him. Do you hear? I would be sorry to rob you of your living.

WAGNER
Sirrah, I say in stavesacre.

CLOWN
Oho! Oho! Stavesacre! Why, then, belike if I were your man I should be full of vermin.

WAGNER
So thou shalt, whether thou beest with me or no. But, sirrah, leave your jesting, and bind yourself presently unto me for seven years, or I'll turn all the lice about thee into familiars, and they shall tear thee in pieces.

CLOWN
Do your hear, sir? You may save that labour; they are too familiar with me already. Swowns! they are as bold with my flesh as if they had paid for [their] meat and drink.

WAGNER
Well, do you hear, sirrah? Hold, take these guilders. [Gives money.]

CLOWN
Gridirons! what be they?

WAGNER
Why, French crowns.

CLOWN
Mass, but for the name of French crowns, a man were as good have as many English counters. And what should I do with these?

WAGNER
Why, now, sirrah, thou art at an hour's warning, whensoever and wheresoever the Devil shall fetch thee.

CLOWN
No, no. Here, take your gridirons again.

WAGNER
Truly I'll none of them.

---

[50] A mean street in London.

CLOWN

Truly but you shall.

WAGNER

Bear witness I gave them him.

CLOWN

Bear witness I gave them you again.

WAGNER

Well, I will cause two devils presently to fetch thee away—Baliol and Belcher.

CLOWN

Let your Baliol and your Belcher come here, and I'll knock them, they were never so knock'd since they were devils. Say I should kill one of them, what would folks say? "Do you see yonder tall fellow in the round slop [51] —he has kill'd the devil." So I should be called Kill-devil all the parish over.

Enter two Devils
the Clown runs up and down crying

WAGNER

Baliol and Belcher! Spirits, away! [Exeunt Devils]

CLOWN. What, are they gone? A vengeance on them, they have vile long nails! There was a he-devil, and a she-devil! I'll tell you how you shall know them all he-devils has horns, and all she-devils has clifts and cloven feet.

WAGNER

Well, sirrah, follow me.

CLOWN

But, do you hear—if I should serve you, would you teach me to raise up Banios and Belcheos?

WAGNER

I will teach thee to turn thyself to anything; to a dog, or a cat, or a mouse, or a rat, or anything.

CLOWN

---

[51] Short wide breeches.

How! a Christian fellow to a dog or a cat, a mouse or a rat! No, no, sir. If you turn me into anything, let it be in the likeness of a little pretty frisky flea, that I may be here and there and everywhere. Oh, I'll tickle the pretty wenches' plackets; I'll be amongst them, i' faith.

WAGNER

Well, sirrah, come.

CLOWN

But, do you hear, Wagner?

WAGNER

How! Baliol and Belcher!

CLOWN

O Lord! I pray, sir, let Banio and Belcher go sleep.

WAGNER

Villain—call me Master Wagner, and let thy left eye be diametarily [52] fixed upon my right heel, with quasi vestigias nostras insistere. [53][Exit]

CLOWN

God forgive me, he speaks Dutch fustian. Well, I'll follow him, I'll serve him, that's flat. Exit.

---

[52] For diametrically.
[53] "As if to tread in my tracks."

SCENE V

FAUSTUS [discovered] in his Study

FAUSTUS
  Now, Faustus, must Thou needs be damn'd, and canst thou not be sav'd
  What boots it then to think of God or Heaven? Away with such vain fancies, and despair
  Despair in God, and trust in Belzebub. Now go not backward
  no, Faustus, be resolute. Why waverest thou? O, something soundeth in mine ears "Abjure this magic, turn to God again!" Ay, and Faustus will turn to God again. To God?—He loves thee not— The God thou serv'st is thine own appetite, Wherein is fix'd the love of Belzebub; To him I'll build an altar and a church, And offer lukewarm blood of new-born babes.

Enter GOOD ANGEL and EVIL ANGEL

GOOD ANGEL
  Sweet Faustus, leave that execrable art.

FAUSTUS
  Contrition, prayer, repentance! What of them?

GOOD ANGEL
  O, they are means to bring thee unto Heaven.

EVIL ANGEL
  Rather, illusions, fruits of lunacy,   That makes men foolish that do trust them most.

GOOD ANGEL
  Sweet Faustus, think of Heaven, and heavenly things.

EVIL ANGEL
  No, Faustus, think of honour and of wealth. [Exeunt ANGELS]

FAUSTUS
  Of wealth!
  What the signiory of Embden[54] shall be mine.   When Mephistophilis shall stand by me, What God can hurt thee, Faustus? Thou art safe; Cast no more

---

[54] Emden, near the mouth of the river Ems, was an important commercial town in Elizabethan times.

doubts. Come, Mephistophilis, And bring glad tidings from great Lucifer;—
Is't not midnight? Come, Mephistophilis; Veni, veni, Mephistophile!

Enter MEPHISTOPHILIS

Now tell me, what says Lucifer thy lord?

MEPHISTOPHILIS
  That I shall wait on Faustus whilst he lives, So he will buy my service with his
soul.

FAUSTUS
  Already Faustus hath hazarded that for thee.

MEPHISTOPHILIS
  But, Faustus, thou must bequeath it solemnly, And write a deed of gift with
thine own blood, For that security craves great Lucifer.
  If thou deny it, I will back to hell.

FAUSTUS
  Stay, Mephistophilis! and tell me what good Will my soul do thy lord.

MEPHISTOPHILIS
  Enlarge his kingdom.

FAUSTUS
  Is that the reason why he tempts us thus?

MEPHISTOPHILIS
  Solamen miseris socios habuisse doloris.[55]

FAUSTUS
  Why, have you any pain that torture others?

MEPHISTOPHILIS
  As great as have the human souls of men.bBut tell me, Faustus, shall I have
thy soul? And I will be thy slave, and wait on thee, And give thee more than
thou hast wit to ask.

FAUSTUS
Ay, Mephistophilis, I give it thee.

---

[55] "Misery loves company."

MEPHISTOPHILIS

Then, Faustus, stab thine arm courageously. And bind thy soul that at some certain day Great Lucifer may claim it as his own; And then be thou as great as Lucifer.

FAUSTUS

[stabbing his arm.] Lo, Mephistophilis, for love of thee, I cut mine arm, and with my proper blood Assure my soul to be great Lucifer's, Chief lord and regent of perpetual night! View here the blood that trickles from mine arm. And let it be propitious for my wish.

MEPHISTOPHILIS

But, Faustus, thou must Write it in manner of a deed of gift.

FAUSTUS

Ay, so I will. [Writes.] But, Mephistophilis, My blood congeals, and I can write no more.

MEPHISTOPHILIS

I'll fetch thee fire to dissolve it straight. [Exit]

FAUSTUS

What might the staying of my blood portend? Is it unwilling I should write this bill? Why streams it not that I may write afresh?   Faustus gives to thee his soul. Ah, there it stay'd. Why should'st thou not? Is not thy soul thine own? Then write again. Faustus gives to thee his soul.

Re-enter MEPHISTOPHILIS with a chafer of coals

MEPHISTOPHILIS

Here's fire. Come, Faustus, set it on.

FAUSTUS

So now the blood begins to clear again;
Now will I make an end immediately. [Writes.]

MEPHISTOPHILIS

O what will not I do to obtain his soul. [Aside.]

FAUSTUS

Consummatum est

[56] this bill is ended, And Faustus hath bequeath'd his soul to Lucifer—
But what is this inscription on mine arm? Homo, fuge![57] Whither should I fly?
If unto God, he'll throw me down to hell. My senses are deceiv'd; here's nothing writ
— I see it plain; here in this place is writ Homo, fuge! Yet shall not Faustus fly.

MEPHISTOPHILIS

I'll fetch him somewhat to delight his mind. [Exit]

Re-enter [MEPHISTOPHILIS] with Devils, giving crowns and rich apparel to FAUSTUS, dance, and depart

FAUSTUS

Speak Mephistophilis, what means this show?

MEPHISTOPHILIS

Nothing, Faustus, but to delight thy mind withal, And to show thee what magic can perform.

FAUSTUS

But may I raise up spirits when I please?

MEPHISTOPHILIS

Ay, Faustus, and do greater things than these.

FAUSTUS

Then there's enough for a thousand souls.
Here, Mephistophilis, receive this scroll, A deed of gift of body and of soul
But yet conditionally that thou perform All articles prescrib'd between us both.

MEPHISTOPHILIS

Faustus, I swear by hell and Lucifer To effect all promises between us made.

FAUSTUS

Then hear me read them
On these conditions following. First, that Faustus may be a spirit in form and substance. Secondly, that Mephistophilis shall be his servant, and at his command. Thirdly, that Mephistophilis shall do for him and bring him whatsoever [he desires]. Fourthly, that he shall be in his chamber or house

---

[56] "It is finished."
[57] "Man, fly!"

34

invisible. Lastly, that he shall appear to the said John Faustus, at all times, and in what form or shape soever he pleases. I, John Faustus, of Wittenberg, Doctor, by these presents do give both body and soul to Lucifer, Prince of the East, and his minister, Mephistophilis; and furthermore grant unto them, that twenty-four years being expired, the articles above written inviolate, full power to fetch or carry the said John Faustus, body and soul, flesh, blood, or goods, into their habitation wheresoever. By me, John Faustus.

MEPHISTOPHILIS

Speak, Faustus, do you deliver this as your deed?

FAUSTUS

Ay, take it, and the Devil give thee good on't.

MEPHISTOPHILIS

Now, Faustus, ask what thou wilt.

FAUSTUS

First will I question with thee about hell.   Tell me where is the place that men call hell?

MEPHISTOPHILIS

Under the Heaven.

FAUSTUS

Ay, but whereabout?

MEPHISTOPHILIS

Within the bowels of these elements, Where we are tortur'd and remain for ever; Hell hath no limits, nor is circumscrib'd In one self place; for where we are is hell, And where hell is there must we ever be
And, to conclude, when all the world dissolves, And every creature shall be purified, All places shall be hell that is not Heaven.

FAUSTUS

Come, I think hell's a fable.

MEPHISTOPHILIS

Ay, think so still, till experience change thy mind.

FAUSTUS

Why, think'st thou then that Faustus shall be damn'd?

MEPHISTOPHILIS

Ay, of necessity, for here's the scroll Wherein thou hast given thy soul to
Lucifer.

FAUSTUS

Ay, and body too; but what of that? Think'st thou that Faustus is so fond [58]
to imagine That, after this life, there is any pain? Tush; these are trifles, and
mere old wives' tales.

MEPHISTOPHILIS

But, Faustus, I am an instance to prove the contrary, For I am damned, and
am now in hell.

FAUSTUS

How! now in hell! Nay, an this be hell, I'll willingly be damn'd here; What?
walking, disputing, &c.? But, leaving off this, let me have a wife, The fairest
maid in Germany; For I am wanton and lascivious, And cannot live without a
wife.

MEPHISTOPHILIS

How—a wife? I prithee, Faustus, talk not of a wife.

FAUSTUS

Nay, sweet Mephistophilis, fetch me one, for I will have one.

MEPHISTOPHILIS

Well—thou wilt have one. Sit there till I come
I'll fetch thee a wife in the Devil's name. [Exit.]

Re-enter MEPHISTOPHILIS with a DEVIL dressed like a woman, with
fireworks

MEPHISTOPHILIS

Tell me, Faustus, how dost thou like thy wife?

FAUSTUS

A plague on her for a hot whore!

MEPHISTOPHILIS

Tut, Faustus, Marriage is but a ceremonial toy; And if thou lovest me, think
no more of it. I'll cull thee out the fairest courtesans, And bring them every
morning to thy bed; She whom thine eye shall like, thy heart shall have, Be she

---

[58] Foolish.

as chaste as was Penelope, As wise as Saba, [59]or as beautiful As was bright Lucifer before his fall. Here, take this book peruse it thoroughly

[Gives a book.] The iterating[60] of these lines brings gold; The framing of this circle on the ground Brings whirlwinds, tempests, thunder and lightning; Pronounce this thrice devoutly to thyself, And men in armour shall appear to thee, Ready to execute what thou desir'st.

FAUSTUS

Thanks, Mephistophilis; yet fain would I have a book wherein I might behold all spells and incantations, that I might raise up spirits when I please.

MEPHISTOPHILIS

Here they are, in this book. Turns to them.

FAUSTUS

Now would I have a book where I might see all characters and planets of the heavens, that I might know their motions and dispositions.

MEPHISTOPHILIS

Here they are too. Turns to them.

FAUSTUS

Nay, let me have one book more,—and then I have done,—wherein I might see all plants, herbs, and trees that grow upon the earth.

MEPHISTOPHILIS

Here they be.

FAUSTUS

O, thou art deceived.

MEPHISTOPHILIS

Tut, I warrant thee. Turns to them. [Exeunt]

---

[59] The Queen of Sheba.
[60] Repeating.

SCENE VI

[The Same.]

Enter FAUSTUS and MEPHISTOPHILIS

FAUSTUS
  When I behold the heavens, then I repent,
  And curse thee, wicked Mephistophilis,
  Because thou hast depriv'd me of those joys.

MEPHISTOPHILIS
  Why, Faustus, Thinkest thou Heaven is such a glorious thing? I tell thee 'tis not half so fair as thou, Or any man that breathes on earth.

FAUSTUS
  How Provest thou that?

MEPHISTOPHILIS
  'Twas made for man, therefore is man more excellent.

FAUSTUS
  If it were made for man, 'twas made for me
  I will renounce this magic and repent.

Enter GOOD ANGEL and EVIL ANGEL

GOOD ANGEL
  Faustus, repent; yet God will pity thee.

EVIL ANGEL
  Thou art a spirit; God can not pity thee.

FAUSTUS
  Who buzzeth in mine ears I am a spirit? Be I a devil, yet God may pity me; Ay, God will pity me if I repent.

EVIL ANGEL
  Ay, but Faustus never shall repent. [Exeunt ANGELS]

FAUSTUS
  My heart's so hard'ned I cannot repent.   Scarce can I name salvation, faith, or heaven, But fearful echoes thunder in mine ears "Faustus, thou art damn'd!" Then swords and knives, Poison, gun, halters, and envenom'd steel Are laid

38

before me to despatch myself, And long ere this I should have slain myself, Had not sweet pleasure conquer'd deep despair. Have I not made blind Homer sing to me Of Alexander's love and Oenon's death? And hath not he that built the walls of Thebes With ravishing sound of his melodious harp, Made music with my Mephistophilis? Why should I die then, or basely despair? I am resolv'd

Faustus shall ne'er repent. Come, Mephistophilis, let us dispute again, And argue of divine astrology. Tell me, are there many heavens above the moon? Are all celestial bodies but one globe, As is the substance of this centric earth?

MEPHISTOPHILIS

As are the elements, such are the spheres Mutually folded in each other's orb, And, Faustus, All jointly move upon one axletree Whose terminine is termed the world's wide pole; Nor are the names of Saturn, Mars, or Jupiter Feign'd but are erring stars.

FAUSTUS

But tell me, have they all one motion, both situ et tempore?[61]

MEPHISTOPHILIS

All jointly move from east to west in twenty-four hours upon the poles of the world; but differ in their motion upon the poles of the zodiac.

FAUSTUS

Tush! These slender trifles Wagner can decide;

Hath Mephistophilis no greater skill? Who knows not the double motion of the planets? The first is finish'd in a natural day; The second thus

as Saturn in thirty years; Jupiter in twelve; Mars in four; the Sun, Venus, and Mercury in a year; the moon in twenty-eight days. Tush, these are freshmen's suppositions. But tell me, hath every sphere a dominion or intelligentia?

MEPHISTOPHILIS

Ay.

FAUSTUS

How many heavens, or spheres, are there?

MEPHISTOPHILIS

Nine

the seven planets, the firmament, and the empyreal heaven.

---

[61] "In direction and in time?"

FAUSTUS

Well, resolve me in this question
Why have we not conjunctions, oppositions, aspects, eclipses, all at one time,
but in some years we have more, in some less?

MEPHISTOPHILIS

Per inæqualem motum respectu totius. [62]

FAUSTUS

Well, I am answered. Tell me who made the world.

MEPHISTOPHILIS

I will not.

FAUSTUS

Sweet Mephistophilis, tell me.

MEPHISTOPHILIS

Move me not, for I will not tell thee.

FAUSTUS

Villain, have I not bound thee to tell me anything?

MEPHISTOPHILIS

Ay, that is not against our kingdom; but this is. Think thou on hell, Faustus,
for thou art damn'd.

FAUSTUS

Think, Faustus, upon God that made the world.

MEPHISTOPHILIS

Remember this.

FAUSTUS

Ay, go, accursed spirit, to ugly hell. 'Tis thou hast damn'd distressed Faustus'
soul. Is't not too late?

Re-enter GOOD ANGEL and EVIL ANGEL.

EVIL ANGEL

Too late.

---

[62] "On account of their unequal motion in relation to the whole."

GOOD ANGEL

Never too late, if Faustus can repent.

EVIL ANGEL

If thou repent, devils shall tear thee in pieces.

GOOD ANGEL

Repent, and they shall never raze thy skin. [Exeunt ANGELS.]

FAUSTUS

Ah, Christ, my Saviour, Seek to save distressed Faustus' soul.

Enter LUCIFER, BELZEBUB, and MEPHISTOPHILIS.

LUCIFER

Christ cannot save thy soul, for he is just; There's none but I have interest in the same.

FAUSTUS

O, who art thou that look'st so terrible?

LUCIFER

I am Lucifer,
And this is my companion-prince in hell.

FAUSTUS

O Faustus! they are come to fetch away thy soul!

LUCIFER

We come to tell thee thou dost injure us;
Thou talk'st of Christ contrary to thy promise; Thou should'st not think of God. Think of the Devil, And of his dam, too.

FAUSTUS

Nor will I henceforth
pardon me in this,   And Faustus vows never to look to Heaven, Never to name God, or to pray to him, To burn his Scriptures, slay his ministers, And make my spirits pull his churches down.

LUCIFER

Do so, and we will highly gratify thee. Faustus, we are come from hell to show thee some pastime. Sit down, and thou shalt see all the Seven Deadly Sins appear in their proper shapes.

41

FAUSTUS

That sight will be as pleasing unto me, As Paradise was to Adam the first day Of his creation.

LUCIFER

Talk not of Paradise nor creation, but mark this show talk of the Devil, and nothing else.—Come away!

Enter the SEVEN DEADLY SINS.

Now, Faustus, examine them of their several names and dispositions.

FAUSTUS

What art thou—the first?

PRIDE

I am Pride. I disdain to have any parents. I am like to Ovid's flea I can creep into every corner of a wench; sometimes, like a periwig, I sit upon her brow; or like a fan of feathers, I kiss her lips; indeed I do—what do I not? But, fie, what a scent is here! I'll not speak another word, except the ground were perfum'd, and covered with cloth of arras.

FAUSTUS

What art thou—the second?

COVETOUSNESS

I am Covetousness, begotten of an old churl in an old leathern bag; and might I have my wish I would desire that this house and all the people in it were turn'd to gold, that I might lock you up in my good chest. O, my sweet gold!

FAUSTUS

What art thou—the third?

WRATH

I am Wrath. I had neither father nor mother I leapt out of a lion's mouth when I was scarce half an hour old; and ever since I have run up and down the world with this case [63] of rapiers, wounding myself when I had nobody to fight withal. I was born in hell; and look to it, for some of you shall be my father.

FAUSTUS

What art thou—the fourth?

---

[63] Pair.

42

ENVY

I am Envy, begotten of a chimney sweeper and an oyster-wife. I cannot read, and therefore wish all books were burnt. I am lean with seeing others eat. O that there would come a famine through all the world, that all might die, and I live alone! then thou should'st see how fat I would be. But must thou sit and I stand! Come down with a vengeance!

FAUSTUS

Away, envious rascal! What art thou—the fifth?

GLUTTONY

Who, I, sir? I am Gluttony. My parents are all dead, and the devil a penny they have left me, but a bare pension, and that is thirty meals a day and ten bevers [64] —a small trifle to suffice nature. O, I come of a royal parentage! My grandfather was a Gammon of Bacon, my grandmother a Hogshead of Claret-wine; my godfathers were these, Peter Pickleherring, and Martin Martlemas-beef. [65] O, but my godmother, she was a jolly gentlewoman, and well beloved in every good town and city; her name was Mistress Margery Marchbeer. Now, Faustus, thou hast heard all my progeny, wilt thou bid me to supper?

FAUSTUS

No, I'll see thee hanged
thou wilt eat up all my victuals.

GLUTTONY

Then the Devil choke thee!

FAUSTUS

Choke thyself, glutton! Who art thou—the sixth?

SLOTH

I am Sloth. I was begotten on a sunny bank, where I have lain ever since; and you have done me great injury to bring me from thence
let me be carried thither again by Gluttony and Lechery. I'll not speak another word for a king's ransom.

FAUSTUS

What are you, Mistress Minx, the seventh and last?

---

[64] Refreshments between meals.

[65] Martlemas or Martinmas was "the customary time for hanging up provisions to dry which had been salted for the winter."—Nares.

LECHERY

Who, I, sir? I am one that loves an inch of raw mutton better than an ell of fried stockfish; and the first letter of my name begins with Lechery.

LUCIFER

Away to hell, to hell!—Now, Faustus, how dost thou like this? [Exeunt the SINS.]

FAUSTUS

O, this feeds my soul!

LUCIFER

Tut, Faustus, in hell is all manner of delight.

FAUSTUS

O might I see hell, and return again, How happy were I then!

LUCIFER

Thou shalt; I will send for thee at midnight. In meantime take this book; peruse it throughly, And thou shalt turn thyself into what shape thou wilt.

FAUSTUS

Great thanks, mighty Lucifer!
This will I keep as chary as my life.

LUCIFER

Farewell, Faustus, and think on the Devil.

FAUSTUS

Farewell, great Lucifer! Come, Mephistophilis. [Exeunt.]

Enter CHORUS

CHORUS

Learned Faustus, To know the secrets of astronomy, Graven in the book of Jove's high firmament, Did mount himself to scale Olympus' top, Being seated in a chariot burning bright, Drawn by the strength of yoky dragons' necks. He now is gone to prove cosmography, And, as I guess, will first arrive at Rome, To see the Pope and manner of his court, And take some part of holy Peter's feast, That to this day is highly solemnis'd. [Exit.]

SCENE VII

[The Pope's Privy-chamber.]

Enter FAUSTUS and MEPHISTOPHILIS

FAUSTUS

Having now, my good Mephistophilis, Passed with delight the stately town of Trier, [66]Environ'd round with airy mountain-tops, With walls of flint, and deep entrenched lakes, Not to be won by any conquering prince; From Paris next, coasting the realm of France, We saw the river Maine fall into Rhine, Whose banks are set with groves of fruitful vines; Then up to Naples, rich Campania, Whose buildings fair and gorgeous to the eye, The streets straight forth, and pav'd with finest brick, Quarter the town in four equivalents. There saw we learned Maro's[67] golden tomb, The way he cut, an English mile in length, Thorough a rock of stone in one night's space; From thence to Venice, Padua, and the rest, In one of which a sumptuous temple stands, That threats the stars with her aspiring top. Thus hitherto has Faustus spent his time

But tell me, now, what resting-place is this? Hast thou, as erst I did command, Conducted me within the walls of Rome?

MEPHISTOPHILIS

Faustus, I have; and because we will not be unprovided, I have taken up his Holiness' privy-chamber for our use.

FAUSTUS

I hope his Holiness will bid us welcome.

MEPHISTOPHILIS

Tut, 'tis no matter, man, we'll be bold with his good cheer. And now, my Faustus, that thou may'st perceive What Rome containeth to delight thee with, Know that this city stands upon seven hills That underprop the groundwork of the same. [Just through the midst runs flowing Tiber's stream, With winding banks that cut it in two parts

]

Over the which four stately bridges lean, That make safe passage to each part of Rome

Upon the bridge called Ponte Angelo Erected is a castle passing strong, Within whose walls such store of ordnance are, And double cannons fram'd of carved brass, As match the days within one complete year; Besides the gates and high pyramides, Which Julius Cæsar brought from Africa.

---

[66] Treves.
[67] Virgil, who was reputed a magician in the Middle Ages, was buried at Naples.

FAUSTUS

Now by the kingdoms of infernal rule, Of Styx, of Acheron, and the fiery lake Of ever-burning Phlegethon, I swear That I do long to see the monuments And situation of bright-splendent Rome
Come therefore, let's away.

MEPHISTOPHILIS

Nay, Faustus, stay
I know you'd see the Pope, And take some part of holy Peter's feast, Where thou shalt see a troop of bald-pate friars, Whose summum bonum is in belly-cheer.

FAUSTUS

Well, I'm content to compass then some sport, And by their folly make us merriment. Then charm me, [Mephistophilis,] that I May be invisible, to do what I please Unseen of any whilst I stay in Rome. [MEPHISTOPHILIS charms him.]

MEPHISTOPHILIS

So, Faustus, now Do what thou wilt, thou shalt not be discern'd.
Sound a sennett. [68]

Enter the POPE and the CARDINAL of LORRAIN to the banquet, with FRIARS attending Pope.

My Lord of Lorrain, wilt please you draw near?

FAUSTUS

Fall to, and the devil choke you an [69] you spare!

POPE

How now! Who's that which spake?-Friars, look about.

FIRST FRIAR

Here's nobody, if it like your Holiness.

POPE

My lord, here is a dainty dish was sent me from the Bishop of Milan.

FAUSTUS

---

[68] "A particular set of notes on the trumpet or cornet, different from a flourish."—Nares.
[69] If.

I thank you, sir. [Snatches the dish.]

POPE

How now! Who's that which snatched the meat from me? Will no man look? My lord, this dish was sent me from the Cardinal of Florence.

FAUSTUS

You say true; I'll ha't. [Snatches the dish.]

POPE

What, again! My lord, I'll drink to your Grace.

FAUSTUS

I'll pledge your Grace. [Snatches the cup.]

CARDINAL OF LORRRAIN

My lord, it may be some ghost newly crept out of purgatory, come to beg a pardon of your Holiness.

POPE

It may be so. Friars, prepare a dirge to lay the fury of this ghost. Once again, my lord, fall to. The POPE crosses himself.

FAUSTUS

What, are you crossing of yourself? Well, use that trick no more I would advise you. The POPE crosses himself again. Well, there's the second time. Aware the third, I give you fair warning. The POPE crosses himself again, and Faustus hits him a box 'f the ear; and they all run away. Come on, Mephistophilis, what shall we do?

MEPHISTOPHILIS

Nay, I know not. We shall be curs'd with bell, book, and candle.

FAUSTUS

How! bell, book, and candle,—candle, book, and bell, Forward and backward to curse Faustus to hell! Anon you shall hear a hog grunt, a calf bleat, and an ass bray, Because it is Saint Peter's holiday.

Re-enter all the FRIARS to sing the Dirge

IST FRIAR

Come, brethren, let's about our business with good devotion.

THEY SING

Cursed be he that stole away his Holiness' meat from the table! Maledicat Dominus! [70]Cursed be he that struck his Holiness a blow on the face! Maledicat Dominus! Cursed be he that took Friar Sandelo a blow on the pate! Maledicat Dominus! Cursed be he that disturbeth our holy dirge! Maledicat Dominus! Cursed be he that took away his Holiness' wine! Maledicat Dominus! Et omnes sancti! [71]Amen! [MEPHISTOPHILIS and FAUSTUS beat the FRIARS, and fling fireworks among them
and so exeunt.]

Enter CHORUS

CHORUS

When Faustus had with pleasure ta'en the view Of rarest things, and royal courts of kings, He stay'd his course, and so returned home; Where such as bear his absence but with grief, I mean his friends, and near'st companions, Did gratulate his safety with kind words, And in their conference of what befell, Touching his journey through the world and air, They put forth questions of Astrology, Which Faustus answer'd with such learned skill, As they admir'd and wond'red at his wit. Now is his fame spread forth in every land; Amongst the rest the Emperor is one, Carolus the Fifth, at whose palace now Faustus is feasted 'mongst his noblemen. What there he did in trial of his art, I leave untold—your eyes shall see perform'd. [Exit.]

---

[70] "May the Lord curse him."
[71] "And all the saints."

SCENE VIII

[An Inn-yard.]

Enter ROBIN the Ostler with a book in his hand

ROBIN
O, this is admirable! here I ha' stolen one of Dr. Faustus' conjuring books, and i' faith I mean to search come circles for my own use. Now will I make all the maidens in our parish dance at my pleasure, stark naked before me; and so by that means I shall see more than e'er I felt or saw yet.

Enter RALPH calling ROBIN

RALPH
Robin, prithee come away; there's a gentleman tarries to have his horse, and he would have his things rubb'd and made clean. He keeps such a chafing with my mistress about it; and she has sent me to look thee out; prithee come away.

ROBIN
Keep out, keep out, or else you are blown up; you are dismemb'red, Ralph keep out, for I am about a roaring piece of work.

RALPH
Come, what dost thou with that same book? Thou canst not read.

ROBIN
Yes, my master and mistress shall find that I can read, he for his forehead, she for her private study; she's born to bear with me, or else my art fails.

RALPH
Why, Robin, what book is that?

ROBIN
What book! Why, the most intolerable book for conjuring that e'er was invented by any brimstone devil.

RALPH
Canst thou conjure with it?

ROBIN
I can do all these things easily with it

first, I can make thee drunk with ippocras [72] at any tabern [73] in Europe for nothing; that's one of my conjuring works.

RALPH

Our Master Parson says that's nothing.

ROBIN

True, Ralph; and more, Ralph, if thou hast any mind to Nan Spit, our kitchenmaid, then turn her and wind her to thy own use as often as thou wilt, and at midnight.

RALPH

O brave Robin, shall I have Nan Spit, and to mine own use? On that condition I'll feed thy devil with horsebread as long as he lives, of free cost.

ROBIN

No more, sweet Ralph
let's go and make clean our boots, which lie foul upon our hands, and then to our conjuring in the Devil's name. [Exeunt.]

---

[72] Wine mixed with sugar and spices.
[73] Tavern.

SCENE IX

[An Inn.]

Enter ROBIN and RALPH with a silver goblet.

ROBIN. Come, Ralph, did not I tell thee we were for ever made by this Doctor Faustus' book? Ecce signum, [74]here's a simple purchase [75] for horsekeepers; our horses shall eat not hay as long as this lasts.

Enter the VINTNER

RALPH
But, Robin, here come the vintner.

ROBIN
Hush! I'll gull him supernaturally.
Drawer, I hope all is paid
God be with you. Come, Ralph.

VINTNER
Soft, sir; a word with you. I must yet have a goblet paid from you, ere you go.

ROBIN
I, a goblet, Ralph; I, a goblet! I scorn you, and you are but a, [76]&c. I, a goblet! search me.

VINTNER
I mean so, sir, with your favour. [Searches him.]

ROBIN
How say you now?

VINTNER
I must say somewhat to your fellow. You, sir!

RALPH
Me, sir! me, sir! search your fill. [VINTNER searches him.] Now, sir, you may be ashamed to burden honest men with a matter of truth.

---

[74] "Behold a sign."
[75] Gain.
[76] The abuse was left to the actor's inventiveness.

51

VINTNER

Well, t'one of you hath this goblet about you.

ROBIN

You lie, drawer, 'tis afore me. [Aside.] Sirrah you, I'll teach ye to impeach honest men;—stand by;—I'll scour you for a goblet!—stand aside you had best, I charge you in the name of Belzebub. Look to the goblet, Ralph. [Aside to RALPH.]

VINTNER

What mean you, sirrah?

ROBIN

I'll tell you what I mean. Reads [from a book.]
Sanctobulorum. Periphrasticon—Nay, I'll tickle you, vintner. Look to the goblet, Ralph. [Aside to RALPH.] Polypragmos Belseborams framanto pacostiphos tostu, Mephistophilis, &c. [Reads.]

Enter MEPHISTOPHILIS, sets squibs at their backs, [and then exit]. They run about

VINT. O nomine Domini! [77]what meanest thou, Robin? Thou hast no goblet.

RALPH. Peccatum peccatorum! [78]Here's thy goblet, good vintner. [Gives the goblet to VINTNER, who exit.]

ROBIN. Misericordia pro nobis! [79]What shall I do? Good Devil, forgive me now, and I'll never rob thy library more.

Re-enter MEPHISTOPHILIS

MEPHISTOPHILIS

Monarch of hell, under whose black survey Great potentates do kneel with awful fear, Upon whose altars thousand souls do lie, How am I vexed with these villains' charms? From Constantinople am I hither come Only for pleasure of these damned slaves.

ROBIN

---

[77] "In the name of the Lord."
[78] "Sin of sins."
[79] "Mercy on us."

How from Constantinople? You have had a great journey. Will you take sixpence in your purse to pay for you supper, and begone?

MEPHISTOPHILIS

Well, villains, for your presumption, I transform thee into an ape, and thee into a dog; and so begone. [Exit.]

ROBIN

How, into an ape? That's brave! I'll have fine sport with the boys. I'll get nuts and apples enow.

RALPH

And I must be a dog.

ROBIN

I'faith thy head will never be out of the pottage pot. [Exeunt]

SCENE X

[The Court of the Emperor.]

Enter EMPEROR, FAUSTUS, and a KNIGHT with attendants

EMPEROR

Master Doctor Faustus, I have heard strange report of thy knowledge in the black art, how that none in my empire nor in the whole world can compare with thee for the rare effects of magic; they say thou hast a familiar spirit, by whom thou canst accomplish what thou list. This therefore is my request, that thou let me see some proof of thy skill, that mine eyes may be witnesses to confirm what mine ears have heard reported; and here I swear to thee by the honour of mine imperial crown, that, whatever thou doest, thou shalt be no ways prejudiced or endamaged.

KNIGHT

I'faith he looks much like a conjuror. [Aside.]

FAUSTUS

My gracious sovereign, though I must confess myself far inferior to the report men have published, and nothing answerable [80] to the honour of your imperial majesty, yet for that love and duty binds me thereunto, I am content to do whatsoever your majesty shall command me.

EMPEROR

Then, Doctor Faustus, mark what I shall say. As I was sometime solitary set Within my closet, sundry thoughts arose About the honour of mine ancestors, How they had won by prowess such exploits, Got such riches, subdued so many kingdoms As we that do succeed, or they that shall Hereafter possess our throne, shall (I fear me) ne'er attain to that degree Of high renown and great authority; Amongst which kings is Alexander the Great, Chief spectacle of the world's pre-eminence,
The bright shining of whose glorious acts Lightens the world with his [81] reflecting beams, As when I heard but motion [82] made of him It grieves my soul I never saw the man. If therefore thou by cunning of thine art Canst raise this man from hollow vaults below, Where lies entomb'd this famous conqueror, And bring with him his beauteous paramour, Both in their right shapes, gesture, and attire They us'd to wear during their time of life, Thou shalt both satisfy my just desire, And give me cause to praise thee whilst I live.

---

[80] Proportionate.
[81] Its.
[82] Mention.

54

FAUSTUS

My gracious lord, I am ready to accomplish your request so far forth as by art, and power of my Spirit, I am able to perform.

KNIGHT

I'faith that's just nothing at all. [Aside.]

FAUSTUS

But, if it like your Grace, it is not in my ability to present before your eyes the true substantial bodies of those two deceased princes, which long since are consumed to dust.

KNIGHT

Ay, marry, Master Doctor, now there's a sign of grace in you, when you will confess the truth. [Aside.]

FAUSTUS

But such spirits as can lively resemble Alexander and his paramour shall appear before your Grace in that manner that they [best] live in, in their most flourishing estate; which I doubt not shall sufficiently content your imperial majesty.

EMPEROR

Go to, Master Doctor, let me see them presently.

KNIGHT

Do you hear, Master Doctor? You bring Alexander and his paramour before the Emperor!

FAUSTUS

How then, sir?

KNIGHT

I'faith that's as true as Diana turn'd me to a stag!

FAUSTUS

No, sir, but when Actaeon died, he left the horns for you. Mephistophilis, begone. [Exit Mephistophilis.]

KNIGHT

Nay, an you go to conjuring. I'll begone. [Exit.]

FAUSTUS

I'll meet with you anon for interrupting me so. Here they are, my gracious lord.

Re-enter MEPHISTOPHILIS with [SPIRITS in the shape of] ALEXANDER and his PARAMOUR

EMPEROR

Master Doctor, I heard this lady while she liv'd had a wart or mole in her neck

how shall I know whether it be so or no?

FAUSTUS

Your Highness may boldly go and see.

EMPEROR

Sure these are no spirits, but the true substantial bodies of those two deceased princes. [Exeunt Spirits.]

FAUSTUS

Will't please your highness now to send for the knight that was so pleasant with me here of late?

EMPEROR

One of you call him forth. [Exit Attendant.]

Re-enter the KNIGHT with a pair of horns on his head

How now, sir knight! why I had thought thou had'st been a bachelor, but now I see thou hast a wife, that not only gives thee horns, but makes thee wear them. Feel on thy head.

KNIGHT

Thou damned wretch and execrable dog, Bred in the concave of some monstrous rock, How darest thou thus abuse a gentleman? Villain, I say, undo what thou hast done!

FAUSTUS

O, not so fast, sir; there's no haste; but, good, are you rememb'red how you crossed me in my conference with the Emperor? I think I have met with you for it.

EMPEROR

Good Master Doctor, at my entreaty release him; he hath done penance sufficient.

FAUSTUS

My gracious lord, not so much for the injury he off'red me here in your presence, as to delight you with some mirth, hath Faustus worthily requited this injurious knight; which, being all I desire, I am content to release him of his horns
and, sir knight, hereafter speak well of scholars. Mephistophilis, transform him straight. [MEPHISTOPHILIS removes the horns.] Now, my good lord, having done my duty I humbly take my leave.

EMPEROR

Farewell, Master Doctor; yet, ere you go, Expect from me a bounteous reward. [Exeunt.]

SCENE XI

[A Green; afterwards the House of Faustus]

[Enter FAUSTUS and MEPHISTOPHILIS]

FAUSTUS

Now, Mephistophilis, the restless course That Time doth run with calm and silent foot, Short'ning my days and thread of vital life, Calls for the payment of my latest years; Therefore, sweet Mephistophilis, let us Make haste to Wittenberg.

MEPHISTOPHILIS

What, will you go on horseback or on foot?

FAUSTUS

Nay, till I'm past this fair and pleasant green, I'll walk on foot.

Enter a HORSE-COURSER

HORSE-COURSER

I have been all this day seeking one Master Fustian
mass, see where he is! God save you, Master Doctor!

FAUSTUS

What, horse-courser! You are well met.

HORSE-COURSER

Do you hear, sir? I have brought you forty dollars for your horse.

FAUSTUS

I cannot sell him so
if thou likest him for fifty take him.

HORSE-COURSER

Alas, sir, I have no more.—I pray you speak for me.

MEPHISTOPHILIS

I pray you let him have him
he is an honest fellow, and he has a great charge, neither wife nor child.

FAUSTUS

Well, come, give me your money. [HORSE-COURSER gives FAUSTUS the money.] My boy will deliver him to you. But I must tell you one thing before you have him; ride him not into the water at any hand.

HORSE-COURSER

Why, sir, will he not drink of all waters?

FAUSTUS

O yes, he will drink of all waters, but ride him not into the water
ride him over hedge or ditch, or where thou wilt, but not into the water.

HORSE-COURSER

Well, sir.—Now I am made man for ever. I'll not leave my horse for forty. If he had but the quality of hey-ding-ding, hey-ding-ding, I'd made a brave living on him
he has a buttock as slick as an eel. [Aside.] Well, God b' wi' ye, sir, your boy will deliver him me
but hark you, sir; if my horse be sick or ill at ease, if I bring his water to you, you'll tell me what it is.

FAUSTUS

Away, you villain; what, dost think I am a horse-doctor? [Exit HORSE-COURSER] What art thou, Faustus, but a man condemn'd to die? Thy fatal time doth draw to final end; Despair doth drive distrust unto my thoughts
Confound these passions with a quiet sleep
Tush, Christ did call the thief upon the cross; Then rest thee, Faustus, quiet in conceit. Sleeps in his chair.

Re-enter HORSE-COURSER, all wet, crying

HORSE-COURSER

Alas, alas! Doctor Fustian quotha? Mass, Doctor Lopus [83] was never such a doctor. Has given me a purgation has purg'd me of forty dollars; I shall never see them more. But yet, like an ass as I was, I would not be ruled by him, for he bade me I should ride him into no water. Now I, thinking my horse had had some rare quality that he would not have had me known of, I, like a venturous youth rid him into the deep pond at the town's end. I was no sooner in the middle of the pond, but my horse vanished away, and I sat upon a bottle of hay, never so near drowning in my life. But I'll seek out my Doctor, and have

---

[83] Dr. Lopez, physician to Queen Elizabeth, was hanged in 1594 on the charge of conspiring to poison the Queen.

my forty dollars again, or I'll make it the dearest horse!—O, yonder is his snipper-snapper.—Do you hear? You hey-pass, [84]where's your master?

MEPHISTOPHILIS

Why, sir, what would you? You cannot speak with him.

HORSE-COURSER

But I will speak with him.

MEPHISTOPHILIS

Why, he's fast asleep. Come some other time.

HORSE-COURSER

I'll speak with him now, or I'll break his glass windows about his ears.

MEPHISTOPHILIS

I tell thee he has not slept this eight nights.

HORSE-COURSER

An he have not slept this eight weeks, I'll speak with him.

MEPHISTOPHILIS

See where he is, fast asleep.

HORSE-COURSER

Ay, this is he. God save you, Master Doctor! Master Doctor, Master Doctor Fustian!—Forty dollars, forty dollars for a bottle of hay!

MEPHISTOPHILIS

Why, thou seest he hears thee not.

HORSE-COURSER

So ho, ho!—so ho, ho! (Hollas in his ear.) No, will you not wake? I'll make you wake ere I go. (Pulls FAUSTUS by the leg, and pulls it away.) Alas, I am undone! What shall I do?

FAUSTUS

O my leg, my leg! Help, Mephistophilis! call the officers. My leg, my leg!

MEPHISTOPHILIS

Come, villain, to the constable.

---

[84] A juggler's term, like "presto, fly!" Hence applied to the juggler himself.—Bullen.

HORSE-COURSER

O lord, sir, let me go, and I'll give you forty dollars more.

MEPHISTOPHILIS

Where be they?

HORSE-COURSER

I have none about me. Come to my ostry [85] and I'll give them you.

MEPHISTOPHILIS

Begone quickly.

[HORSE-COURSER runs away.]

FAUSTUS

What, is he gone? Farewell he! Faustus has his leg again, and the horse-courser, I take it, a bottle of hay for his labour. Well, this trick shall cost him forty dollars more.

Enter WAGNER

How now, Wagner, what's the news with thee?

WAGNER

Sir, the Duke of Vanholt doth earnestly entreat your company.

FAUSTUS

The Duke of Vanholt! an honourable gentleman, to whom I must be no niggard of my cunning. Come, Mephistophilis, let's away to him.

[Exeunt.]

---

[85] Inn.

SCENE XII

[The Court of the Duke of Vanholt.]

Enter the DUKE [of VANHOLT], the DUCHESS, FAUSTUS, and
MEPHISTOPHILIS

DUKE

Believe me, Master Doctor, this merriment hath much pleased me.

FAUSTUS

My gracious lord, I am glad it contents you so well.—But it may be, madam,
you take no delight in this. I have heard that great-bellied women do long for
some dainties or other. What is it, madam? Tell me, and you shall have it.

DUCHESS

Thanks, good Master Doctor; and for I see your courteous intent to pleasure
me, I will not hide from you the thing my heart desires; and were it now
summer, as it is January and the dead time of the winter, I would desire no
better meat than a dish of ripe grapes.

FAUSTUS

Alas, madam, that's nothing! Mephistophilis, begone. (Exit
MEPHISTOPHILIS.) Were it a greater thing than this, so it would content
you, you should have it.

Re-enter MEPHISTOPHILIS with the grapes

Here they be, madam; wilt please you taste on them?

DUKE

Believe me, Master Doctor, this makes me wonder above the rest, that being
in the dead time of winter, and in the month of January, how you should come
by these grapes.

FAUSTUS

If it like your Grace, the year is divided into two circles over the whole world,
that, when it is here winter with us, in the contrary circle it is summer with
them, as in India, Saba, and farther countries in the East; and by means of a
swift spirit that I have I had them brought hither, as ye see.—How do you like
them, madam; be they good?

DUCHESS

Believe me, Master Doctor, they be the best grapes that I e'er tasted in my life before.

FAUSTUS

I am glad they content you so, madam.

DUKE

Come, madam, let us in, where you must well reward this learned man for the great kindness he hath show'd to you.

DUCHESS

And so I will, my lord; and, whilst I live, rest beholding for this courtesy.

FAUSTUS

I humbly thank your Grace.

DUKE

Come, Master Doctor, follow us and receive your reward. [Exeunt.]

SCENE XIII

[A room in Faustus' House.]

Enter WAGNER

WAGNER

I think my master shortly means to die, For he hath given to me all his goods; And yet, methinks, if that death were so near, He would not banquet and carouse and swill Amongst the students, as even now he doth, Who are at supper with such belly-cheer As Wagner ne'er beheld in all his life. See where they come! Belike the feast is ended.

Enter FAUSTUS, with two or three SCHOLARS [and MEPHISTOPHILIS]

1ST SCHOLAR

Master Doctor Faustus, since our conference about fair ladies, which was the beautifullest in all the world, we have determined with ourselves that Helen of Greece was the admirablest lady that ever lived

therefore, Master Doctor, if you will do us that favour, as to let us see that peerless dame of Greece, whom all the world admires for majesty, we should think ourselves much beholding unto you.

FAUSTUS

Gentlemen, For that I know your friendship is unfeigned, And Faustus' custom is not to deny The just requests of those that wish him well, You shall behold that peerless dame of Greece, No otherways for pomp and majesty Than when Sir Paris cross'd the seas with her, And brought the spoils to rich Dardania. Be silent, then, for danger is in words.

Music sounds, and HELEN passeth over the stage.

2ND SCHOLAR

Too simple is my wit to tell her praise, Whom all the world admires for majesty.

3RD SCHOLAR

No marvel though the angry Greeks pursued With ten years' war the rape of such a queen, Whose heavenly beauty passeth all compare.

1ST SCHOLAR

Since we have seen the pride of Nature's works, And only paragon of excellence, Let us depart; and for this glorious deed Happy and blest be Faustus evermore.

FAUSTUS

Gentlemen, farewell—the same I wish to you.

Exeunt SCHOLARS [and WAGNER].

Enter an OLD MAN

OLD MAN

Ah, Doctor Faustus, that I might prevail To guide thy steps unto the way of life, By which sweet path thou may'st attain the goal That shall conduct thee to celestial rest! Break heart, drop blood, and mingle it with tears, Tears falling from repentant heaviness Of thy most vile and loathsome filthiness, The stench whereof corrupts the inward soul With such flagitious crimes of heinous sins As no commiseration may expel, But mercy, Faustus, of thy Saviour sweet, Whose blood alone must wash away thy guilt.

FAUSTUS

Where art thou, Faustus? Wretch, what hast thou done? Damn'd art thou, Faustus, damn'd; despair and die! Hell calls for right, and with a roaring voice Says "Faustus! come! thine hour is [almost] come!" And Faustus [now] will come to do the right.

MEPHISTOPHILIS gives him a dagger.

OLD MAN

Ah stay, good Faustus, stay thy desperate steps! I see an angel hovers o'er thy head, And, with a vial full of precious grace, Offers to pour the same into thy soul
Then call for mercy, and avoid despair.

FAUSTUS

Ah, my sweet friend, I feel Thy words do comfort my distressed soul. Leave me a while to ponder on my sins.

OLD MAN

I go, sweet Faustus, but with heavy cheer, Fearing the ruin of thy hopeless soul. [Exit.]

FAUSTUS

Accursed Faustus, where is mercy now? I do repent; and yet I do despair; Hell strives with grace for conquest in my breast
What shall I do to shun the snares of death?

MEPHISTOPHILIS

Thou traitor, Faustus, I arrest thy soul For disobedience to my sovereign lord; Revolt, or I'll in piecemeal tear thy flesh.

FAUSTUS

Sweet Mephistophilis, entreat thy lord To pardon my unjust presumption. And with my blood again I will confirm My former vow I made to Lucifer.

MEPHISTOPHILIS

Do it then quickly, with unfeigned heart, Lest greater danger do attend thy drift. [FAUSTUS stabs his arm and writes on a paper with his blood.]

FAUSTUS

Torment, sweet friend, that base and crooked age, [86] That durst dissuade me from my Lucifer, With greatest torments that our hell affords.

MEPHISTOPHILIS

His faith is great, I cannot touch his soul; But what I may afflict his body with I will attempt, which is but little worth.

FAUSTUS

One thing, good servant, let me crave of thee, To glut the longing of my heart's desire,—That I might have unto my paramour That heavenly Helen, Which I saw of late, Whose sweet embracings may extinguish clean These thoughts that do dissuade me from my vow, And keep mine oath I made to Lucifer.

MEPHISTOPHILIS

Faustus, this or what else thou shalt desire Shall be perform'd in twinkling of an eye.

Re-enter HELEN

FAUSTUS

Was this the face that launched a thousand ships And burnt the topless [87] towers of Ilium? Sweet Helen, make me immortal with a kiss. [Kisses her.] Her lips suck forth my soul; see where it flies!— Come, Helen, come, give me my soul again. Here will I dwell, for Heaven is in these lips, And all is dross that is not Helena.

Enter OLD MAN.

---

[86] Old man.
[87] Unsurpassed in height.

I will be Paris, and for love of thee, Instead of Troy, shall Wittenberg be sack'd; And I will combat with weak Menelaus, And wear thy colours on my plumed crest; Yea, I will wound Achilles in the heel, And then return to Helen for a kiss. Oh, thou art fairer than the evening air Clad in the beauty of a thousand stars; Brighter art thou than flaming Jupiter When he appear'd to hapless Semele

More lovely than the monarch of the sky In wanton Arethusa's azured arms

And none but thou shalt be my paramour. [Exeunt.]

OLD MAN

Accursed Faustus, miserable man, That from thy soul exclud'st the grace of Heaven, And fly'st the throne of his tribunal seat!

Enter DEVILS

Satan begins to sift me with his pride

As in this furnace God shall try my faith, My faith, vile hell, shall triumph over thee. Ambitious fiends! see how the heavens smiles At your repulse, and laughs your state to scorn! Hence, hell! for hence I fly unto my God. Exeunt [on one side DEVILS, on the other, OLD MAN].

SCENE XIV

[The Same.]

Enter FAUSTUS with SCHOLARS

FAUSTUS
Ah, gentlemen!

1ST SCHOLAR
What ails Faustus?

FAUSTUS
Ah, my sweet chamber-fellow, had I lived with thee, then had I lived still! but now I die eternally. Look, comes he not, comes he not?

2ND SCHOLAR
What means Faustus?

3RD SCHOLAR
Belike he is grown into some sickness by being over solitary.

1ST SCHOLAR
If it be so, we'll have physicians to cure him. 'Tis but a surfeit. Never fear, man.

FAUSTUS
A surfeit of deadly sin that hath damn'd both body and soul.

2ND SCHOLAR
Yet, Faustus, look up to Heaven; remember God's mercies are infinite.

FAUSTUS
But Faustus' offenses can never be pardoned
the serpent that tempted Eve may be sav'd, but not Faustus. Ah, gentlemen, hear me with patience, and tremble not at my speeches! Though my heart pants and quivers to remember that I have been a student here these thirty years, oh, would I had never seen Wittenberg, never read book! And what wonders I have done, All Germany can witness, yea, the world; for which Faustus hath lost both Germany and the world, yea Heaven itself, Heaven, the seat of God, the throne of the blessed, the kingdom of joy; and must remain in hell for ever, hell, ah, hell, for ever! Sweet friends! what shall become of Faustus being in hell for ever?

3RD SCHOLAR

Yet, Faustus, call on God.

FAUSTUS

On God, whom Faustus hath abjur'd! on God, whom Faustus hath blasphemed! Ah, my God, I would weep, but the Devil draws in my tears. Gush forth blood instead of tears! Yea, life and soul! Oh, he stays my tongue! I would lift up my hands, but see, they hold them, they hold them!

ALL

Who, Faustus?

FAUSTUS

Lucifer and Mephistophilis. Ah, gentlemen, I gave them my soul for my cunning!

ALL

God forbid!

FAUSTUS

God forbade it indeed; but Faustus hath done it. For vain pleasure of twenty-four years hath Faustus lost eternal joy and felicity. I writ them a bill with mine own blood
the date is expired; the time will come, and he will fetch me.

1ST SCHOLAR

Why did not Faustus tell us of this before, that divines might have pray'd for thee?

FAUSTUS

Oft have I thought to have done so; but the Devil threat'ned to tear me in pieces if I nam'd God; to fetch both body and soul if I once gave ear to divinity and now 'tis too late. Gentlemen, away! lest you perish with me.

2ND SCHOLAR

Oh, what shall we do to save Faustus?

FAUSTUS

Talk not of me, but save yourselves, and depart.

3RD SCHOLAR

God will strengthen me. I will stay with Faustus.

1ST SCHOLAR

Tempt not God, sweet friend; but let us into the next room, and there pray for him.

FAUSTUS

Ay, pray for me, pray for me! and what noise soever ye hear, come not unto me, for nothing can rescue me.

2ND SCHOLAR

Pray thou, and we will pray that God may have mercy upon thee.

FAUSTUS

Gentlemen, farewell! If I live till morning I'll visit you
if not—Faustus is gone to hell.

ALL

Faustus, farewell! [Exeunt SCHOLARS. The clock strikes eleven]

FAUSTUS

Ah, Faustus, Now hast thou but one bare hour to live, And then thou must be damn'd perpetually! Stand still, you ever-moving spheres of Heaven, That time may cease, and midnight never come; Fair Nature's eye, rise, rise again and make Perpetual day; or let this hour be but A year, a month, a week, a natural day, That Faustus may repent and save his soul! O lente, lente, curite noctis equi. [88]The stars move still, [89]time runs, the clock will strike, The Devil will come, and Faustus must be damn'd. O, I'll leap up to my God! Who pulls me down? See, see where Christ's blood streams in the firmament! One drop would save my soul—half a drop
ah, my Christ! Ah, rend not my heart for naming of my Christ! Yet will I call on him
O spare me, Lucifer!— Where is it now? 'Tis gone; and see where God Stretcheth out his arm, and bends his ireful brows! Mountain and hills come, come and fall on me, And hide me from the heavy wrath of God! No! no! Then will I headlong run into the earth; Earth gape! O no, it will not harbour me! You stars that reign'd at my nativity, Whose influence hath alloted death and hell, Now draw up Faustus like a foggy mist Into the entrails of yon labouring clouds, That when they vomit forth into the air, My limbs may issue from their smoky mouths, So that my soul may but ascend to Heaven. The watch strikes [the half hour]. Ah, half the hour is past! 'Twill all be past anon! O God! If thou wilt not have mercy on my soul, Yet for Christ's sake whose blood hath ransom'd me, Impose some end to my incessant pain; Let Faustus live in hell a thousand years— A hundred thousand, and—at last—be sav'd!

---

[88] "Run softly, softly, horses of the night."—Ovid's Amores, i, 13.
[89] Without ceasing.

O, no end is limited to damned souls! Why wert thou not a creature wanting soul? Or why is this immortal that thou hast? Ah, Pythogoras' metempsychosis! were that true, This soul should fly from me, and I be chang'd Unto some brutish beast! All beasts are happy, For when they die, Their souls are soon dissolv'd in elements; But mine must live, still to be plagu'd in hell. Curst be the parents that engend'red me! No, Faustus
curse thyself
curse Lucifer That hath depriv'd thee of the joys of Heaven. The clock striketh twelve. O, it strikes, it strikes! Now, body, turn to air, Or Lucifer will bear thee quick to hell. Thunder and lightning. O soul, be chang'd into little water-drops, And fall into the ocean—ne'er be found. My God! my God! look not so fierce on me!

Enter DEVILS.

Adders and serpents, let me breathe awhile! Ugly hell, gape not! come not, Lucifer! I'll burn my books!—Ah Mephistophilis! [Exeunt DEVILS with FAUSTUS.]

Enter CHORUS

CHORUS
Cut is the branch that might have grown full straight, And burned is Apollo's laurel bough, That sometime grew within this learned man. Faustus is gone; regard his hellish fall, Whose fiendfull fortune may exhort the wise Only to wonder at unlawful things, Whose deepness doth entice such forward wits To practise more than heavenly power permits. [Exit.]

Faust

Part the First

Johann Wolfgang von Goethe

Faust

Part the First

Johann Wolfgang von Goethe

Translated into English ,
in the Original Metres,
by

Bayard Taylor

FAUST

It is twenty years since I first determined to attempt the translation of Faust, in the original metres. At that time, although more than a score of English translations of the First Part, and three or four of the Second Part, were in existence, the experiment had not yet been made. The prose version of Hayward seemed to have been accepted as the standard, in default of anything more satisfactory: the English critics, generally sustaining the translator in his views concerning the secondary importance of form in Poetry, practically discouraged any further attempt; and no one, familiar with rhythmical expression through the needs of his own nature, had devoted the necessary love and patience to an adequate reproduction of the great work of Goethe's life.

Mr. Brooks was the first to undertake the task, and the publication of his translation of the First Part (in 1856) induced me, for a time, to give up my own design. No previous English version exhibited such abnegation of the translator's own tastes and habits of thought, such reverent desire to present the original in its purest form. The care and conscience with which the work had been performed were so apparent, that I now state with reluctance what then seemed to me to be its only deficiencies,--a lack of the lyrical fire and fluency of the original in some passages, and an occasional lowering of the tone through the use of words which are literal, but not equivalent. The plan of translation adopted by Mr. Brooks was so entirely my own, that when further residence in Germany and a more careful study of both parts of Faust had satisfied me that the field was still open,--that the means furnished by the poetical affinity of the two languages had not yet been exhausted,--nothing remained for me but to follow him in all essential particulars. His example confirmed me in the belief that there were few difficulties in the way of a nearly literal yet thoroughly rhythmical version of Faust, which might not be overcome by loving labor. A comparison of seventeen English translations, in the arbitrary metres adopted by the translators, sufficiently showed the danger of allowing license in this respect: the white light of Goethe's thought was thereby passed through the tinted glass of other minds, and assumed the coloring of each. Moreover, the plea of selecting different metres in the hope of producing a similar effect is unreasonable, where the identical metres are possible.

The value of form, in a poetical work, is the first question to be considered. No poet ever understood this question more thoroughly than Goethe himself, or expressed a more positive opinion in regard to it. The alternative modes of translation which he presents (reported by Riemer, quoted by Mrs. Austin, in her "Characteristics of Goethe," and accepted by Mr. Hayward),[90] are quite independent of his views concerning the value of form, which we find given elsewhere, in the clearest and most emphatic manner.[91] Poetry is not simply a fashion of expression: it is the form of expression absolutely required by a certain class of ideas. Poetry, indeed, may be distinguished from Prose by the single circumstance, that it is the utterance of whatever in man cannot be perfectly uttered in any other than a rhythmical form: it is useless to say that the naked meaning is independent of the form: on the contrary, the form contributes essentially to the fullness of the meaning. In Poetry which endures through its own inherent vitality, there is no forced union of these two elements. They are as intimately blended, and with the same mysterious beauty, as the sexes in the ancient Hermaphroditus. To attempt to represent Poetry in Prose, is very much like attempting to translate music into speech.[92]

"The rhythm," said Goethe, "is an unconscious result of the poetic mood. If one should stop to consider it mechanically, when about to write a poem, one would become bewildered and accomplish nothing of real poetical value."--Ibid.

"All that is poetic in character should be rythmically treated! Such is my conviction; and if even a sort of poetic prose should be gradually introduced, it would only show that the distinction between prose and poetry had been completely lost sight of."--Goethe to Schiller, 1797. Tycho Mommsen, in his excellent essay, Die Kunst des Deutschen Uebersetzers aus neueren Sprachen, goes so far as to say: "The metrical or rhymed modelling of a poetical work is so essentially the germ of its being, that, rather than by giving it up, we might hope to construct a similar work of art before the eyes of our countrymen, by

---

[90] "'There are two maxims of translation,' says he: 'the one requires that the author, of a foreign nation, be brought to us in such a manner that we may regard him as our own; the other, on the contrary, demands of us that we transport ourselves over to him, and adopt his situation, his mode of speaking, and his peculiarities. The advantages of both are sufficiently known to all instructed persons, from masterly examples.'" Is it necessary, however, that there should always be this alternative? Where the languages are kindred, and equally capable of all varieties of metrical expression, may not both these "maxims" be observed in the same translation? Goethe, it is true, was of the opinion that Faust ought to be given, in French, in the manner of Clement Marot; but this was undoubtedly because he felt the inadequacy of modern French to express the naive, simple realism of many passages. The same objection does not apply to English. There are a few archaic expressions in Faust, but no more than are still allowed--nay, frequently encouraged--in the English of our day.

[91] "You are right," said Goethe; "there are great and mysterious agencies included in the various forms of Poetry. If the substance of my 'Roman Elegies' were to be expressed in the tone and measure of Byron's 'Don Juan,' it would really have an atrocious effect."--Eckermann.

[92] "Goethe's poems exercise a great sway over me, not only by their meaning, but also by their rhythm. It is a language which stimulates me to composition."--Beethoven.

giving up or changing the substance. The immeasurable result which has followed works wherein the form has been retained--such as the Homer of Voss, and the Shakespeare of Tieck and Schlegel--is an incontrovertible evidence of the vitality of the endeavor."

The various theories of translation from the Greek and Latin poets have been admirably stated by Dryden in his Preface to the "Translations from Ovid's Epistles," and I do not wish to continue the endless discussion,--especially as our literature needs examples, not opinions. A recent expression, however, carries with it so much authority, that I feel bound to present some considerations which the accomplished scholar seems to have overlooked. Mr. Lewes[93] justly says: "The effect of poetry is a compound of music and suggestion; this music and this suggestion are intermingled in words, which to alter is to alter the effect. For words in poetry are not, as in prose, simple representatives of objects and ideas: they are parts of an organic whole,--they are tones in the harmony." He thereupon illustrates the effect of translation by changing certain well-known English stanzas into others, equivalent in meaning, but lacking their felicity of words, their grace and melody. I cannot accept this illustration as valid, because Mr. Lewes purposely omits the very quality which an honest translator should exhaust his skill in endeavoring to reproduce. He turns away from the one best word or phrase in the English lines he quotes, whereas the translator seeks precisely that one best word or phrase (having all the resources of his language at command), to represent what is said in another language. More than this, his task is not simply mechanical: he must feel, and be guided by, a secondary inspiration. Surrendering himself to the full possession of the spirit which shall speak through him, he receives, also, a portion of the same creative power. Mr. Lewes reaches this conclusion: "If, therefore, we reflect what a poem Faust is, and that it contains almost every variety of style and metre, it will be tolerably evident that no one unacquainted with the original can form an adequate idea of it from translation,"[94] which is certainly correct of any translation wherein something of the rhythmical variety and beauty of the original is not retained. That very much of the rhythmical character may be retained in English, was long ago shown by Mr. Carlyle,[95] in the passages which he translated, both literally and rhythmically, from the Helena (Part Second). In fact, we have so many instances of the possibility of reciprocally transferring the finest qualities of English and German poetry, that there is no sufficient excuse for an unmetrical translation of Faust. I refer

---

[93] Life of Goethe (Book VI.).

[94] Mr. Lewes gives the following advice: "The English reader would perhaps best succeed who should first read Dr. Anster's brilliant paraphrase, and then carefully go through Hayward's prose translation." This is singularly at variance with the view he has just expressed. Dr. Anster's version is an almost incredible dilution of the original, written in other metres; while Hayward's entirely omits the element of poetry.

[95] Foreign Review, 1828.

especially to such subtile and melodious lyrics as "The Castle by the Sea," of Uhland, and the "Silent Land" of Salis, translated by Mr. Longfellow; Goethe's "Minstrel" and "Coptic Song," by Dr. Hedge; Heine's "Two Grenadiers," by Dr. Furness and many of Heine's songs by Mr Leland; and also to the German translations of English lyrics, by Freiligrath and Strodtmann.[96]

I have a more serious objection, however, to urge against Mr. Hayward's prose translation. Where all the restraints of verse are flung aside, we should expect, at least, as accurate a reproduction of the sense, spirit, and tone of the original, as the genius of our language will permit. So far from having given us such a reproduction, Mr. Hayward not only occasionally mistakes the exact meaning of the German text,[97] but, wherever two phrases may be used to express the meaning with equal fidelity, he very frequently selects that which has the less grace, strength, or beauty.[98] For there are few things which may not be said, in

---

[96] When Freiligrath can thus give us Walter Scott:--

"Kommt, wie der Wind kommt, Wenn Wälder erzittern Kommt, wie die Brandung Wenn Flotten zersplittern! Schnell heran, schnell herab, Schneller kommt Al'e!--Häuptling und Bub' und Knapp, Herr und Vasalle!"

or Strodtmann thus reproduce Tennyson:--

"Es fällt der Strahl auf Burg und Thal, Und schneeige Gipfel, reich an Sagen; Viel' Lichter wehn auf blauen Seen, Bergab die Wasserstürze jagen! Blas, Hüfthorn, blas, in Wiederhall erschallend: Blas, Horn--antwortet, Echos, hallend, hallend, hallend!"

--it must be a dull ear which would be satisfied with the omission of rhythm and rhyme.

[97] On his second page, the line Mein Lied ertönt der unbekannten Menge, "My song sounds to the unknown multitude," is translated: "My sorrow voices itself to the strange throng." Other English translators, I notice, have followed Mr. Hayward in mistaking Lied for Leid.

[98] I take but one out of numerous instances, for the sake of illustration. The close of the Soldier's Song (Part I. Scene II.) is:--

> "Kühn is das Mühen,
> Herrlich der Lohn!
> Und die Soldaten
> Ziehen davon."

Literally:

> Bold is the endeavor,
> Splendid the pay!
> And the soldiers

English, in a twofold manner,--one poetic, and the other prosaic. In German, equally, a word which in ordinary use has a bare prosaic character may receive a fairer and finer quality from its place in verse. The prose translator should certainly be able to feel the manifestation of this law in both languages, and should so choose his words as to meet their reciprocal requirements. A man, however, who is not keenly sensible to the power and beauty and value of rhythm, is likely to overlook these delicate yet most necessary distinctions. The author's thought is stripped of a last grace in passing through his mind, and frequently presents very much the same resemblance to the original as an unhewn shaft to the fluted column. Mr. Hayward unconsciously illustrates his lack of a refined appreciation of verse, "in giving," as he says, "a sort of rhythmical arrangement to the lyrical parts," his object being "to convey some notion of the variety of versification which forms one great charm of the poem." A literal translation is always possible in the unrhymed passages; but even here Mr. Hayward's ear did not dictate to him the necessity of preserving the original rhythm.

While, therefore, I heartily recognize his lofty appreciation of Faust,--while I honor him for the patient and conscientious labor he has bestowed upon his translation,--I cannot but feel that he has himself illustrated the unsoundness of his argument. Nevertheless, the circumstance that his prose translation of Faust has received so much acceptance proves those qualities of the original work which cannot be destroyed by a test so violent. From the cold bare outline thus produced, the reader unacquainted with the German language would scarcely guess what glow of color, what richness of changeful life, what fluent grace and energy of movement have been lost in the process. We must, of course, gratefully receive such an outline, where a nearer approach to the form of the original is impossible, but, until the latter has been demonstrated, we are wrong to remain content with the cheaper substitute. It seems to me that in all discussions upon this subject the capacities of the English language have received but scanty justice. The intellectual tendencies of our race have always been somewhat conservative, and its standards of literary taste or belief, once set up, are not varied without a struggle. The English ear is suspicious of new metres and unaccustomed forms of expression: there are critical detectives on the track of every author, and a violation of the accepted canons is followed

---

March away.

This Mr. Hayward translates:--

Bold the adventure,
Noble the reward--
And the soldiers
Are off.

by a summons to judgment. Thus the tendency is to contract rather than to expand the acknowledged excellences of the language.[99]

The difficulties in the way of a nearly literal translation of Faust in the original metres have been exaggerated, because certain affinities between the two languages have not been properly considered. With all the splendor of versification in the work, it contains but few metres of which the English tongue is not equally capable. Hood has familiarized us with dactylic (triple) rhymes, and they are remarkably abundant and skillful in Mr. Lowell's "Fable for the Critics": even the unrhymed iambic hexameter of the Helena occurs now and then in Milton's Samson Agonistes. It is true that the metrical foot into which the German language most naturally falls is the trochaic, while in English it is the iambic: it is true that German is rich, involved, and tolerant of new combinations, while English is simple, direct, and rather shy of compounds; but precisely these differences are so modified in the German of Faust that there is a mutual approach of the two languages. In Faust, the iambic measure predominates; the style is compact; the many licenses which the author allows himself are all directed towards a shorter mode of construction. On the other hand, English metre compels the use of inversions, admits many verbal liberties prohibited to prose, and so inclines towards various flexible features of its sister-tongue that many lines of Faust may be repeated in English without the slightest change of meaning, measure, or rhyme. There are words, it is true, with so delicate a bloom upon them that it can in no wise be preserved; but even such words will always lose less when they carry with them

---

[99] I cannot resist the temptation of quoting the following passage from Jacob Grimm: "No one of all the modern languages has acquired a greater force and strength than the English, through the derangement and relinquishment of its ancient laws of sound. The unteachable (nevertheless learnable) profusion of its middle-tones has conferred upon it an intrinsic power of expression, such as no other human tongue ever possessed. Its entire, thoroughly intellectual and wonderfully successful foundation and perfected development issued from a marvelous union of the two noblest tongues of Europe, the Germanic and the Romanic. Their mutual relation in the English language is well known, since the former furnished chiefly the material basis, while the latter added the intellectual conceptions. The English language, by and through which the greatest and most eminent poet of modern times--as contrasted with ancient classical poetry--(of course I can refer only to Shakespeare) was begotten and nourished, has a just claim to be called a language of the world; and it appears to be destined, like the English race, to a higher and broader sway in all quarters of the earth. For in richness, in compact adjustment of parts, and in pure intelligence, none of the living languages can be compared with it,--not even our German, which is divided even as we are divided, and which must cast off many imperfections before it can boldly enter on its career."--Ueber den Ursprung der Sprache.

their rhythmical atmosphere. The flow of Goethe's verse is sometimes so similar to that of the corresponding English metre, that not only its harmonies and caesural pauses, but even its punctuation, may be easily retained.

I am satisfied that the difference between a translation of Faust in prose or metre is chiefly one of labor,--and of that labor which is successful in proportion as it is joyously performed. My own task has been cheered by the discovery, that the more closely I reproduced the language of the original, the more of its rhythmical character was transferred at the same time. If, now and then, there was an inevitable alternative of meaning or music, I gave the preference to the former. By the term "original metres" I do not mean a rigid, unyielding adherence to every foot, line, and rhyme of the German original, although this has very nearly been accomplished. Since the greater part of the work is written in an irregular measure, the lines varying from three to six feet, and the rhymes arranged according to the author's will, I do not consider that an occasional change in the number of feet, or order of rhyme, is any violation of the metrical plan. The single slight liberty I have taken with the lyrical passages is in Margaret's song,--"The King of Thule,"--in which, by omitting the alternate feminine rhymes, yet retaining the metre, I was enabled to make the translation strictly literal. If, in two or three instances, I have left a line unrhymed, I have balanced the omission by giving rhymes to other lines which stand unrhymed in the original text. For the same reason, I make no apology for the imperfect rhymes, which are frequently a translation as well as a necessity. With all its supreme qualities, Faust is far from being a technically perfect work.[100]

The feminine and dactylic rhymes, which have been for the most part omitted by all metrical translators except Mr. Brooks, are indispensable. The characteristic tone of many passages would be nearly lost, without them. They give spirit and grace to the dialogue, point to the aphoristic portions (especially in the Second Part), and an ever-changing music to the lyrical passages. The English language, though not so rich as the German in such rhymes, is less deficient than is generally supposed. The difficulty to be overcome is one of construction rather than of the vocabulary. The present participle can only be used to a limited extent, on account of its weak termination, and the want of

---

[100] "At present, everything runs in technical grooves, and the critical gentlemen begin to wrangle whether in a rhyme an s should correspond with an s and not with sz. If I were young and reckless enough, I would purposely offend all such technical caprices: I would use alliteration, assonance, false rhyme, just according to my own will or convenience--but, at the same time, I would attend to the main thing, and endeavor to say so many good things that every one would be attracted to read and remember them."--Goethe, in 1831.

an accusative form to the noun also restricts the arrangement of words in English verse. I cannot hope to have been always successful; but I have at least labored long and patiently, bearing constantly in mind not only the meaning of the original and the mechanical structure of the lines, but also that subtile and haunting music which seems to govern rhythm instead of being governed by it.

B.T.

AN GOETHE

I

Erhabener Geist, im Geisterreich verloren!
Wo immer Deine lichte Wohnung sey,
Zum höh'ren Schaffen bist Du neugeboren,
Und singest dort die voll're Litanei.
Von jenem Streben das Du auserkoren,
Vom reinsten Aether, drin Du athmest frei,
O neige Dich zu gnädigem Erwiedern
Des letzten Wiederhalls von Deinen Liedern!

II

Den alten Musen die bestäubten Kronen
Nahmst Du, zu neuem Glanz, mit kühner Hand:
Du löst die Räthsel ältester Aeonen
Durch jüngeren Glauben, helleren Verstand,
Und machst, wo rege Menschengeister wohnen,
Die ganze Erde Dir zum Vaterland;
Und Deine Jünger sehn in Dir, verwundert,
Verkörpert schon das werdende Jahrhundert.

III

Was Du gesungen, Aller Lust und Klagen,
Des Lebens Wiedersprüche, neu vermählt,--
Die Harfe tausendstimmig frisch geschlagen,
Die Shakspeare einst, die einst Homer gewählt,--
Darf ich in fremde Klänge übertragen
Das Alles, wo so Mancher schon gefehlt?
Lass Deinen Geist in meiner Stimme klingen,
Und was Du sangst, lass mich es Dir nachsingen!

B.T.

DEDICATION

Again ye come, ye hovering Forms! I find ye,
As early to my clouded sight ye shone!
Shall I attempt, this once, to seize and bind ye?
Still o'er my heart is that illusion thrown?
Ye crowd more near! Then, be the reign assigned ye,
And sway me from your misty, shadowy zone!
My bosom thrills, with youthful passion shaken,
From magic airs that round your march awaken.

Of joyous days ye bring the blissful vision;
The dear, familiar phantoms rise again,
And, like an old and half-extinct tradition,
First Love returns, with Friendship in his train.
Renewed is Pain: with mournful repetition
Life tracks his devious, labyrinthine chain,
And names the Good, whose cheating fortune tore them
From happy hours, and left me to deplore them.

They hear no longer these succeeding measures,
The souls, to whom my earliest songs I sang:

Dispersed the friendly troop, with all its pleasures,
And still, alas! the echoes first that rang!
I bring the unknown multitude my treasures;
Their very plaudits give my heart a pang,
And those beside, whose joy my Song so flattered,
If still they live, wide through the world are scattered.

And grasps me now a long-unwonted yearning
For that serene and solemn Spirit-Land:
My song, to faint Aeolian murmurs turning,
Sways like a harp-string by the breezes fanned.
I thrill and tremble; tear on tear is burning,
And the stern heart is tenderly unmanned.
What I possess, I see far distant lying,
And what I lost, grows real and undying.

PRELUDE AT THE THEATRE

MANAGER   DRAMATIC POET   MERRY-ANDREW

MANAGER

You two, who oft a helping hand
Have lent, in need and tribulation.
Come, let me know your expectation
Of this, our enterprise, in German land!
I wish the crowd to feel itself well treated,
Especially since it lives and lets me live;
The posts are set, the booth of boards completed.
And each awaits the banquet I shall give.
Already there, with curious eyebrows raised,
They sit sedate, and hope to be amazed.
I know how one the People's taste may flatter,
Yet here a huge embarrassment I feel:
What they're accustomed to, is no great matter,
But then, alas! they've read an awful deal.
How shall we plan, that all be fresh and new,--
Important matter, yet attractive too?
For 'tis my pleasure-to behold them surging,
When to our booth the current sets apace,
And with tremendous, oft-repeated urging,
Squeeze onward through the narrow gate of grace:
By daylight even, they push and cram in
To reach the seller's box, a fighting host,
And as for bread, around a baker's door, in famine,
To get a ticket break their necks almost.
This miracle alone can work the Poet
On men so various: now, my friend, pray show it.

POET

Speak not to me of yonder motley masses,
Whom but to see, puts out the fire of Song!
Hide from my view the surging crowd that passes,
And in its whirlpool forces us along!
No, lead me where some heavenly silence glasses
The purer joys that round the Poet throng,--
Where Love and Friendship still divinely fashion
The bonds that bless, the wreaths that crown his passion!
Ah, every utterance from the depths of feeling
The timid lips have stammeringly expressed,--
Now failing, now, perchance, success revealing,--

Gulps the wild Moment in its greedy breast;
Or oft, reluctant years its warrant sealing,
Its perfect stature stands at last confessed!
What dazzles, for the Moment spends its spirit:
What's genuine, shall Posterity inherit.

MERRY-ANDREW

Posterity! Don't name the word to me!
If I should choose to preach Posterity,
Where would you get contemporary fun?
That men will have it, there's no blinking:
A fine young fellow's presence, to my thinking,
Is something worth, to every one.
Who genially his nature can outpour,
Takes from the People's moods no irritation;
The wider circle he acquires, the more
Securely works his inspiration.
Then pluck up heart, and give us sterling coin!
Let Fancy be with her attendants fitted,--
Sense, Reason, Sentiment, and Passion join,--
But have a care, lest Folly be omitted!

MANAGER

Chiefly, enough of incident prepare!
They come to look, and they prefer to stare.
Reel off a host of threads before their faces,
So that they gape in stupid wonder: then
By sheer diffuseness you have won their graces,
And are, at once, most popular of men.
Only by mass you touch the mass; for any
Will finally, himself, his bit select:
Who offers much, brings something unto many,
And each goes home content with the effect,
If you've a piece, why, just in pieces give it:
A hash, a stew, will bring success, believe it!
'Tis easily displayed, and easy to invent.
What use, a Whole compactly to present?
Your hearers pick and pluck, as soon as they receive it!

POET

You do not feel, how such a trade debases;
How ill it suits the Artist, proud and true!
The botching work each fine pretender traces
Is, I perceive, a principle with you.

MANAGER

Such a reproach not in the least offends;
A man who some result intends
Must use the tools that best are fitting.
Reflect, soft wood is given to you for splitting,
And then, observe for whom you write!
If one comes bored, exhausted quite,
Another, satiate, leaves the banquet's tapers,
And, worst of all, full many a wight
Is fresh from reading of the daily papers.
Idly to us they come, as to a masquerade,
Mere curiosity their spirits warming:
The ladies with themselves, and with their finery, aid,
Without a salary their parts performing.
What dreams are yours in high poetic places?
You're pleased, forsooth, full houses to behold?
Draw near, and view your patrons' faces!
The half are coarse, the half are cold.
One, when the play is out, goes home to cards;
A wild night on a wench's breast another chooses:
Why should you rack, poor, foolish bards,
For ends like these, the gracious Muses?
I tell you, give but more--more, ever more, they ask:
Thus shall you hit the mark of gain and glory.
Seek to confound your auditory!
To satisfy them is a task.--
What ails you now? Is't suffering, or pleasure?

POET

Go, find yourself a more obedient slave!
What! shall the Poet that which Nature gave,
The highest right, supreme Humanity,
Forfeit so wantonly, to swell your treasure?
Whence o'er the heart his empire free?
The elements of Life how conquers he?
Is't not his heart's accord, urged outward far and dim,
To wind the world in unison with him?
When on the spindle, spun to endless distance,
By Nature's listless hand the thread is twirled,
And the discordant tones of all existence
In sullen jangle are together hurled,
Who, then, the changeless orders of creation
Divides, and kindles into rhythmic dance?

Who brings the One to join the general ordination,
Where it may throb in grandest consonance?
Who bids the storm to passion stir the bosom?
In brooding souls the sunset burn above?
Who scatters every fairest April blossom
Along the shining path of Love?
Who braids the noteless leaves to crowns, requiting
Desert with fame, in Action's every field?
Who makes Olympus sure, the Gods uniting?
The might of Man, as in the Bard revealed.

MERRY-ANDREW

So, these fine forces, in conjunction,
Propel the high poetic function,
As in a love-adventure they might play!
You meet by accident; you feel, you stay,
And by degrees your heart is tangled;
Bliss grows apace, and then its course is jangled;
You're ravished quite, then comes a touch of woe,
And there's a neat romance, completed ere you know!
Let us, then, such a drama give!
Grasp the exhaustless life that all men live!
Each shares therein, though few may comprehend:
Where'er you touch, there's interest without end.
In motley pictures little light,
Much error, and of truth a glimmering mite,
Thus the best beverage is supplied,
Whence all the world is cheered and edified.
Then, at your play, behold the fairest flower
Of youth collect, to hear the revelation!
Each tender soul, with sentimental power,
Sucks melancholy food from your creation;
And now in this, now that, the leaven works.
For each beholds what in his bosom lurks.
They still are moved at once to weeping or to laughter,
Still wonder at your flights, enjoy the show they see:
A mind, once formed, is never suited after;
One yet in growth will ever grateful be.

POET

Then give me back that time of pleasures,
While yet in joyous growth I sang,--
When, like a fount, the crowding measures
Uninterrupted gushed and sprang!

Then bright mist veiled the world before me,
In opening buds a marvel woke,
As I the thousand blossoms broke,
Which every valley richly bore me!
I nothing had, and yet enough for youth--
Joy in Illusion, ardent thirst for Truth.
Give, unrestrained, the old emotion,
The bliss that touched the verge of pain,
The strength of Hate, Love's deep devotion,--
O, give me back my youth again!

MERRY ANDREW

Youth, good my friend, you certainly require
When foes in combat sorely press you;
When lovely maids, in fond desire,
Hang on your bosom and caress you;
When from the hard-won goal the wreath
Beckons afar, the race awaiting;
When, after dancing out your breath,
You pass the night in dissipating:--
But that familiar harp with soul
To play,--with grace and bold expression,
And towards a self-erected goal
To walk with many a sweet digression,--
This, aged Sirs, belongs to you,
And we no less revere you for that reason:
Age childish makes, they say, but 'tis not true;
We're only genuine children still, in Age's season!

MANAGER

The words you've bandied are sufficient;
'Tis deeds that I prefer to see:
In compliments you're both proficient,
But might, the while, more useful be.
What need to talk of Inspiration?
'Tis no companion of Delay.
If Poetry be your vocation,
Let Poetry your will obey!
Full well you know what here is wanting;
The crowd for strongest drink is panting,
And such, forthwith, I'd have you brew.
What's left undone to-day, To-morrow will not do.
Waste not a day in vain digression:
With resolute, courageous trust

Seize every possible impression,
And make it firmly your possession;
You'll then work on, because you must.
Upon our German stage, you know it,
Each tries his hand at what he will;
So, take of traps and scenes your fill,
And all you find, be sure to show it!
Use both the great and lesser heavenly light,--
Squander the stars in any number,
Beasts, birds, trees, rocks, and all such lumber,
Fire, water, darkness, Day and Night!
Thus, in our booth's contracted sphere,
The circle of Creation will appear,
And move, as we deliberately impel,
From Heaven, across the World, to Hell!

PROLOGUE IN HEAVEN

THE LORD THE HEAVENLY HOST Afterwards
MEPHISTOPHELES

(The THREE ARCHANGELS come forward.)

RAPHAEL

The sun-orb sings, in emulation,
'Mid brother-spheres, his ancient round:
His path predestined through Creation
He ends with step of thunder-sound.
The angels from his visage splendid
Draw power, whose measure none can say;
The lofty works, uncomprehended,
Are bright as on the earliest day.

GABRIEL

And swift, and swift beyond conceiving,
The splendor of the world goes round,
Day's Eden-brightness still relieving
The awful Night's intense profound:
The ocean-tides in foam are breaking,
Against the rocks' deep bases hurled,
And both, the spheric race partaking,
Eternal, swift, are onward whirled!

MICHAEL

And rival storms abroad are surging
From sea to land, from land to sea.
A chain of deepest action forging
Round all, in wrathful energy.
There flames a desolation, blazing
Before the Thunder's crashing way:
Yet, Lord, Thy messengers are praising
The gentle movement of Thy Day.

THE THREE

Though still by them uncomprehended,
From these the angels draw their power,
And all Thy works, sublime and splendid,
Are bright as in Creation's hour.

MEPHISTOPHELES

Since Thou, O Lord, deign'st to approach again
And ask us how we do, in manner kindest,
And heretofore to meet myself wert fain,
Among Thy menials, now, my face Thou findest.
Pardon, this troop I cannot follow after
With lofty speech, though by them scorned and spurned:
My pathos certainly would move Thy laughter,
If Thou hadst not all merriment unlearned.
Of suns and worlds I've nothing to be quoted;
How men torment themselves, is all I've noted.
The little god o' the world sticks to the same old way,
And is as whimsical as on Creation's day.
Life somewhat better might content him,
But for the gleam of heavenly light which Thou hast lent
  him:
He calls it Reason--thence his power's increased,
To be far beastlier than any beast.
Saving Thy Gracious Presence, he to me
A long-legged grasshopper appears to be,
That springing flies, and flying springs,
And in the grass the same old ditty sings.
Would he still lay among the grass he grows in!
Each bit of dung he seeks, to stick his nose in.

THE LORD

Hast thou, then, nothing more to mention?
Com'st ever, thus, with ill intention?
Find'st nothing right on earth, eternally?

MEPHISTOPHELES

No, Lord! I find things, there, still bad as they can be.
Man's misery even to pity moves my nature;
I've scarce the heart to plague the wretched creature.

THE LORD

Know'st Faust?

MEPHISTOPHELES

The Doctor Faust?

THE LORD

My servant, he!

MEPHISTOPHELES

Forsooth! He serves you after strange devices:
No earthly meat or drink the fool suffices:
His spirit's ferment far aspireth;
Half conscious of his frenzied, crazed unrest,
The fairest stars from Heaven he requireth,
From Earth the highest raptures and the best,
And all the Near and Far that he desireth
Fails to subdue the tumult of his breast.

THE LORD

Though still confused his service unto Me,
I soon shall lead him to a clearer morning.
Sees not the gardener, even while buds his tree,
Both flower and fruit the future years adorning?

MEPHISTOPHELES

What will you bet? There's still a chance to gain him,
If unto me full leave you give,
Gently upon my road to train him!

THE LORD

As long as he on earth shall live,
So long I make no prohibition.
While Man's desires and aspirations stir,
He cannot choose but err.

MEPHISTOPHELES

My thanks! I find the dead no acquisition,
And never cared to have them in my keeping.
I much prefer the cheeks where ruddy blood is leaping,
And when a corpse approaches, close my house:
It goes with me, as with the cat the mouse.

THE LORD

Enough! What thou hast asked is granted.
Turn off this spirit from his fountain-head;
To trap him, let thy snares be planted,
And him, with thee, be downward led;
Then stand abashed, when thou art forced to say:
A good man, through obscurest aspiration,
Has still an instinct of the one true way.

MEPHISTOPHELES

Agreed! But 'tis a short probation.

About my bet I feel no trepidation.
If I fulfill my expectation,
You'll let me triumph with a swelling breast:
Dust shall he eat, and with a zest,
As did a certain snake, my near relation.

THE LORD
Therein thou'rt free, according to thy merits;
The like of thee have never moved My hate.
Of all the bold, denying Spirits,
The waggish knave least trouble doth create.
Man's active nature, flagging, seeks too soon the level;
Unqualified repose he learns to crave;
Whence, willingly, the comrade him I gave,
Who works, excites, and must create, as Devil.
But ye, God's sons in love and duty,
Enjoy the rich, the ever-living Beauty!
Creative Power, that works eternal schemes,
Clasp you in bonds of love, relaxing never,
And what in wavering apparition gleams
Fix in its place with thoughts that stand forever!

(Heaven closes: the ARCHANGELS separate.)

MEPHISTOPHELES (solus)
I like, at times, to hear The Ancient's word,
And have a care to be most civil:
It's really kind of such a noble Lord
So humanly to gossip with the Devil!

FIRST PART OF THE TRAGEDY

I

NIGHT

(A lofty-arched, narrow, Gothic chamber. FAUST, in a chair at his desk, restless.)

FAUST
I've studied now Philosophy
And Jurisprudence, Medicine,--
And even, alas! Theology,--
From end to end, with labor keen;
And here, poor fool! with all my lore
I stand, no wiser than before:
I'm Magister--yea, Doctor--hight,
And straight or cross-wise, wrong or right,
These ten years long, with many woes,
I've led my scholars by the nose,--
And see, that nothing can be known!
That knowledge cuts me to the bone.
I'm cleverer, true, than those fops of teachers,
Doctors and Magisters, Scribes and Preachers;
Neither scruples nor doubts come now to smite me,
Nor Hell nor Devil can longer affright me.

For this, all pleasure am I foregoing;
I do not pretend to aught worth knowing,
I do not pretend I could be a teacher
To help or convert a fellow-creature.
Then, too, I've neither lands nor gold,
Nor the world's least pomp or honor hold--
No dog would endure such a curst existence!
Wherefore, from Magic I seek assistance,
That many a secret perchance I reach
Through spirit-power and spirit-speech,
And thus the bitter task forego
Of saying the things I do not know,--
That I may detect the inmost force
Which binds the world, and guides its course;
Its germs, productive powers explore,
And rummage in empty words no more!

O full and splendid Moon, whom I
Have, from this desk, seen climb the sky
So many a midnight,--would thy glow
For the last time beheld my woe!
Ever thine eye, most mournful friend,
O'er books and papers saw me bend;
But would that I, on mountains grand,
Amid thy blessed light could stand,
With spirits through mountain-caverns hover,
Float in thy twilight the meadows over,
And, freed from the fumes of lore that swathe me,
To health in thy dewy fountains bathe me!

Ah, me! this dungeon still I see.
This drear, accursed masonry,
Where even the welcome daylight strains
But duskly through the painted panes.
Hemmed in by many a toppling heap
Of books worm-eaten, gray with dust,
Which to the vaulted ceiling creep,
Against the smoky paper thrust,--
With glasses, boxes, round me stacked,
And instruments together hurled,
Ancestral lumber, stuffed and packed--
Such is my world: and what a world!

And do I ask, wherefore my heart
Falters, oppressed with unknown needs?
Why some inexplicable smart
All movement of my life impedes?
Alas! in living Nature's stead,
Where God His human creature set,
In smoke and mould the fleshless dead
And bones of beasts surround me yet!

Fly! Up, and seek the broad, free land!
And this one Book of Mystery
From Nostradamus' very hand,
Is't not sufficient company?
When I the starry courses know,
And Nature's wise instruction seek,
With light of power my soul shall glow,
As when to spirits spirits speak.
Tis vain, this empty brooding here,

Though guessed the holy symbols be:
Ye, Spirits, come--ye hover near--
Oh, if you hear me, answer me!

(He opens the Book, and perceives the sign of the Macrocosm.)

Ha! what a sudden rapture leaps from this
I view, through all my senses swiftly flowing!
I feel a youthful, holy, vital bliss
In every vein and fibre newly glowing.
Was it a God, who traced this sign,
With calm across my tumult stealing,
My troubled heart to joy unsealing,
With impulse, mystic and divine,
The powers of Nature here, around my path, revealing?
Am I a God?--so clear mine eyes!
In these pure features I behold
Creative Nature to my soul unfold.
What says the sage, now first I recognize:
"The spirit-world no closures fasten;
Thy sense is shut, thy heart is dead:
Disciple, up! untiring, hasten
To bathe thy breast in morning-red!"

(He contemplates the sign.)

How each the Whole its substance gives,
Each in the other works and lives!
Like heavenly forces rising and descending,
Their golden urns reciprocally lending,
With wings that winnow blessing
From Heaven through Earth I see them pressing,
Filling the All with harmony unceasing!
How grand a show! but, ah! a show alone.
Thee, boundless Nature, how make thee my own?
Where you, ye beasts? Founts of all Being, shining,
Whereon hang Heaven's and Earth's desire,
Whereto our withered hearts aspire,--
Ye flow, ye feed: and am I vainly pining?

(He turns the leaves impatiently, and perceives the sign of the
Earth-Spirit.)

How otherwise upon me works this sign!

Thou, Spirit of the Earth, art nearer:
Even now my powers are loftier, clearer;
I glow, as drunk with new-made wine:
New strength and heart to meet the world incite me,
The woe of earth, the bliss of earth, invite me,
And though the shock of storms may smite me,
No crash of shipwreck shall have power to fright me!
Clouds gather over me--
The moon conceals her light--
The lamp's extinguished!--
Mists rise,--red, angry rays are darting
Around my head!--There falls
A horror from the vaulted roof,
And seizes me!
I feel thy presence, Spirit I invoke!
Reveal thyself!
Ha! in my heart what rending stroke!
With new impulsion
My senses heave in this convulsion!
I feel thee draw my heart, absorb, exhaust me:
Thou must! thou must! and though my life it cost me!

(He seizes the book, and mysteriously pronounces the sign of
the Spirit. A ruddy flame flashes: the Spirit appears in
the flame.)

SPIRIT
Who calls me?

FAUST (with averted head)
Terrible to see!

SPIRIT
Me hast thou long with might attracted,
Long from my sphere thy food exacted,
And now--

FAUST
  Woe! I endure not thee!

SPIRIT
To view me is thine aspiration,
My voice to hear, my countenance to see;
Thy powerful yearning moveth me,

Here am I!--what mean perturbation
Thee, superhuman, shakes? Thy soul's high calling, where?
Where is the breast, which from itself a world did bear,
And shaped and cherished--which with joy expanded,
To be our peer, with us, the Spirits, banded?
Where art thou, Faust, whose voice has pierced to me,
Who towards me pressed with all thine energy?
He art thou, who, my presence breathing, seeing,
Trembles through all the depths of being,
A writhing worm, a terror-stricken form?

FAUST
Thee, form of flame, shall I then fear?
Yes, I am Faust: I am thy peer!

SPIRIT
  In the tides of Life, in Action's storm,
  A fluctuant wave,
  A shuttle free,
  Birth and the Grave,
  An eternal sea,
  A weaving, flowing
  Life, all-glowing,
Thus at Time's humming loom 'tis my hand prepares
The garment of Life which the Deity wears!

FAUST
Thou, who around the wide world wendest,
Thou busy Spirit, how near I feel to thee!

SPIRIT
Thou'rt like the Spirit which thou comprehendest,
Not me!

(Disappears.)

FAUST (overwhelmed)

Not thee!
Whom then?
I, image of the Godhead!
Not even like thee!

(A knock).

O Death!--I know it--'tis my Famulus!
My fairest luck finds no fruition:
In all the fullness of my vision
The soulless sneak disturbs me thus!

(Enter WAGNER, in dressing-gown and night-cap, a lamp in
his hand. FAUST turns impatiently.)

WAGNER

Pardon, I heard your declamation;
'Twas sure an old Greek tragedy you read?
In such an art I crave some preparation,
Since now it stands one in good stead.
I've often heard it said, a preacher
Might learn, with a comedian for a teacher.

FAUST

Yes, when the priest comedian is by nature,
As haply now and then the case may be.

WAGNER

Ah, when one studies thus, a prisoned creature,
That scarce the world on holidays can see,--
Scarce through a glass, by rare occasion,
How shall one lead it by persuasion?

FAUST

You'll ne'er attain it, save you know the feeling,
Save from the soul it rises clear,
Serene in primal strength, compelling
The hearts and minds of all who hear.
You sit forever gluing, patching;
You cook the scraps from others' fare;
And from your heap of ashes hatching
A starveling flame, ye blow it bare!
Take children's, monkeys' gaze admiring,
If such your taste, and be content;
But ne'er from heart to heart you'll speak inspiring,
Save your own heart is eloquent!

WAGNER

Yet through delivery orators succeed;
I feel that I am far behind, indeed.

FAUST

Seek thou the honest recompense!
Beware, a tinkling fool to be!
With little art, clear wit and sense
Suggest their own delivery;
And if thou'rt moved to speak in earnest,
What need, that after words thou yearnest?
Yes, your discourses, with their glittering show,
Where ye for men twist shredded thought like paper,
Are unrefreshing as the winds that blow
The rustling leaves through chill autumnal vapor!

WAGNER

Ah, God! but Art is long,
And Life, alas! is fleeting.
And oft, with zeal my critic-duties meeting,
In head and breast there's something wrong.

How hard it is to compass the assistance
Whereby one rises to the source!
And, haply, ere one travels half the course
Must the poor devil quit existence.

FAUST

Is parchment, then, the holy fount before thee,
A draught wherefrom thy thirst forever slakes?
No true refreshment can restore thee,
Save what from thine own soul spontaneous breaks.

WAGNER

Pardon! a great delight is granted
When, in the spirit of the ages planted,
We mark how, ere our times, a sage has thought,
And then, how far his work, and grandly, we have brought.

FAUST

O yes, up to the stars at last!
Listen, my friend: the ages that are past
Are now a book with seven seals protected:
What you the Spirit of the Ages call
Is nothing but the spirit of you all,
Wherein the Ages are reflected.
So, oftentimes, you miserably mar it!

At the first glance who sees it runs away.
An offal-barrel and a lumber-garret,
Or, at the best, a Punch-and-Judy play,
With maxims most pragmatical and hitting,
As in the mouths of puppets are befitting!

WAGNER

But then, the world--the human heart and brain!
Of these one covets some slight apprehension.

FAUST

Yes, of the kind which men attain!
Who dares the child's true name in public mention?
The few, who thereof something really learned,
Unwisely frank, with hearts that spurned concealing,
And to the mob laid bare each thought and feeling,
Have evermore been crucified and burned.
I pray you, Friend, 'tis now the dead of night;
Our converse here must be suspended.

WAGNER

I would have shared your watches with delight,
That so our learned talk might be extended.
To-morrow, though, I'll ask, in Easter leisure,
This and the other question, at your pleasure.
Most zealously I seek for erudition:
Much do I know--but to know all is my ambition.

[Exit.

FAUST (solus)

That brain, alone, not loses hope, whose choice is
To stick in shallow trash forevermore,--
Which digs with eager hand for buried ore,
And, when it finds an angle-worm, rejoices!

Dare such a human voice disturb the flow,
Around me here, of spirit-presence fullest?
And yet, this once my thanks I owe
To thee, of all earth's sons the poorest, dullest!
For thou hast torn me from that desperate state
Which threatened soon to overwhelm my senses:
The apparition was so giant-great,
It dwarfed and withered all my soul's pretences!

I, image of the Godhead, who began--
Deeming Eternal Truth secure in nearness--
Ye choirs, have ye begun the sweet, consoling chant,
Which, through the night of Death, the angels ministrant
Sang, God's new Covenant repeating?

CHORUS OF WOMEN

With spices and precious
Balm, we arrayed him;
Faithful and gracious,
We tenderly laid him:
Linen to bind him
Cleanlily wound we:
Ah! when we would find him,
Christ no more found we!

CHORUS OF ANGELS

Christ is ascended!
Bliss hath invested him,--
Woes that molested him,
Trials that tested him,
Gloriously ended!

FAUST

Why, here in dust, entice me with your spell,
Ye gentle, powerful sounds of Heaven?
Peal rather there, where tender natures dwell.
Your messages I hear, but faith has not been given;
The dearest child of Faith is Miracle.
I venture not to soar to yonder regions
Whence the glad tidings hither float;
And yet, from childhood up familiar with the note,
To Life it now renews the old allegiance.
Once Heavenly Love sent down a burning kiss
Upon my brow, in Sabbath silence holy;
And, filled with mystic presage, chimed the church-bell slowly,
And prayer dissolved me in a fervent bliss.
A sweet, uncomprehended yearning
Drove forth my feet through woods and meadows free,
And while a thousand tears were burning,
I felt a world arise for me.
These chants, to youth and all its sports appealing,
Proclaimed the Spring's rejoicing holiday;

And Memory holds me now, with childish feeling,
Back from the last, the solemn way.
Sound on, ye hymns of Heaven, so sweet and mild!
My tears gush forth: the Earth takes back her child!

CHORUS OF DISCIPLES

Has He, victoriously,
Burst from the vaulted
Grave, and all-gloriously
Now sits exalted?
Is He, in glow of birth,
Rapture creative near?
Ah! to the woe of earth
Still are we native here.
We, his aspiring
Followers, Him we miss;
Weeping, desiring,
Master, Thy bliss!

CHORUS OF ANGELS

Christ is arisen,
Out of Corruption's womb:
Burst ye the prison,
Break from your gloom!
Praising and pleading him,
Lovingly needing him,
Brotherly feeding him,
Preaching and speeding him,
Blessing, succeeding Him,
Thus is the Master near,--
Thus is He here!

II

BEFORE THE CITY-GATE

(Pedestrians of all kinds come forth.)

SEVERAL APPRENTICES
Why do you go that way?

OTHERS
We're for the Hunters' lodge, to-day.

THE FIRST
We'll saunter to the Mill, in yonder hollow.

AN APPRENTICE
Go to the River Tavern, I should say.

SECOND APPRENTICE
But then, it's not a pleasant way.

THE OTHERS
And what will you?

A THIRD
As goes the crowd, I follow.

A FOURTH
Come up to Burgdorf? There you'll find good cheer,
The finest lasses and the best of beer,
And jolly rows and squabbles, trust me!

A FIFTH

You swaggering fellow, is your hide
A third time itching to be tried?
I won't go there, your jolly rows disgust me!

SERVANT-GIRL

No,--no! I'll turn and go to town again.

ANOTHER
We'll surely find him by those poplars yonder.

THE FIRST

That's no great luck for me, 'tis plain.
You'll have him, when and where you wander:
His partner in the dance you'll be,--
But what is all your fun to me?

THE OTHER

He's surely not alone to-day:
He'll be with Curly-head, I heard him say.

A STUDENT

Deuce! how they step, the buxom wenches!
Come, Brother! we must see them to the benches.
A strong, old beer, a pipe that stings and bites,
A girl in Sunday clothes,--these three are my delights.

CITIZEN'S DAUGHTER

Just see those handsome fellows, there!
It's really shameful, I declare;--
To follow servant-girls, when they
Might have the most genteel society to-day!

SECOND STUDENT (to the First)

Not quite so fast! Two others come behind,--
Those, dressed so prettily and neatly.
My neighbor's one of them, I find,
A girl that takes my heart, completely.
They go their way with looks demure,
But they'll accept us, after all, I'm sure.

THE FIRST

No, Brother! not for me their formal ways.
Quick! lest our game escape us in the press:
The hand that wields the broom on Saturdays
Will best, on Sundays, fondle and caress.

CITIZEN

He suits me not at all, our new-made Burgomaster!
Since he's installed, his arrogance grows faster.
How has he helped the town, I say?
Things worsen,--what improvement names he?
Obedience, more than ever, claims he,

And more than ever we must pay!

BEGGAR (sings)
  Good gentlemen and lovely ladies,
  So red of cheek and fine of dress,
  Behold, how needful here your aid is,
  And see and lighten my distress!
  Let me not vainly sing my ditty;
  He's only glad who gives away:
  A holiday, that shows your pity,
  Shall be for me a harvest-day!

ANOTHER CITIZEN

On Sundays, holidays, there's naught I take delight in,
Like gossiping of war, and war's array,
When down in Turkey, far away,
The foreign people are a-fighting.
One at the window sits, with glass and friends,
And sees all sorts of ships go down the river gliding:
And blesses then, as home he wends
At night, our times of peace abiding.

THIRD CITIZEN
Yes, Neighbor! that's my notion, too:
Why, let them break their heads, let loose their passions,
And mix things madly through and through,
So, here, we keep our good old fashions!

OLD WOMAN (to the Citizen's Daughter)
Dear me, how fine! So handsome, and so young!
Who wouldn't lose his heart, that met you?
Don't be so proud! I'll hold my tongue,
And what you'd like I'll undertake to get you.

CITIZEN'S DAUGHTER
Come, Agatha! I shun the witch's sight
Before folks, lest there be misgiving:
'Tis true, she showed me, on Saint Andrew's Night,
My future sweetheart, just as he were living.

THE OTHER
She showed me mine, in crystal clear,
With several wild young blades, a soldier-lover:

I seek him everywhere, I pry and peer,
And yet, somehow, his face I can't discover.

SOLDIERS

Castles, with lofty
Ramparts and towers,
Maidens disdainful
In Beauty's array,
Both shall be ours!
Bold is the venture,
Splendid the pay!
Lads, let the trumpets
For us be suing,--
Calling to pleasure,
Calling to ruin.
Stormy our life is;
Such is its boon!
Maidens and castles
Capitulate soon.
Bold is the venture,
Splendid the pay!
And the soldiers go marching,
Marching away!

FAUST AND WAGNER

FAUST

Released from ice are brook and river
By the quickening glance of the gracious Spring;
The colors of hope to the valley cling,
And weak old Winter himself must shiver,
Withdrawn to the mountains, a crownless king:
Whence, ever retreating, he sends again
Impotent showers of sleet that darkle
In belts across the green o' the plain.
But the sun will permit no white to sparkle;
Everywhere form in development moveth;
He will brighten the world with the tints he loveth,
And, lacking blossoms, blue, yellow, and red,
He takes these gaudy people instead.
Turn thee about, and from this height
Back on the town direct thy sight.
Out of the hollow, gloomy gate,
The motley throngs come forth elate:

Each will the joy of the sunshine hoard,
To honor the Day of the Risen Lord!
They feel, themselves, their resurrection:
From the low, dark rooms, scarce habitable;
From the bonds of Work, from Trade's restriction;
From the pressing weight of roof and gable;
From the narrow, crushing streets and alleys;
From the churches' solemn and reverend night,
All come forth to the cheerful light.
How lively, see! the multitude sallies,
Scattering through gardens and fields remote,
While over the river, that broadly dallies,
Dances so many a festive boat;
And overladen, nigh to sinking,
The last full wherry takes the stream.
Yonder afar, from the hill-paths blinking,
Their clothes are colors that softly gleam.
I hear the noise of the village, even;
Here is the People's proper Heaven;
Here high and low contented see!
Here I am Man,--dare man to be!

WAGNER

To stroll with you, Sir Doctor, flatters;
'Tis honor, profit, unto me.
But I, alone, would shun these shallow matters,
Since all that's coarse provokes my enmity.
This fiddling, shouting, ten-pin rolling
I hate,--these noises of the throng:
They rave, as Satan were their sports controlling.
And call it mirth, and call it song!

PEASANTS, UNDER THE LINDEN-TREE
(Dance and Song.)

All for the dance the shepherd dressed,
In ribbons, wreath, and gayest vest
  Himself with care arraying:
Around the linden lass and lad
Already footed it like mad:
  Hurrah! hurrah!
  Hurrah--tarara-la!
The fiddle-bow was playing.

He broke the ranks, no whit afraid,
And with his elbow punched a maid,
   Who stood, the dance surveying:
The buxom wench, she turned and said:
"Now, you I call a stupid-head!"
   Hurrah! hurrah!
   Hurrah--tarara-la!
"Be decent while you're staying!"

Then round the circle went their flight,
They danced to left, they danced to right:
Their kirtles all were playing.
They first grew red, and then grew warm,
And rested, panting, arm in arm,--
   Hurrah! hurrah!
   Hurrah--tarara-la!
And hips and elbows straying.

Now, don't be so familiar here!
How many a one has fooled his dear,
Waylaying and betraying!

And yet, he coaxed her soon aside,
And round the linden sounded wide.
   Hurrah! hurrah!
   Hurrah--tarara-la!
And the fiddle-bow was playing.

OLD PEASANT

Sir Doctor, it is good of you,
That thus you condescend, to-day,
Among this crowd of merry folk,
A highly-learned man, to stray.
Then also take the finest can,
We fill with fresh wine, for your sake:
I offer it, and humbly wish
That not alone your thirst is slake,--
That, as the drops below its brink,
So many days of life you drink!

FAUST

I take the cup you kindly reach,
With thanks and health to all and each.

(The People gather in a circle about him.)

OLD PEASANT
In truth, 'tis well and fitly timed,
That now our day of joy you share,
Who heretofore, in evil days,
Gave us so much of helping care.
Still many a man stands living here,
Saved by your father's skillful hand,
That snatched him from the fever's rage
And stayed the plague in all the land.
Then also you, though but a youth,
Went into every house of pain:
Many the corpses carried forth,
But you in health came out again.

FAUST
No test or trial you evaded:
A Helping God the helper aided.

ALL
Health to the man, so skilled and tried.
That for our help he long may abide!

FAUST
To Him above bow down, my friends,
Who teaches help, and succor sends!

(He goes on with WAGNER.)

WAGNER
With what a feeling, thou great man, must thou
Receive the people's honest veneration!
How lucky he, whose gifts his station
With such advantages endow!
Thou'rt shown to all the younger generation:
Each asks, and presses near to gaze;
The fiddle stops, the dance delays.
Thou goest, they stand in rows to see,
And all the caps are lifted high;
A little more, and they would bend the knee
As if the Holy Host came by.
FAUST
A few more steps ascend, as far as yonder stone!--

Here from our wandering will we rest contented.
Here, lost in thought, I've lingered oft alone,
When foolish fasts and prayers my life tormented.
Here, rich in hope and firm in faith,
With tears, wrung hands and sighs, I've striven,
The end of that far-spreading death
Entreating from the Lord of Heaven!
Now like contempt the crowd's applauses seem:
Couldst thou but read, within mine inmost spirit,
How little now I deem,
That sire or son such praises merit!
My father's was a sombre, brooding brain,
Which through the holy spheres of Nature groped and wandered,
And honestly, in his own fashion, pondered
With labor whimsical, and pain:
Who, in his dusky work-shop bending,
With proved adepts in company,
Made, from his recipes unending,
Opposing substances agree.
There was a Lion red, a wooer daring,
Within the Lily's tepid bath espoused,
And both, tormented then by flame unsparing,
By turns in either bridal chamber housed.
If then appeared, with colors splendid,
The young Queen in her crystal shell,
This was the medicine--the patients' woes soon ended,
And none demanded: who got well?
Thus we, our hellish boluses compounding,
Among these vales and hills surrounding,
Worse than the pestilence, have passed.
Thousands were done to death from poison of my giving;
And I must hear, by all the living,
The shameless murderers praised at last!

WAGNER

Why, therefore, yield to such depression?
A good man does his honest share
In exercising, with the strictest care,
The art bequeathed to his possession!
Dost thou thy father honor, as a youth?
Then may his teaching cheerfully impel thee:
Dost thou, as man, increase the stores of truth?
Then may thine own son afterwards excel thee.

FAUST

O happy he, who still renews
The hope, from Error's deeps to rise forever!
That which one does not know, one needs to use;
And what one knows, one uses never.
But let us not, by such despondence, so
The fortune of this hour embitter!
Mark how, beneath the evening sunlight's glow,
The green-embosomed houses glitter!
The glow retreats, done is the day of toil;
It yonder hastes, new fields of life exploring;
Ah, that no wing can lift me from the soil,
Upon its track to follow, follow soaring!
Then would I see eternal Evening gild
The silent world beneath me glowing,
On fire each mountain-peak, with peace each valley filled,
The silver brook to golden rivers flowing.
The mountain-chain, with all its gorges deep,
Would then no more impede my godlike motion;
And now before mine eyes expands the ocean
With all its bays, in shining sleep!
Yet, finally, the weary god is sinking;
The new-born impulse fires my mind,--
I hasten on, his beams eternal drinking,
The Day before me and the Night behind,
Above me heaven unfurled, the floor of waves beneath me,--
A glorious dream! though now the glories fade.
Alas! the wings that lift the mind no aid
Of wings to lift the body can bequeath me.
Yet in each soul is born the pleasure
Of yearning onward, upward and away,
When o'er our heads, lost in the vaulted azure,
The lark sends down his flickering lay,--
When over crags and piny highlands
The poising eagle slowly soars,
And over plains and lakes and islands
The crane sails by to other shores.

WAGNER

I've had, myself, at times, some odd caprices,
But never yet such impulse felt, as this is.
One soon fatigues, on woods and fields to look,
Nor would I beg the bird his wing to spare us:
How otherwise the mental raptures bear us

From page to page, from book to book!
Then winter nights take loveliness untold,
As warmer life in every limb had crowned you;
And when your hands unroll some parchment rare and old,
All Heaven descends, and opens bright around you!

FAUST

One impulse art thou conscious of, at best;
O, never seek to know the other!
Two souls, alas! reside within my breast,
And each withdraws from, and repels, its brother.
One with tenacious organs holds in love
And clinging lust the world in its embraces;
The other strongly sweeps, this dust above,
Into the high ancestral spaces.
If there be airy spirits near,
'Twixt Heaven and Earth on potent errands fleeing,
Let them drop down the golden atmosphere,
And bear me forth to new and varied being!
Yea, if a magic mantle once were mine,
To waft me o'er the world at pleasure,
I would not for the costliest stores of treasure--
Not for a monarch's robe--the gift resign.

WAGNER

Invoke not thus the well-known throng,
Which through the firmament diffused is faring,
And danger thousand-fold, our race to wrong.
In every quarter is preparing.
Swift from the North the spirit-fangs so sharp
Sweep down, and with their barbéd points assail you;
Then from the East they come, to dry and warp
Your lungs, till breath and being fail you:
If from the Desert sendeth them the South,
With fire on fire your throbbing forehead crowning,
The West leads on a host, to cure the drouth
Only when meadow, field, and you are drowning.
They gladly hearken, prompt for injury,--
Gladly obey, because they gladly cheat us;
From Heaven they represent themselves to be,
And lisp like angels, when with lies they meet us.
But, let us go! 'Tis gray and dusky all:
The air is cold, the vapors fall.
At night, one learns his house to prize:--

Why stand you thus, with such astonished eyes?
What, in the twilight, can your mind so trouble?

FAUST

Seest thou the black dog coursing there, through corn and stubble?

WAGNER

Long since: yet deemed him not important in the least.

FAUST

Inspect him close: for what tak'st thou the beast?

WAGNER

Why, for a poodle who has lost his master,
And scents about, his track to find.

FAUST

Seest thou the spiral circles, narrowing faster,
Which he, approaching, round us seems to wind?
A streaming trail of fire, if I see rightly,
Follows his path of mystery.

WAGNER

It may be that your eyes deceive you slightly;
Naught but a plain black poodle do I see.

FAUST

It seems to me that with enchanted cunning
He snares our feet, some future chain to bind.

WAGNER

I see him timidly, in doubt, around us running,
Since, in his master's stead, two strangers doth he find.

FAUST

The circle narrows: he is near!

WAGNER

A dog thou seest, and not a phantom, here!
Behold him stop--upon his belly crawl--His
tail set wagging: canine habits, all!

FAUST

Come, follow us! Come here, at least!

WAGNER

'Tis the absurdest, drollest beast.
Stand still, and you will see him wait;
Address him, and he gambols straight;
If something's lost, he'll quickly bring it,--
Your cane, if in the stream you fling it.

FAUST

No doubt you're right: no trace of mind, I own,
Is in the beast: I see but drill, alone.

WAGNER

The dog, when he's well educated,
Is by the wisest tolerated.
Yes, he deserves your favor thoroughly,--
The clever scholar of the students, he!

(They pass in the city-gate.)

III

THE STUDY

FAUST
(Entering, with the poodle.)

> Behind me, field and meadow sleeping,
> I leave in deep, prophetic night,
> Within whose dread and holy keeping
> The better soul awakes to light.
> The wild desires no longer win us,
> The deeds of passion cease to chain;
> The love of Man revives within us,
> The love of God revives again.

Be still, thou poodle; make not such racket and riot!
Why at the threshold wilt snuffing be?
Behind the stove repose thee in quiet!
My softest cushion I give to thee.
As thou, up yonder, with running and leaping
Amused us hast, on the mountain's crest,

So now I take thee into my keeping,
A welcome, but also a silent, guest.

> Ah, when, within our narrow chamber
> The lamp with friendly lustre glows,
> Flames in the breast each faded ember,
> And in the heart, itself that knows.
> Then Hope again lends sweet assistance,
> And Reason then resumes her speech:
> One yearns, the rivers of existence,
> The very founts of Life, to reach.

Snarl not, poodle! To the sound that rises,
The sacred tones that my soul embrace,
This bestial noise is out of place.
We are used to see, that Man despises
What he never comprehends,
And the Good and the Beautiful vilipends,
Finding them often hard to measure:
Will the dog, like man, snarl his displeasure?

But ah! I feel, though will thereto be stronger,
Contentment flows from out my breast no longer.
Why must the stream so soon run dry and fail us,
And burning thirst again assail us?
Therein I've borne so much probation!
And yet, this want may be supplied us;
We call the Supernatural to guide us;
We pine and thirst for Revelation,
Which nowhere worthier is, more nobly sent,
Than here, in our New Testament.
I feel impelled, its meaning to determine,--
With honest purpose, once for all,
The hallowed Original
To change to my beloved German.

(He opens a volume, and commences.)
'Tis written: "In the Beginning was the Word."
Here am I balked: who, now can help afford?
The Word?--impossible so high to rate it;
And otherwise must I translate it.
If by the Spirit I am truly taught.
Then thus: "In the Beginning was the Thought"
This first line let me weigh completely,
Lest my impatient pen proceed too fleetly.
Is it the Thought which works, creates, indeed?
"In the Beginning was the Power," I read.
Yet, as I write, a warning is suggested,
That I the sense may not have fairly tested.
The Spirit aids me: now I see the light!
"In the Beginning was the Act," I write.

If I must share my chamber with thee,
Poodle, stop that howling, prithee!
Cease to bark and bellow!
Such a noisy, disturbing fellow
I'll no longer suffer near me.
One of us, dost hear me!
Must leave, I fear me.
No longer guest-right I bestow;
The door is open, art free to go.
But what do I see in the creature?
Is that in the course of nature?
Is't actual fact? or Fancy's shows?

How long and broad my poodle grows!
He rises mightily:
A canine form that cannot be!
What a spectre I've harbored thus!
He resembles a hippopotamus,
With fiery eyes, teeth terrible to see:
O, now am I sure of thee!
For all of thy half-hellish brood
The Key of Solomon is good.

SPIRITS (in the corridor)
 Some one, within, is caught!
 Stay without, follow him not!
 Like the fox in a snare,
 Quakes the old hell-lynx there.
 Take heed--look about!
 Back and forth hover,
 Under and over,
 And he'll work himself out.
 If your aid avail him,
 Let it not fail him;
 For he, without measure,
 Has wrought for our pleasure.

FAUST
First, to encounter the beast,
The Words of the Four be addressed:
 Salamander, shine glorious!
 Wave, Undine, as bidden!
 Sylph, be thou hidden!
 Gnome, be laborious!

Who knows not their sense
(These elements),--
Their properties
And power not sees,--
No mastery he inherits
Over the Spirits.

 Vanish in flaming ether,
 Salamander!
 Flow foamingly together,
 Undine!
 Shine in meteor-sheen,

Sylph!
Bring help to hearth and shelf.
Incubus! Incubus!
Step forward, and finish thus!

Of the Four, no feature
Lurks in the creature.
Quiet he lies, and grins disdain:
Not yet, it seems, have I given him pain.
Now, to undisguise thee,
Hear me exorcise thee!
Art thou, my gay one,
Hell's fugitive stray-one?
The sign witness now,
Before which they bow,
The cohorts of Hell!

With hair all bristling, it begins to swell.

Base Being, hearest thou?
Knowest and fearest thou
The One, unoriginate,
Named inexpressibly,
Through all Heaven impermeate,
Pierced irredressibly!

Behind the stove still banned,
See it, an elephant, expand!
It fills the space entire,
Mist-like melting, ever faster.
'Tis enough: ascend no higher,--
Lay thyself at the feet of the Master!
Thou seest, not vain the threats I bring thee:
With holy fire I'll scorch and sting thee!
Wait not to know
The threefold dazzling glow!
Wait not to know
The strongest art within my hands!

MEPHISTOPHELES
(while the vapor is dissipating, steps forth from behind the
stove, in the costume of a Travelling Scholar.)
Why such a noise? What are my lord's commands?

FAUST

This was the poodle's real core,
A travelling scholar, then? The casus is diverting.

MEPHISTOPHELES

The learned gentleman I bow before:
You've made me roundly sweat, that's certain!

FAUST

What is thy name?

MEPHISTOPHELES

A question small, it seems,
For one whose mind the Word so much despises;
Who, scorning all external gleams,
The depths of being only prizes.

FAUST

With all you gentlemen, the name's a test,
Whereby the nature usually is expressed.
Clearly the latter it implies
In names like Beelzebub, Destroyer, Father of Lies.
Who art thou, then?

MEPHISTOPHELES

Part of that Power, not understood,
Which always wills the Bad, and always works the Good.

FAUST

What hidden sense in this enigma lies?

MEPHISTOPHELES

I am the Spirit that Denies!
And justly so: for all things, from the Void
Called forth, deserve to be destroyed:
'Twere better, then, were naught created.
Thus, all which you as Sin have rated,--
Destruction,--aught with Evil blent,--
That is my proper element.

FAUST

Thou nam'st thyself a part, yet show'st complete to me?

MEPHISTOPHELES

The modest truth I speak to thee.
If Man, that microcosmic fool, can see
Himself a whole so frequently,
Part of the Part am I, once All, in primal Night,--
Part of the Darkness which brought forth the Light,
The haughty Light, which now disputes the space,
And claims of Mother Night her ancient place.
And yet, the struggle fails; since Light, howe'er it weaves,
Still, fettered, unto bodies cleaves:
It flows from bodies, bodies beautifies;
By bodies is its course impeded;
And so, but little time is needed,
I hope, ere, as the bodies die, it dies!

FAUST

I see the plan thou art pursuing:
Thou canst not compass general ruin,
And hast on smaller scale begun.

MEPHISTOPHELES

And truly 'tis not much, when all is done.
That which to Naught is in resistance set,--
The Something of this clumsy world,--has yet,
With all that I have undertaken,
Not been by me disturbed or shaken:
From earthquake, tempest, wave, volcano's brand,
Back into quiet settle sea and land!
And that damned stuff, the bestial, human brood,--
What use, in having that to play with?
How many have I made away with!
And ever circulates a newer, fresher blood.
It makes me furious, such things beholding:
From Water, Earth, and Air unfolding,
A thousand germs break forth and grow,
In dry, and wet, and warm, and chilly;
And had I not the Flame reserved, why, really,
There's nothing special of my own to show!

FAUST

So, to the actively eternal
Creative force, in cold disdain
You now oppose the fist infernal,
Whose wicked clench is all in vain!

Some other labor seek thou rather,
Queer Son of Chaos, to begin!

MEPHISTOPHELES
Well, we'll consider: thou canst gather
My views, when next I venture in.
Might I, perhaps, depart at present?

FAUST
Why thou shouldst ask, I don't perceive.
Though our acquaintance is so recent,
For further visits thou hast leave.
The window's here, the door is yonder;
A chimney, also, you behold.

MEPHISTOPHELES
I must confess that forth I may not wander,
My steps by one slight obstacle controlled,--
The wizard's-foot, that on your threshold made is.

FAUST
The pentagram prohibits thee?
Why, tell me now, thou Son of Hades,
If that prevents, how cam'st thou in to me?
Could such a spirit be so cheated?

MEPHISTOPHELES
Inspect the thing: the drawing's not completed.
The outer angle, you may see,
Is open left--the lines don't fit it.

FAUST
Well,--Chance, this time, has fairly hit it!
And thus, thou'rt prisoner to me?
It seems the business has succeeded.

MEPHISTOPHELES
The poodle naught remarked, as after thee he speeded;
But other aspects now obtain:
The Devil can't get out again.

FAUST
Try, then, the open window-pane!

MEPHISTOPHELES

For Devils and for spectres this is law:
Where they have entered in, there also they withdraw.
The first is free to us; we're governed by the second.

FAUST

In Hell itself, then, laws are reckoned?
That's well! So might a compact be
Made with you gentlemen--and binding,--surely?

MEPHISTOPHELES

All that is promised shall delight thee purely;
No skinflint bargain shalt thou see.
But this is not of swift conclusion;
We'll talk about the matter soon.
And now, I do entreat this boon--
Leave to withdraw from my intrusion.

FAUST

One moment more I ask thee to remain,
Some pleasant news, at least, to tell me.

MEPHISTOPHELES

Release me, now! I soon shall come again;
Then thou, at will, mayst question and compel me.

FAUST

I have not snares around thee cast;
Thyself hast led thyself into the meshes.
Who traps the Devil, hold him fast!
Not soon a second time he'll catch a prey so precious.

MEPHISTOPHELES

An't please thee, also I'm content to stay,
And serve thee in a social station;
But stipulating, that I may
With arts of mine afford thee recreation.

FAUST

Thereto I willingly agree,
If the diversion pleasant be.

MEPHISTOPHELES

My friend, thou'lt win, past all pretences,

More in this hour to soothe thy senses,
Than in the year's monotony.
That which the dainty spirits sing thee,
The lovely pictures they shall bring thee,
Are more than magic's empty show.
Thy scent will be to bliss invited;
Thy palate then with taste delighted,
Thy nerves of touch ecstatic glow!
All unprepared, the charm I spin:
We're here together, so begin!

SPIRITS

    Vanish, ye darking
Arches above him!
Loveliest weather,
Born of blue ether,
Break from the sky!
O that the darkling
Clouds had departed!
Starlight is sparkling,
Tranquiller-hearted
Suns are on high.
Heaven's own children
In beauty bewildering,
Waveringly bending,
Pass as they hover;
Longing unending
Follows them over.
They, with their glowing
Garments, out-flowing,
Cover, in going,
Landscape and bower,
Where, in seclusion,
Lovers are plighted,
Lost in illusion.
Bower on bower!
Tendrils unblighted!
Lo! in a shower
Grapes that o'ercluster
Gush into must, or
Flow into rivers
Of foaming and flashing
Wine, that is dashing
Gems, as it boundeth

Down the high places,
And spreading, surroundeth
With crystalline spaces,
In happy embraces,
Blossoming forelands,
Emerald shore-lands!
And the winged races
Drink, and fly onward--
Fly ever sunward
To the enticing
Islands, that flatter,
Dipping and rising
Light on the water!
Hark, the inspiring
Sound of their quiring!
See, the entrancing
Whirl of their dancing!
All in the air are
Freer and fairer.
Some of them scaling
Boldly the highlands,
Others are sailing,
Circling the islands;
Others are flying;
Life-ward all hieing,--
All for the distant
Star of existent
Rapture and Love!

MEPHISTOPHELES

He sleeps! Enough, ye fays! your airy number
Have sung him truly into slumber:
For this performance I your debtor prove.--
Not yet art thou the man, to catch the Fiend and hold him!--
With fairest images of dreams infold him,
Plunge him in seas of sweet untruth!
Yet, for the threshold's magic which controlled him,
The Devil needs a rat's quick tooth.
I use no lengthened invocation:
Here rustles one that soon will work my liberation.

The lord of rats and eke of mice,
Of flies and bed-bugs, frogs and lice,
Summons thee hither to the door-sill,

To gnaw it where, with just a morsel
Of oil, he paints the spot for thee:--
There com'st thou, hopping on to me!
To work, at once! The point which made me craven
Is forward, on the ledge, engraven.
Another bite makes free the door:
So, dream thy dreams, O Faust, until we meet once more!

FAUST (awaking)
Am I again so foully cheated?
Remains there naught of lofty spirit-sway,
But that a dream the Devil counterfeited,
And that a poodle ran away?

IV

THE STUDY

FAUST MEPHISTOPHELES

FAUST

A knock? Come in! Again my quiet broken?

MEPHISTOPHELES

'Tis I!

FAUST

Come in!

MEPHISTOPHELES

Thrice must the words be spoken.

FAUST

Come in, then!

MEPHISTOPHELES

Thus thou pleasest me.
I hope we'll suit each other well;
For now, thy vapors to dispel,
I come, a squire of high degree,
In scarlet coat, with golden trimming,
A cloak in silken lustre swimming,
A tall cock's-feather in my hat,
A long, sharp sword for show or quarrel,--
And I advise thee, brief and flat,
To don the self-same gay apparel,
That, from this den released, and free,
Life be at last revealed to thee!

FAUST

This life of earth, whatever my attire,
Would pain me in its wonted fashion.
Too old am I to play with passion;
Too young, to be without desire.
What from the world have I to gain?
Thou shalt abstain--renounce--refrain!
Such is the everlasting song

That in the ears of all men rings,--
That unrelieved, our whole life long,
Each hour, in passing, hoarsely sings.
In very terror I at morn awake,
Upon the verge of bitter weeping,
To see the day of disappointment break,
To no one hope of mine--not one--its promise keeping:--
That even each joy's presentiment
With wilful cavil would diminish,
With grinning masks of life prevent
My mind its fairest work to finish!
Then, too, when night descends, how anxiously
Upon my couch of sleep I lay me:
There, also, comes no rest to me,
But some wild dream is sent to fray me.
The God that in my breast is owned
Can deeply stir the inner sources;
The God, above my powers enthroned,
He cannot change external forces.
So, by the burden of my days oppressed,
Death is desired, and Life a thing unblest!

MEPHISTOPHELES
And yet is never Death a wholly welcome guest.

FAUST
O fortunate, for whom, when victory glances,
The bloody laurels on the brow he bindeth!
Whom, after rapid, maddening dances,
In clasping maiden-arms he findeth!
O would that I, before that spirit-power,
Ravished and rapt from life, had sunken!

MEPHISTOPHELES
And yet, by some one, in that nightly hour,
A certain liquid was not drunken.

FAUST
Eavesdropping, ha! thy pleasure seems to be.

MEPHISTOPHELES
Omniscient am I not; yet much is known to me.

FAUST

Though some familiar tone, retrieving
My thoughts from torment, led me on,
And sweet, clear echoes came, deceiving
A faith bequeathed from Childhood's dawn,
Yet now I curse whate'er entices
And snares the soul with visions vain;
With dazzling cheats and dear devices
Confines it in this cave of pain!
Cursed be, at once, the high ambition
Wherewith the mind itself deludes!
Cursed be the glare of apparition
That on the finer sense intrudes!
Cursed be the lying dream's impression
Of name, and fame, and laurelled brow!
Cursed, all that flatters as possession,
As wife and child, as knave and plow!
Cursed Mammon be, when he with treasures
To restless action spurs our fate!
Cursed when, for soft, indulgent leisures,
He lays for us the pillows straight!
Cursed be the vine's transcendent nectar,--
The highest favor Love lets fall!
Cursed, also, Hope!--cursed Faith, the spectre!
And cursed be Patience most of all!

CHORUS OF SPIRITS (invisible)

Woe! woe!
Thou hast it destroyed,
The beautiful world,
With powerful fist:
In ruin 'tis hurled,
By the blow of a demigod shattered!
The scattered
Fragments into the Void we carry,
Deploring
The beauty perished beyond restoring.
Mightier
For the children of men,
Brightlier
Build it again,
In thine own bosom build it anew!
Bid the new career
Commence,

With clearer sense,
And the new songs of cheer
Be sung thereto!

MEPHISTOPHELES

These are the small dependants
Who give me attendance.
Hear them, to deeds and passion
Counsel in shrewd old-fashion!
Into the world of strife,
Out of this lonely life
That of senses and sap has betrayed thee,
They would persuade thee.
This nursing of the pain forego thee,
That, like a vulture, feeds upon thy breast!
The worst society thou find'st will show thee
Thou art a man among the rest.
But 'tis not meant to thrust
Thee into the mob thou hatest!
I am not one of the greatest,
Yet, wilt thou to me entrust
Thy steps through life, I'll guide thee,--
Will willingly walk beside thee,--
Will serve thee at once and forever
With best endeavor,
And, if thou art satisfied,
Will as servant, slave, with thee abide.

FAUST

And what shall be my counter-service therefor?

MEPHISTOPHELES

The time is long: thou need'st not now insist.

FAUST

No--no! The Devil is an egotist,
And is not apt, without a why or wherefore,
"For God's sake," others to assist.
Speak thy conditions plain and clear!
With such a servant danger comes, I fear.

MEPHISTOPHELES

Here, an unwearied slave, I'll wear thy tether,
And to thine every nod obedient be:

When There again we come together,
Then shalt thou do the same for me.

FAUST

The There my scruples naught increases.
When thou hast dashed this world to pieces,
The other, then, its place may fill.
Here, on this earth, my pleasures have their sources;
Yon sun beholds my sorrows in his courses;
And when from these my life itself divorces,
Let happen all that can or will!
I'll hear no more: 'tis vain to ponder
If there we cherish love or hate,
Or, in the spheres we dream of yonder,
A High and Low our souls await.

MEPHISTOPHELES

In this sense, even, canst thou venture.
Come, bind thyself by prompt indenture,
And thou mine arts with joy shalt see:
What no man ever saw, I'll give to thee.

FAUST

Canst thou, poor Devil, give me whatsoever?
When was a human soul, in its supreme endeavor,
E'er understood by such as thou?
Yet, hast thou food which never satiates, now,--
The restless, ruddy gold hast thou,
That runs, quicksilver-like, one's fingers through,--
A game whose winnings no man ever knew,--
A maid that, even from my breast,
Beckons my neighbor with her wanton glances,
And Honor's godlike zest,
The meteor that a moment dances,--
Show me the fruits that, ere they're gathered, rot,
And trees that daily with new leafage clothe them!

MEPHISTOPHELES

Such a demand alarms me not:
Such treasures have I, and can show them.
But still the time may reach us, good my friend.
When peace we crave and more luxurious diet.

FAUST

When on an idler's bed I stretch myself in quiet.
There let, at once, my record end!
Canst thou with lying flattery rule me,
Until, self-pleased, myself I see,--
Canst thou with rich enjoyment fool me,
Let that day be the last for me!
The bet I offer.

MEPHISTOPHELES
Done!

FAUST
And heartily!
When thus I hail the Moment flying:
"Ah, still delay--thou art so fair!"
Then bind me in thy bonds undying,
My final ruin then declare!
Then let the death-bell chime the token.
Then art thou from thy service free!
The clock may stop, the hand be broken,
Then Time be finished unto me!

MEPHISTOPHELES
Consider well: my memory good is rated.

FAUST
Thou hast a perfect right thereto.
My powers I have not rashly estimated:
A slave am I, whate'er I do--
If thine, or whose? 'tis needless to debate it.

MEPHISTOPHELES
Then at the Doctors'-banquet I, to-day,
Will as a servant wait behind thee.
But one thing more! Beyond all risk to bind thee,
Give me a line or two, I pray.

FAUST
Demand'st thou, Pedant, too, a document?
Hast never known a man, nor proved his word's intent?
Is't not enough, that what I speak to-day
Shall stand, with all my future days agreeing?
In all its tides sweeps not the world away,
And shall a promise bind my being?

Yet this delusion in our hearts we bear:
Who would himself therefrom deliver?
Blest he, whose bosom Truth makes pure and fair!
No sacrifice shall he repent of ever.
Nathless a parchment, writ and stamped with care,
A spectre is, which all to shun endeavor.
The word, alas! dies even in the pen,
And wax and leather keep the lordship then.
What wilt from me, Base Spirit, say?--
Brass, marble, parchment, paper, clay?
The terms with graver, quill, or chisel, stated?
I freely leave the choice to thee.

MEPHISTOPHELES

Why heat thyself, thus instantly,
With eloquence exaggerated?
Each leaf for such a pact is good;
And to subscribe thy name thou'lt take a drop of blood.

FAUST

If thou therewith art fully satisfied,
So let us by the farce abide.

MEPHISTOPHELES

Blood is a juice of rarest quality.

FAUST

Fear not that I this pact shall seek to sever?
The promise that I make to thee
Is just the sum of my endeavor.
I have myself inflated all too high;
My proper place is thy estate:
The Mighty Spirit deigns me no reply,
And Nature shuts on me her gate.
The thread of Thought at last is broken,
And knowledge brings disgust unspoken.
Let us the sensual deeps explore,
To quench the fervors of glowing passion!
Let every marvel take form and fashion
Through the impervious veil it wore!
Plunge we in Time's tumultuous dance,
In the rush and roll of Circumstance!
Then may delight and distress,
And worry and success,

Alternately follow, as best they can:
Restless activity proves the man!

MEPHISTOPHELES

For you no bound, no term is set.
Whether you everywhere be trying,
Or snatch a rapid bliss in flying,
May it agree with you, what you get!
Only fall to, and show no timid balking.

FAUST

But thou hast heard, 'tis not of joy we're talking.
I take the wildering whirl, enjoyment's keenest pain,
Enamored hate, exhilarant disdain.
My bosom, of its thirst for knowledge sated,
Shall not, henceforth, from any pang be wrested,
And all of life for all mankind created
Shall be within mine inmost being tested:
The highest, lowest forms my soul shall borrow,
Shall heap upon itself their bliss and sorrow,
And thus, my own sole self to all their selves expanded,
I too, at last, shall with them all be stranded!

MEPHISTOPHELES

Believe me, who for many a thousand year
The same tough meat have chewed and tested,
That from the cradle to the bier
No man the ancient leaven has digested!
Trust one of us, this Whole supernal
Is made but for a God's delight!
He dwells in splendor single and eternal,
But us he thrusts in darkness, out of sight,
And you he dowers with Day and Night.

FAUST

Nay, but I will!

MEPHISTOPHELES

A good reply!
One only fear still needs repeating:
The art is long, the time is fleeting.
Then let thyself be taught, say I!
Go, league thyself with a poet,
Give the rein to his imagination,

Then wear the crown, and show it,
Of the qualities of his creation,--
The courage of the lion's breed,
The wild stag's speed,
The Italian's fiery blood,
The North's firm fortitude!
Let him find for thee the secret tether
That binds the Noble and Mean together.
And teach thy pulses of youth and pleasure
To love by rule, and hate by measure!
I'd like, myself, such a one to see:
Sir Microcosm his name should be.

FAUST

What am I, then, if 'tis denied my part
The crown of all humanity to win me,
Whereto yearns every sense within me?

MEPHISTOPHELES

Why, on the whole, thou'rt--what thou art.
Set wigs of million curls upon thy head, to raise thee,
Wear shoes an ell in height,--the truth betrays thee,
And thou remainest--what thou art.

FAUST

I feel, indeed, that I have made the treasure
Of human thought and knowledge mine, in vain;
And if I now sit down in restful leisure,
No fount of newer strength is in my brain:
I am no hair's-breadth more in height,
Nor nearer, to the Infinite,

MEPHISTOPHELES

Good Sir, you see the facts precisely
As they are seen by each and all.
We must arrange them now, more wisely,
Before the joys of life shall pall.
Why, Zounds! Both hands and feet are, truly--
And head and virile forces--thine:
Yet all that I indulge in newly,
Is't thence less wholly mine?
If I've six stallions in my stall,
Are not their forces also lent me?
I speed along, completest man of all,

As though my legs were four-and-twenty.
Take hold, then! let reflection rest,
And plunge into the world with zest!
I say to thee, a speculative wight
Is like a beast on moorlands lean,
That round and round some fiend misleads to evil plight,
While all about lie pastures fresh and green.

FAUST
Then how shall we begin?

MEPHISTOPHELES
We'll try a wider sphere.
What place of martyrdom is here!
Is't life, I ask, is't even prudence,
To bore thyself and bore the students?
Let Neighbor Paunch to that attend!
Why plague thyself with threshing straw forever?
The best thou learnest, in the end
Thou dar'st not tell the youngsters--never!
I hear one's footsteps, hither steering.

FAUST
To see him now I have no heart.

MEPHISTOPHELES
So long the poor boy waits a hearing,
He must not unconsoled depart.
Thy cap and mantle straightway lend me!
I'll play the comedy with art.

(He disguises himself.)

My wits, be certain, will befriend me.
But fifteen minutes' time is all I need;
For our fine trip, meanwhile, prepare thyself with speed!

[Exit FAUST.

MEPHISTOPHELES
(In FAUST'S long mantle.)

Reason and Knowledge only thou despise,
The highest strength in man that lies!

Let but the Lying Spirit bind thee
With magic works and shows that blind thee,
And I shall have thee fast and sure!--
Fate such a bold, untrammelled spirit gave him,
As forwards, onwards, ever must endure;
Whose over-hasty impulse drave him
Past earthly joys he might secure.
Dragged through the wildest life, will I enslave him,
Through flat and stale indifference;
With struggling, chilling, checking, so deprave him
That, to his hot, insatiate sense,
The dream of drink shall mock, but never lave him:
Refreshment shall his lips in vain implore--
Had he not made himself the Devil's, naught could save
him,
Still were he lost forevermore!

(A STUDENT enters.)

STUDENT
A short time, only, am I here,
And come, devoted and sincere,
To greet and know the man of fame,
Whom men to me with reverence name.

MEPHISTOPHELES
Your courtesy doth flatter me:
You see a man, as others be.
Have you, perchance, elsewhere begun?

STUDENT
Receive me now, I pray, as one
Who comes to you with courage good,
Somewhat of cash, and healthy blood:
My mother was hardly willing to let me;
But knowledge worth having I fain would get me.

MEPHISTOPHELES
Then you have reached the right place now.

STUDENT
I'd like to leave it, I must avow;
I find these walls, these vaulted spaces
Are anything but pleasant places.

Tis all so cramped and close and mean;
One sees no tree, no glimpse of green,
And when the lecture-halls receive me,
Seeing, hearing, and thinking leave me.

MEPHISTOPHELES

All that depends on habitude.
So from its mother's breasts a child
At first, reluctant, takes its food,
But soon to seek them is beguiled.
Thus, at the breasts of Wisdom clinging,
Thou'lt find each day a greater rapture bringing.

STUDENT

I'll hang thereon with joy, and freely drain them;
But tell me, pray, the proper means to gain them.

MEPHISTOPHELES

Explain, before you further speak,
The special faculty you seek.

STUDENT

I crave the highest erudition;
And fain would make my acquisition
All that there is in Earth and Heaven,
In Nature and in Science too.

MEPHISTOPHELES

Here is the genuine path for you;
Yet strict attention must be given.

STUDENT

Body and soul thereon I'll wreak;
Yet, truly, I've some inclination
On summer holidays to seek
A little freedom and recreation.

MEPHISTOPHELES

Use well your time! It flies so swiftly from us;
But time through order may be won, I promise.
So, Friend (my views to briefly sum),
First, the collegium logicum.
There will your mind be drilled and braced,
As if in Spanish boots 'twere laced,

And thus, to graver paces brought,
'Twill plod along the path of thought,
Instead of shooting here and there,
A will-o'-the-wisp in murky air.
Days will be spent to bid you know,
What once you did at a single blow,
Like eating and drinking, free and strong,--
That one, two, three! thereto belong.
Truly the fabric of mental fleece
Resembles a weaver's masterpiece,
Where a thousand threads one treadle throws,
Where fly the shuttles hither and thither.
Unseen the threads are knit together.
And an infinite combination grows.
Then, the philosopher steps in
And shows, no otherwise it could have been:
The first was so, the second so,
Therefore the third and fourth are so;
Were not the first and second, then
The third and fourth had never been.
The scholars are everywhere believers,
But never succeed in being weavers.
He who would study organic existence,
First drives out the soul with rigid persistence;
Then the parts in his hand he may hold and class,
But the spiritual link is lost, alas!
Encheiresin natures, this Chemistry names,
Nor knows how herself she banters and blames!

STUDENT

I cannot understand you quite.

MEPHISTOPHELES

Your mind will shortly be set aright,
When you have learned, all things reducing,
To classify them for your using.

STUDENT

I feel as stupid, from all you've said,
As if a mill-wheel whirled in my head!

MEPHISTOPHELES

And after--first and foremost duty--Of
Metaphysics learn the use and beauty!

See that you most profoundly gain
What does not suit the human brain!
A splendid word to serve, you'll find
For what goes in--or won't go in--your mind.
But first, at least this half a year,
To order rigidly adhere;
Five hours a day, you understand,
And when the clock strikes, be on hand!
Prepare beforehand for your part
With paragraphs all got by heart,
So you can better watch, and look
That naught is said but what is in the book:
Yet in thy writing as unwearied be,
As did the Holy Ghost dictate to thee!

STUDENT

No need to tell me twice to do it!
I think, how useful 'tis to write;
For what one has, in black and white,
One carries home and then goes through it.

MEPHISTOPHELES

Yet choose thyself a faculty!

STUDENT

I cannot reconcile myself to Jurisprudence.

MEPHISTOPHELES

Nor can I therefore greatly blame you students:
I know what science this has come to be.
All rights and laws are still transmitted
Like an eternal sickness of the race,--
From generation unto generation fitted,
And shifted round from place to place.
Reason becomes a sham, Beneficence a worry:
Thou art a grandchild, therefore woe to thee!
The right born with us, ours in verity,
This to consider, there's, alas! no hurry.

STUDENT

My own disgust is strengthened by your speech:
O lucky he, whom you shall teach!
I've almost for Theology decided.

MEPHISTOPHELES

I should not wish to see you here misguided:
For, as regards this science, let me hint
'Tis very hard to shun the false direction;
There's so much secret poison lurking in 't,
So like the medicine, it baffles your detection.
Hear, therefore, one alone, for that is best, in sooth,
And simply take your master's words for truth.
On words let your attention centre!
Then through the safest gate you'll enter
The temple-halls of Certainty.

STUDENT

Yet in the word must some idea be.

MEPHISTOPHELES

Of course! But only shun too over-sharp a tension,
For just where fails the comprehension,
A word steps promptly in as deputy.
With words 'tis excellent disputing;
Systems to words 'tis easy suiting;
On words 'tis excellent believing;
No word can ever lose a jot from thieving.

STUDENT

Pardon! With many questions I detain you.
Yet must I trouble you again.
Of Medicine I still would fain
Hear one strong word that might explain you.
Three years is but a little space.
And, God! who can the field embrace?
If one some index could be shown,
'Twere easier groping forward, truly.

MEPHISTOPHELES (aside)

I'm tired enough of this dry tone,--
Must play the Devil again, and fully.

(Aloud)

To grasp the spirit of Medicine is easy:
Learn of the great and little world your fill,
To let it go at last, so please ye,
Just as God will!

In vain that through the realms of science you may drift;
Each one learns only--just what learn he can:
Yet he who grasps the Moment's gift,
He is the proper man.
Well-made you are, 'tis not to be denied,
The rest a bold address will win you;
If you but in yourself confide,
At once confide all others in you.
To lead the women, learn the special feeling!
Their everlasting aches and groans,
In thousand tones,
Have all one source, one mode of healing;
And if your acts are half discreet,
You'll always have them at your feet.
A title first must draw and interest them,
And show that yours all other arts exceeds;
Then, as a greeting, you are free to touch and test them,
While, thus to do, for years another pleads.
You press and count the pulse's dances,
And then, with burning sidelong glances,
You clasp the swelling hips, to see
If tightly laced her corsets be.

STUDENT
That's better, now! The How and Where, one sees.

MEPHISTOPHELES
My worthy friend, gray are all theories,
And green alone Life's golden tree.

STUDENT
I swear to you, 'tis like a dream to me.
Might I again presume, with trust unbounded,
To hear your wisdom thoroughly expounded?

MEPHISTOPHELES
Most willingly, to what extent I may.

STUDENT
I cannot really go away:
Allow me that my album first I reach you,--
Grant me this favor, I beseech you!

MEPHISTOPHELES

Assuredly.

(He writes, and returns the book.)

STUDENT (reads)
Eritis sicut Deus, scientes bonum et malum.
(Closes the book with reverence, and withdraws)

MEPHISTOPHELES
Follow the ancient text, and the snake thou wast ordered to trample!
With all thy likeness to God, thou'lt yet be a sorry example!

(FAUST enters.)

FAUST
Now, whither shall we go?

MEPHISTOPHELES
As best it pleases thee.
The little world, and then the great, we'll see.
With what delight, what profit winning,
Shalt thou sponge through the term beginning!

FAUST
Yet with the flowing beard I wear,
Both ease and grace will fail me there.
The attempt, indeed, were a futile strife;
I never could learn the ways of life.
I feel so small before others, and thence
Should always find embarrassments.

MEPHISTOPHELES
My friend, thou soon shalt lose all such misgiving:
Be thou but self-possessed, thou hast the art of living!

FAUST
How shall we leave the house, and start?
Where hast thou servant, coach and horses?

MEPHISTOPHELES
We'll spread this cloak with proper art,
Then through the air direct our courses.
But only, on so bold a flight,
Be sure to have thy luggage light.

A little burning air, which I shall soon prepare us,
Above the earth will nimbly bear us,
And, if we're light, we'll travel swift and clear:
I gratulate thee on thy new career!

V

AUERBACH'S CELLAR IN LEIPZIG
CAROUSAL OF JOLLY COMPANIONS

FROSCH

I no one laughing? no one drinking?
I'll teach you how to grin, I'm thinking.
To-day you're like wet straw, so tame;
And usually you're all aflame.

BRANDER

Now that's your fault; from you we nothing see,
No beastliness and no stupidity.

FROSCH

(Pours a glass of wine over BRANDER'S head.)
There's both together!

BRANDER

Twice a swine!

FROSCH

You wanted them: I've given you mine.

SIEBEL

Turn out who quarrels--out the door!
With open throat sing chorus, drink and roar!
Up! holla! ho!

ALTMAYER

Woe's me, the fearful bellow!
Bring cotton, quick! He's split my ears, that fellow.

SIEBEL

When the vault echoes to the song,
One first perceives the bass is deep and strong.

FROSCH

Well said! and out with him that takes the least offence!
Ah, tara, lara da!

ALTMAYER

Ah, tara, lara, da!

FROSCH
The throats are tuned, commence!
(Sings.)
The dear old holy Roman realm,
How does it hold together?

BRANDER
A nasty song! Fie! a political song--
A most offensive song! Thank God, each morning, therefore,
That you have not the Roman realm to care for!
At least, I hold it so much gain for me,
That I nor Chancellor nor Kaiser be.
Yet also we must have a ruling head, I hope,
And so we'll choose ourselves a Pope.
You know the quality that can
Decide the choice, and elevate the man.

FROSCH (sings)
Soar up, soar up, Dame Nightingale!
Ten thousand times my sweetheart hail!

SIEBEL
No, greet my sweetheart not! I tell you, I'll resent it.

FROSCH
My sweetheart greet and kiss! I dare you to prevent it!

(Sings.)

Draw the latch! the darkness makes:
Draw the latch! the lover wakes.
Shut the latch! the morning breaks.

SIEBEL
Yes, sing away, sing on, and praise, and brag of her!
I'll wait my proper time for laughter:
Me by the nose she led, and now she'll lead you after.
Her paramour should be an ugly gnome,
Where four roads cross, in wanton play to meet her:
An old he-goat, from Blocksberg coming home,
Should his good-night in lustful gallop bleat her!
A fellow made of genuine flesh and blood

Is for the wench a deal too good.
Greet her? Not I: unless, when meeting,
To smash her windows be a greeting!

BRANDER (pounding on the table)
Attention! Hearken now to me!
Confess, Sirs, I know how to live.
Enamored persons here have we,
And I, as suits their quality,
Must something fresh for their advantage give.
Take heed! 'Tis of the latest cut, my strain,
And all strike in at each refrain!

(He sings.)

There was a rat in the cellar-nest,
Whom fat and butter made smoother:
He had a paunch beneath his vest
Like that of Doctor Luther.
The cook laid poison cunningly,
And then as sore oppressed was he
As if he had love in his bosom.

CHORUS (shouting)
As if he had love in his bosom!

BRANDER
He ran around, he ran about,
His thirst in puddles laving;
He gnawed and scratched the house throughout.
But nothing cured his raving.
He whirled and jumped, with torment mad,
And soon enough the poor beast had,
As if he had love in his bosom.

CHORUS
As if he had love in his bosom!

BRANDER
And driven at last, in open day,
He ran into the kitchen,
Fell on the hearth, and squirming lay,
In the last convulsion twitching.
Then laughed the murderess in her glee:

"Ha! ha! he's at his last gasp," said she,
"As if he had love in his bosom!"

CHORUS
As if he had love in his bosom!

SIEBEL
How the dull fools enjoy the matter!
To me it is a proper art
Poison for such poor rats to scatter.

BRANDER
Perhaps you'll warmly take their part?

ALTMAYER
The bald-pate pot-belly I have noted:
Misfortune tames him by degrees;
For in the rat by poison bloated
His own most natural form he sees.

FAUST AND MEPHISTOPHELES

MEPHISTOPHELES
Before all else, I bring thee hither
Where boon companions meet together,
To let thee see how smooth life runs away.
Here, for the folk, each day's a holiday:
With little wit, and ease to suit them,
They whirl in narrow, circling trails,
Like kittens playing with their tails?
And if no headache persecute them,
So long the host may credit give,
They merrily and careless live.

BRANDER
The fact is easy to unravel,
Their air's so odd, they've just returned from travel:
A single hour they've not been here.

FROSCH
You've verily hit the truth! Leipzig to me is dear:
Paris in miniature, how it refines its people!

SIEBEL

Who are the strangers, should you guess?

FROSCH
Let me alone! I'll set them first to drinking,
And then, as one a child's tooth draws, with cleverness,
I'll worm their secret out, I'm thinking.
They're of a noble house, that's very clear:
Haughty and discontented they appear.

BRANDER
They're mountebanks, upon a revel.

ALTMAYER
Perhaps.

FROSCH
Look out, I'll smoke them now!

MEPHISTOPHELES (to FAUST)
Not if he had them by the neck, I vow,
Would e'er these people scent the Devil!

FAUST
Fair greeting, gentlemen!

SIEBEL
Our thanks: we give the same.
(Murmurs, inspecting MEPHISTOPHELES from the side.)
In one foot is the fellow lame?

MEPHISTOPHELES
Is it permitted that we share your leisure?
In place of cheering drink, which one seeks vainly here,
Your company shall give us pleasure.

ALTMAYER
A most fastidious person you appear.

FROSCH
No doubt 'twas late when you from Rippach started?
And supping there with Hans occasioned your delay?

MEPHISTOPHELES

We passed, without a call, to-day.
At our last interview, before we parted
Much of his cousins did he speak, entreating
That we should give to each his kindly greeting.

(He bows to FROSCH.)

ALTMAYER (aside)
You have it now! he understands.

SIEBEL
A knave sharp-set!

FROSCH
Just wait awhile: I'll have him yet.

MEPHISTOPHELES
If I am right, we heard the sound
Of well-trained voices, singing chorus;
And truly, song must here rebound
Superbly from the arches o'er us.

FROSCH
Are you, perhaps, a virtuoso?

MEPHISTOPHELES
O no! my wish is great, my power is only so-so.

ALTMAYER
Give us a song!

MEPHISTOPHELES
If you desire, a number.

SIEBEL
So that it be a bran-new strain!

MEPHISTOPHELES
We've just retraced our way from. Spain,
The lovely land of wine, and song, and slumber.

(Sings.)

There was a king once reigning,

Who had a big black flea--

FROSCH
Hear, hear! A flea! D'ye rightly take the jest?
I call a flea a tidy guest.

MEPHISTOPHELES (sings)
> There was a king once reigning,
> Who had a big black flea,
> And loved him past explaining,
> As his own son were he.
> He called his man of stitches;
> The tailor came straightway:
> Here, measure the lad for breeches.
> And measure his coat, I say!

BRANDER
But mind, allow the tailor no caprices:
Enjoin upon him, as his head is dear,
To most exactly measure, sew and shear,
So that the breeches have no creases!

MEPHISTOPHELES
> In silk and velvet gleaming
> He now was wholly drest--
> Had a coat with ribbons streaming,
> A cross upon his breast.
> He had the first of stations,
> A minister's star and name;
> And also all his relations
> Great lords at court became.
>
> And the lords and ladies of honor
> Were plagued, awake and in bed;
> The queen she got them upon her,
> The maids were bitten and bled.
> And they did not dare to brush them,
> Or scratch them, day or night:
> We crack them and we crush them,
> At once, whene'er they bite.

CHORUS (shouting)
> We crack them and we crush them,
> At once, whene'er they bite!

155

FROSCH Bravo! bravo! that was fine.

SIEBEL
Every flea may it so befall!

BRANDER
Point your fingers and nip them all!

ALTMAYER
Hurrah for Freedom! Hurrah for wine!

MEPHISTOPHELES
I fain would drink with you, my glass to Freedom clinking,
If 'twere a better wine that here I see you drinking.

SIEBEL
Don't let us hear that speech again!

MEPHISTOPHELES
Did I not fear the landlord might complain,
I'd treat these worthy guests, with pleasure,
To some from out our cellar's treasure.

SIEBEL
Just treat, and let the landlord me arraign!

FROSCH
And if the wine be good, our praises shall be ample.
But do not give too very small a sample;
For, if its quality I decide,
With a good mouthful I must be supplied.

ALTMAYER (aside)
They're from the Rhine! I guessed as much, before.

MEPHISTOPHELES
Bring me a gimlet here!

BRANDER
What shall therewith be done?
You've not the casks already at the door?

ALTMAYER

Yonder, within the landlord's box of tools, there's one!

MEPHISTOPHELES (takes the gimlet)
(To FROSCH.)

Now, give me of your taste some intimation.

FROSCH
How do you mean? Have you so many kinds?

MEPHISTOPHELES
The choice is free: make up your minds.

ALTMAYER (to FROSCH)
Aha! you lick your chops, from sheer anticipation.

FROSCH
Good! if I have the choice, so let the wine be Rhenish!
Our Fatherland can best the sparkling cup replenish.

MEPHISTOPHELES
(boring a hole in the edge of the table, at the place where
FROSCH sits)

Get me a little wax, to make the stoppers, quick!

ALTMAYER
Ah! I perceive a juggler's trick.

MEPHISTOPHELES (to BRANDER)
And you?

BRANDER
Champagne shall be my wine,
And let it sparkle fresh and fine!

MEPHISTOPHELES
(bores: in the meantime one has made the wax stoppers, and
plugged the holes with them.)

BRANDER
What's foreign one can't always keep quite clear of,
For good things, oft, are not so near;
A German can't endure the French to see or hear of,

Yet drinks their wines with hearty cheer.

SIEBEL
(as MEPHISTOPHELES *approaches his seat)*
For me, I grant, sour wine is out of place;
Fill up my glass with sweetest, will you?

MEPHISTOPHELES (boring)
Tokay shall flow at once, to fill you!

ALTMAYER
No--look me, Sirs, straight in the face!
I see you have your fun at our expense.

MEPHISTOPHELES
O no! with gentlemen of such pretence,
That were to venture far, indeed.
Speak out, and make your choice with speed!
With what a vintage can I serve you?

ALTMAYER
With any--only satisfy our need.

(After the holes have been bored and plugged)

MEPHISTOPHELES *(with singular gestures)*
Grapes the vine-stem bears,
Horns the he-goat wears!
The grapes are juicy, the vines are wood,
The wooden table gives wine as good!
Into the depths of Nature peer,--
Only believe there's a miracle here!

Now draw the stoppers, and drink your fill!

ALL
(as they draw out the stoppers, and the wine which has been desired flows into the glass of each)

O beautiful fountain, that flows at will!

MEPHISTOPHELES
But have a care that you nothing spill!

(They drink repeatedly.)

ALL (sing)
> As 'twere five hundred hogs, we feel
> So cannibalic jolly!

MEPHISTOPHELES
See, now, the race is happy--it is free!

FAUST
To leave them is my inclination.

MEPHISTOPHELES
Take notice, first! their bestiality
Will make a brilliant demonstration.

SIEBEL
(drinks carelessly: the wine spills upon the earth, and turns to flame)

Help! Fire! Help! Hell-fire is sent!

MEPHISTOPHELES (charming away the flame)
Be quiet, friendly element!

(To the revellers)

A bit of purgatory 'twas for this time, merely.

SIEBEL
What mean you? Wait!--you'll pay for't dearly!
You'll know us, to your detriment.

FROSCH
Don't try that game a second time upon us!

ALTMAYER
I think we'd better send him packing quietly.

SIEBEL
What, Sir! you dare to make so free,
And play your hocus-pocus on us!

MEPHISTOPHELES

Be still, old wine-tub.

SIEBEL
Broomstick, you!
You face it out, impertinent and heady?

BRANDER
Just wait! a shower of blows is ready.

ALTMAYER
(draws a stopper out of the table: fire flies in his face.)
I burn! I burn!

SIEBEL
'Tis magic! Strike--
The knave is outlawed! Cut him as you like!
(They draw their knives, and rush upon MEPHISTOPHELES.)

MEPHISTOPHELES (with solemn gestures)
    False word and form of air,
    Change place, and sense ensnare!
    Be here--and there!

(They stand amazed and look at each other.)

ALTMAYER
Where am I? What a lovely land!

FROSCH
Vines? Can I trust my eyes?

SIEBEL
And purple grapes at hand!

BRANDER
Here, over this green arbor bending,
See what a vine! what grapes depending!

(He takes SIEBEL by the nose: the others do the same reciprocally,
and raise their knives.)

MEPHISTOPHELES (as above)
Loose, Error, from their eyes the band,
And how the Devil jests, be now enlightened!

160

(He disappears with FAUST: the revellers start and separate.)

SIEBEL
What happened?

ALTMAYER
How?

FROSCH
Was that your nose I tightened?

BRANDER (to SIEBEL)
And yours that still I have in hand?

ALTMAYER
It was a blow that went through every limb!
Give me a chair! I sink! my senses swim.

FROSCH
But what has happened, tell me now?

SIEBEL
Where is he? If I catch the scoundrel hiding,
He shall not leave alive, I vow.

ALTMAYER
I saw him with these eyes upon a wine-cask riding
Out of the cellar-door, just now.
Still in my feet the fright like lead is weighing.
(He turns towards the table.)
Why! If the fount of wine should still be playing?

SIEBEL
'Twas all deceit, and lying, false design!

FROSCH
And yet it seemed as I were drinking wine.

BRANDER
But with the grapes how was it, pray?

ALTMAYER
Shall one believe no miracles, just say!

VI

WITCHES' KITCHEN

(Upon a low hearth stands a great caldron, under which a fire
is burning. Various figures appear in the vapors which
rise from the caldron. An ape sits beside it, skims it, and
watches lest it boil over. The he-ape, with the young
ones, sits near and warms himself. Ceiling and walls are
covered with the most fantastic witch-implements.)

FAUST MEPHISTOPHELES

FAUST

These crazy signs of witches' craft repel me!
I shall recover, dost thou tell me,
Through this insane, chaotic play?
From an old hag shall I demand assistance?
And will her foul mess take away
Full thirty years from my existence?
Woe's me, canst thou naught better find!
Another baffled hope must be lamented:
Has Nature, then, and has a noble mind
Not any potent balsam yet invented?

MEPHISTOPHELES

Once more, my friend, thou talkest sensibly.
There is, to make thee young, a simpler mode and apter;
But in another book 'tis writ for thee,
And is a most eccentric chapter.

FAUST

Yet will I know it.

MEPHISTOPHELES

Good! the method is revealed
Without or gold or magic or physician.
Betake thyself to yonder field,
There hoe and dig, as thy condition;
Restrain thyself, thy sense and will
Within a narrow sphere to flourish;
With unmixed food thy body nourish;
Live with the ox as ox, and think it not a theft

That thou manur'st the acre which thou reapest;--
That, trust me, is the best mode left,
Whereby for eighty years thy youth thou keepest!

FAUST

I am not used to that; I cannot stoop to try it--
To take the spade in hand, and ply it.
The narrow being suits me not at all.

MEPHISTOPHELES

Then to thine aid the witch must call.

FAUST

Wherefore the hag, and her alone?
Canst thou thyself not brew the potion?

MEPHISTOPHELES

That were a charming sport, I own:
I'd build a thousand bridges meanwhile, I've a notion.
Not Art and Science serve, alone;
Patience must in the work be shown.
Long is the calm brain active in creation;
Time, only, strengthens the fine fermentation.
And all, belonging thereunto,
Is rare and strange, howe'er you take it:
The Devil taught the thing, 'tis true,
And yet the Devil cannot make it.
(Perceiving the Animals)
See, what a delicate race they be!
That is the maid! the man is he!
(To the Animals)
It seems the mistress has gone away?

THE ANIMALS

Carousing, to-day!
Off and about,
By the chimney out!

MEPHISTOPHELES

What time takes she for dissipating?

THE ANIMALS

While we to warm our paws are waiting.

MEPHISTOPHELES (to FAUST)
How findest thou the tender creatures?

FAUST
Absurder than I ever yet did see.

MEPHISTOPHELES
Why, just such talk as this, for me,
Is that which has the most attractive features!

(To the Animals)

But tell me now, ye cursed puppets,
Why do ye stir the porridge so?

THE ANIMALS
We're cooking watery soup for beggars.

MEPHISTOPHELES
Then a great public you can show.

THE HE-APE
(comes up and fawns on MEPHISTOPHELES)

O cast thou the dice!
Make me rich in a trice,
Let me win in good season!
Things are badly controlled,
And had I but gold,
So had I my reason.

MEPHISTOPHELES
How would the ape be sure his luck enhances.
Could he but try the lottery's chances!

(In the meantime the young apes have been playing with a large ball, which they now roll forward.)

THE HE-APE
The world's the ball:
Doth rise and fall,
And roll incessant:
Like glass doth ring,
A hollow thing,--

How soon will't spring,
And drop, quiescent?
Here bright it gleams,
Here brighter seems:
I live at present!
Dear son, I say,
Keep thou away!
Thy doom is spoken!
'Tis made of clay,
And will be broken.

MEPHISTOPHELES
What means the sieve?

THE HE-APE (taking it down)
Wert thou the thief,
I'd know him and shame him.

(He runs to the SHE-APE, and lets her look through it.)

Look through the sieve!
Know'st thou the thief,
And darest not name him?

MEPHISTOPHELES (approaching the fire)
And what's this pot?

HE-APE AND SHE-APE
The fool knows it not!
He knows not the pot,
He knows not the kettle!

MEPHISTOPHELES
Impertinent beast!

THE HE-APE
Take the brush here, at least,
And sit down on the settle!

(He invites MEPHISTOPHELES to sit down.)

FAUST
(who during all this time has been standing before a mirror,
now approaching and now retreating from it)

165

What do I see? What heavenly form revealed
Shows through the glass from Magic's fair dominions!
O lend me, Love, the swiftest of thy pinions,
And bear me to her beauteous field!
Ah, if I leave this spot with fond designing,
If I attempt to venture near,
Dim, as through gathering mist, her charms appear!--
A woman's form, in beauty shining!
Can woman, then, so lovely be?
And must I find her body, there reclining,
Of all the heavens the bright epitome?
Can Earth with such a thing be mated?

MEPHISTOPHELES
Why, surely, if a God first plagues Himself six days,
Then, self-contented, Bravo! says,
Must something clever be created.
This time, thine eyes be satiate!
I'll yet detect thy sweetheart and ensnare her,
And blest is he, who has the lucky fate,
Some day, as bridegroom, home to bear her.

(FAUST gazes continually in the mirror. MEPHISTOPHELES,
stretching himself out on the settle, and playing with the
brush, continues to speak.)

So sit I, like the King upon his throne:
I hold the sceptre, here,--and lack the crown alone.

THE ANIMALS
(who up to this time have been making all kinds of fantastic
movements together bring a crown to MEPHISTOPHELES
with great noise.)

    O be thou so good
    With sweat and with blood
    The crown to belime!

(They handle the crown awkwardly and break it into two
pieces, with which they spring around.)

    'Tis done, let it be!
    We speak and we see,

166

We hear and we rhyme!

FAUST (before the mirror)
Woe's me! I fear to lose my wits.

MEPHISTOPHELES (pointing to the Animals)
My own head, now, is really nigh to sinking.

THE ANIMALS
    If lucky our hits,
    And everything fits,
    'Tis thoughts, and we're thinking!

FAUST (as above)
My bosom burns with that sweet vision;
Let us, with speed, away from here!

MEPHISTOPHELES (in the same attitude)
One must, at least, make this admission--
They're poets, genuine and sincere.

(The caldron, which the SHE-APE has up to this time neglected
to watch, begins to boil over: there ensues a great flame,
which blazes out the chimney. The WITCH comes careering
down through the flame, with terrible cries.)

THE WITCH
    Ow! ow! ow! ow!
    The damnéd beast--the curséd sow!
    To leave the kettle, and singe the Frau!
    Accurséd fere!

(Perceiving FAUST and MEPHISTOPHELES.)

    What is that here?
    Who are you here?
    What want you thus?
    Who sneaks to us?
    The fire-pain
    Burn bone and brain!

(She plunges the skimming-ladle into the caldron, and scatters
flames towards FAUST, MEPHISTOPHELES, and the Animals.
The Animals whimper.)

MEPHISTOPHELES
(reversing the brush, which he has been holding in his hand,
and striding among the jars and glasses)

In two! in two!
There lies the brew!
There lies the glass!
The joke will pass,
As time, foul ass!
To the singing of thy crew.

(As the WITCH starts back, full of wrath and horror)

Ha! know'st thou me? Abomination, thou!
Know'st thou, at last, thy Lord and Master?
What hinders me from smiting now
Thee and thy monkey-sprites with fell disaster?
Hast for the scarlet coat no reverence?
Dost recognize no more the tall cock's-feather?
Have I concealed this countenance?--
Must tell my name, old face of leather?

THE WITCH
O pardon, Sir, the rough salute!
Yet I perceive no cloven foot;
And both your ravens, where are they now?

MEPHISTOPHELES
This time, I'll let thee 'scape the debt;
For since we two together met,
'Tis verily full many a day now.
Culture, which smooth the whole world licks,
Also unto the Devil sticks.
The days of that old Northern phantom now are over:
Where canst thou horns and tail and claws discover?
And, as regards the foot, which I can't spare, in truth,
'Twould only make the people shun me;
Therefore I've worn, like many a spindly youth,
False calves these many years upon me.

THE WITCH (dancing)
Reason and sense forsake my brain,
Since I behold Squire Satan here again!

MEPHISTOPHELES

Woman, from such a name refrain!

THE WITCH

Why so? What has it done to thee?

MEPHISTOPHELES

It's long been written in the Book of Fable;
Yet, therefore, no whit better men we see:
The Evil One has left, the evil ones are stable.
Sir Baron call me thou, then is the matter good;
A cavalier am I, like others in my bearing.
Thou hast no doubt about my noble blood:
See, here's the coat-of-arms that I am wearing!

(He makes an indecent gesture.)

THE WITCH (laughs immoderately)

Ha! ha! That's just your way, I know:
A rogue you are, and you were always so.

MEPHISTOPHELES (to FAUST)

My friend, take proper heed, I pray!
To manage witches, this is just the way.

THE WITCH

Wherein, Sirs, can I be of use?

MEPHISTOPHELES

Give us a goblet of the well-known juice!
But, I must beg you, of the oldest brewage;
The years a double strength produce.

THE WITCH

With all my heart! Now, here's a bottle,
Wherefrom, sometimes, I wet my throttle,
Which, also, not the slightest, stinks;
And willingly a glass I'll fill him.

(Whispering)

Yet, if this man without due preparation drinks,
As well thou know'st, within an hour 'twill kill him.

MEPHISTOPHELES
He is a friend of mine, with whom it will agree,
And he deserves thy kitchen's best potation:
Come, draw thy circle, speak thine adjuration,
And fill thy goblet full and free!

THE WITCH
(with fantastic gestures draws a circle and places mysterious
articles therein; meanwhile the glasses begin to ring, the
caldron to sound, and make a musical accompaniment.
Finally she brings a great book, and stations in the circle
the Apes, who are obliged to serve as reading-desk, and to
hold the torches. She then beckons FAUST to approach.)

FAUST (to MEPHISTOPHELES)
Now, what shall come of this? the creatures antic,
The crazy stuff, the gestures frantic,--
All the repulsive cheats I view,--
Are known to me, and hated, too.

MEPHISTOPHELES
O, nonsense! That's a thing for laughter;
Don't be so terribly severe!
She juggles you as doctor now, that, after,
The beverage may work the proper cheer.

(He persuades FAUST to step into the circle.)

THE WITCH
(begins to declaim, with much emphasis, from the book)

    See, thus it's done!
    Make ten of one,
    And two let be,
    Make even three,
    And rich thou 'lt be.
    Cast o'er the four!
    From five and six
    (The witch's tricks)
    Make seven and eight,
    'Tis finished straight!
    And nine is one,
    And ten is none.

This is the witch's once-one's-one!

FAUST

She talks like one who raves in fever.

MEPHISTOPHELES

Thou'lt hear much more before we leave her.
'Tis all the same: the book I can repeat,
Such time I've squandered o'er the history:
A contradiction thus complete
Is always for the wise, no less than fools, a mystery.
The art is old and new, for verily
All ages have been taught the matter,--
By Three and One, and One and Three,
Error instead of Truth to scatter.
They prate and teach, and no one interferes;
All from the fellowship of fools are shrinking.
Man usually believes, if only words he hears,
That also with them goes material for thinking!

THE WITCH (continues)

   The lofty skill
   Of Science, still
   From all men deeply hidden!
   Who takes no thought,
   To him 'tis brought,
   'Tis given unsought, unbidden!

FAUST

What nonsense she declaims before us!
My head is nigh to split, I fear:
It seems to me as if I hear
A hundred thousand fools in chorus.

MEPHISTOPHELES

O Sibyl excellent, enough of adjuration!
But hither bring us thy potation,
And quickly fill the beaker to the brim!
This drink will bring my friend no injuries:
He is a man of manifold degrees,
And many draughts are known to him.

(The WITCH, with many ceremonies, pours the drink into a
cup; as FAUST sets it to his lips, a light flame arises.)

Down with it quickly! Drain it off!
'Twill warm thy heart with new desire:
Art with the Devil hand and glove,
And wilt thou be afraid of fire?

(The WITCH breaks the circle: FAUST steps forth.)

MEPHISTOPHELES
And now, away! Thou dar'st not rest.

THE WITCH
And much good may the liquor do thee!

MEPHISTOPHELES (to the WITCH)
Thy wish be on Walpurgis Night expressed;
What boon I have, shall then be given unto thee.

THE WITCH
Here is a song, which, if you sometimes sing,
You'll find it of peculiar operation.

MEPHISTOPHELES (to FAUST)
Come, walk at once! A rapid occupation
Must start the needful perspiration,
And through thy frame the liquor's potence fling.
The noble indolence I'll teach thee then to treasure,
And soon thou'lt be aware, with keenest thrills of pleasure,
How Cupid stirs and leaps, on light and restless wing.

FAUST
One rapid glance within the mirror give me,
How beautiful that woman-form!

MEPHISTOPHELES
No, no! The paragon of all, believe me,
Thou soon shalt see, alive and warm.

(Aside)

Thou'lt find, this drink thy blood compelling,
Each woman beautiful as Helen!

VII

STREET

FAUST MARGARET (passing by)

FAUST
Fair lady, let it not offend you,
That arm and escort I would lend you!

MARGARET
I'm neither lady, neither fair,
And home I can go without your care.

[She releases herself, and exit.

FAUST
By Heaven, the girl is wondrous fair!
Of all I've seen, beyond compare;
So sweetly virtuous and pure,
And yet a little pert, be sure!
The lip so red, the cheek's clear dawn,
[Illustration:]
I'll not forget while the world rolls on!
How she cast down her timid eyes,
Deep in my heart imprinted lies:
How short and sharp of speech was she,
Why, 'twas a real ecstasy!

(MEPHISTOPHELES enters)

FAUST
Hear, of that girl I'd have possession!

MEPHISTOPHELES
Which, then?

FAUST
The one who just went by.

MEPHISTOPHELES
She, there? She's coming from confession,
Of every sin absolved; for I,

Behind her chair, was listening nigh.
So innocent is she, indeed,
That to confess she had no need.
I have no power o'er souls so green.

FAUST

And yet, she's older than fourteen.

MEPHISTOPHELES

How now! You're talking like Jack Rake,
Who every flower for himself would take,
And fancies there are no favors more,
Nor honors, save for him in store;
Yet always doesn't the thing succeed.

FAUST

Most Worthy Pedagogue, take heed!
Let not a word of moral law be spoken!
I claim, I tell thee, all my right;
And if that image of delight
Rest not within mine arms to-night,
At midnight is our compact broken.

MEPHISTOPHELES

But think, the chances of the case!
I need, at least, a fortnight's space,
To find an opportune occasion.

FAUST

Had I but seven hours for all,
I should not on the Devil call,
But win her by my own persuasion.

MEPHISTOPHELES

You almost like a Frenchman prate;
Yet, pray, don't take it as annoyance!
Why, all at once, exhaust the joyance?
Your bliss is by no means so great
As if you'd use, to get control,
All sorts of tender rigmarole,
And knead and shape her to your thought,
As in Italian tales 'tis taught.

FAUST

Without that, I have appetite.

MEPHISTOPHELES
But now, leave jesting out of sight!
I tell you, once for all, that speed
With this fair girl will not succeed;
By storm she cannot captured be;
We must make use of strategy.

FAUST
Get me something the angel keeps!
Lead me thither where she sleeps!
Get me a kerchief from her breast,--
A garter that her knee has pressed!

MEPHISTOPHELES
That you may see how much I'd fain
Further and satisfy your pain,
We will no longer lose a minute;
I'll find her room to-day, and take you in it.

FAUST
And shall I see--possess her?

MEPHISTOPHELES

No!
Unto a neighbor she must go,
And meanwhile thou, alone, mayst glow
With every hope of future pleasure,
Breathing her atmosphere in fullest measure.

FAUST
Can we go thither?

MEPHISTOPHELES
'Tis too early yet.

FAUST
A gift for her I bid thee get!
[Exit.

MEPHISTOPHELES
Presents at once? That's good: he's certain to get at her!

Full many a pleasant place I know,
And treasures, buried long ago:
I must, perforce, look up the matter. [Exit.

VIII

EVENING A SMALL, NEATLY KEPT CHAMBER

MARGARET
(plaiting and binding up the braids of her hair)

I'd something give, could I but say
Who was that gentleman, to-day.
Surely a gallant man was he,
And of a noble family;
And much could I in his face behold,--
And he wouldn't, else, have been so bold!

[Exit

MEPHISTOPHELES FAUST

MEPHISTOPHELES
Come in, but gently: follow me!

FAUST (after a moment's silence)
Leave me alone, I beg of thee!

MEPHISTOPHELES (prying about)
Not every girl keeps things so neat.

FAUST (looking around)
O welcome, twilight soft and sweet,
That breathes throughout this hallowed shrine!
Sweet pain of love, bind thou with fetters fleet
The heart that on the dew of hope must pine!
How all around a sense impresses
Of quiet, order, and content!
This poverty what bounty blesses!
What bliss within this narrow den is pent!

(He throws himself into a leathern arm-chair near the bed.)

Receive me, thou, that in thine open arms
Departed joy and pain wert wont to gather!
How oft the children, with their ruddy charms,
Hung here, around this throne, where sat the father!

Perchance my love, amid the childish band,
Grateful for gifts the Holy Christmas gave her,
Here meekly kissed the grandsire's withered hand.
I feel, O maid! thy very soul
Of order and content around me whisper,--
Which leads thee with its motherly control,
The cloth upon thy board bids smoothly thee unroll,
The sand beneath thy feet makes whiter, crisper.
O dearest hand, to thee 'tis given
To change this hut into a lower heaven!
And here!

(He lifts one of the bed-curtains.)

What sweetest thrill is in my blood!
Here could I spend whole hours, delaying:
Here Nature shaped, as if in sportive playing,
The angel blossom from the bud.
Here lay the child, with Life's warm essence
The tender bosom filled and fair,
And here was wrought, through holier, purer presence,
The form diviner beings wear!

And I? What drew me here with power?
How deeply am I moved, this hour!
What seek I? Why so full my heart, and sore?
Miserable Faust! I know thee now no more.

Is there a magic vapor here?
I came, with lust of instant pleasure,
And lie dissolved in dreams of love's sweet leisure!
Are we the sport of every changeful atmosphere?

And if, this moment, came she in to me,
How would I for the fault atonement render!
How small the giant lout would be,
Prone at her feet, relaxed and tender!

MEPHISTOPHELES
Be quick! I see her there, returning.

FAUST
Go! go! I never will retreat.

MEPHISTOPHELES

Here is a casket, not unmeet,
Which elsewhere I have just been earning.
Here, set it in the press, with haste!
I swear, 'twill turn her head, to spy it:
Some baubles I therein had placed,
That you might win another by it.
True, child is child, and play is play.

FAUST

I know not, should I do it?

MEPHISTOPHELES

Ask you, pray?
Yourself, perhaps, would keep the bubble?
Then I suggest, 'twere fair and just
To spare the lovely day your lust,
And spare to me the further trouble.
You are not miserly, I trust?
I rub my hands, in expectation tender--

(He places the casket in the press, and locks it again.)

Now quick, away!
The sweet young maiden to betray,
So that by wish and will you bend her;
And you look as though
To the lecture-hall you were forced to go,--
As if stood before you, gray and loath,
Physics and Metaphysics both!
But away! [Exeunt.

MARGARET (with a lamp)

It is so close, so sultry, here!

(She opens the window)

And yet 'tis not so warm outside.
I feel, I know not why, such fear!--
Would mother came!--where can she bide?
My body's chill and shuddering,--
I'm but a silly, fearsome thing!

(She begins to sing while undressing)

There was a King in Thule,
Was faithful till the grave,--
To whom his mistress, dying,
A golden goblet gave.

Naught was to him more precious;
He drained it at every bout:
His eyes with tears ran over,
As oft as he drank thereout.

When came his time of dying,
The towns in his land he told,
Naught else to his heir denying
Except the goblet of gold.

He sat at the royal banquet
With his knights of high degree,
In the lofty hall of his fathers
In the Castle by the Sea.

There stood the old carouser,
And drank the last life-glow;
And hurled the hallowed goblet
Into the tide below.

He saw it plunging and filling,
And sinking deep in the sea:
Then fell his eyelids forever,
And never more drank he!

(She opens the press in order to arrange her clothes, and perceives
the casket of jewels.)

How comes that lovely casket here to me?
I locked the press, most certainly.
'Tis truly wonderful! What can within it be?
Perhaps 'twas brought by some one as a pawn,
And mother gave a loan thereon?
And here there hangs a key to fit:
I have a mind to open it.
What is that? God in Heaven! Whence came
Such things? Never beheld I aught so fair!
Rich ornaments, such as a noble dame

On highest holidays might wear!
How would the pearl-chain suit my hair?
Ah, who may all this splendor own?

(She adorns herself with the jewelry, and steps before the mirror.)

Were but the ear-rings mine, alone!
One has at once another air.
What helps one's beauty, youthful blood?
One may possess them, well and good;
But none the more do others care.
They praise us half in pity, sure:
To gold still tends,
On gold depends
All, all! Alas, we poor!

PROMENADE

(FAUST, walking thoughtfully up and down. To him MEPHISTOPHELES.)

MEPHISTOPHELES
By all love ever rejected! By hell-fire hot and unsparing!
I wish I knew something worse, that I might use it for
swearing!

FAUST
What ails thee? What is't gripes thee, elf?
A face like thine beheld I never.

MEPHISTOPHELES
I would myself unto the Devil deliver,
If I were not a Devil myself!

FAUST
Thy head is out of order, sadly:
It much becomes thee to be raving madly.

MEPHISTOPHELES
Just think, the pocket of a priest should get
The trinkets left for Margaret!
The mother saw them, and, instanter,
A secret dread began to haunt her.
Keen scent has she for tainted air;
She snuffs within her book of prayer,
And smells each article, to see
If sacred or profane it be;
So here she guessed, from every gem,
That not much blessing came with them.
"My child," she said, "ill-gotten good
Ensnares the soul, consumes the blood.
Before the Mother of God we'll lay it;
With heavenly manna she'll repay it!"
But Margaret thought, with sour grimace,
"A gift-horse is not out of place,
And, truly! godless cannot be
The one who brought such things to me."
A parson came, by the mother bidden:

He saw, at once, where the game was hidden,
And viewed it with a favor stealthy.
He spake: "That is the proper view,--
Who overcometh, winneth too.
The Holy Church has a stomach healthy:
Hath eaten many a land as forfeit,
And never yet complained of surfeit:
The Church alone, beyond all question,
Has for ill-gotten goods the right digestion."

FAUST

A general practice is the same,
Which Jew and King may also claim.

MEPHISTOPHELES

Then bagged the spangles, chains, and rings,
As if but toadstools were the things,
And thanked no less, and thanked no more
Than if a sack of nuts he bore,--
Promised them fullest heavenly pay,
And deeply edified were they.

FAUST

And Margaret?

MEPHISTOPHELES

Sits unrestful still,
And knows not what she should, or will;
Thinks on the jewels, day and night,
But more on him who gave her such delight.

FAUST

The darling's sorrow gives me pain.
Get thou a set for her again!
The first was not a great display.

MEPHISTOPHELES

O yes, the gentleman finds it all child's-play!

FAUST

Fix and arrange it to my will;
And on her neighbor try thy skill!
Don't be a Devil stiff as paste,
But get fresh jewels to her taste!

MEPHISTOPHELES
Yes, gracious Sir, in all obedience!

[Exit FAUST.

Such an enamored fool in air would blow
Sun, moon, and all the starry legions,
To give his sweetheart a diverting show.

[Exit.

X

THE NEIGHBOR'S HOUSE

MARTHA (solus)
God forgive my husband, yet he
Hasn't done his duty by me!
Off in the world he went straightway,--
Left me lie in the straw where I lay.
And, truly, I did naught to fret him:
God knows I loved, and can't forget him!

(She weeps.)

Perhaps he's even dead! Ah, woe!--
Had I a certificate to show!

MARGARET (comes)
Dame Martha!

MARTHA
Margaret! what's happened thee?

MARGARET
I scarce can stand, my knees are trembling!
I find a box, the first resembling,
Within my press! Of ebony,--
And things, all splendid to behold,
And richer far than were the old.

MARTHA
You mustn't tell it to your mother!
'Twould go to the priest, as did the other.

MARGARET
Ah, look and see--just look and see!

MARTHA (adorning her)
O, what a blessed luck for thee!

MARGARET
But, ah! in the streets I dare not bear them,
Nor in the church be seen to wear them.

MARTHA
Yet thou canst often this way wander,
And secretly the jewels don,
Walk up and down an hour, before the mirror yonder,--
We'll have our private joy thereon.
And then a chance will come, a holiday,
When, piece by piece, can one the things abroad display,
A chain at first, then other ornament:
Thy mother will not see, and stories we'll invent.

MARGARET
Whoever could have brought me things so precious?
That something's wrong, I feel suspicious.

(A knock)

Good Heaven! My mother can that have been?

MARTHA (peeping through the blind)
'Tis some strange gentleman.--Come in!

(MEPHISTOPHELES enters.)

MEPHISTOPHELES
That I so boldly introduce me,
I beg you, ladies, to excuse me.

(Steps back reverently, on seeing MARGARET.)

For Martha Schwerdtlein I'd inquire!

MARTHA
I'm she: what does the gentleman desire?

MEPHISTOPHELES (aside to her)
It is enough that you are she:
You've a visitor of high degree.
Pardon the freedom I have ta'en,--
Will after noon return again.

MARTHA (aloud)
Of all things in the world! Just hear--
He takes thee for a lady, dear!

MARGARET

I am a creature young and poor:
The gentleman's too kind, I'm sure.
The jewels don't belong to me.

MEPHISTOPHELES

Ah, not alone the jewelry!
The look, the manner, both betray--
Rejoiced am I that I may stay!

MARTHA

What is your business? I would fain--

MEPHISTOPHELES

I would I had a more cheerful strain!
Take not unkindly its repeating:
Your husband's dead, and sends a greeting.

MARTHA

Is dead? Alas, that heart so true!
My husband dead! Let me die, too!

MARGARET

Ah, dearest dame, let not your courage fail!

MEPHISTOPHELES

Hear me relate the mournful tale!

MARGARET

Therefore I'd never love, believe me!
A loss like this to death would grieve me.

MEPHISTOPHELES

Joy follows woe, woe after joy comes flying.

MARTHA

Relate his life's sad close to me!

MEPHISTOPHELES

In Padua buried, he is lying
Beside the good Saint Antony,
Within a grave well consecrated,

For cool, eternal rest created.

MARTHA
He gave you, further, no commission?

MEPHISTOPHELES
Yes, one of weight, with many sighs:
Three hundred masses buy, to save him from perdition!
My hands are empty, otherwise.

MARTHA
What! Not a pocket-piece? no jewelry?
What every journeyman within his wallet spares,
And as a token with him bears,
And rather starves or begs, than loses?

MEPHISTOPHELES
Madam, it is a grief to me;
Yet, on my word, his cash was put to proper uses.
Besides, his penitence was very sore,
And he lamented his ill fortune all the more.

MARGARET
Alack, that men are so unfortunate!
Surely for his soul's sake full many a prayer I'll proffer.

MEPHISTOPHELES
You well deserve a speedy marriage-offer:
You are so kind, compassionate.

MARGARET
O, no! As yet, it would not do.

MEPHISTOPHELES
If not a husband, then a beau for you!
It is the greatest heavenly blessing,
To have a dear thing for one's caressing.

MARGARET
The country's custom is not so.

MEPHISTOPHELES
Custom, or not! It happens, though.

MARTHA

Continue, pray!

MEPHISTOPHELES

I stood beside his bed of dying.
'Twas something better than manure,--
Half-rotten straw: and yet, he died a Christian, sure,
And found that heavier scores to his account were lying.
He cried: "I find my conduct wholly hateful!
To leave my wife, my trade, in manner so ungrateful!
Ah, the remembrance makes me die!
Would of my wrong to her I might be shriven!"

MARTHA (weeping)

The dear, good man! Long since was he forgiven.

MEPHISTOPHELES

"Yet she, God knows! was more to blame than I."

MARTHA

He lied! What! On the brink of death he slandered?

MEPHISTOPHELES

In the last throes his senses wandered,
If I such things but half can judge.
He said: "I had no time for play, for gaping freedom:
First children, and then work for bread to feed 'em,--
For bread, in the widest sense, to drudge,
And could not even eat my share in peace and quiet!"

MARTHA

Had he all love, all faith forgotten in his riot?
My work and worry, day and night?

MEPHISTOPHELES

Not so: the memory of it touched him quite.
Said he: "When I from Malta went away
My prayers for wife and little ones were zealous,
And such a luck from Heaven befell us,
We made a Turkish merchantman our prey,
That to the Soldan bore a mighty treasure.
Then I received, as was most fit,
Since bravery was paid in fullest measure,
My well-apportioned share of it."

MARTHA

Say, how? Say, where? If buried, did he own it?

MEPHISTOPHELES

Who knows, now, whither the four winds have blown it?
A fair young damsel took him in her care,
As he in Naples wandered round, unfriended;
And she much love, much faith to him did bear,
So that he felt it till his days were ended.

MARTHA

The villain! From his children thieving!
Even all the misery on him cast
Could not prevent his shameful way of living!

MEPHISTOPHELES

But see! He's dead therefrom, at last.
Were I in your place, do not doubt me,
I'd mourn him decently a year,
And for another keep, meanwhile, my eyes about me.

MARTHA

Ah, God! another one so dear
As was my first, this world will hardly give me.
There never was a sweeter fool than mine,
Only he loved to roam and leave me,
And foreign wenches and foreign wine,
And the damned throw of dice, indeed.

MEPHISTOPHELES

Well, well! That might have done, however,
If he had only been as clever,
And treated your slips with as little heed.
I swear, with this condition, too,
I would, myself, change rings with you.

MARTHA

The gentleman is pleased to jest.

MEPHISTOPHELES

I'll cut away, betimes, from here:
She'd take the Devil at his word, I fear.

(To MARGARET)

How fares the heart within your breast?

MARGARET
What means the gentleman?

MEPHISTOPHELES (aside)
 Sweet innocent, thou art!

(Aloud.)

 Ladies, farewell!

MARGARET
Farewell!

MARTHA
A moment, ere we part!
I'd like to have a legal witness,
Where, how, and when he died, to certify his fitness.
Irregular ways I've always hated;
I want his death in the weekly paper stated.

MEPHISTOPHELES
Yes, my good dame, a pair of witnesses
Always the truth establishes.
I have a friend of high condition,
Who'll also add his deposition.
I'll bring him here.

MARTHA
Good Sir, pray do!

MEPHISTOPHELES
And this young lady will be present, too?
A gallant youth! has travelled far:
Ladies with him delighted are.

MARGARET
Before him I should blush, ashamed.

MEPHISTOPHELES
Before no king that could be named!

MARTHA
Behind the house, in my garden, then,
This eve we'll expect the gentlemen.

XI

A STREET

FAUST MEPHISTOPHELES

FAUST
How is it? under way? and soon complete?

MEPHISTOPHELES
Ah, bravo! Do I find you burning?
Well, Margaret soon will still your yearning:
At Neighbor Martha's you'll this evening meet.
A fitter woman ne'er was made
To ply the pimp and gypsy trade!

FAUST
Tis well.

MEPHISTOPHELES
Yet something is required from us.

FAUST
One service pays the other thus.

MEPHISTOPHELES
We've but to make a deposition valid
That now her husband's limbs, outstretched and pallid,
At Padua rest, in consecrated soil.

FAUST
Most wise! And first, of course, we'll make the journey
  thither?

MEPHISTOPHELES
Sancta simplicitas! no need of such a toil;
Depose, with knowledge or without it, either!

FAUST
If you've naught better, then, I'll tear your pretty plan!

MEPHISTOPHELES
Now, there you are! O holy man!

Is it the first time in your life you're driven
To bear false witness in a case?
Of God, the world and all that in it has a place,
Of Man, and all that moves the being of his race,
Have you not terms and definitions given
With brazen forehead, daring breast?
And, if you'll probe the thing profoundly,
Knew you so much--and you'll confess it roundly!--
As here of Schwerdtlein's death and place of rest?

FAUST
Thou art, and thou remain'st, a sophist, liar.

MEPHISTOPHELES
Yes, knew I not more deeply thy desire.
For wilt thou not, no lover fairer,
Poor Margaret flatter, and ensnare her,
And all thy soul's devotion swear her?

FAUST
And from my heart.

MEPHISTOPHELES
'Tis very fine!
Thine endless love, thy faith assuring,
The one almighty force enduring,--
Will that, too, prompt this heart of thine?

FAUST
Hold! hold! It will!--If such my flame,
And for the sense and power intense
I seek, and cannot find, a name;
Then range with all my senses through creation,
Craving the speech of inspiration,
And call this ardor, so supernal,
Endless, eternal and eternal,--
Is that a devilish lying game?

MEPHISTOPHELES
And yet I'm right!

FAUST
Mark this, I beg of thee!
And spare my lungs henceforth: whoever

Intends to have the right, if but his
 tongue be clever,
Will have it, certainly.
But come: the further talking brings
 disgust,
For thou art right, especially since I
 must.

XII

GARDEN

(MARGARET on FAUST'S arm. MARTHA and MEPHISTOPHELES walking up and down.)

MARGARET
I feel, the gentleman allows for me,
Demeans himself, and shames me by it;
A traveller is so used to be
Kindly content with any diet.
I know too well that my poor gossip can
Ne'er entertain such an experienced man.

FAUST
A look from thee, a word, more entertains
Than all the lore of wisest brains.

(He kisses her hand.)

MARGARET
Don't incommode yourself! How could you ever kiss it!
It is so ugly, rough to see!
What work I do,--how hard and steady is it!
Mother is much too close with me.

[They pass.

MARTHA
And you, Sir, travel always, do you not?

MEPHISTOPHELES
Alas, that trade and duty us so harry!
With what a pang one leaves so many a spot,
And dares not even now and then to tarry!

MARTHA
In young, wild years it suits your ways,
This round and round the world in freedom sweeping;
But then come on the evil days,
And so, as bachelor, into his grave a-creeping,
None ever found a thing to praise.

MEPHISTOPHELES

I dread to see how such a fate advances.

MARTHA

Then, worthy Sir, improve betimes your chances!

[They pass.

MARGARET

Yes, out of sight is out of mind!
Your courtesy an easy grace is;
But you have friends in other places,
And sensibler than I, you'll find.

FAUST

Trust me, dear heart! what men call sensible
Is oft mere vanity and narrowness.

MARGARET

  How so?

FAUST

Ah, that simplicity and innocence ne'er know
Themselves, their holy value, and their spell!
That meekness, lowliness, the highest graces
Which Nature portions out so lovingly--

MARGARET

So you but think a moment's space on me,
All times I'll have to think on you, all places!

FAUST

No doubt you're much alone?

MARGARET

Yes, for our household small has grown,
Yet must be cared for, you will own.
We have no maid: I do the knitting, sewing, sweeping,
The cooking, early work and late, in fact;
And mother, in her notions of housekeeping,
Is so exact!
Not that she needs so much to keep expenses down:
We, more than others, might take comfort, rather:

A nice estate was left us by my father,
A house, a little garden near the town.
But now my days have less of noise and hurry;
My brother is a soldier,
My little sister's dead.
True, with the child a troubled life I led,
Yet I would take again, and willing, all the worry,
So very dear was she.

FAUST

An angel, if like thee!

MARGARET

I brought it up, and it was fond of me.
Father had died before it saw the light,
And mother's case seemed hopeless quite,
So weak and miserable she lay;
And she recovered, then, so slowly, day by day.
She could not think, herself, of giving
The poor wee thing its natural living;
And so I nursed it all alone
With milk and water: 'twas my own.
Lulled in my lap with many a song,
It smiled, and tumbled, and grew strong.

FAUST

The purest bliss was surely then thy dower.

MARGARET

But surely, also, many a weary hour.
I kept the baby's cradle near
My bed at night: if 't even stirred, I'd guess it,
And waking, hear.
And I must nurse it, warm beside me press it,
And oft, to quiet it, my bed forsake,
And dandling back and forth the restless creature take,
Then at the wash-tub stand, at morning's break;
And then the marketing and kitchen-tending,
Day after day, the same thing, never-ending.
One's spirits, Sir, are thus not always good,
But then one learns to relish rest and food.

[They pass.

MARTHA

Yes, the poor women are bad off, 'tis true:
A stubborn bachelor there's no converting.

MEPHISTOPHELES

It but depends upon the like of you,
And I should turn to better ways than flirting.

MARTHA

Speak plainly, Sir, have you no one detected?
Has not your heart been anywhere subjected?

MEPHISTOPHELES

The proverb says: One's own warm hearth
And a good wife, are gold and jewels worth.

MARTHA

I mean, have you not felt desire, though ne'er so slightly?

MEPHISTOPHELES

I've everywhere, in fact, been entertained politely.

MARTHA

I meant to say, were you not touched in earnest, ever?

MEPHISTOPHELES

One should allow one's self to jest with ladies never.

MARTHA

Ah, you don't understand!

MEPHISTOPHELES

I'm sorry I'm so blind:
But I am sure--that you are very kind.

[They pass.

FAUST

And me, thou angel! didst thou recognize,
As through the garden-gate I came?

MARGARET

Did you not see it? I cast down my eyes.

FAUST

And thou forgiv'st my freedom, and the blame
To my impertinence befitting,
As the Cathedral thou wert quitting?

MARGARET

I was confused, the like ne'er happened me;
No one could ever speak to my discredit.
Ah, thought I, in my conduct has he read it--
Something immodest or unseemly free?
He seemed to have the sudden feeling
That with this wench 'twere very easy dealing.
I will confess, I knew not what appeal
On your behalf, here, in my bosom grew;
But I was angry with myself, to feel
That I could not be angrier with you.

FAUST

Sweet darling!

MARGARET

Wait a while!

(She plucks a star-flower, and pulls off the leaves, one after
the other.)

FAUST

Shall that a nosegay be?

MARGARET

No, it is just in play.

FAUST

How?

MARGARET

Go! you'll laugh at me.
(She pulls off the leaves and murmurs.)

FAUST

What murmurest thou?

MARGARET (half aloud)

He loves me--loves me not.

FAUST

Thou sweet, angelic soul!

MARGARET (continues)

Loves me--not--loves me--not--
(plucking the last leaf, she cries with frank delight:)

He loves me!

FAUST

Yes, child! and let this blossom-word
For thee be speech divine! He loves thee!
Ah, know'st thou what it means? He loves thee!

(He grasps both her hands.)

MARGARET

I'm all a-tremble!

FAUST

O tremble not! but let this look,
Let this warm clasp of hands declare thee
What is unspeakable!
To yield one wholly, and to feel a rapture
In yielding, that must be eternal!
Eternal!--for the end would be despair.
No, no,--no ending! no ending!

MARTHA (coming forward)

The night is falling.

MEPHISTOPHELES

Ay! we must away.

MARTHA

I'd ask you, longer here to tarry,
But evil tongues in this town have full play.
It's as if nobody had nothing to fetch and carry,
Nor other labor,
But spying all the doings of one's neighbor:
And one becomes the talk, do whatsoe'er one may.
Where is our couple now?

MEPHISTOPHELES
Flown up the alley yonder,
The wilful summer-birds!

MARTHA
He seems of her still fonder.

MEPHISTOPHELES
And she of him. So runs the world away!

XIII

A GARDEN-ARBOR

(MARGARET comes in, conceals herself behind the door, puts her finger to her lips, and peeps through the crack.)

MARGARET
He comes!

FAUST (entering)
Ah, rogue! a tease thou art:
I have thee!
(He kisses her.)

MARGARET (clasping him, and returning the kiss)
 Dearest man! I love thee from my heart.

(MEPHISTOPHELES knocks)

FAUST (stamping his foot)
Who's there?

MEPHISTOPHELES
A friend!

FAUST
A beast!

MEPHISTOPHELES
Tis time to separate.

MARTHA (coming)
Yes, Sir, 'tis late.

FAUST
May I not, then, upon you wait?

MARGARET
My mother would--farewell!

FAUST
Ah, can I not remain?

Farewell!

MARTHA
Adieu!

MARGARET
And soon to meet again!

[Exeunt FAUST and MEPHISTOPHELES.

MARGARET
Dear God! However is it, such
A man can think and know so much?
I stand ashamed and in amaze,
And answer "Yes" to all he says,
A poor, unknowing child! and he--
I can't think what he finds in me! [Exit.

XIV

FOREST AND CAVERN

FAUST (solus)
Spirit sublime, thou gav'st me, gav'st me all
For which I prayed. Not unto me in vain
Hast thou thy countenance revealed in fire.
Thou gav'st me Nature as a kingdom grand,
With power to feel and to enjoy it. Thou
Not only cold, amazed acquaintance yield'st,
But grantest, that in her profoundest breast
I gaze, as in the bosom of a friend.
The ranks of living creatures thou dost lead
Before me, teaching me to know my brothers
In air and water and the silent wood.
And when the storm in forests roars and grinds,
The giant firs, in falling, neighbor boughs
And neighbor trunks with crushing weight bear down,
And falling, fill the hills with hollow thunders,--
Then to the cave secure thou leadest me,
Then show'st me mine own self, and in my breast
The deep, mysterious miracles unfold.
And when the perfect moon before my gaze
Comes up with soothing light, around me float
From every precipice and thicket damp
The silvery phantoms of the ages past,
And temper the austere delight of thought.

That nothing can be perfect unto Man
I now am conscious. With this ecstasy,
Which brings me near and nearer to the Gods,
Thou gav'st the comrade, whom I now no more
Can do without, though, cold and scornful, he
Demeans me to myself, and with a breath,
A word, transforms thy gifts to nothingness.
Within my breast he fans a lawless fire,
Unwearied, for that fair and lovely form:
Thus in desire I hasten to enjoyment,
And in enjoyment pine to feel desire.

(MEPHISTOPHELES enters.)

MEPHISTOPHELES

Have you not led this life quite long enough?
How can a further test delight you?
'Tis very well, that once one tries the stuff,
But something new must then requite you.

FAUST

Would there were other work for thee!
To plague my day auspicious thou returnest.

MEPHISTOPHELES

Well! I'll engage to let thee be:
Thou darest not tell me so in earnest.
The loss of thee were truly very slight,--
comrade crazy, rude, repelling:

One has one's hands full all the day and night;
If what one does, or leaves undone, is right,
From such a face as thine there is no telling.

FAUST

There is, again, thy proper tone!--
That thou hast bored me, I must thankful be!

MEPHISTOPHELES

Poor Son of Earth, how couldst thou thus alone
Have led thy life, bereft of me?
I, for a time, at least, have worked thy cure;
Thy fancy's rickets plague thee not at all:
Had I not been, so hadst thou, sure,
Walked thyself off this earthly ball
Why here to caverns, rocky hollows slinking,
Sit'st thou, as 'twere an owl a-blinking?
Why suck'st, from sodden moss and dripping stone,
Toad-like, thy nourishment alone?
A fine way, this, thy time to fill!
The Doctor's in thy body still.

FAUST

What fresh and vital forces, canst thou guess,
Spring from my commerce with the wilderness?
But, if thou hadst the power of guessing,
Thou wouldst be devil enough to grudge my soul the blessing.

MEPHISTOPHELES

A blessing drawn from supernatural fountains!
In night and dew to lie upon the mountains;
All Heaven and Earth in rapture penetrating;
Thyself to Godhood haughtily inflating;
To grub with yearning force through Earth's dark marrow,
Compress the six days' work within thy bosom narrow,--
To taste, I know not what, in haughty power,
Thine own ecstatic life on all things shower,
Thine earthly self behind thee cast,
And then the lofty instinct, thus--

(With a gesture:)

at last,--
daren't say how--to pluck the final flower!

FAUST

Shame on thee!

MEPHISTOPHELES

Yes, thou findest that unpleasant!
Thou hast the moral right to cry me "shame!" at present.
One dares not that before chaste ears declare,
Which chaste hearts, notwithstanding, cannot spare;
And, once for all, I grudge thee not the pleasure
Of lying to thyself in moderate measure.
But such a course thou wilt not long endure;
Already art thou o'er-excited,
And, if it last, wilt soon be plighted
To madness and to horror, sure.
Enough of that! Thy love sits lonely yonder,
By all things saddened and oppressed;
Her thoughts and yearnings seek thee, tenderer, fonder,--
mighty love is in her breast.
First came thy passion's flood and poured around her
As when from melted snow a streamlet overflows;
Thou hast therewith so filled and drowned her,
That now thy stream all shallow shows.
Methinks, instead of in the forests lording,
The noble Sir should find it good,
The love of this young silly blood
At once to set about rewarding.
Her time is miserably long;

She haunts her window, watching clouds that stray
O'er the old city-wall, and far away.
"Were I a little bird!" so runs her song,
Day long, and half night long.
Now she is lively, mostly sad,
Now, wept beyond her tears;
Then again quiet she appears,--Always
love-mad.

FAUST
Serpent! Serpent!

MEPHISTOPHELES (aside)
Ha! do I trap thee!

FAUST
Get thee away with thine offences,
Reprobate! Name not that fairest thing,
Nor the desire for her sweet body bring
Again before my half-distracted senses!

MEPHISTOPHELES
What wouldst thou, then? She thinks that thou art flown;
And half and half thou art, I own.

FAUST
Yet am I near, and love keeps watch and ward;
Though I were ne'er so far, it cannot falter:
I envy even the Body of the Lord
The touching of her lips, before the altar.

MEPHISTOPHELES
'Tis very well! My envy oft reposes
On your twin-pair, that feed among the roses.

FAUST
Away, thou pimp!

MEPHISTOPHELES
You rail, and it is fun to me.
The God, who fashioned youth and maid,
Perceived the noblest purpose of His trade,
And also made their opportunity.
Go on! It is a woe profound!

'Tis for your sweetheart's room you're bound,
And not for death, indeed.

FAUST

What are, within her arms, the heavenly blisses?
Though I be glowing with her kisses,
Do I not always share her need?
I am the fugitive, all houseless roaming,
The monster without air or rest,
That like a cataract, down rocks and gorges foaming,
Leaps, maddened, into the abyss's breast!
And side-wards she, with young unwakened senses,
Within her cabin on the Alpine field
Her simple, homely life commences,
Her little world therein concealed.
And I, God's hate flung o'er me,
Had not enough, to thrust
The stubborn rocks before me
And strike them into dust!
She and her peace I yet must undermine:
Thou, Hell, hast claimed this sacrifice as thine!
Help, Devil! through the coming pangs to push me;
What must be, let it quickly be!
Let fall on me her fate, and also crush me,--
One ruin whelm both her and me!

MEPHISTOPHELES

Again it seethes, again it glows!
Thou fool, go in and comfort her!
When such a head as thine no outlet knows,
It thinks the end must soon occur.
Hail him, who keeps a steadfast mind!
Thou, else, dost well the devil-nature wear:
Naught so insipid in the world I find
As is a devil in despair.

XV

MARGARET'S ROOM

MARGARET (at the spinning-wheel, alone)

My peace is gone,
My heart is sore:
I never shall find it,
Ah, nevermore!

Save I have him near.
The grave is here;
The world is gall
And bitterness all.

My poor weak head
Is racked and crazed;
My thought is lost,
My senses mazed.

My peace is gone,
My heart is sore:
I never shall find it,
Ah, nevermore!

To see him, him only,
At the pane I sit;
To meet him, him only,
The house I quit.

His lofty gait,
His noble size,
The smile of his mouth,
The power of his eyes,

And the magic flow
Of his talk, the bliss
In the clasp of his hand,
And, ah! his kiss!

My peace is gone,
My heart is sore:

I never shall find it,
Ah, nevermore!

My bosom yearns
For him alone;
Ah, dared I clasp him,
And hold, and own!

And kiss his mouth,
To heart's desire,
And on his kisses
At last expire!

XVI

MARTHA'S GARDEN

MARGARET FAUST

MARGARET
Promise me, Henry!--

FAUST
What I can!

MARGARET
How is't with thy religion, pray?
Thou art a dear, good-hearted man,
And yet, I think, dost not incline that way.

FAUST
Leave that, my child! Thou know'st my love is tender;
For love, my blood and life would I surrender,
And as for Faith and Church, I grant to each his own.

MARGARET
That's not enough: we must believe thereon.

FAUST
Must we?

MARGARET
Would that I had some influence!
Then, too, thou honorest not the Holy Sacraments.

FAUST
I honor them.

MARGARET
Desiring no possession
'Tis long since thou hast been to mass or to confession.
Believest thou in God?

FAUST
My darling, who shall dare
"I believe in God!" to say?

Ask priest or sage the answer to declare,
And it will seem a mocking play,
A sarcasm on the asker.

MARGARET
Then thou believest not!

FAUST
Hear me not falsely, sweetest countenance!
Who dare express Him?
And who profess Him,
Saying: I believe in Him!
Who, feeling, seeing,
Deny His being,
Saying: I believe Him not!
The All-enfolding,
The All-upholding,
Folds and upholds he not
Thee, me, Himself?
Arches not there the sky above us?
Lies not beneath us, firm, the earth?
And rise not, on us shining,
Friendly, the everlasting stars?
Look I not, eye to eye, on thee,
And feel'st not, thronging
To head and heart, the force,
Still weaving its eternal secret,
Invisible, visible, round thy life?
Vast as it is, fill with that force thy heart,
And when thou in the feeling wholly blessed art,
Call it, then, what thou wilt,--
Call it Bliss! Heart! Love! God!
I have no name to give it!
Feeling is all in all:
The Name is sound and smoke,
Obscuring Heaven's clear glow.

MARGARET
All that is fine and good, to hear it so:
Much the same way the preacher spoke,
Only with slightly different phrases.

FAUST
The same thing, in all places,

All hearts that beat beneath the heavenly day--
Each in its language--say;
Then why not I, in mine, as well?

MARGARET

To hear it thus, it may seem passable;
And yet, some hitch in't there must be
For thou hast no Christianity.

FAUST

Dear love!

MARGARET

I've long been grieved to see
That thou art in such company.

FAUST

How so?

MARGARET

The man who with thee goes, thy mate,
Within my deepest, inmost soul I hate.
In all my life there's nothing
Has given my heart so keen a pang of loathing,
As his repulsive face has done.

FAUST

Nay, fear him not, my sweetest one!

MARGARET

I feel his presence like something ill.
I've else, for all, a kindly will,
But, much as my heart to see thee yearneth,
The secret horror of him returneth;
And I think the man a knave, as I live!
If I do him wrong, may God forgive!

FAUST

There must be such queer birds, however.

MARGARET

Live with the like of him, may I never!
When once inside the door comes he,
He looks around so sneeringly,

And half in wrath:
One sees that in nothing no interest he hath:
'Tis written on his very forehead
That love, to him, is a thing abhorréd.
I am so happy on thine arm,
So free, so yielding, and so warm,
And in his presence stifled seems my heart.

FAUST
Foreboding angel that thou art!

MARGARET
It overcomes me in such degree,
That wheresoe'er he meets us, even,
I feel as though I'd lost my love for thee.
When he is by, I could not pray to Heaven.
That burns within me like a flame,
And surely, Henry, 'tis with thee the same.

FAUST
There, now, is thine antipathy!

MARGARET
But I must go.

FAUST
Ah, shall there never be
A quiet hour, to see us fondly plighted,
With breast to breast, and soul to soul united?

MARGARET
Ah, if I only slept alone!
I'd draw the bolts to-night, for thy desire;
But mother's sleep so light has grown,
And if we were discovered by her,
'Twould be my death upon the spot!

FAUST
Thou angel, fear it not!
Here is a phial: in her drink
But three drops of it measure,
And deepest sleep will on her senses sink.

MARGARET

What would I not, to give thee pleasure?
It will not harm her, when one tries it?

FAUST
If 'twould, my love, would I advise it?

MARGARET
Ah, dearest man, if but thy face I see,
I know not what compels me to thy will:
So much have I already done for thee,
That scarcely more is left me to fulfil.

(Enter MEPHISTOPHELES.) [Exit.

MEPHISTOPHELES
The monkey! Is she gone?

FAUST
Hast played the spy again?

MEPHISTOPHELES
I've heard, most fully, how she drew thee.
The Doctor has been catechised, 'tis plain;
Great good, I hope, the thing will do thee.
The girls have much desire to ascertain
If one is prim and good, as ancient rules compel:
If there he's led, they think, he'll follow them as well.

FAUST
Thou, monster, wilt nor see nor own
How this pure soul, of faith so lowly,
So loving and ineffable,--
The faith alone
That her salvation is,--with scruples holy
Pines, lest she hold as lost the man she loves so well!

MEPHISTOPHELES
Thou, full of sensual, super-sensual desire,
A girl by the nose is leading thee.

FAUST
Abortion, thou, of filth and fire!

MEPHISTOPHELES

And then, how masterly she reads physiognomy!
When I am present she's impressed, she knows not how;
She in my mask a hidden sense would read:
She feels that surely I'm a genius now,--
Perhaps the very Devil, indeed!
Well, well,--to-night--?

FAUST
What's that to thee?

MEPHISTOPHELES
Yet my delight 'twill also be!

XVII

AT THE FOUNTAIN

MARGARET and LISBETH With pitchers.

LISBETH
Hast nothing heard of Barbara?

MARGARET
No, not a word. I go so little out.

LISBETH
It's true, Sibylla said, to-day.
She's played the fool at last, there's not a doubt.
Such taking-on of airs!

MARGARET
How so?

LISBETH
It stinks!
She's feeding two, whene'er she eats and drinks.

MARGARET
Ah!

LISBETH
 And so, at last, it serves her rightly.
She clung to the fellow so long and tightly!
That was a promenading!
At village and dance parading!
As the first they must everywhere shine,
And he treated her always to pies and wine,
And she made a to-do with her face so fine;
So mean and shameless was her behavior,
She took all the presents the fellow gave her.
'Twas kissing and coddling, on and on!
So now, at the end, the flower is gone.

MARGARET
The poor, poor thing!

LISBETH

Dost pity her, at that?
When one of us at spinning sat,
And mother, nights, ne'er let us out the door
She sported with her paramour.
On the door-bench, in the passage dark,
The length of the time they'd never mark.
So now her head no more she'll lift,
But do church-penance in her sinner's shift!

MARGARET

He'll surely take her for his wife.

LISBETH

He'd be a fool! A brisk young blade
Has room, elsewhere, to ply his trade.
Besides, he's gone.

MARGARET

That is not fair!

LISBETH

If him she gets, why let her beware!
The boys shall dash her wreath on the floor,
And we'll scatter chaff before her door!
                                    [Exit.

MARGARET (returning home)

How scornfully I once reviled,
When some poor maiden was beguiled!
More speech than any tongue suffices
I craved, to censure others' vices.
Black as it seemed, I blackened still,
And blacker yet was in my will;
And blessed myself, and boasted high,--
And now--a living sin am I!
Yet--all that drove my heart thereto,
God! was so good, so dear, so true!

XVIII

DONJON

(In a niche of the wall a shrine, with an image of the Mater Dolorosa. Pots of flowers before it.)

MARGARET
(putting fresh flowers in the pots)

Incline, O Maiden,
Thou sorrow-laden,
Thy gracious countenance upon my pain!

The sword Thy heart in,
With anguish smarting,
Thou lookest up to where Thy Son is slain!

Thou seest the Father;
Thy sad sighs gather,
And bear aloft Thy sorrow and His pain!

Ah, past guessing,
Beyond expressing,
The pangs that wring my flesh and bone!
Why this anxious heart so burneth,
Why it trembleth, why it yearneth,
Knowest Thou, and Thou alone!

Where'er I go, what sorrow,
What woe, what woe and sorrow
Within my bosom aches!
Alone, and ah! unsleeping,
I'm weeping, weeping, weeping,
The heart within me breaks.

The pots before my window,
Alas! my tears did wet,
As in the early morning
For thee these flowers I set.

Within my lonely chamber
The morning sun shone red:

I sat, in utter sorrow,
Already on my bed.

Help! rescue me from death and stain!
O Maiden!
Thou sorrow-laden,
Incline Thy countenance upon my pain!

XIX

NIGHT

STREET BEFORE MARGARET'S DOOR

VALENTINE (a soldier, MARGARET'S brother)
When I have sat at some carouse.
Where each to each his brag allows,
And many a comrade praised to me
His pink of girls right lustily,
With brimming glass that spilled the toast,
And elbows planted as in boast:
I sat in unconcerned repose,
And heard the swagger as it rose.
And stroking then my beard, I'd say,
Smiling, the bumper in my hand:
"Each well enough in her own way.
But is there one in all the land
Like sister Margaret, good as gold,--
One that to her can a candle hold?"
Cling! clang! "Here's to her!" went around
The board: "He speaks the truth!" cried some;
"In her the flower o' the sex is found!"
And all the swaggerers were dumb.
And now!--I could tear my hair with vexation.
And dash out my brains in desperation!
With turned-up nose each scamp may face me,
With sneers and stinging taunts disgrace me,
And, like a bankrupt debtor sitting,
A chance-dropped word may set me sweating!
Yet, though I thresh them all together,
I cannot call them liars, either.

But what comes sneaking, there, to view?
If I mistake not, there are two.
If he's one, let me at him drive!
He shall not leave the spot alive.

FAUST MEPHISTOPHELES

FAUST
How from the window of the sacristy

Upward th'eternal lamp sends forth a glimmer,
That, lessening side-wards, fainter grows and dimmer,
Till darkness closes from the sky!
The shadows thus within my bosom gather.

MEPHISTOPHELES

I'm like a sentimental tom-cat, rather,
That round the tall fire-ladders sweeps,
And stealthy, then, along the coping creeps:
Quite virtuous, withal, I come,
A little thievish and a little frolicsome.
I feel in every limb the presage
Forerunning the grand Walpurgis-Night:
Day after to-morrow brings its message,
And one keeps watch then with delight.

FAUST

Meanwhile, may not the treasure risen be,
Which there, behind, I glimmering see?

MEPHISTOPHELES

Shalt soon experience the pleasure,
To lift the kettle with its treasure.
I lately gave therein a squint--
Saw splendid lion-dollars in 't.

FAUST

Not even a jewel, not a ring,
To deck therewith my darling girl?

MEPHISTOPHELES

I saw, among the rest, a thing
That seemed to be a chain of pearl.

FAUST

That's well, indeed! For painful is it
To bring no gift when her I visit.

MEPHISTOPHELES

Thou shouldst not find it so annoying,
Without return to be enjoying.
Now, while the sky leads forth its starry throng,
Thou'lt hear a masterpiece, no work completer:
I'll sing her, first, a moral song,

The surer, afterwards, to cheat her.

(Sings to the cither.)

> What dost thou here
> In daybreak clear,
> Kathrina dear,
> Before thy lover's door?
> Beware! the blade
> Lets in a maid.
> That out a maid
> Departeth nevermore!
>
> The coaxing shun
> Of such an one!
> When once 'tis done
> Good-night to thee, poor thing!
> Love's time is brief:
> Unto no thief
> Be warm and lief,
> But with the wedding-ring!

VALENTINE (comes forward)
Whom wilt thou lure? God's-element!
Rat-catching piper, thou!--perdition!
To the Devil, first, the instrument!
To the Devil, then, the curst musician!

MEPHISTOPHELES
The cither's smashed! For nothing more 'tis fitting.

VALENTINE
There's yet a skull I must be splitting!

MEPHISTOPHELES (to FAUST)
Sir Doctor, don't retreat, I pray!
Stand by: I'll lead, if you'll but tarry:
Out with your spit, without delay!
You've but to lunge, and I will parry.

VALENTINE
Then parry that!

MEPHISTOPHELES

Why not? 'tis light.

VALENTINE
That, too!

MEPHISTOPHELES
Of course.

VALENTINE
I think the Devil must fight!
How is it, then? my hand's already lame:

MEPHISTOPHELES (to FAUST)
Thrust home!

VALENTINE (jails)
O God!

MEPHISTOPHELES
Now is the lubber tame!
But come, away! 'Tis time for us to fly;
For there arises now a murderous cry.
With the police 'twere easy to compound it,
But here the penal court will sift and sound it.

[Exit with FAUST.

MARTHA (at the window)
Come out! Come out!

MARGARET (at the window)
Quick, bring a light!

MARTHA (as above)
They swear and storm, they yell and fight!

PEOPLE
Here lies one dead already--see!

MARTHA (coming from the house)
The murderers, whither have they run?

MARGARET (coming out)
Who lies here?

PEOPLE
'Tis thy mother's son!

MARGARET
Almighty God! what misery!

VALENTINE
I'm dying! That is quickly said,
And quicker yet 'tis done.
Why howl, you women there? Instead,
Come here and listen, every one!

(All gather around him)

My Margaret, see! still young thou art,
But not the least bit shrewd or smart,
Thy business thus to slight:
So this advice I bid thee heed--
Now that thou art a whore indeed,
Why, be one then, outright!

MARGARET
My brother! God! such words to me?

VALENTINE
In this game let our Lord God be!
What's done's already done, alas!
What follows it, must come to pass.
With one begin'st thou secretly,
Then soon will others come to thee,
And when a dozen thee have known,
Thou'rt also free to all the town.
When Shame is born and first appears,
She is in secret brought to light,
And then they draw the veil of night
Over her head and ears;
Her life, in fact, they're loath to spare her.
But let her growth and strength display,
She walks abroad unveiled by day,
Yet is not grown a whit the fairer.
The uglier she is to sight,
The more she seeks the day's broad light.
The time I verily can discern

When all the honest folk will turn
From thee, thou jade! and seek protection
As from a corpse that breeds infection.
Thy guilty heart shall then dismay thee.
When they but look thee in the face:--
Shalt not in a golden chain array thee,
Nor at the altar take thy place!
Shalt not, in lace and ribbons flowing,
Make merry when the dance is going!
But in some corner, woe betide thee!
Among the beggars and cripples hide thee;
And so, though even God forgive,
On earth a damned existence live!

MARTHA

Commend your soul to God for pardon,
That you your heart with slander harden!

VALENTINE

Thou pimp most infamous, be still!
Could I thy withered body kill,
'Twould bring, for all my sinful pleasure,
Forgiveness in the richest measure.

MARGARET

My brother! This is Hell's own pain!

VALENTINE

I tell thee, from thy tears refrain!
When thou from honor didst depart
It stabbed me to the very heart.
Now through the slumber of the grave
I go to God as a soldier brave.

(Dies.)

XX

CATHEDRAL

SERVICE, ORGAN and ANTHEM.

(MARGARET among much people: the EVIL SPIRIT behind
MARGARET.)

EVIL SPIRIT
HOW otherwise was it, Margaret,
When thou, still innocent,
Here to the altar cam'st,
And from the worn and fingered book
Thy prayers didst prattle,
Half sport of childhood,
Half God within thee!
Margaret!
Where tends thy thought?
Within thy bosom
What hidden crime?
Pray'st thou for mercy on thy mother's soul,
That fell asleep to long, long torment, and through thee?
Upon thy threshold whose the blood?
And stirreth not and quickens
Something beneath thy heart,
Thy life disquieting
With most foreboding presence?

MARGARET
Woe! woe!
Would I were free from the thoughts
That cross me, drawing hither and thither
Despite me!

CHORUS
Diesira, dies illa,
Solvet soeclum in favilla!
(Sound of the organ.)

EVIL SPIRIT
Wrath takes thee!
The trumpet peals!

228

The graves tremble!
And thy heart
From ashy rest
To fiery torments
Now again requickened,
Throbs to life!

MARGARET

Would I were forth!
I feel as if the organ here
My breath takes from me,
My very heart
Dissolved by the anthem!

CHORUS

Judex ergo cum sedebit,
Quidquid latet, ad parebit,
Nil inultum remanebit.

MARGARET

I cannot breathe!
The massy pillars
Imprison me!
The vaulted arches
Crush me!--Air!

EVIL SPIRIT

Hide thyself! Sin and shame
Stay never hidden.
Air? Light?
Woe to thee!

CHORUS

Quid sum miser tunc dicturus,
Quem patronem rogaturus,
Cum vix Justus sit securus?

EVIL SPIRIT

They turn their faces,
The glorified, from thee:
The pure, their hands to offer,
Shuddering, refuse thee!
Woe!

CHORUS
Quid sum miser tune dicturus?

MARGARET
Neighbor! your cordial! (She falls in a swoon.)

XXI

WALPURGIS-NIGHT

THE HARTZ MOUNTAINS.

DISTRICT OF SCHIERKE AND ELEND.

FAUST MEPHISTOPHELES

MEPHISTOPHELES
DOST thou not wish a broomstick-steed's assistance?
The sturdiest he-goat I would gladly see:
The way we take, our goal is yet some distance.

FAUST
So long as in my legs I feel the fresh existence.
This knotted staff suffices me.
What need to shorten so the way?
Along this labyrinth of vales to wander,
Then climb the rocky ramparts yonder,
Wherefrom the fountain flings eternal spray,
Is such delight, my steps would fain delay.
The spring-time stirs within the fragrant birches,
And even the fir-tree feels it now:
Should then our limbs escape its gentle searches?

MEPHISTOPHELES
I notice no such thing, I vow!
'Tis winter still within my body:
Upon my path I wish for frost and snow.
How sadly rises, incomplete and ruddy,
The moon's lone disk, with its belated glow,
And lights so dimly, that, as one advances,
At every step one strikes a rock or tree!
Let us, then, use a Jack-o'-lantern's glances:
I see one yonder, burning merrily.
Ho, there! my friend! I'll levy thine attendance:
Why waste so vainly thy resplendence?
Be kind enough to light us up the steep!

WILL-O'-THE-WISP
My reverence, I hope, will me enable

231

To curb my temperament unstable;
For zigzag courses we are wont to keep.

MEPHISTOPHELES
Indeed? he'd like mankind to imitate!
Now, in the Devil's name, go straight,
Or I'll blow out his being's flickering spark!

WILL-O'-THE-WISP
You are the master of the house, I mark,
And I shall try to serve you nicely.
But then, reflect: the mountain's magic-mad to-day,
And if a will-o'-the-wisp must guide you on the way,
You mustn't take things too precisely.

FAUST, MEPHISTOPHELES, WILL-O'-THE-WISP
(in alternating song)

We, it seems, have entered newly
In the sphere of dreams enchanted.
Do thy bidding, guide us truly,
That our feet be forwards planted
In the vast, the desert spaces!
See them swiftly changing places,
Trees on trees beside us trooping,
And the crags above us stooping,
And the rocky snouts, outgrowing,--
Hear them snoring, hear them blowing!
O'er the stones, the grasses, flowing
Stream and streamlet seek the hollow.
Hear I noises? songs that follow?
Hear I tender love-petitions?
Voices of those heavenly visions?
Sounds of hope, of love undying!
And the echoes, like traditions
Of old days, come faint and hollow.

Hoo-hoo! Shoo-hoo! Nearer hover
Jay and screech-owl, and the plover,--
Are they all awake and crying?
Is't the salamander pushes,
Bloated-bellied, through the bushes?
And the roots, like serpents twisted,
Through the sand and boulders toiling,

Fright us, weirdest links uncoiling
To entrap us, unresisted:
Living knots and gnarls uncanny
Feel with polypus-antennae
For the wanderer. Mice are flying,
Thousand-colored, herd-wise hieing
Through the moss and through the heather!

And the fire-flies wink and darkle,
Crowded swarms that soar and sparkle,
And in wildering escort gather!

Tell me, if we still are standing,
Or if further we're ascending?
All is turning, whirling, blending,
Trees and rocks with grinning faces,
Wandering lights that spin in mazes,
Still increasing and expanding!

MEPHISTOPHELES

Grasp my skirt with heart undaunted!
Here a middle-peak is planted,
Whence one seeth, with amaze,
Mammon in the mountain blaze.

FAUST

How strangely glimmers through the hollows
A dreary light, like that of dawn!
Its exhalation tracks and follows
The deepest gorges, faint and wan.
Here steam, there rolling vapor sweepeth;
Here burns the glow through film and haze:
Now like a tender thread it creepeth,
Now like a fountain leaps and plays.
Here winds away, and in a hundred
Divided veins the valley braids:
There, in a corner pressed and sundered,
Itself detaches, spreads and fades.
Here gush the sparkles incandescent
Like scattered showers of golden sand;--
But, see! in all their height, at present,
The rocky ramparts blazing stand.

[Illustration: Under the old ribs of the rock retreating,]

MEPHISTOPHELES

Has not Sir Mammon grandly lighted
His palace for this festal night?
'Tis lucky thou hast seen the sight;
The boisterous guests approach that were invited.

FAUST

How raves the tempest through the air!
With what fierce blows upon my neck 'tis beating!

MEPHISTOPHELES

Under the old ribs of the rock retreating,
Hold fast, lest thou be hurled down the abysses there!
The night with the mist is black;
Hark! how the forests grind and crack!
Frightened, the owlets are scattered:
Hearken! the pillars are shattered.
The evergreen palaces shaking!
Boughs are groaning and breaking,
The tree-trunks terribly thunder,
The roots are twisting asunder!
In frightfully intricate crashing
Each on the other is dashing,
And over the wreck-strewn gorges
The tempest whistles and surges!
Hear'st thou voices higher ringing?
Far away, or nearer singing?
Yes, the mountain's side along,
Sweeps an infuriate glamouring song!

WITCHES (in chorus)

    The witches ride to the Brocken's top,
    The stubble is yellow, and green the crop.
    There gathers the crowd for carnival:
    Sir Urian sits over all.

    And so they go over stone and stock;
    The witch she-----s, and-----s the buck.

A VOICE

    Alone, old Baubo's coming now;
    She rides upon a farrow-sow.

CHORUS

Then honor to whom the honor is due!
Dame Baubo first, to lead the crew!
A tough old sow and the mother thereon,
Then follow the witches, every one.

A VOICE

Which way com'st thou hither?

VOICE

O'er the Ilsen-stone.
I peeped at the owl in her nest alone:
How she stared and glared!

VOICE

Betake thee to Hell!
Why so fast and so fell?

VOICE

She has scored and has flayed me:
See the wounds she has made me!

WITCHES (chorus)

The way is wide, the way is long:
See, what a wild and crazy throng!
The broom it scratches, the fork it thrusts,
The child is stifled, the mother bursts.

WIZARDS (semichorus)

As doth the snail in shell, we crawl:
Before us go the women all.
When towards the Devil's House we tread,
Woman's a thousand steps ahead.

OTHER SEMICHORUS

We do not measure with such care:
Woman in thousand steps is theft.
But howsoe'er she hasten may,
Man in one leap has cleared the way.

VOICE (from above)

Come on, come on, from Rocky Lake!

VOICE (from below)

235

Aloft we'd fain ourselves betake.
We've washed, and are bright as ever you will,
Yet we're eternally sterile still.

BOTH CHORUSES

The wind is hushed, the star shoots by.
The dreary moon forsakes the sky;
The magic notes, like spark on spark,
Drizzle, whistling through the dark.

VOICE (from below)
Halt, there! Ho, there!

VOICE (from above)
Who calls from the rocky cleft below there?

VOICE (below)
Take me, too! take me, too!
I'm climbing now three hundred years,
And yet the summit cannot see:
Among my equals I would be.

BOTH CHORUSES

Bears the broom and bears the stock,
Bears the fork and bears the buck:
Who cannot raise himself to-night
Is evermore a ruined wight.

HALF-WITCH (below)
So long I stumble, ill bestead,
And the others are now so far ahead!
At home I've neither rest nor cheer,
And yet I cannot gain them here.

CHORUS OF WITCHES

To cheer the witch will salve avail;
A rag will answer for a sail;
Each trough a goodly ship supplies;
He ne'er will fly, who now not flies.

BOTH CHORUSES

When round the summit whirls our flight,
Then lower, and on the ground alight;
And far and wide the heather press

With witchhood's swarms of wantonness!

(They settle down.)

MEPHISTOPHELES
They crowd and push, they roar and clatter!
They whirl and whistle, pull and chatter!
They shine, and spirt, and stink, and burn!
The true witch-element we learn.
Keep close! or we are parted, in our turn,
Where art thou?

FAUST (in the distance)
Here!

MEPHISTOPHELES
What! whirled so far astray?
Then house-right I must use, and clear the way.
Make room! Squire Voland comes! Room, gentle rabble,
room!

Here, Doctor, hold to me: in one jump we'll resume
An easier space, and from the crowd be free:
It's too much, even for the like of me.
Yonder, with special light, there's something shining clearer
Within those bushes; I've a mind to see.
Come on! well slip a little nearer.

FAUST
Spirit of Contradiction! On! I'll follow straight.
'Tis planned most wisely, if I judge aright:
We climb the Brocken's top in the Walpurgis-Night,
That arbitrarily, here, ourselves we isolate.

MEPHISTOPHELES
But see, what motley flames among the heather!
There is a lively club together:
In smaller circles one is not alone.

FAUST
Better the summit, I must own:
There fire and whirling smoke I see.
They seek the Evil One in wild confusion:
Many enigmas there might find solution.

MEPHISTOPHELES

But there enigmas also knotted be.
Leave to the multitude their riot!
Here will we house ourselves in quiet.
It is an old, transmitted trade,
That in the greater world the little worlds are made.
I see stark-nude young witches congregate,
And old ones, veiled and hidden shrewdly:
On my account be kind, nor treat them rudely!
The trouble's small, the fun is great.
I hear the noise of instruments attuning,--
Vile din! yet one must learn to bear the crooning.
Come, come along! It must be, I declare!
I'll go ahead and introduce thee there,
Thine obligation newly earning.
That is no little space: what say'st thou, friend?
Look yonder! thou canst scarcely see the end:
A hundred fires along the ranks are burning.
They dance, they chat, they cook, they drink, they court:
Now where, just tell me, is there better sport?

FAUST

Wilt thou, to introduce us to the revel,
Assume the part of wizard or of devil?

MEPHISTOPHELES

I'm mostly used, 'tis true, to go incognito,
But on a gala-day one may his orders show.
The Garter does not deck my suit,
But honored and at home is here the cloven foot.
Perceiv'st thou yonder snail? It cometh, slow and steady;
So delicately its feelers pry,
That it hath scented me already:
I cannot here disguise me, if I try.
But come! we'll go from this fire to a newer:
I am the go-between, and thou the wooer.

(To some, who are sitting around dying embers:)

Old gentlemen, why at the outskirts? Enter!
I'd praise you if I found you snugly in the centre,
With youth and revel round you like a zone:
You each, at home, are quite enough alone.

GENERAL

Say, who would put his trust in nations,
Howe'er for them one may have worked and planned?
For with the people, as with women,
Youth always has the upper hand.

MINISTER

They're now too far from what is just and sage.
I praise the old ones, not unduly:
When we were all-in-all, then, truly,
Then was the real golden age.

PARVENU

We also were not stupid, either,
And what we should not, often did;
But now all things have from their bases slid,
Just as we meant to hold them fast together.

AUTHOR

Who, now, a work of moderate sense will read?
Such works are held as antiquate and mossy;
And as regards the younger folk, indeed,
They never yet have been so pert and saucy.

MEPHISTOPHELES

(who all at once appears very old)

I feel that men are ripe for Judgment-Day,
Now for the last time I've the witches'-hill ascended:
Since to the lees my cask is drained away,
The world's, as well, must soon be ended.

HUCKSTER-WITCH

Ye gentlemen, don't pass me thus!
Let not the chance neglected be!
Behold my wares attentively:
The stock is rare and various.
And yet, there's nothing I've collected--
No shop, on earth, like this you'll find!--
Which has not, once, sore hurt inflicted
Upon the world, and on mankind.
No dagger's here, that set not blood to flowing;
No cup, that hath not once, within a healthy frame

Poured speedy death, in poison glowing:
No gems, that have not brought a maid to shame;
No sword, but severed ties for the unwary,
Or from behind struck down the adversary.

MEPHISTOPHELES
Gossip! the times thou badly comprehendest:
What's done has happed--what haps, is done!
'Twere better if for novelties thou sendest:
By such alone can we be won.

FAUST
Let me not lose myself in all this pother!
This is a fair, as never was another!

MEPHISTOPHELES
The whirlpool swirls to get above:
Thou'rt shoved thyself, imagining to shove.

FAUST
But who is that?

MEPHISTOPHELES
Note her especially,
Tis Lilith.

FAUST
Who?

MEPHISTOPHELES
Adam's first wife is she.
Beware the lure within her lovely tresses,
The splendid sole adornment of her hair!
When she succeeds therewith a youth to snare,
Not soon again she frees him from her jesses.

FAUST
Those two, the old one with the young one sitting,
They've danced already more than fitting.

MEPHISTOPHELES
No rest to-night for young or old!
They start another dance: come now, let us take hold!

FAUST (dancing with the young witch)

A lovely dream once came to me;
I then beheld an apple-tree,
And there two fairest apples shone:
They lured me so, I climbed thereon.

THE FAIR ONE

Apples have been desired by you,
Since first in Paradise they grew;
And I am moved with joy, to know
That such within my garden grow.

MEPHISTOPHELES (dancing with the old one)

A dissolute dream once came to me:
Therein I saw a cloven tree,
Which had a----------------;
Yet,-----as 'twas, I fancied it.

THE OLD ONE

I offer here my best salute
Unto the knight with cloven foot!
Let him a-----------prepare,
If him-----------------does not scare.

PROKTOPHANTASMIST

Accurséd folk! How dare you venture thus?
Had you not, long since, demonstration
That ghosts can't stand on ordinary foundation?
And now you even dance, like one of us!

THE FAIR ONE (dancing)

Why does he come, then, to our ball?

FAUST (dancing)

O, everywhere on him you fall!
When others dance, he weighs the matter:
If he can't every step bechatter,
Then 'tis the same as were the step not made;
But if you forwards go, his ire is most displayed.
If you would whirl in regular gyration
As he does in his dull old mill,
He'd show, at any rate, good-will,--
Especially if you heard and heeded his hortation.

PROKTOPHANTASMIST

You still are here? Nay, 'tis a thing unheard!
Vanish, at once! We've said the enlightening word.
The pack of devils by no rules is daunted:
We are so wise, and yet is Tegel haunted.
To clear the folly out, how have I swept and stirred!
Twill ne'er be clean: why, 'tis a thing unheard!

THE FAIR ONE
Then cease to bore us at our ball!

PROKTOPHANTASMIST

I tell you, spirits, to your face,
I give to spirit-despotism no place;
My spirit cannot practise it at all.

(The dance continues)

Naught will succeed, I see, amid such revels;
Yet something from a tour I always save,
And hope, before my last step to the grave,
To overcome the poets and the devils.

MEPHISTOPHELES

He now will seat him in the nearest puddle;
The solace this, whereof he's most assured:
And when upon his rump the leeches hang and fuddle,
He'll be of spirits and of Spirit cured.

(To FAUST, who has left the dance:)

Wherefore forsakest thou the lovely maiden,
That in the dance so sweetly sang?

FAUST
Ah! in the midst of it there sprang
A red mouse from her mouth--sufficient reason.

MEPHISTOPHELES
That's nothing! One must not so squeamish be;
So the mouse was not gray, enough for thee.

Who'd think of that in love's selected season?

FAUST
Then saw I--.

MEPHISTOPHELES
What?

FAUST
Mephisto, seest thou there,
Alone and far, a girl most pale and fair?
She falters on, her way scarce knowing,
As if with fettered feet that stay her going.
I must confess, it seems to me
As if my kindly Margaret were she.

MEPHISTOPHELES
Let the thing be! All thence have evil drawn:
It is a magic shape, a lifeless eidolon.
Such to encounter is not good:
Their blank, set stare benumbs the human blood,
And one is almost turned to stone.
Medusa's tale to thee is known.

FAUST
Forsooth, the eyes they are of one whom, dying,
No hand with loving pressure closed;
That is the breast whereon I once was lying,--
The body sweet, beside which I reposed!

MEPHISTOPHELES
Tis magic all, thou fool, seduced so easily!
Unto each man his love she seems to be.

FAUST
The woe, the rapture, so ensnare me,
That from her gaze I cannot tear me!
And, strange! around her fairest throat
A single scarlet band is gleaming,
No broader than a knife-blade seeming!

MEPHISTOPHELES
Quite right! The mark I also note.
Her head beneath her arm she'll sometimes carry;

Twas Perseus lopped it, her old adversary.
Thou crav'st the same illusion still!
Come, let us mount this little hill;
The Prater shows no livelier stir,
And, if they've not bewitched my sense,
I verily see a theatre.
What's going on?

SERVIBILIS

'Twill shortly recommence:
A new performance--'tis the last of seven.
To give that number is the custom here:
'Twas by a Dilettante written,
And Dilettanti in the parts appear.
That now I vanish, pardon, I entreat you!
As Dilettante I the curtain raise.

MEPHISTOPHELES

When I upon the Blocksberg meet you,
I find it good: for that's your proper place.

XXII

WALPURGIS-NIGHT'S DREAM

OBERON AND TITANIA's GOLDEN WEDDING

INTERMEZZO

MANAGER

Sons of Mieding, rest to-day!
Needless your machinery:
Misty vale and mountain gray,
That is all the scenery.

HERALD

That the wedding golden be.
Must fifty years be rounded:
But the Golden give to me,
When the strife's compounded.

OBERON

Spirits, if you're here, be seen--
Show yourselves, delighted!
Fairy king and fairy queen,
They are newly plighted.

PUCK

Cometh Puck, and, light of limb,
Whisks and whirls in measure:
Come a hundred after him,
To share with him the pleasure.

ARIEL

Ariel's song is heavenly-pure,
His tones are sweet and rare ones:
Though ugly faces he allure,
Yet he allures the fair ones.

OBERON

Spouses, who would fain agree,
Learn how we were mated!
If your pairs would loving be,
First be separated!

TITANIA

If her whims the wife control,
And the man berate her,
Take him to the Northern Pole,
And her to the Equator!

ORCHESTRA. TUTTI.

Fortissimo.

Snout of fly, mosquito-bill,
And kin of all conditions,
Frog in grass, and cricket-trill,--
These are the musicians!

SOLO

See the bagpipe on our track!
'Tis the soap-blown bubble:
Hear the schnecke-schnicke-schnack
Through his nostrils double!

SPIRIT, JUST GROWING INTO FORM

Spider's foot and paunch of toad,
And little wings--we know 'em!
A little creature 'twill not be,
But yet, a little poem.

A LITTLE COUPLE

Little step and lofty leap
Through honey-dew and fragrance:
You'll never mount the airy steep
With all your tripping vagrance.

INQUISITIVE TRAVELLER

Is't but masquerading play?
See I with precision?
Oberon, the beauteous fay,
Meets, to-night, my vision!

ORTHODOX

Not a claw, no tail I see!
And yet, beyond a cavil,
Like "the Gods of Greece," must he
Also be a devil.

NORTHERN ARTIST

I only seize, with sketchy air,
Some outlines of the tourney;
Yet I betimes myself prepare
For my Italian journey.

PURIST

My bad luck brings me here, alas!
How roars the orgy louder!
And of the witches in the mass,
But only two wear powder.

YOUNG WITCH

Powder becomes, like petticoat,
A gray and wrinkled noddy;
So I sit naked on my goat,
And show a strapping body.

MATRON

We've too much tact and policy
To rate with gibes a scolder;
Yet, young and tender though you be,
I hope to see you moulder.

LEADER OF THE BAND

Fly-snout and mosquito-bill,
Don't swarm so round the Naked!
Frog in grass and cricket-trill,
Observe the time, and make it!

WEATHERCOCK (towards one side)

Society to one's desire!
Brides only, and the sweetest!
And bachelors of youth and fire.
And prospects the completest!

WEATHERCOCK (towards the other side)

And if the Earth don't open now
To swallow up each ranter,
Why, then will I myself, I vow,
Jump into hell instanter!

XENIES

Us as little insects see!
With sharpest nippers flitting,
That our Papa Satan we
May honor as is fitting.

HENNINGS

How, in crowds together massed,
They are jesting, shameless!
They will even say, at last,
That their hearts are blameless.

MUSAGETES

Among this witches' revelry
His way one gladly loses;
And, truly, it would easier be
Than to command the Muses.

CI-DEVANT GENIUS OF THE AGE

The proper folks one's talents laud:
Come on, and none shall pass us!
The Blocksberg has a summit broad,
Like Germany's Parnassus.

INQUISITIVE TRAVELLER

Say, who's the stiff and pompous man?
He walks with haughty paces:
He snuffles all he snuffle can:
"He scents the Jesuits' traces."

CRANE

Both clear and muddy streams, for me
Are good to fish and sport in:
And thus the pious man you see
With even devils consorting.

WORLDLING

Yes, for the pious, I suspect,
All instruments are fitting;
And on the Blocksberg they erect
Full many a place of meeting.

DANCER

A newer chorus now succeeds!
I hear the distant drumming.

"Don't be disturbed! 'tis, in the reeds,
The bittern's changeless booming."

DANCING-MASTER

How each his legs in nimble trip
Lifts up, and makes a clearance!
The crooked jump, the heavy skip,
Nor care for the appearance.

GOOD FELLOW

The rabble by such hate are held,
To maim and slay delights them:
As Orpheus' lyre the brutes compelled,
The bagpipe here unites them.

DOGMATIST

I'll not be led by any lure
Of doubts or critic-cavils:
The Devil must be something, sure,--
Or how should there be devils?

IDEALIST

This once, the fancy wrought in me
Is really too despotic:
Forsooth, if I am all I see,
I must be idiotic!

REALIST

This racking fuss on every hand,
It gives me great vexation;
And, for the first time, here I stand
On insecure foundation.

SUPERNATURALIST

With much delight I see the play,
And grant to these their merits,
Since from the devils I also may
Infer the better spirits.

SCEPTIC

The flame they follow, on and on,
And think they're near the treasure:
But Devil rhymes with Doubt alone,
So I am here with pleasure.

LEADER OF THE BAND

Frog in green, and cricket-trill.
Such dilettants!--perdition!
Fly-snout and mosquito-bill,--
Each one's a fine musician!

THE ADROIT

Sans souci, we call the clan
Of merry creatures so, then;
Go a-foot no more we can,
And on our heads we go, then.

THE AWKWARD

Once many a bit we sponged, but now,
God help us! that is done with:
Our shoes are all danced out, we trow,
We've but naked soles to run with.

WILL-O'-THE WISPS

From the marshes we appear,
Where we originated;
Yet in the ranks, at once, we're here
As glittering gallants rated.

SHOOTING-STAR

Darting hither from the sky,
In star and fire light shooting,
Cross-wise now in grass I lie:
Who'll help me to my footing?

THE HEAVY FELLOWS

Room! and round about us, room!
Trodden are the grasses:
Spirits also, spirits come,
And they are bulky masses.

PUCK

Enter not so stall-fed quite,
Like elephant-calves about one!
And the heaviest weight to-night
Be Puck, himself, the stout one!

ARIEL

If loving Nature at your back,
Or Mind, the wings uncloses,
Follow up my airy track
To the mount of roses!

ORCHESTRA
pianissimo
Cloud and trailing mist o'erhead
Are now illuminated:
Air in leaves, and wind in reed,
And all is dissipated.

XXIII

DREARY DAY

A FIELD

FAUST MEPHISTOPHELES

FAUST

In misery! In despair! Long wretchedly astray on the face of the earth, and now imprisoned! That gracious, ill-starred creature shut in a dungeon as a criminal, and given up to fearful torments! To this has it come! to this!--Treacherous, contemptible spirit, and thou hast concealed it from me!--Stand, then,--stand! Roll the devilish eyes wrathfully in thy head! Stand and defy me with thine intolerable presence! Imprisoned! In irretrievable misery! Delivered up to evil spirits, and to condemning, unfeeling Man! And thou hast lulled me, meanwhile, with the most insipid dissipations, hast concealed from me her increasing wretchedness, and suffered her to go helplessly to ruin! [Illustration: Roll the devilish eyes wrathfully in thy head]

MEPHISTOPHELES

She is not the first.

FAUST

Dog! Abominable monster! Transform him, thou Infinite Spirit! transform the reptile again into his dog-shape? in which it pleased him often at night to scamper on before me, to roll himself at the feet of the unsuspecting wanderer, and hang upon his shoulders when he fell! Transform him again into his favorite likeness, that he may crawl upon his belly in the dust before me,--that I may trample him, the outlawed, under foot! Not the first! O woe! woe which no human soul can grasp, that more than one being should sink into the depths of this misery,--that the first, in its writhing death-agony under the eyes of the Eternal Forgiver, did not expiate the guilt of all others! The misery of this single one pierces to the very marrow of my life; and thou art calmly grinning at the fate of thousands!

MEPHISTOPHELES

Now we are already again at the end of our wits, where the understanding of you men runs wild. Why didst thou enter into fellowship with us, if thou canst not carry it out? Wilt fly, and art not secure against dizziness? Did we thrust ourselves upon thee, or thou thyself upon us?

FAUST

Gnash not thus thy devouring teeth at me? It fills me with horrible disgust. Mighty, glorious Spirit, who hast vouchsafed to me Thine apparition, who knowest my heart and my soul, why fetter me to the felon-comrade, who feeds on mischief and gluts himself with ruin?

MEPHISTOPHELES

Hast thou done?

FAUST

Rescue her, or woe to thee! The fearfullest curse be upon thee for thousands of ages!

MEPHISTOPHELES

I cannot loosen the bonds of the Avenger, nor undo his bolts. Rescue her? Who was it that plunged her into ruin? I, or thou?

(FAUST looks around wildly.)

Wilt thou grasp the thunder? Well that it has not been given to you, miserable mortals! To crush to pieces the innocent respondent--that is the tyrant-fashion of relieving one's self in embarrassments.

FAUST

Take me thither! She shall be free!

MEPHISTOPHELES

And the danger to which thou wilt expose thyself? Know that the guilt of blood, from thy hand, still lies upon the town! Avenging spirits hover over the spot where the victim fell, and lie in wait for the returning murderer.

FAUST

That, too, from thee? Murder and death of a world upon thee, monster! Take me thither, I say, and liberate her!

MEPHISTOPHELES

I will convey thee there; and hear, what I can do! Have I all the power in Heaven and on Earth? I will becloud the jailer's senses: get possession of the key, and lead her forth with human hand! I will keep watch: the magic steeds are ready, I will carry you off. So much is in my power.

FAUST
Up and away!

XXIV

NIGHT

OPEN FIELD

(FAUST and MEPHISTOPHELES speeding onward on black horses.)

FAUST

What weave they there round the raven-stone?

MEPHISTOPHELES

I know not what they are brewing and doing.

FAUST

Soaring up, sweeping down, bowing and bending!

MEPHISTOPHELES

A witches'-guild.

FAUST

They scatter, devote and doom!

MEPHISTOPHELES

On! on!

XXV

DUNGEON

FAUST

(with a bunch of keys and a lamp, before an iron door)

A shudder, long unfelt, comes o'er me;
Mankind's collected woe o'erwhelms me, here.
She dwells within the dark, damp walls before me,
And all her crime was a delusion dear!
What! I delay to free her?
I dread, once again to see her?
On! my shrinking but lingers Death more near.

(He grasps the lock: the sound of singing is heard inside.)

My mother, the harlot,
Who put me to death;
My father, the varlet,
Who eaten me hath!
Little sister, so good,
Laid my bones in the wood,
In the damp moss and clay:
Then was I a beautiful bird o' the wood;
Fly away! Fly away!

FAUST (unlocking)
She does not dream her lover listens near;
That he the rattling chain, the rustling straw, can hear.

(He enters.)

MARGARET (hiding herself on the pallet)
Woe! woe! They come. O death of bitterness!

FAUST (whispering)
Hush! hush! The hour is come that frees thee.

MARGARET (throwing herself before him)
Art thou a man, then pity my distress!

FAUST
Thy cries will wake the guards, and they will seize thee!
(He takes hold of the fetters to unlock them.)

MARGARET (on her knees)
Who, headsman! unto thee such power
Over me could give?
Thou'rt come for me at midnight-hour:
Have mercy on me, let me live!
Is't not soon enough when morning chime has run?

(She rises.)

And I am yet so young, so young!
And now Death comes, and ruin!
I, too, was fair, and that was my undoing.
My love was near, but now he's far;
Torn lies the wreath, scattered the blossoms are.
Seize me not thus so violently!
Spare me! What have I done to thee?
Let me not vainly entreat thee!
I never chanced, in all my days, to meet thee!

FAUST
Shall I outlive this misery?

MARGARET
Now am I wholly in thy might.
But let me suckle, first, my baby!
I blissed it all this livelong night;
They took 't away, to vex me, maybe,
And now they say I killed the child outright.
And never shall I be glad again.
They sing songs about me! 'tis bad of the folk to do it!
There's an old story has the same refrain;
Who bade them so construe it?

FAUST (falling upon his knees)
Here lieth one who loves thee ever,
The thraldom of thy woe to sever.

MARGARET (flinging herself beside him)
O let us kneel, and call the Saints to hide us!
Under the steps beside us,

The threshold under,
Hell heaves in thunder!
The Evil One
With terrible wrath
Seeketh a path
His prey to discover!

FAUST (aloud)
Margaret! Margaret!

MARGARET (attentively listening)
That was the voice of my lover!

(She springs to her feet: the fetters fall off.)

Where is he? I heard him call me.
I am free! No one shall enthrall me.
To his neck will I fly,
On his bosom lie!
On the threshold he stood, and Margaret! calling,
Midst of Hell's howling and noises appalling,
Midst of the wrathful, infernal derision,
I knew the sweet sound of the voice of the vision!

FAUST
'Tis I!

MARGARET

'Tis thou! O, say it once again!

(Clasping him.)

'Tis he! 'tis he! Where now is all my pain?
The anguish of the dungeon, and the chain?
'Tis thou! Thou comest to save me,
And I am saved!--
Again the street I see
Where first I looked on thee;
And the garden, brightly blooming,
Where I and Martha wait thy coming.

FAUST (struggling to leave)
Come! Come with me!

MARGARET

Delay, now!
So fain I stay, when thou delayest!

 (Caressing him.)

FAUST

Away, now!
If longer here thou stayest,
We shall be made to dearly rue it.

MARGARET

Kiss me!--canst no longer do it?
My friend, so short a time thou'rt missing,
And hast unlearned thy kissing?
Why is my heart so anxious, on thy breast?
Where once a heaven thy glances did create me,
A heaven thy loving words expressed,
And thou didst kiss, as thou wouldst suffocate me--
Kiss me!
Or I'll kiss thee!

(She embraces him.)

Ah, woe! thy lips are chill,
And still.
How changed in fashion
Thy passion!
Who has done me this ill?

(She turns away from him.)

FAUST

Come, follow me! My darling, be more bold:
I'll clasp thee, soon, with warmth a thousand-fold;
But follow now! 'Tis all I beg of thee.

MARGARET (turning to him)
And is it thou? Thou, surely, certainly?

FAUST
'Tis I! Come on!

MARGARET

Thou wilt unloose my chain,
And in thy lap wilt take me once again.
How comes it that thou dost not shrink from me?--
Say, dost thou know, my friend, whom thou mak'st free?

FAUST

Come! come! The night already vanisheth.

MARGARET

My mother have I put to death;
I've drowned the baby born to thee.
Was it not given to thee and me?
Thee, too!--'Tis thou! It scarcely true doth seem--
Give me thy hand! 'Tis not a dream!
Thy dear, dear hand!--But, ah, 'tis wet!
Why, wipe it off! Methinks that yet
There's blood thereon.
Ah, God! what hast thou done?
Nay, sheathe thy sword at last!
Do not affray me!

FAUST

O, let the past be past!
Thy words will slay me!

MARGARET

No, no! Thou must outlive us.
Now I'll tell thee the graves to give us:
Thou must begin to-morrow
The work of sorrow!
The best place give to my mother,
Then close at her side my brother,
And me a little away,
But not too very far, I pray!
And here, on my right breast, my baby lay!
Nobody else will lie beside me!--
Ah, within thine arms to hide me,
That was a sweet and a gracious bliss,
But no more, no more can I attain it!
I would force myself on thee and constrain it,
And it seems thou repellest my kiss:
And yet 'tis thou, so good, so kind to see!

FAUST

If thou feel'st it is I, then come with me!

MARGARET

Out yonder?

FAUST

To freedom.

MARGARET

  If the grave is there,
Death lying in wait, then come!
From here to eternal rest:
No further step--no, no!
Thou goest away! O Henry, if I could go!

FAUST

Thou canst! Just will it! Open stands the door.

MARGARET

I dare not go: there's no hope any more.
Why should I fly? They'll still my steps waylay!
It is so wretched, forced to beg my living,
And a bad conscience sharper misery giving!
It is so wretched, to be strange, forsaken,
And I'd still be followed and taken!

FAUST

I'll stay with thee.

MARGARET

Be quick! Be quick!
Save thy perishing child!
Away! Follow the ridge
Up by the brook,
Over the bridge,
Into the wood,
To the left, where the plank is placed
In the pool!
Seize it in haste!
'Tis trying to rise,
'Tis struggling still!

Save it! Save it!

FAUST

Recall thy wandering will!
One step, and thou art free at last!

MARGARET

If the mountain we had only passed!
There sits my mother upon a stone,--
I feel an icy shiver!
There sits my mother upon a stone,
And her head is wagging ever.
She beckons, she nods not, her heavy head falls o'er;
She slept so long that she wakes no more.
She slept, while we were caressing:
Ah, those were the days of blessing!

FAUST

Here words and prayers are nothing worth;
I'll venture, then, to bear thee forth.

MARGARET

No--let me go! I'll suffer no force!
Grasp me not so murderously!
I've done, else, all things for the love of thee.

FAUST

The day dawns: Dearest! Dearest!

MARGARET

Day? Yes, the day comes,--the last day breaks for me!
My wedding-day it was to be!
Tell no one thou has been with Margaret!
Woe for my garland! The chances
Are over--'tis all in vain!
We shall meet once again,
But not at the dances!
The crowd is thronging, no word is spoken:
The square below
And the streets overflow:
The death-bell tolls, the wand is broken.
I am seized, and bound, and delivered--

Shoved to the block--they give the sign!
Now over each neck has quivered
The blade that is quivering over mine.
Dumb lies the world like the grave!

FAUST
O had I ne'er been born!

MEPHISTOPHELES (appears outside)
Off! or you're lost ere morn.
Useless talking, delaying and praying!
My horses are neighing:
The morning twilight is near.

MARGARET
What rises up from the threshold here?
He! he! suffer him not!
What does he want in this holy spot?
He seeks me!

FAUST
Thou shalt live.

MARGARET
Judgment of God! myself to thee I give.

MEPHISTOPHELES (to FAUST)
Come! or I'll leave her in the lurch, and thee!

MARGARET
Thine am I, Father! rescue me!
Ye angels, holy cohorts, guard me,
Camp around, and from evil ward me!
Henry! I shudder to think of thee.

MEPHISTOPHELES
She is judged!

VOICE (from above)
She is saved!

MEPHISTOPHELES (to FAUST)
Hither to me!

(He disappears with FAUST.)

VOICE (from within, dying away)
Henry! Henry!

Faust

Part the Second

Johann Wolfgang von Goethe

Faust

Part the Second

Johann Wolfgang von Goethe

Translated into English ,
in the Original Metres,
by

Bayard Taylor

I

A Pleasant Landscape

(Faust is lying on flowery turf, tired and restless, trying to sleep. A circle of tiny, graceful spirits hovers round him.)

ARIEL (Chanting, accompanied by Aeolian Harps.)
When the springtime blossoms, falling,
Shower down, and cover all things,
When the fields with greener blessing
Dazzle all the world of earthlings,
Little elves, but great in spirit,
Haste to help, where help they can,
And, be he holy, be he wicked,
Pity they the luckless man.

You, hovering in airy circles, round his head
Show yourselves in proud elf-form, instead,
Calm all the fierce resistance of his heart,
Remove the bitter barbs of sharp remorse,
Free him from past terrors, by your art.
Four are the watches night makes in its course,
At once, now, mercifully, let the dark depart.
Let his head sink down on pillow's coolness,
Next sprinkle him with dew from Lethe's stream:
Then let his joints be free of cramps and stiffness,
So that he's strong enough to greet day's gleam:
Elves exert your sweetest right,
Return him to the holy light!

CHOIR (Singly, and two or more, alternately and together.)
When the balmy breezes smother
All the green-encircled land,
Sweetly fragrant and mist-covered,
Twilight gathers all around.
Sweet peace then whispers softly,
Rocks the heart on childhood's shores,
And on the eyelids, tired and weary,

Closes daylight's golden doors.

Here the night's already passing,
Sacred stars set, star by star,
Great lights, and the lesser glittering,
Sparkling near, and gleaming far:
Sparkling, where the lake reflects her,
Gleaming bright in cloudless height,
Protecting the deep bliss of rest, there,
Moon, in splendour, rules the night.

The hours have vanished now, already
Joy and pain have flown away,
You are whole! Recover, wholly:
Trust the sight of breaking day.
Greening valleys, swelling hills there,
Rise from out their shadowy sleep:
And, drifting in its waves of silver,
On to harvest, flows the wheat.

Wish then, to achieve your wishes,
Gaze up, at the brightness there!
You are lightly tangled: this is
Sleep, a shell, so now emerge!
Don't delay, walk bravely, tall,
When the crowd waits, hesitating:
The noblest man achieves his all,
By seeing, and then, swiftly, taking.

ARIEL
Listen! Hear the hour nearing!
Ringing out to spirit-hearing,
Now, the new day is appearing.
Doors of stone creak and chatter,
Phoebus' wheels roll and clatter,
What a din the daylight's bringing!
Trombone- and trumpeting,
Eyes amazed, and ears ringing,
The Unheard drops out of hearing.
Slip into the flowers presence,
Deeper, deeper, lie there silent,
In the pebbles, where the leaves bend:
If it strikes you, you'll be deafened.

FAUST

Life's pulses beating now, with new existence,
Greet the mild ethereal half-light round me:
You, Earth, stood firm tonight, as well: I sense
Your breath is quickening all the things about me,
Already, with that joy you give, beginning
To stir the strengthening resolution in me,
That strives, forever, towards highest Being. –
Now the world unfolds, in half-light's gleam,
The wood's alive, its thousand harmonies singing,
While through the valleys, misted ribbons stream:
And heavenly light now penetrates the deep:
Twigs, branches shoot, with fresher life it seems,
From fragrant gulfs, where they were sunk in sleep:
Colour on colour lifts now from the ground,
As leaf and flower with trembling dewdrops weep –
And a paradise reveals itself, all round.
Gaze upwards! – The vast mountain heights
Already with the solemn hour resound:
They are the first to enjoy the eternal light
That later, for us, will work its way below.
Now, to the sloping Alpine meadows bright,
It gives a fresh clarity, a newer glow,
And step by step it reaches us down here: –
It blazes out! – Ah, already blinded, though
I turn away, my eyesight wounded, pierced.
So it is, when to the thing we yearn for
The highest wish so intimately rehearsed,
We find fulfilment opening wide the door:
And then, from eternal space, there breaks
A flood of flame, we stand amazed before:
We wished to set the torch of life ablaze,
A sea of fire consumes us, and such fire!
Love, is it, then? Or hate? This fierce embrace,
The joy and pain of alternating pyres,
So that, gazing back to earth again,
We seek to veil ourselves in youth's desire.
Let the sun shine on, behind me, then!
The waterfall that splits the cliffs' broad edge,
I gaze at with a growing pleasure, when
A thousand torrents plunge from ledge to ledge,
And still a thousand more pour down that stair,
Spraying the bright foam skywards from their beds.
And in lone splendour, through the tumult there,

The rainbow's arch of colour, bending brightly,
Is clearly marked, and then dissolved in air,
Around it the cool showers, falling lightly.
There the efforts of mankind they mirror.
Reflect on it, you'll understand precisely:
We live our life amongst refracted colour.

II

The Emperor's Castle: The Throne Room

(A council of state waits for the Emperor. Trumpets.)

(Enter court attendants of all kinds, splendidly dressed. The Emperor approaches the throne: the Astrologer is to his right.)

THE EMPEROR
I greet you all, the loved, and true,
Gathered here from far and wide: -
I see a wise man's at my side,
But where on earth's the fool?

ATTENDANT
Right behind your mantle there,
He suddenly tumbled on the stair,
They dragged away the pile of fat.
Dead: or drunk? No man knows that.

A SECOND ATTENDANT
At once, and at a wondrous pace,
Another came to take his place.
Quite extravagantly dressed,
Yet troubling, since he's so grotesque:
Guards closed the door in his face,
Their halberds held crosswise too –
Yet here he comes, the daring fool!

MEPHISTOPHELES (Kneeling in front of the throne.)
What is cursed, and yet is welcomed?
What's desired, yet chased away?
What's always carefully defended?
What's abused: condemned, I say?
What do you not dare appeal to?
What will all, happily, hear named?
What stands on the step before you?
What's banished from here, all the same?

THE EMPEROR
For once, at least, spare us your babble!

This is no time or place for riddles,
They're a matter for these gentlemen. –
Solve it! I'll gladly hear it all again.
I fear my old fool's wandered far in space:
Come to my side, here, and take his place.

(Mephistopheles places himself on the Emperor's left.)

MURMURS FROM THE CROWD
A newer fool – for newer cares –
Where's he from? – How'd he get there? –
The old one fell – He's all done in –
He was fat – Now this one's thin –

THE EMPEROR
So now, my faithful and beloved,
Welcome here from near and far!
We meet beneath a lucky star,
Since health and luck are written above.
But tell me, why in days like these,
When we've conquered care,
And carnival masks are all our wear,
And delightful things are waiting,
We trouble ourselves with debating?
Yet since you say we have to do it,
It's settled then, and we'll go to it.

THE CHANCELLOR
The highest virtue, like a sacred halo
Circles the Emperor's head: and so
He alone may validly exercise it:
Justice! – All men love and prize it,
What all ask, yet wish they could do without,
The people look to him to hand it out.
But ah! What help can human wit deliver,
Or kindly heart, or willing hand, if fever
Rages wildly through the state, and evil
Itself is broodingly preparing evil?
Look about, from this height's extreme,
Across the realm: it seems like some bad dream,
Where one deformity acts on another,
Where lawlessness by law is furthered,
And an age of crime is discovered.
Here one steals cattle, there, a wife,

274

Cross, cup and candlestick, from the altar,
And boasts of it for many a year,
His skin's intact, and so's his life.
Then they take their claims to court
The judge, in pomp, on his high cushion,
Meanwhile there grows a furious roar,
From swelling tides of revolution.
They insist it's crime and disgrace,
With their accomplices beside them,
And 'Guilty!' is the verdict in a case,
Only where Innocence is its own defence.
So all the world will slash and chop,
Destroying just what suits themselves:
How then can that true sense develop
That shows the morally acceptable?
At last the well-intentioned man
Yields to the bribe, the flatterer:
And the judge who can't convict, is hand
In hand with the criminal offender.
I've painted in black, but I'd rather draw
Its image in the deeper colour that I saw.

(Pause)

The conclusion's inescapable:
If all men suffer when all cause trouble,
Then His Majesty himself is harmed.

THE COMMANDER IN CHIEF
How riotous things are in this wild age!
They all lash out, and are lashed, these days,
And everyone is deaf to all command.
The citizen behind his wall,
The knight in his cliff-top tower,
Have sworn to defy us all,
And hold fast to their power.
The impatient mercenaries
Impetuously demand their pay,
And if we owed them less, already
They'd be off, and march away.
If one forbids what all desire,
He's disturbed a hornet's nest:
The kingdom, they should keep entire,
Is plundered, and distressed.

They'd like to wreak a wild disorder,
Half the world has been dissolved:
There are still kings beyond our border,
But none of them think they're involved.

THE TREASURER

In allies, then, who'd put their trust!
The subsidies they promised us,
Like water pipes are all blocked up.
And, Sire, in all your wide estate,
Who's benefited from the take?
Wherever you go, there's some new pup,
Who declares his independence.
We watch, while they carry on:
We've given away our rights, and hence,
No rights are left for us, not one.
Our parties too, however called,
Can't be depended on today:
They like to praise, and blame: it's all
Impartial both their love and hate.
They're resting: they take cover,
The Ghibelline, and Guelph.
Now, who'll help his neighbour?
Each man just helps himself.
The golden doors are fastened tight,
Men scrape and scratch and glean, all right,
But our coffers still are empty.

THE STEWARD

What evils, too, I must endure!
We try to save each day, I'm sure,
But every day sees greater need:
So, daily, some new torment's mine.
The cooks, alas, have all they want:
Boar, pheasant, hare and venison,
Ducks and peacocks, chickens, geese,
Payment in kind, and guaranteed,
They keep coming all the time,
But in the end we're short of wine.
Though cask on cask once filled the cellar,
The best of vintages, and names, there,
These noble lords can drink forever,
And haven't left a single drop.
The council too must have their fill,

They grasp their tankards tight until,
Under the table, they have to stop.
Now I'll count the cost, you'll see,
The moneylenders won't spare me,
The advances that they give gladly,
Will eat the future years, on top.
Pigs don't have time to fatten: instead
Men seize the pillows from your bed,
Even the bread from your table's gone.

THE EMPEROR (After reflection, to Mephistopheles.)
Fool, do you know anything else that's wrong?

MEPHISTOPHELES
Me? Nothing at all! I see splendour, as I must,
Around me, of you and yours! — Lack trust,
Where Majesty commands so, without question,
Where ready force scatters the enemy faction?
Where strong wills, with wit to understand,
Active and various, are all at hand?
What, for some evil purpose, could combine,
For darkness, then, where such stars shine?

MURMURS
Here's a rogue — who understands —
He'll tell lies — as long as he can —
I wonder too — what lies behind —
And what's in front? — A project of some kind —

MEPHISTOPHELES
In this world, what isn't lacking, somewhere, though?
Sometimes it's this, or that: here what's missing's gold.
True you can't just rake it up from the floor,
But wisdom knows the mines where one gets more.
In mountain veins, foundation walls,
Coined and un-coined golden hoards,
And ask me, now, who'll bring it to the light:
One gifted with Mind's power and Nature's might.

THE CHANCELLOR
Mind and Nature — don't speak to Christians so.
That's why men burn atheists, below,
Such speech is dangerous, all right,
Nature is sin, and Mind's the devil,

It harbours within it, Doubt, that evil,
Their misshapen hermaphrodite.
Not so with us! – In the Emperor's land
Two kinds of men are still at hand
Worthy alone to defend the throne:
The Saints are they, and the Knights:
They enter life's uncertain fights,
Rewards of Church and State they own:
Firm in their resistance, check
The confused aims of everyman.
No, Nature and Mind are heretics!
Wizards! Ruining town and land.
And you, with brazen impudence still
Invoke them here in this high circle:
You're fostering the corrupted will,
Fools are always hand in hand.

MEPHISTOPHELES

By this I recognise a most learned lord!
What you can't feel lies miles abroad,
What you can't grasp, you think, is done with too.
What you don't count on can't be true,
What you can't weigh won't weigh, of old,
What you don't coin: that can't be gold.

THE EMPEROR

You won't sort out our faults like that,
Will Lenten sermons make men fat?
I'm tired of the eternal 'if and when':
We're short of gold, well fine, so fetch some then.

MEPHISTOPHELES

I'll fetch what you wish, and I'll fetch more:
Easy it's true, but then easy things weigh more:
It's there already, yet how we might achieve it,
That's the tricky thing, knowing how to seize it.
Just think how, in those times of consternation,
When a human flood drowned land and nation,
People were so terrified, everywhere,
They hid their treasures, here and there.
So it was when mighty Rome held sway,
And so it goes on, yesterday and today.
Still buried in the earth, why, there it is:

The earth is the Emperor's, so it's his.

THE TREASURER
For a Fool his aim's not out of sight:
It's true, that's an old Imperial right.

THE CHANCELLOR
Satan lays out his gilded nets, for you,
These things don't square with what's good and true.

THE STEWARD
Only bring them to court: I'll welcome the sight,
And I'll gladly accept the thing as not quite right. The Commander in Chief

The Fool's clever, to promise what each of us needs:
A soldier will never ask from whence it all proceeds.

MEPHISTOPHELES
If you think I'm cheating you, maybe,
Why here's the man: ask Astrology!
He knows each circling hour and house:
So ask him: how are the Heavens now?

MURMURS
Two rogues, there – already known –
Fool and Dreamer – so near the throne –
An idle song – an ancient rhyme –
The Fool plays – the Wise Man speaks, in time –

THE ASTROLOGER (Speaks, with Mephistopheles prompting him.)
The Sun, himself, he is of purest gold:
Mercury, messenger, of riches told:
Venus has bewitched you all, and she
Looks on you, soon and late, quite lovingly:
The chaste Moon's mood holds fast:
Mars won't harm: his strength won't last:
And Jupiter remains the loveliest sight:
While Saturn's great, but far away and slight.
His metal we don't greatly venerate,
Light of worth, though leaden in its weight.
Yes! When Sun and Moon are conjoined fine,
Silver and gold will make the whole world shine:
The rest as well in turn are all achieved,
Palaces, gardens proud, and rosy cheeks:

All this he brings this highly knowledgeable man:
He can deliver, too, what nobody else here can.

THE EMPEROR
The words they say, I hear them twice,
And yet I'm not convinced they're right.

MURMURS
What's all that? - A joke gone flat –
Horoscopy – And Chemistry –
I've heard that vein – Hoped in vain –
Come, quick – It's still a trick –

MEPHISTOPHELES
They stand around: they're all amazed,
They don't trust what can be found,
One babbles about deadly nightshade,
The other of some jet-black hound.
What matter if one thinks I'm jesting,
Or another calls it sorcery,
If the soles of their feet are itching,
If their firm step totters towards me.
All can feel the secret working
Of Nature's everlasting power,
And from its deepest lurking,
A living vein shall rise and flower.
When every member twitches,
When all looks strange to your eyes,
Make up your minds, be delvers,
Here the players, there the prize!

MURMURS
It's like a lead-weight on my feet –
My arm's swollen – but then, it's gouty –
There's a tickle here in my big toe –
All the way down my back it goes –
From these signs, I'd say we're near
A rich vein of treasure, here.

THE EMPEROR
Quick then! Don't slope off there!
Let's test your froth of lies,
Show us, all, this rarest prize.
I'll lay down the sword and sceptre,

With my own noble hands, as well,
If you don't lie, complete the work myself,
And, if you lie, then send you down to Hell!

MEPHISTOPHELES

I'll find the way there anyway –
Yet I really can't exaggerate
What's lying round ownerless, everywhere.
The farmer, ploughing the furrows, lays bare
A crock of gold the clods unfold:
Seeks saltpetre from damp limy walls,
And finds there golden rolls of gold,
In his poor hands: frightened by all.
What caverns exist to be blown open,
Through what shafts and cuttings then,
Burrow those gold-divining men,
Those neighbours of the Underworld!
Secure in vast ancient cellars, find,
Golden plates, bowls, cups for wine,
In rows, and heaps where they were hurled:
Goblets fashioned out of rubies,
And if they wants to try their uses,
Beside them there's the ancient fluid.
Yet – I would trust the expert though –
The wooden casks rotted long ago,
The wine makes tartar, in the liquid.
Not just gold, and jewels, fine
But the essence then of noble wine
Terror hides, and night, as stark.
So quiz the wise untiringly:
It's trivial, by day, to see:
Mystery: houses in the dark.

THE EMPEROR

See to it then! What use is it out of sight?
Whatever's valuable must see the light.
Who knows a rogue for certain but by day?
At night all cows are black, and cats are grey.
The pots down there, full of golden weight –
Drive your plough, and, ploughing, excavate.

MEPHISTOPHELES

Take hoe and spade: and dig yourself,
Labouring will make you great,

A herd of golden calves, you'll help
To rise from out their buried state.
Then with delight, without delay,
You can, yourself, your love array:
Glittering colours, shining gems, will best
Enhance your majesty, and her loveliness.

THE EMPEROR
Quick then, quick! How slow it always is!

THE ASTROLOGER (Prompted by Mephistopheles.)
Sire, restrain your urgent passion, please.
First let all your pleasant pastimes go:
Distracted natures won't achieve the goal.
First we must atone for them in quiet,
Lower things are gained by the higher.
Who wants the good, must first be good:
Who wants delight, must calm the blood:
Who longs for wine, treads ripened grapes:
Who hopes for miracles, strengthens then his faith.

THE EMPEROR
So let the time be passed in merriment!
Ash Wednesday will achieve our grave intent.
And we can celebrate, wild Carnival,
More riotously, meanwhile, after all.

(They exit to the sound of trumpets.)

MEPHISTOPHELES
How merit and luck are linked together
These fools can't see, no, not a one:
If they'd the Philosopher's Stone, as ever,
There'd lack a philosopher for the stone.

III

A Spacious Hall with Adjoining Rooms

(Arranged and decorated for a Carnival Masque.)

HERALD
In our German lands, fear no evil,
Dance of Death or Fool, or Devil:
There's a cheerful feast, here: wait.
Our Sire, on his Roman travels,
Has, for his profit, and our revels,
Crossed the highest Alpine levels,
And gained himself a happier State.
The Emperor kissed the holy slipper,
First, won sovereign rights, and as,
He was gifted with the crown, there,
Accepted a fool's cap, for us.
We're all newly born, now:
Every sophisticated man,
Pulls it snug over ears and brow:
He seems a poor fool, but he'll vow
To wear it wisely as he can.
I see they're gathering already,
Hesitant alone, or paired off intimately:
Chorus on chorus pushing through.
In, and out, quite undeterred:
And end up where they were before, too.
With its hundred thousand scenes of the absurd,
The World itself is just one giant Fool.

FLOWER GIRLS (Singing, accompanied by mandolins.)
Dressed to win your praises,
We are here tonight,
Young Florentine ladies,
At the German Court of light.

Many a bright flower we wear
To adorn our tawny hair:
Silken threads, silken gear,
They play their own part here.

Then our position's well deserved, oh,

Worth your praise, without a doubt,
Our shining-flowers, by hand we sew,
So they bloom year in, year out.

All kinds of coloured snippets,
Placed with perfect symmetry:
You might mock us bit by bit, yes,
But the whole attracts you see.

We are pretty things to look on,
Flower Girls, and very smart:
Then, the temperament of Woman
Is so very close to Art.

HERALD

Let's see those trays of flowers
That you carry on your heads,
That paint your arms with colours:
What each likes, let her select.
Quick: in walks and branches
What a garden we will share!
They are fit to crowd around us,
Flower sellers and their wares.

THE FLOWER GIRLS

Haggle in this cheerful place,
But seek no market here!
At a quick and witty pace,
Let all know what you bear.

AN OLIVE-BRANCH WITH OLIVES

I don't envy flowery ones,
Every kind of strife I shun:
It's unnatural, to me:
So I am the sign of nations,
And I seal their obligations,
Mark of peace in any field.
I hope I'm worth good luck today:
Some lovely head I might array.

A GARLAND OF WHEAT-EARS (Golden)

Ceres gift, for you to wear,
Charming, sweet, we were all sent:
The most desired of uses, here

As your beautiful adornment.

A FANCY GARLAND
Like a mallow, bright with colour,
A marvellous flower grew from the moss!
Never known before to Nature,
Yet Fashion brought it us.

A FANCY BOUQUET
My name's for you to know,
Theophrastus couldn't tell you though:
Yet I hope, if not all do,
Many of us will still please you,
She, I'd like, most to possess us,
Who might twine us in her tresses:
Or if she should so decide,
Set beside her heart, I'd ride.

ROSEBUDS
Many-coloured fancies may
Form the fashion of the day,
Strange and curious of shape,
Such as Nature never made:
Stalks of green and bells of gold,
Show in tresses all untold! –
Yet we – remain here, covered up:
Lucky those who first discover us.
When the summer is proclaimed,
Then the rosebuds are in flame,
Who would do without such pleasures?
Promises, and yielded treasures,
That, in the flowery kingdom, rule,
Mind and heart and glances, too.

(The Flower Girls garland themselves, and show their wares, gracefully, in the
green leafy arcades.)

THE GARDENERS (Singing, accompanied by lutes.)
See the flowers quietly growing,
On your brows, sweetly amuse you,
And their fruit will not seduce you,
One may taste delight in knowing.

Sunburned faces offer up,

Peaches, plums, and cherries, yet.
Buy! Against the tongue and palate,
The eye is the worst way to judge.

Come, of all this ripest fruit,
Eat with taste, and delight!
Poems on roses might still suit,
But on the apple man must bite.

So then let us join with their
Flowering youth itself,
And we'll dress our riper wares
In our neighbour's wealth.

Dressed in cheerful garlands, there,
Along this jewelled leafy route,
All things can be found together,
Buds and leaves, and flowers and fruit.

(Both choruses set out their goods on the flight of steps, with alternating song
accompanied by the lutes and mandolins, and offer their wares to the
spectators.)

A MOTHER (With her daughter.)
Child, when you came to light,
I dressed you in your little hat:
Your face was so sweet and bright,
And your body was soft at that.
I thought you'd soon be a bride,
To the wealthiest of men allied,
I thought you'd find a match.

Ah! Now already many a year
Has flown by, uselessly,
The motley crowd of suitors here,
Pass you quickly by, I see:
With him you danced a lively dance,
Gave that other a knowing glance
With your elbow, sharply.

I've thought about the many feasts
We went to, all in vain,
Forfeits, and Hide and Seek,
Couldn't help, that's plain:

Today the fools are out the trap,
Darling, open then your lap,
There's someone you can gain.

(Other young and lovely girls join the Flower Girls, and they gossip together.
Fishermen and bird-catchers with fishing rods, nests, limed twigs and other
implements appear, and scatter themselves among the girls. Mutual attempts to
win over, catch, escape and embrace, allow the most agreeable conversation.)

WOOD-CUTTERS (Entering, loudly and boisterously.)
Make way! Stand back!
We must be free,
We fell the trees,
They crash, and smash:
And when we pass,
Expect a smack.
To give us praise
Consider this:
If coarser ways,
Weren't in this land,
How'd the finest,
Have means to stand,
Despite they're jesting?
So learn our meaning!
For you'd be freezing,
If we weren't sweating.

PULCINELLI
You're fools, a troop,
That's born to stoop.
We're the wise,
We see through lies:
And then our bags
Our caps and rags,
Are light to wear:
And free from care,
We're always idle,
Slippered, we sidle,
Through market crowds,
Slithering about,
Standing to gaze,
And croak, amazed:
And at that sound,
Through heaving mounds,

287

Eel-like slipping,
Lightly skipping,
We romp together.
Praise us ever,
Or scold us so,
We let both go.

THE PARASITICAL (Fawning, and lustful.)
You brave woodsmen,
And your next of kin,
The charcoal-burners,
You're the men for us.
Since all the stooping,
The ready nodding,
The winding phrase,
That plays both ways,
That warms or chills,
Just as one feels,
What profit is it then?
The mighty fire
From heaven or higher,
Might come in vain
Without logs again,
And coal heaps there,
To light the oven
And make it glare.
It roasts and steams,
It boils and teems.
The finger-picker,
The plate-licker,
He sniffs the fry,
Suspects the fish:
Rules, by and by,
The patron's dish.

A DRUNK (Confused.)
Nothing seems bad to me today!
I feel so frank, and free:
New joys, and happy songs, I say.
I brought them both with me!
So let's drink! Drink, and drink!
Drink up, you! Clink, and clink!
You behind me, come around!
Drink it up, and send it down.

My wife was so outraged, she screamed,
When I turned up, dressed so funny,
However much I boasted, she
Kept calling me a tailor's dummy.
So I drink! Drink, and drink!
Clink the tankards! Clink, and clink!
Tailor's dummy: swill it round!
When it's clinked, drink it down!

Don't you say, I've lost my way:
I'm here, where I've got it made.
If host and hostess won't play,
I'll get credit from the maid.
Always drinking! Drink, and drink!
Lift, you others! Clink, and clink!
Each to each! So it goes round!
Too soon, I know, it's all gone down.

However I please myself, may I
Have it happen at my command:
Let me lie here, where I lie,
If I can't, any longer, stand.

CHORUS
Every pal, now: drink and drink!
A toast again, a clink and clink!
Hold tight now to bench and ground!
Under the table, he'll be found.

(The Herald announces sundry poets – Poets of Nature, and Court, and
Minstrels, Sentimentalists and Enthusiasts. In this competitive crowd no one
allows anyone else to start reciting. One slips by with a few words.)

A SATIRICAL POET
As a poet, do you know
What I'd most enjoy, here?
If I dared to sing, or bellow
What no one wants to hear.

(The Night and Church Poets excuse themselves having become engaged in a
very interesting conversation with a newly-risen Vampire, from which a new
school of poetry might derive. The Herald has to accept their excuses, and
meanwhile calls on characters from Greek Mythology, who even in modern

masks lose neither their character nor power to charm.)

(The Three Graces appear.)

AGLAIA
Grace it is we bring, to living:
So be graceful in your giving.

HEGEMONE
Gracefully may you receive:
Lovely is the wish achieved.

EUPHROSYNE
And in quieter hours, and places,
Chiefly, in your thanks, be gracious.

(The Three Fates appear)

ATROPOS
I, the eldest, I, the spinning
Am lumbered with this time: I've
Need of lots of pondering, thinking,
To yield the tender threads of life.

So you may be soft and supple,
I sift through the finest flax:
Drawn through clever fingers, double
Fine, and even, smooth as wax.

If you wish all joy and dancing,
Excessive now, in what you take,
Think about those threads: their ending.
Then, take care! The threads might break.

CLOTHO
Know that in these latter days,
I was trusted with the shears:
Since our eldest sister's ways,
Failed to help men, it appears.

She dragged all her useless spinning,
Endlessly to air and light,
While the hopes of wondrous winnings,
Were clipped and buried out of sight.

I too made a host of errors:
Myself, in my younger years,
But, to keep myself in check, there's
The case, in which I keep my shears.

And so, willingly restrained,
I look kindly on this place,
In these hours, your freedom gained,
Run on and on, at your wild pace.

LACHESIS

I, the only one with sense,
To twist the threads am left:
My ways brook no nonsense,
I've never hurried yet.

Threads they come, threads I wind,
Guiding each one on its track,
Letting no thread wander blind,
Twining each one in the pack.

If I, once, forgot myself, my fears
For the world would give me pause:
Counting hours, measuring years,
So the Weaver holds her course.

HERALD

You wouldn't recognise the ones who come now,
However much you know of ancient troubles,
To look at them, the cause of many evils,
You'd call them welcome guests, and bow.

They're the Furies: no one will believe me,
Pretty, shapely, friendly, young in years:
But meet with them, you'll quickly learn I fear,
How serpent-like these doves are to hurt freely.

Though they're malicious, in modernity,
Where fools now boast about their sinful stories,
They too have ceased to want the Angels' glories:
Confess themselves the plague of land and city.

(The Furies approach.)

ALECTO

What does that matter? You still believe in us:
Then, we're pretty, young, and fawning kittens:
If one of you has a lover, with whom he's smitten,
We'll tickle his ears at length, sweetly fuss,

Till it would be safe to tell him, eye to eye,
That she waves to him, and him, the same,
She's thick up top, a crooked back, and lame,
And married, she'd be no good, by and by.

We know how to pester the bride-to-be as well:
Scarcely a week ago, her lover himself,
Said nasty things to her about herself! –
They're reconciled, but something rankles still.

MEGAERA

That's a joke! Let them be married, any way,
I'll take it up, and know, whatever may befall,
Through wilfulness the sweetest joys will pall,
Man's changeable, and changeable the day.

And no one holds the desired one in his arms,
Without longing, foolishly, for the more-desired,
Leave's his good fortune, with which he was fired:
Flies from the sun, and asks the frost for warmth.

I know how to give birth to those things: there,
Is Asmodi, who is my faithful servant,
To work true mischief at the proper moment,
And send to ruin all Mankind, in pairs.

TISIPHONE

Instead of malice: poison and the knife
I'm mixing, sharpening for that betrayer:
Love another, and sooner now or later,
Ruin itself will penetrate your life.

Gall and wormwood they must roam
Through all those sweetest moments!
No bargaining here, no bartering, come –
The perpetrator must atone.

Let no one sing about forgiveness!
I cry my cause to the cliffs again,
Echo! Hear! Reply: Avenge!
Let him who alters, cease existence.

THE HERALD

I'll ask you please, to move aside,
Since what comes next, is otherwise.
You can see, here's a mountain coming,
Decked with princely coloured trappings,
A tusked head, snaking trunk, there too,
A mystery, but I'll reveal the key to you.
A delicate and dainty girl sits on its neck,
And with a thin wand keeps the beast in check:
Another, up there, standing, wonderfully,
Surrounded with light, almost blinding me.
Beside it, two girls walk in chains, one fearful,
While the other girl seems quite cheerful:
One wishes to be, and one feels she is, free.
Let each of them declare who they might be.

FEAR

Smoking torches, flares and lights,
Are burning at the troubled feast:
Among all these deceptive sights,
Ah, I'm held fast by the feet.

Away, you ridiculous smilers!
I suspect those grins so bright:
All my enemies, beguilers,
Press towards me through the night.

Here! A friend becomes a foe,
Yet I know that mask, I'd say:
One that wants to kill me, though,
Now unmasked he creeps away.

Gladly, heedless of direction
I'd escape from out this world:
But, beyond, there roars destruction:
In mists of terror I am furled.

HOPE

I greet you, sisters! Though today,
And the whole of yesterday,
You enjoyed the masquerade,
I know all will be displayed:
In the morning you'll unveil.
And if, in the torchlight, we
Don't feel particular delight,
Yet the days to come, so bright,
More wholly suited, we shall hail,
Now as one, now solitary,
Through fair fields, we'll roam loose,
To act, or rest, as we choose,
And in that carefree way of living,
Dispense with nothing, go on striving:
Guests are welcome everywhere,
Confidently, let's appear:
Surely, the best anywhere,
Must be somewhere, here.

INTELLIGENCE

Two of Man's worst enemies,
Fear and Hope, I bind for you,
Now this country worries me.
Make room! I'll rescue you.

I lead the living Colossus,
Turret-crowned, as you see,
Step by step, he crosses,
The highest passes, tirelessly.

But above me, on the summit,
Is a goddess, there, who's bearing
Outspread wings, and turns about,
Everywhere, to see who's winning.

Ringed by splendour, and by glory,
Shining far, on every side:
She calls herself – Victory,
Goddess of the active life.

ZOILO-THERSITES (An Ugly Dwarfish Warrior.)

Ah, ha! I've come just in time,
I hold you all guilty of crime!

Yet my goal I assume to be
Her up there: Queen Victory.
With her pair of snowy wings,
She's an eagle, she must think:
And that whenever she's on hand,
To her belong the folk and land:
But when famous deeds are done,
At once I'm here with armour on,
When low is high, and high is low,
Bent is straight, and straight not so,
That alone fills me with mirth,
I wish it so throughout the Earth.

THE HERALD

So I'll lend you, dog from birth,
This good baton's masterstroke!
Twist and turn now: it's no joke! –
See how the twin dwarfish ape,
Rolls into a foul lumpish shape!
A wonder – the lump's an egg, on cue,
It swells and then it cracks in two:
Now a pair of twins appear,
An adder and a bat roll clear.
One through the dust is swiftly winding,
The black one's flitting round the ceiling.
They hurry outside, in company,
I wouldn't choose to be number three.

MURMURS

Lively now! There's dancing there –
No! I'd much rather be elsewhere –
Can't you feel some ghostly race
Fly about us, through this place? –
Something just rushed through my hair –
Round my feet, it's flying, where? –
None of us are injured though –
But we all are frightened so –
All the fun is spoilt completely –
As those creatures wished, you see.

THE HERALD

Since I play the herald's role,
As this masquerade unfolds,
I watch sternly at the door,

In case some devious outlaw
To this happy place, comes creeping:
Never yielding, never wavering.
Through the window, though, I fear
Airborne spectres enter here:
From magic and from devilry
Alas, I cannot set you free.
All this makes the dwarf suspicious,
Now! From behind, a new masque issues.
And I must dutifully explain
The meaning of the forms, again.
But I can't easily announce
What cannot be understood:
Help me explain it, if you would! –
See it wander through the crowd?
A splendid chariot, a four-in-hand,
Rolling through them, where they stand:
But it doesn't split the people,
I see no one's crushed at all.
Colours glitter in the distance,
Sundry wandering stars for instance,
A magic-lantern-like performance.
It blows along, a storm's assault.
Make way, there! I shudder!

THE BOY CHARIOTEER
Halt!
Dragons, your wings restrain,
Feel your accustomed rein,
Control yourselves, if I control you,
Sweep away when I inspire you –
Let us do honour to this place!
Look round, a widening display
Of admirers, circle now on circle.
Herald, now, then! As you will,
Before we leave you all,
Describe us, and say our name:
Since we're allegorical,
You should know us, plain.

HERALD
No, indeed, I can't tell your name:
I'll try and describe you all the same.
The Boy Charioteer

So try!

THE HERALD
I must confess
To young and handsome, before the rest.
You're a half-grown boy: yet a woman
Would prefer to see you fully grown.
You seem to me a wooer, in future,
Out of her house, a real seducer.

THE BOY CHARIOTEER
Let's hear more! Go on: go on,
Find the riddle's bright solution.

THE HERALD
Dark eyes that shine: night-black hair
Which brightly jewelled bands enclose:
And what a dainty garment flows
From shoulder down to ankle, there:
With purple hem its glittering shows!
One might take you for a girl:
Yet for good or ill, you'd be,
Prized already by any girl,
She'd teach you your ABC.

THE BOY CHARIOTEER
And he, who like a splendid vision,
Sits on the chariot, enthroned there?

THE HERALD
He seems a king, a rich and kind one,
Blessed are they who gain his favour!
He has no further need to strive,
His eyes observe whatever's lacking,
And to spread his pure delight,
Is more to him than joy and owning.

THE BOY CHARIOTEER
You daren't stop there: what you see,
You must describe it precisely.

THE HERALD
I can't express all the dignity.

But the glowing moon face, I see,
The full mouth, the bright cheeks, then
That shine beneath the jewelled turban:
Rich comfort in the clothes he's wearing!
What shall I say about his bearing?
As a ruler he seems known to me.

THE BOY CHARIOTEER
Plutus the God of Riches, this is he!
He's come himself in all his splendour,
The Emperor wished greatly he were here.

THE HERALD
Explain your own what and how to me!

THE BOY CHARIOTEER
I am Extravagance: I am Poetry:
I am the Poet, who is self-perfected
When his special gift is squandered.
Yet I'm immeasurably wealthy,
Like Plutus, worth as much as he,
I adorn, enliven, dance and feast,
And whatever he lacks, I complete.

HERALD
Your boasting makes you handsomer,
But let's see all your skill appear.

THE BOY CHARIOTEER
Just watch me snap my fingers, now,
The chariot will gleam and glow.
There a string of pearls appear!

(He continues to snap his fingers, in all directions.)

Golden jewels for neck and ear:
Flawless combs and diadems,
Set in a ring, rare precious gems:
I scatter flames too, here and there,
Waiting for their chance to flare.

THE HERALD
How the dear crowd snatch, I see!
The giver's soon in difficulty.

He snaps out jewels, as in a dream,
And they all snatch them, in a stream.
But now a different trick, you see:
What each has grasped so eagerly,
Has gained him but a poor reward,
The gifts already fluttering skyward.
The pearls are loosened from their band,
And beetles crawl there in his hand,
The poor man shakes them off, instead
They're humming now around his head.
Another, for some solid thing,
Catches at a butterfly's wing.
That's what the rascal's promise means:
He only lends them golden gleams!

THE BOY CHARIOTEER

You know how to announce masks: it's true,
But it's not the herald's task to search below
The outer surface of existence:
That requires a keener sense.
Still I'm wary of all disputes.
Lord, I'll direct my speech and questioning to you.

(Turning towards Plutus.)

Have you not trusted me with the task, to stand
And guide the tempest of your four-in-hand?
Don't I steer well, as you direct?
Am I not there, when you expect?
And don't I know how to win
The palm, for you, on daring wing?
When I've fought for you in war, now,
I've been successful every time:
When laurel wreaths adorn your brow
Have I not fashioned them with hand and mind?

PLUTUS

If I'm required to be a witness to it,
I'd say: You are the spirit of my spirit.
You always act according to my wishes,
And as I gain myself, you too are richer.
To reward your services, I value now
The green branch higher than my crown.
One true word, then, for everyone:

I've found delight in you, dear Son.

THE BOY CHARIOTEER
The greatest gifts from my hand,
See! I've scattered them around.
On every head there's the glow
Of some little flame I throw:
Leaping from one brow to another,
Halts on him, then leaves his brother,
But rarely does the flame-let rise,
And briefly flower in bright skies:
For many, before they know, it's vanished,
Sadly, it's burnt out, and finished.

WOMEN (Chatting to each other.)
Up there, on the four-in-hand,
He's certainly a charlatan:
And there's a clown perched behind,
By hunger and thirst he's been refined,
Like nothing one's ever seen before:
Pinch, and he'll feel nothing at all.

THE STARVELING
Disgusting women, leave me alone!
Not to come here again, I'll know.
When women kept to their hearths, then
Avaritia, Greed: was my name:
The houses were fine, all about,
Lots came in, nothing went out!
I took care of cupboard and chest:
That was a burden, to top the rest.
But now in this younger age,
Wives don't know how to save,
And like all those wicked students,
They have more desires than 'talents',
And their men have much to suffer,
Their debts are left about all over.
They spend whatever they can extract,
On their lovers, and on their backs:
They eat of the best, and drink deeper,
With their wretched army of admirers:
Which adds to the value of gold, for me:
We're manly fellows, the Miserly!

LEADER OF THE WOMEN

Let dragon be miserly with dragon:
In the end it's merely lies, illusion!
Men flock around, and turn the charm on,
But they're soon annoyance and confusion.

THE CROWD OF WOMEN

That Scarecrow! Give him a poke!
What's the Wooden Rake threaten?
We'll all shun his ugly looks, then!
Dragons of wood and paper: a joke!
Look lively, now, and we'll do him in!

THE HERALD

By my wand! Keep the peace! —
Though there's no need for my assistance:
Look at those grim monsters, how each
Clears round itself a proper distance,
Unfolding its quadruple wings, the beast.
The dragons shake themselves, indignant,
With fiery throats, their tails rampant:
The place is cleared: the people flee.

(Plutus descends from the chariot.)

THE HERALD

He steps down, in a kingly manner!
He beckons, and the dragons stir:
From the chariot bearing Avarice,
And gold, down comes the chest,
See, there at his feet, it's landed:
It's a wonder how it happened.

PLUTUS (To the Boy Charioteer)

Now you've left that troubling burden here,
You're free: so, fly now to your own sphere!
Not this! Where, confused, motley, wild,
Distorted objects crowd around us, child.
No: where you see clear, with sweetest Clarity,
Self-possessed, trusting in your own self: flee,
Where Goodness and Beauty may be viewed,
And there create your world — in Solitude!

THE BOY CHARIOTEER

So, I'll be your worthy envoy then,
So, I'll love you like my dearest kin.
Where you live, is Plenty: and where
I am, all feel they gain in splendour.
And often hesitate in life's uncertainty:
Should they yield to you, or yield to me?
Certainly your followers will have rest:
Who follows me, with work's forever blessed.
My actions are never kept a secret,
I only have to breathe and I'm apparent.
Farewell, then! You granted me my joy:
But whisper low, and you shall have your boy!

(He exits as he came.)

PLUTUS (Faust in disguise.)
And now it's time to reveal the treasure!
I strike the lock with the herald's wand.
It's open! Look! Vessels of noblest measure,
Pour the golden blood through your hands,
First it swells, roars, writhes as if it's molten:
A jewelled hoard of crowns, rings, and chains.

VARIOUS SHOUTS FROM THE CROWD.
Look here, oh, there! How rich it flows:
The chest, right to the brim, it glows. –
Golden vessels, molten too,
Rolls of coins, turning too. –
Minted ducats leaping,
Oh, how my heart is beating –
I see all, for which I'm yearning,
On the floor there, burning! –
It's offered you, don't be a fool,
Be rich, you only need to stoop. –
For, quick as lightning, all the rest,
Will take possession of the chest.

THE HERALD
What's this, you Fools? Ah, yes,
It's no more than a maskers' jest.
Tonight, don't ask for any more:
Think you, we'd give you golden ore?
In this game there are any amount
Of pennies: too many for you to count.

You clumsy idiots! A fine appearance,
Seems, to you, truth's naked essence.
What is your Truth? – Hollow illusion
Grasps you, with its fool's cap on. –
Heroic Mask, Plutus that conceals,
Drive these folk, then, from the field.

PLUTUS

Your wand's best by a mile,
Lend it me for a little while. –
I'll dip it, quick, in heat and glow. –
You Maskers, all take care then, now!
It gleams and bursts and throws off sparks!
The wand already shines in the dark.
And anyone who gets too near me,
Will be scorched, as well, mercilessly. –
And now I'll sweep with my brand.

SHOUTS AND CONFUSION

Ah! We're done for every man. –
Fly, now, whoever can! –
Back, back, the hindmost man! –
It's shining brightly in my eyes. –
On me the wand's hot weight lies –
We're all lost, lost for good. –
Back, back, you masks in flood!
Back, back, you senseless mob! –
If I'd wings, I'd soar aloft. –

PLUTUS

The circle backwards sinks,
Yet no one's scorched, I think.
The crowd will now give way,
They're only scared I'd say. –
But to guarantee good order,
I'll mark out an unseen border.

THE HERALD

You've done a fine job all right,
Thanks to your cunning, and might.

PLUTUS

Noble friend, you'll still need patience:

All kinds of turmoil still threaten us.

AVARICE

Now, if it pleases you, you may
Cast your eye around with pleasure:
The women are to the fore as ever,
Where they can nibble things, or gaze.
Still, I'm not completely rusty!
A lovely woman's always lovely:
And since, today, it costs me nothing,
With confidence, I too go wooing.
Still, here, in such a crowded space,
Lest words fall in an idle place,
I'll try being clever, attempt success,
And in clear mime make my address.
Hands, feet, gesturing won't cut the ice,
So, I'll have to employ a comical device.
I'll shape the gold like moistened clay,
Since the metal's malleable anyway.

THE HERALD

What's he up to that skinny Fool!
Is there a jest in the starveling too?
He kneads the gold just like dough,
It's soft between his hands, although
However he squeezes and forms it all,
It still remains a shapeless ball.
He turns now towards the women,
They all scream, and start to run,
Gesturing in complete disgust:
That rascal's up to no good.
I fear he'll be in ecstasy
If he can offend morality.
I shan't remain silent, anyway
Give me the wand: I'll drive him away.

PLUTUS

He doesn't see what we threaten here:
Let him pursue his foolishness!
There'll be no room left for his excess:
The law is great, but necessity's greater.

TUMULT AND SINGING

The wild crowd come here, specially,

304

From mountain-top, and wooded valley,
Shouting forcefully, as they can:
They celebrate the great god Pan.
They know what none can know,
And into the empty circle flow.

PLUTUS

'I know you well, and your great Pan!
Together these daring steps you plan.
I know all that no one knows,
And clear for you this narrow close.'
May good fortune follow them too!
The strangest things may happen:
They don't know where they're going to:
Since they never look before them.

WILD SINGING

You plaster people: you tinsel show!
Rough and coarse is how they go,
Leaping: wild is their track ahead,
Solid andsturdy is their tread.

FAUNS

The Faun flocks
In happy dance,
Oaken garlands,
On curlinglocks,
Fine pointed ears
Through tangled hair,
Snub noses, faces broad and flat,
The women can't fault any of that:
When the Fauns begin to prance,
The loveliest won't scorn the dance.

A SATYR

The Satyr's leaping here behind,
Goat's foot, and lean of thigh,
Sinewy, skinny he'll go by,
And chamois-like, on mountain height,
He looks around, and takes delight.
He's alive in the free air,
Mocks at man, child, woman there,
Who deep in the valley's damp flue,
Think, cosily, they're living too,

While, still pure and undisturbed,
To him alone is the upper world.

THE GNOMES
The little crowd trips by there,
They don't like to travel in pairs:
In mossy clothes with lanterns bright,
They pass together, quick and light,
Each one passing on his own,
Like glowing ants swarming home:
And always busy, here and there,
Industrious, and everywhere.
Kin to the 'Little People', known
As surgeons to the rock and stone:
'We bleed the mountains high,
We drain the deep veins dry:
We hurl the metals round,
With hearty greetings: Luck! Well found!
And it's always kindly meant: again,
We're the friends of all good men.
Yet we the gold to light deliver,
So men may steal, and covet ever,
So princely hand won't lack the steel
That worldwide murder longs to deal.
Who those three commandments breaks
Scant heed of the other seven takes.
But of all that we're innocent:
About it all, like us, be patient.'

THE GIANTS
The wild men, we are named,
Known in all the Hartz range:
Natural, plain, in all our antics,
Appearing frightfully gigantic.
A fir-tree trunk in each right hand,
Round our body a thick band,
A solid apron of branches, not
The bodyguard the Pope has got.

NYMPHS IN CHORUS (Surrounding Great Pan, who is the masked Emperor.)
Here he'll stand! –
The world's All,
Is shown to all,

In mighty Pan.
You the happiest, surround him,
In magic dances soar around him:
Here now, serious and good, he
Wishes all men to be happy.
Under the curving roof of blue
He seems endlessly wakeful, too,
Yet the streams flow gently for him,
And the breezes gently rock him,
And, when he sleeps at noon, the leaf
Is motionless in the branches' wreath:
The rich plants' fragrant balsams there
Fill all the still and silent air:
The Nymph no longer dares to leap,
And where she stands, falls fast asleep.
But when his powerful shout,
Unexpectedly, rings out,
Like thunder crack, or wave's roar,
Who knows what's happening any more,
The army's witless in the fight,
The hero in battle's filled with fright.
So honour him, where honour's due,
And hail him, who led us to you!

A DEPUTATION OF GNOMES (To Great Pan.)
When the rich and shining goods,
Spread threadlike through the deep,
Then delicate divining rods,
Reveal what labyrinths keep.

Bending in our dark vaults, there,
As troglodytes we're measured,
While in the purest daylight air,
Gracious, you divide the treasure.

Now we find we've discovered
A marvellous fountain here,
Promising, easily, to deliver
Things that infrequently appear.

It all waits for your command:
Master, take and care for it: do.
Every treasure in your hand,

Helps the whole world too.

PLUTUS (To the Herald.)
We must grasp things in the highest sense,
And let what may come, come, with confidence.
You've shown the highest courage once before.
So now too what is fearful, we must try it:
World, and posterity, will stubbornly deny it,
So pen it faithfully in your report.

THE HERALD (Grasping the wand in Plutus' hand, and assisting with the Masquerade.)
The dwarves lead on great Pan,
Gently, to the fiery fountain:
It boils from the deep profound,
Then sinks again, through the ground,
And gloomy is its open round:
Yet shows again the heat and glow.
Great Pan stands there, well disposed,
Pleased with all this wondrous thing,
Pearl foam, right, left, showering.
How can he trust such a show?
He bends to look inside, and so,
His beard gets caught within! –
Who's made that hairless chin?
His hand hides it from our vision. –
What follows is all clumsy action:
The beard, on fire, flies back, soon
Scorching garland, chest and head:
Delight is turned to pain instead. –
They rush to quench it all again,
But none of them are free of flames,
And how they flare and dart,
Exciting fire in every part:
Wreathed in that element,
The whole masked crowd is burnt.
But what's all this news about,
Ear after ear, mouth after mouth!
O eternally unlucky night
So little of it's turned out right!
Tomorrow's dawn will declare
What nobody wants to hear:
In every ear we'll hear it plain:
'The Emperor is in such pain.'

O, would that it were something other!
Burnt, Emperor and Court together.
Cursed be those who led him astray,
In resinous twigs did him array,
To rage, and bellow out that song,
To the ruin of all that throng.
O Youth, Youth will you never
Restrict joy's purest measure?
O Power, Power, will you never,
Sense and Omnipotence treasure?
The 'forest' too is soon in flames,
The pointed tongues play their games,
To the real wooden beams lick higher:
We're threatened by universal fire.
The cup of misery overflows,
Who will save us? No one knows.
See, Imperial splendour, by dawn's light,
Turned to a heap of ash, in a single night.

PLUTUS

That's enough terror overhead,
Let help arrive here, instead! –
Strike, you heavenly wand, with power,
So the earth will ring and tremor!
You, the wide realms of air,
Fill with cool fragrance there!
Hurry down, to sweep around us,
Cloudy mists and swelling vapours,
Quench the thronging flames!
Murmuring, trickling, fogs gather,
Sliding, rolling, softly drenching,
Slipping everywhere, and quenching.
You, the moist, who soothe forever,
Change them all to gleaming weather,
All these empty fiery games! –
Threatening Spirits, that would harm,
We, by magic, will disarm.

IV

A PLEASURE GARDEN IN THE MORNING SUN

(The Emperor, his Court, Noblemen and Ladies: Faust and Mephistopheles dressed fashionably but not ostentatiously, both kneel.)

FAUST
Sire, forgive the fiery conjuring tricks?

THE EMPEROR (Beckoning to him to rise.)
More fun, in that vein, would be my wish. –
At once, I saw myself in a glowing sphere,
It seemed as if I were divine Pluto, there.
A rocky depth of mine, and darkness, lay
Glowing with flame: out of each vent played
A thousand wild and whirling fires,
And flickered in the vault together, higher,
Licking upwards to the highest dome,
That now seemed there, and now was gone.
Through a far space wound with fiery pillars,
I saw a long line of people approach us,
Crowding till they formed a circle near,
And paid me homage, as they do forever.
From Court, I knew one face, and then another's,
I seemed the Prince of a thousand salamanders.

MEPHISTOPHELES
You are, Sire! Since every element
Knows your Majesty, amongst all men.
You've now proved the fire obedient:
Leap in the sea, in its wildest torrent,
You'll barely touch its pearl-strewn bed,
A noble dome will rise round you, instead:
You'll see green translucent waves swelling
Purple edged, to make the loveliest dwelling,
And you will be its centre. At each step
Wherever you go, the palace follows yet,
The very walls themselves delight in life,
Flash to and fro, in swarming arrow-flight.
Sea-wonders crowd around this sweet new sight,
Shoot past, still not allowed to enter quite.
There, golden-scaled, bright sea-dragons play,

The shark gapes wide, you smile in his face.
However much your court attracts you now,
You've never seen such an amazing crowd.
Nor will you part there from the loveliest:
The Nereids will be gathering, curious,
To this wondrous house, in seas eternally fresh,
The youngest shy and pleasure-loving, like fish,
The old ones: cunning. Thetis at the news,
Gives hand and lips to this second Peleus. –
A seat there, on the height of Olympus, too…
The Emperor

I'll leave the airy spaces all to you:
Soon enough we'll be climbing to that throne.

MEPHISTOPHELES
And, Sire, the Earth already is your own!

THE EMPEROR
What brought you here, now: what good fortune,
Straight from the Thousand Nights and One?
If you're as fertile as Scheherezade
I'll guarantee you a sublime reward.
Be ready then, when your world's light,
As it often does, disappoints me quite.

THE STEWARD (Entering hastily.)
Your Supreme Highness, I never thought
To announce such luck, the finest wrought,
As this is, for me the greatest blessing,
Which I've revealed in your presence:
For debt after debt I've accounted,
The usurer's claws now are blunted,
I'm free of Hell's pain, and then,
It can't be any brighter in Heaven.

THE COMMANDER IN CHIEF (Follows hastily.)
Something's paid of what we owe,
The Army's all renewed their vow,
The Cavalry's fresh blood is up,
And girls and landlords can sup.

THE EMPEROR
Now your chests breathe easier!

Now your furrowed brows are clear!
How quickly you hurried to the hall!

THE TREASURER (Appearing.)
Ask them: it was they who did it all.

FAUST
It's right the Chancellor should read the page.

THE CHANCELLOR (Coming forward slowly.)
I'm happy enough to do so, in my old age. –
See and hear the scroll, heavy with destiny,
That's changed to happiness, our misery.
'To whom it concerns, may you all know,
This paper's worth a thousand crowns, or so.
As a secure pledge, it will underwrite,
All buried treasure, our Emperor's right.
Now, as soon as the treasure's excavated,
It's taken care of, and well compensated.'

THE EMPEROR
I smell a fraud, a monstrous imposture!
Who forged the Emperor's signature?
Have they gone unpunished for their crime?

THE TREASURER
Remember! You yourself it was that signed:
Last night. You acted as great Pan,
Here's how the Chancellor's speech began:
'Grant yourself this great festive pleasure,
The People's Good: a few strokes of the feather.'
You wrote it here, and while night ruled the land,
A thousand artists created another thousand,
So all might benefit from your good deed,
We stamped the whole series with your screed,
Tens, Thirties, Fifties, Hundreds, all are done.
You can't think how well the folk get on.
See your city once half-dead with decay,
Now all's alive, enjoying its new day!
Though your name's long filled the world with glee,
They've never gazed at it so happily.
Now the alphabet's superfluous,
In these marks there's bliss for all of us.

THE EMPEROR

And my people value it as gold, you say?
The Court and Army treat it as real pay?
Then I must yield, though it's wonderful to me.

THE STEWARD

It was impossible to catch the escapee:
It flashed like lightning through the land:
The moneychanger's shops are jammed,
Men pay, themselves, the papers mount
They're gold and silver, and at a discount.
Now used by landlords, butchers, bakers:
Half the world think they're merrymakers,
The others, newly clothed, are on show.
The drapers cut the cloth: the tailors sew.
The toast is 'Hail, the Emperor!' in the bars,
With cooking, roasting, tinkling of jars.

MEPHISTOPHELES

Strolling, lonely, on the terrace,
You see a beauty, smartly dressed,
One eye hidden by her peacock fan,
She smiles sweetly, looks at your hand:
And, quicker than wit or eloquence,
Love's sweetest favour's arranged at once.
You're not plagued with pouch or wallet,
A note beneath the heart, install it,
Paired with love-letters, conveniently.
The priest carries his in a breviary,
And wouldn't the soldier be quicker on his way,
With a lighter belt around his middle, say.
Your Majesty will forgive me if, in miniature,
I produce a low note, in our high adventure.

FAUST

The wealth of treasure that solidifies,
That in your land, in deep earth lies,
Is all unused. In our boldest thought,
Such riches are only feebly caught:
Imagination, in its highest flight,
Strives to, but can't reach that height.
But grasping Spirits, worthy to look deeply,
Trust in things without limit, limitlessly.

MEPHISTOPHELES

Such paper's convenient, for rather than a lot
Of gold and silver, you know what you've got.
You've no need of bartering and exchanging,
Just drown your needs in wine and love-making.
If you lack coin, there's moneychangers' mile,
And if it fails, you dig the ground a while.
Cups and chains are auctioned: well,
Since the paper, in this way, pays for itself,
It shames the doubters, and their acid wit,
People want nothing else, they're used to it.
So now in all of your Imperial land
You've gems, gold, paper enough to hand.

THE EMPEROR

The Empire thanks you deeply for this bliss:
We want the reward to match your service.
We entrust you with the riches underground,
You are the best custodians to be found.
You know the furthest well-concealed hoard,
And when men dig, it's you must give the word.
You masters of our treasure, then, unite,
Accept your roles with honour and delight:
They make the Underworld, and the Upper,
Happy in their agreement, fit together.

THE TREASURER

No dispute will divide us in the future:
I'm happy to have a wizard for a partner.

(He exits with Faust.)

THE EMPEROR

Now, presents for the court: everyone
Confess to me whatever it is you want.

A PAGE (Accepting his present.)
I'll live well, happy, have the best of things.

ANOTHER (Also.)
I'll quickly buy my lover chains and rings.

A CHAMBERLAIN
I'll drink wines that are twice as fine.

A SECOND CHAMBERLAIN
The dice in my pockets itch I find.

A KNIGHT (Thoughtfully.)
My lands and castle will be free of debt.

A SECOND KNIGHT
It's treasure: a second treasure I will get.

THE EMPEROR
I hoped for desire and courage for new deeds:
But whoever knows you, thinks you slight indeed.
I see, clearly: despite this treasure and more,
You're all the same, still, as you were before.

THE FOOL (Recovered, and approaching the throne.)
You're handing presents out: give me one too!

THE EMPEROR
Alive again? You'd drink it all you fool.

THE FOOL
Magic papers! I don't understand them, truly.

THE EMPEROR
That I'd believe: you'll only use them badly.

THE FOOL
Others are falling: I don't know what to do.

THE EMPEROR
Just pick them up: those are all yours too.
(The Emperor exits.)

THE FOOL
Five thousand crowns I'm holding, in my hand!

MEPHISTOPHELES
You two-legged wineskin, so you still stand?

THE FOOL
I've had my luck, but this is the best yet.

MEPHISTOPHELES
You're so delighted: look, it's made you sweat.

THE FOOL
But see here, is it truly worth real gold?

MEPHISTOPHELES
You've there just what belly and throat are owed.

THE FOOL
And can I buy a cottage, cow and field?

MEPHISTOPHELES
Why yes! There's nothing to it: make a bid.

THE FOOL
A castle: with forests, hunting, fishing?

MEPHISTOPHELES
Trust me!
To see you a proper Lord would make me happy!

THE FOOL
Tonight I'll plant my weight on what I'll get! –

(He Exits.)

MEPHISTOPHELES
Who doubts now that our Fool's full of wit!

V
A GLOOMY GALLERY

(Faust. Mephistopheles.)

MEPHISTOPHELES
Why bring me here to this dark passage?
Isn't there fun enough inside,
In the Court's colourful tide,
Opportunities for jests and sharp practice?

FAUST
Don't give me that: in the good old days
You wore us out in a thousand ways:
And now this wandering, there and here,
Is only so I can't catch your ear.
But there's something I need done:
Commander and Chamberlain egg me on.
The Emperor, I must work quickly for him,
Wants Helen and Paris to appear before him:
He wants to see the ideal form of Man
Clearly revealed to him, and Woman.
Get to work! I daren't break my word.

MEPHISTOPHELES
Such a thoughtless promise was absurd.

FAUST
Friend, you haven't considered
Where your powers have lead us:
First we made him rich, and how,
So he wants us to amuse him now.

MEPHISTOPHELES
You think it's fixed that quickly:
We're looking at a deeper track,
To the strangest realm, and wickedly,
Adding new faults to the old,
Do you think it's easy to call Helen back,
Like a pasteboard spirit edged with gold –
Witch-bitches, ghost-hostesses, freely,
Or dwarf-maidens, I'll serve you equally:
But Devil's sweethearts, though you're for them,

317

Still you can't, as heroines, applaud them.

FAUST
Still the same old story, every day!
With you, things are always difficult.
You're the father of all obstacles,
For every miracle you want more pay.
I know: a little muttering, and it's done:
At a blink, you'll bring her here.

MEPHISTOPHELES
With Pagan folk I don't get on:
They live in their own Hell there:
Yet, there is a way.

FAUST
Tell, without delay!

MEPHISTOPHELES
Unwillingly! There's a greater mystery, I say,
Goddesses, enthroned on high, and solitary.
No space round them, not even time: only
To speak of them embarrasses me.
They are The Mothers!

FAUST (Terrified.)
Mothers!

MEPHISTOPHELES
Are you afraid?

FAUST
The Mothers! Mothers! It sounds so strange!

MEPHISTOPHELES
As, it is. Goddesses, unknown, as you see,
To you Mortals, not named by us willingly.
You must dig in the Depths to reach them:
It's your own fault that we need them.

FAUST
Where is the path?

MEPHISTOPHELES

No path! Into the un-enterable,
Never to be entered: One path to the un-askable,
Never to be asked. Are you ready?
No locks, no bolts to manipulate,
You'll drift about in solitary space.
Can you conceive the waste and solitary?

FAUST

I think you might spare the speeches then:
They always smell of the witches' kitchen,
Of a long forgotten time, to me.
Have I not trafficked with the world?
Learned the void, the void unfurled? –
When I spoke with reason, as I descried,
Contradiction, doubly loud, replied:
Have I not fled, from hateful trickery,
Into the wild, into the solitary,
And, not to lose all, and live alone,
Surrendered to the Devil's own?

MEPHISTOPHELES

And if you'd swum through every ocean,
And seen the boundless space all round
You'd still have seen wave on wave in motion,
Though you might have been afraid to drown.
You'd have seen something. Seen, within
The green still seas, the leaping dolphin:
Seen clouds go by, Sun, Moon and star –
You'll see none in the endless void, afar,
Hear not a single footstep fall,
Find no firm place to rest at all.

FAUST

You speak as chief of all Mystagogues, who
Deceive their neophytes, the loyal and true:
Only reversed. You send me to the Void,
So I'll increase the power and skill employed:
To use me, like a cat, that's your desire:
Just to claw your chestnuts from the fire.
The same as ever! I'll find what I'll discover:
In your Nothingness, I hope, the All I will recover.

MEPHISTOPHELES

I'll praise you, before you separate from me,
That you know the Devil, I can truly see:
Here take this key.

FAUST

That tiny thing!

MEPHISTOPHELES

Grasp it, it has a worth you're undervaluing.

FAUST

It's growing in my hand, it shines and glows!

MEPHISTOPHELES

What one possesses in it, would you now know?
The key will sniff the place out, from all others.
Follow it down: it leads you to the Mothers.

FAUST

The Mothers! That always strikes me like a blow!
What is that word that, once heard, scares me so?

MEPHISTOPHELES

Are you so limited one new word disturbs you?
Will you only hear what you're accustomed to?
Don't be troubled, whatever strange sound rings,
You've already long been used to marvellous things.

FAUST

Yes, there's no good for me in lethargy.
A shudder's the truest sign of humanity:
Though the world is such we may not feel it,
Once seized by it, we feel Immensity deeply.

MEPHISTOPHELES

Then, descend! I might as easily say rise!
It's all the same. Escape from what exists,
Into the boundless realm where all Form lies!
Delight in what's no longer on the list:
Where turmoil rolls along all cloudily:
Then, far from your body, swing the key!

FAUST (Inspired.)
Good! I feel new strength, firmly grasped,
My heart expands, on now to the great task.

MEPHISTOPHELES
Sight of a glowing tripod will tell you, finally,
You're in the last deep, deepest there might be.
By its light you'll see the Mothers,
Some sit about, as they wish, the others,
Stand and move. Formation, Transformation,
Eternal minds in eternal recreation.
Images of all creatures float, portrayed:
They'll not see you: they only see a shade.
Be of good heart, the danger there is great,
Go to the tripod: don't hesitate,
And touch it with the key!

(Faust assumes a commanding attitude with the key.)

MEPHISTOPHELES (Watching him.)
That's right!
It will close itself, and follow as a servant might:
Exalted by your good luck, you'll calmly rise,
And be back with it, before you've blinked your eyes.
And, once you've brought it here all right,
Call the Hero and Heroine from the night,
The first man who has ever achieved it:
It's done, and you're the one who did it.
By magic process then you'll surely find,
The incense' vapour will become divine.

FAUST
And now: what?

MEPHISTOPHELES
Strain with all your being: downward.
Stamp to descend, stamp again to go upward.

(Faust stamps and sinks out of sight.)

If he might only gain some good from that key!
I'm curious as to whether he'll return to me.

VI

BRILLIANTLY LIT HALLS

(The Emperor and Princes. The Court in Action.)

THE CHAMBERLAIN (To Mephistopheles)
You still owe us that scene with the Spirits:
The Emperor's impatient. Get on with it!

THE STEWARD
That's what His Grace just now was saying:
You! Don't offend His Majesty by delaying.

MEPHISTOPHELES
That's why my companion has just gone:
He knows how to put the whole thing on,
And has to labour away in silence: still,
All the most special diligence he applies:
He who'd own that treasure, the Beautiful,
Needs highest arts, the magic of the wise.

THE STEWARD
The arts you need are neither here nor there:
The Emperor orders it to be prepared.

A BLONDE LADY (Approaching Mephistopheles.)
Sir, a word! You see a clear complexion,
Yet it's not so in summertime's dejection!
A hundred red-brown freckles all sprout there,
And cover my white skin: I'm in despair.
A cure!

MEPHISTOPHELES
A pity! Such a shining beauty,
Spotted like a panther-cub, in May!
Take frogspawn, toads' tongues, in cohabitation,
Skilfully, under a full moon, make a distillation,
When it wanes, apply it undiluted,
When spring comes, the spots have been uprooted.

A DARK-HAIRED LADY
The crowd are pressing round to squeeze you dry.
I ask a cure! For a frozen foot

That hinders me in dancing, walking by,
And I curtsey awkwardly to boot.

MEPHISTOPHELES
Permit a little kick from my foot.

THE DARK-HAIRED LADY
Well, between lovers that's occurred before.

MEPHISTOPHELES
Child! My kick means something more.
Like cures like, when one's suffering:
Foot heals foot, and so with every member.
Come! Pay attention! No retaliation there.

THE DARK-HAIRED LADY (Crying out.)
Ouch! Ouch! That hurt! I call that kicking
Like a horse's hoof.

MEPHISTOPHELES
With that the cure I bring.
You can indulge in any amount of dancing,
Touch feet under the table with your darling.

A LADY (Pushing forward.)
Let me through! My suffering is so great,
He used to hold me in his heart's embrace:
Yesterday his joy was in my glances,
He turns his back on me: with her romances.

MEPHISTOPHELES
That's serious, but listen to me now.
You must gently press your advances,
Take this charcoal: mark him anyhow,
On his cloak or on his sleeve alight,
He'll feel sweet Remorse's blow.
Swallow the charcoal straight away,
No wine or water on your lips all day:
He'll be sighing at your door tonight.

THE LADY
It's not poisonous?

MEPHISTOPHELES (Offended.)
Respect now, where it's due!
You'd have to travel far to find such charcoal:
It comes from the dying pyre at a funeral,
On which I, once more, diligently blew.

A PAGE
I'm in love: they say I'm not old enough to.

MEPHISTOPHELES (Aside.)
I'm not sure now, whom I should listen to.

(To the Page.)

Don't set your heart on the younger ones.
The older will value what they've won.

(Others crowd round.)

More, already! What a demanding crew!
I'll help myself, and out now with the truth:
The worst expedient! The pain is great, you see. –
O Mothers, Mothers! Just let Faust go free!

(Gazing round him.)

The lights burn dim, already, in the hall,
The Court's moving off, and they're all
Arranged in their proper rank, I see,
Through the far aisles and galleries.
Now they assemble in the largest place,
The vast Hall of the Knights, there's barely space,
Who bought the mass of bright tapestry,
Filled corners, niches like an armoury.
Here I doubt there's need of magic spells:
The ghosts will find this place for themselves.

VII
THE HALL OF THE KNIGHTS, DIMLY LIT

(The Emperor and Court.)

THE HERALD
My ancient duty, to announce the play,
Is thwarted by the Spirits' secret action:
Please forgive: there's no sensible way
To explain such confused transformation.
The chairs are here: the stools and all:
The emperor's high up, by the wall:
He can see the battles on the tapestry
From mighty ages: watching comfortably.
Here they all sit now, Prince, Court around,
Benches packed together, as background:
In this hour of spirits, too, the lovers
Have lovingly found room beside their lovers.
And now that all have found their proper places,
We're ready: let the spirits show their faces!

(Trumpets.)

THE ASTROLOGER
Begin the drama then without delay,
The Emperor commands: take walls away!
No further hindrance, here magic is at hand:
The Tapestry's shrivelled as if by burning brand.
The walls divide, and sweep apart, as one,
An empty stage it seems has been created,
A mysterious light falls on our faces,
And I climb up to the proscenium.

MEPHISTOPHELES (Rising to view in the prompter's box.)
From here I hope for general acclamation,
Prompting is the devil's true oration.

(To the Astrologer.)

You know the measures that all the stars obey,
You'll understand my whispers in a masterly way.

325

THE ASTROLOGER

By miraculous power appears to view,
A massive temple-front: it's ancient too.
Like Atlas, who once held up the sky,
The many rows of columns stand on high.
They might well bear the stony weight,
Since two could raise a building straight.

THE ARCHITECT

That's the antique! It doesn't earn my praise,
Clumsy, overstretched we call it, nowadays.
Men think that crude is noble: bulk is greatness.
I love slender shafts, uplifting, boundless:
A pointed arch sends the spirit to the sky:
Architecture such as that will edify.

THE ASTROLOGER

Receive with reverence these hours the stars allow:
Let words of magic bind pure Reason now:
Let marvellously daring Fantasy,
In return, sweep onward, wide and free.
Your eyes see what you daringly conceived:
It's impossible, so more worthy to be believed.

(Faust rises into view on the other side of the proscenium.)

In priestly vestments, crowned, a wondrous man,
Fulfilling what he confidently began.
A tripod rises with him from deep abyss,
I smell the odour of incense in the dish.
He prepares to bless this sacred labour:
From this moment on it will find favour.

FAUST (Sublimely.)

In your name, Mothers, you enthroned
In boundlessness, set eternally alone,
And yet together. All the Forms of Life
Float round your heads, active, not alive.
Whatever was, in all its glow and gleam,
Moves there still, since it must always be.
And you assign it, with omnipotent might,
To day's pavilion or the vault of night.
Life holds some fast on its sweet track,
Others the bold magician must bring back:

Filled with faith, and richly generous,
He shows, what each desires, the Marvellous.

THE ASTROLOGER
The glowing key has scarcely touched the dish,
At once the room is filled with darkened mist:
It swirls about, as puffs of cloud will do,
Grows, condenses, shrinks, and splits in two.
And now behold a spirit-masterpiece!
As it moves about, there's music without cease.
In heavenly tones, pours out a who-knows-how,
And while it moves, all's turned to melody now.
The pillared shafts, even the tri-glyph, ringing
I think that the whole temple's singing.
The dark sinks down: from the light mist,
A handsome youth steps out in time to it.
I needn't name him, so my task is finished,
Who doesn't know the name of charming Paris!

A LADY
O! What a shining healthy powerful youth!

A SECOND
Like a peach, so fresh and full of juice!

A THIRD
The finely delineated, sweetly swelling lip!

A FOURTH
From such a cup you'd surely like to sip?

A FIFTH
He's quite pretty, but a little unrefined.

A SIXTH
He could be a bit more graceful, to my mind.

A KNIGHT
I sense the shepherd here, I think,
No trace of Courtier or Prince.

ANOTHER
Yes! Half naked the youth's quite handsome

We'd need to see him first with armour on!

A LADY
He sits down so gently and pleasantly.

A KNIGHT
You'd like to sit on his lap, comfortably?

ANOTHER
He lifts his arm so lightly above his head.

A CHAMBERLAIN
The lout! That's not acceptable: how ill-bred!

A LADY
You lords find fault with everything.

THE CHAMBERLAIN
In the Emperor's presence, all that stretching!

THE LADY
He's posed there! He thinks he's quite alone.

THE CHAMBERLAIN
Even a play should be polite in tone.

THE LADY
Now sleep has overcome the charming boy.

THE CHAMBERLAIN
And now he'll snore: that's natural, what joy!

A YOUNG LADY
What refreshes my heart so deeply, that fragrance
Mixed with fumes from the burning incense?

AN OLDER LADY
Truly! It's breath penetrates one's nature,
It comes from him!

AN ELDERLY LADY
It's the sap of nurture,
It's generated in youth, like ambrosia,

And spreads around in the atmosphere.

(Helen emerges.)

MEPHISTOPHELES
So that's her! I'd not lose sleep for that. She
Is quite pretty, true, but doesn't do much for me.

THE ASTROLOGER
There's nothing more now for me to do,
As men of honour confess, I confess it too.
Beauty comes: if only I'd a tongue of fire! –
Beauty so many songs has forever inspired –
Whom she appears to, of self he's dispossessed,
Whom she belonged to, was too greatly blessed.

FAUST
Is this the fount of beauty? Have I still, eyes?
What pours here, through my mind, so richly?
My dreadful journey yields a blessed prize.
How void the world was, undeveloped for me!
What is it now since my priesthood?
Desirable, lasting, solid underfoot!
The power of my life's breath should
Fail, if I'm ever again estranged from you! –
The perfect form that drew me before,
Delighting me, in the magic mirror,
Was only an airy phantom of such beauty! – You
Are the true embodiment of my passion:
Towards you is my powers' whole direction
To you, love, feeling, faith, madness are owed.

MEPHISTOPHELES (From the prompter's box.)
Calm yourself, now, and don't fail in your role!

AN OLDER LADY
Tall, well formed, only the head is small.

A YOUNGER LADY
Just look! Could clumsier feet exist at all?

A DIPLOMAT
I've seen princesses of this kind: though

I think she's beautiful, from head to toe.

A COURTIER
Soft and sly, she goes towards the sleeper.

A LADY
How ugly, near that form so young and pure.

A POET
From her Beauty shines towards him.

A LADY
A picture! Luna and Endymion!

THE POET
Quite so! The goddess seems to descend,
Leans above him to drink his breath, ah then:
Enviable! – A Kiss! – The cup's full to excess.

A DUENNA
In front of everyone! What utter madness!

FAUST
A dreadful favour to grant a boy! –

MEPHISTOPHELES
Quiet now! Be still!
And let the spectre do what it will.

A COURTIER
She slips away, lightly: he awakes.

A LADY
Just as I thought! That glance she takes!

A COURTIER
He stares! It's wonderful what's happening.

A LADY
But not so wonderful what she sees in him.

A COURTIER
She turns towards him now with dignity.

A LADY

I see she'll soon take him through his lesson:
At such times men behave quite stupidly,
Perhaps he even thinks that's he the first one.

A KNIGHT

Let me be worthy! Majestically fine! –

A LADY

The trollop! I'd call that table wine!

A PAGE

I'd like to swap his place for mine!

A COURTIER

Who wouldn't be tangled in such a net?

A LADY

That treasure's been handled often, you forget,
And the gilding's mostly rubbed away.

ANOTHER

Worthless since it was ten years old, I'd say.

A KNIGHT

Sometimes one takes the best that one can get:
I'd be content with the loveliness that's left.

A LEARNED MAN

I see clearly but I'll confess, quite freely
It's doubtful if that's the true one I see.
The Present's tempted to exaggerate,
I hold to what the ancient texts relate.
There I read she gave particular joy
To all the grey-bearded men of Troy:
And that fits perfectly here too, you see:
I'm not young: still she gives joy to me.

THE ASTROLOGER

No longer a boy! A daring hero, he:
Grasped she defends herself, but barely.
He lifts her high in his strong arms, too,
Will he carry her off?

FAUST
Audacious fool!
You dare? Do you hear? Stop! Enough, I say!

MEPHISTOPHELES
You created the mime these phantoms play!

THE ASTROLOGER
A word! After what we've been given,
I'll call this piece: The Rape of Helen.

FAUST
What rape! Am I nothing in this place!
Is this key no longer in my hand!
It led me through terror, waste and wave,
Through solitude, to where, set firm, I stand.
Here's a foothold! Here's reality,
Where spirit dare with spirits disagree,
And prepare itself for its great, dual mastery.
She was so far: how could she closer shine!
I'll rescue her, and she'll be doubly mine.
The risk! The Mothers! They must grant her!
Who knows her once, can never live without her.

THE ASTROLOGER
What are you doing, Faust! Faust! —With force
He seizes her, the form dims in its course.
He turns the key against the youth, and then,
Touches him! – Ah! – Gone, in a moment! Gone!

(An explosion. Faust falls to the ground. The spirits vanish in mist.)

MEPHISTOPHELES (Taking Faust on his shoulders.)
You've done it now! Carrying fools, my friend,
Brings harm to the Devil himself, in the end.

ACT II

I

A HIGH-ARCHED, NARROW, GOTHIC CHAMBER FORMERLY FAUST'S, UNCHANGED

MEPHISTOPHELES (Entering from behind a curtain. As he holds it up and looks behind him, Faust is seen lying stretched out on an antiquated bed.)

Lie there, unlucky man! One tempted by
The bonds of a love not readily undone!
The man whom Helena shall paralyse
Won't find it easy to regain his reason.

(Looking around him.)

I look upwards, here, around me,
All's unaltered, and undamaged:
Stained glass, there, shows darkly,
Spiders have added to their webs:
The ink is dry: the paper's yellow,
But everything's still in its place:
Even the quill-pen's here, on show,
With which Faust and the Devil embraced.
Yes! Deeper in the nib there's still
A drop of blood, I tempted him to spill.
It's a unique piece, in my book,
So I'll wish the great collectors luck.
The old fur-robe, on the hook, too,
Reminds me of a joke or two,
That time when I taught the student,
What, perhaps, in youth, he's glad he learnt.
Truly the same desire is on me, for
You, smoke-singed gown: you and I,
To flaunt ourselves once more as a professor,
And speak as one who's always in the right.
How to achieve that all the learned know:
It's something the Devil lost long ago.

(He shakes the fur as he takes it down, and moths, crickets and beetles fly out.)

CHORUS OF INSECTS

Greetings! We're greeting
Our Patron of old,
We're floating and buzzing,
To us you're well known.
Singly, in silence,
You sowed us like plants.
Father, in thousands
We've come to the dance.
The jester is snugly
Contained in the breast,
The lice in the fur they
Are sooner expressed.

MEPHISTOPHELES

What a nice surprise, this young brood of mine!
One merely sows, and harvests in due time.
I'll shake this ancient fleece about,
Here and there, one flutters out. –
Away! Around! In a hundred leavings,
Hurry and hide yourself, you darlings.
There, where the ancient boxes lie,
Here, in the smoky parchment try,
In that broken dusty old pottery,
Or the skull, its eye-sockets empty.
All this jumbled mildewed existence,
Always gives one whims and fancies.
Again let's dress up as a lecturer!
Today I'll be the Principal, once more.
But it's no use naming myself, you see:
Where are the people, to welcome me?

FAMULUS (A College Servant, tottering here, down the long gallery)

What a noise! What a quake!
The stairs sway, the walls shake:
Through the windows' trembling colours
I see the lightning gleam above us.
The floor leaps, and, on high,
Plaster, rubble from the sky.
And the door, once tightly locked,
By wondrous force is thrown back. –
There! How fearful! A giant
Look, in Faust's old garment!
At his gazing, and his pleas,

I want to sink to my knees.
Shall I go? Shall I remain?
Oh, what will happen to me, then!

MEPHISTOPHELES
Here, my friend! – You're called Nicodemus.

FAMULUS
Honoured Sir! That's my name – Oremus.

MEPHISTOPHELES
Enough of that!

FAMULUS
How pleased I am you knew me!

MEPHISTOPHELES
I know you well: a student still, I see,
Mossy Sir! After all, a learned man
Studies hard, and does the best he can.
So one builds a respectable house of cards,
That greater minds can't finish afterwards.
But he's a witty fellow, is your master,
Who doesn't know the noble Doctor Wagner?
He's the first in all the world of learning!
He's unique: wisdom, each day increasing,
And all of it he still holds together,
Crowds, around him, panting, gather
Listeners, eaves'-droppers, welcome.
Alone, he shines there at the rostrum.
He holds a key, just like Saint Peter,
That unlocks the lower, and the higher.
He glows and sparkles above the rest,
No name and fame has wider standing:
Even that of Faust has dimmed, at best:
He's the one who's always inventing.

FAMULUS
Forgive me, honoured Sir, if I dare
To speak, and contradict you, there:
There's no question of that, I must declare:
Since modesty's his role, as all discern.
Discovering nothing of the circumstances,
Baffled by the great man's disappearance:

335

He seeks all health and comfort in his return.
The room waits for its old master
While Doctor Faustus is away,
Untouched, still, as in his day.
And I scarcely dare to enter.
What can the stars be doing? –
The walls themselves are frightening me:
The doorframes quiver, bolts work free,
Or you yourself couldn't have got in.

MEPHISTOPHELES
And your great man where is he?
Lead me there: or bring him here to me!

FAMULUS
Oh! His warnings are quite clear,
I'm not allowed to interfere.
For months I've left him in utter peace,
Till his great work is complete.
He, the most delicate of scholars,
His face looks like a charcoal burner's,
Blackened now from nose to ears,
Eyes crimson, blowing up the fires,
All the while, so enthusiastic:
Clinking of tongs, that's his music.

MEPHISTOPHELES
Why would he deny an entrance to me?
I'm one who'd speed his luck, you see.

(The Famulus exits: Mephistopheles sits down, gravely.)

I've hardly taken my seat here,
And I see a guest behind my chair.
But he's one of the new school's persuasion:
He'll be arrogant, I think, on this occasion.

BACCALAUREUS (Storming along the corridor.)
I find the gates and doors are open!
Now there's room at last for hope then,
That it won't be merely as before,
A live man, acting as a corpse,
Wasting away, and rotting,
Till he merely dies of living.

These walls and these partitions,
Bow and sink towards perdition,
And if we don't look about us,
Their decline and fall will rout us.
I'm audacious, no one more so,
But no further in do I go.

What will I find here today?
It's years since I've been this way,
Where timid and innocent
As a freshman I was sent!
Where I trusted in my elders,
Edified by all their blather.

From the dry old books, they knew
They lied to me: what they knew,
Not believing in it truly,
Stealing life itself, from me.
What? – There, in his cell,
Sits a darkly bright one still!

With astonishment now, nearer,
See him sitting in his dark fur,
Truly, as I left him sitting
Still in all his coarse wrapping!
Then he seemed a fount of wisdom,
Since I didn't understand him.
He won't find me so today,
Fresh and new, I'm on my way!

Sir, if in Lethe's melancholy stream
That bald nodding head's not swum,
See your grateful scholar come,
Outgrown, his academic dream.
I find you now, as I saw you:
I was another though: that's true.

MEPHISTOPHELES

I'm glad the ringing brought you.
I rated you once before as high:
The caterpillar, the chrysalis too,
Showed the bright future butterfly.
Your curly hair and pointed collar,

337

Made you a childishly pleasing scholar.
You never wore pigtails I believe? –
And today you're cropped like a Swede.
I see you're bold and resolute:
But don't go home too absolute!

BACCALAUREUS

My old master! We're in our old places:
But don't think to renew time's journey,
And spare me words with dual-faces:
I treat them now quite differently.
You teased the true, and honest youth.
It wasn't difficult for you to do
It's what no one dares to do today.

MEPHISTOPHELES

Pure truth on the young is thrown away,
The little beaks don't like it, any way,
But afterwards when years have passed,
And they've learnt it for themselves at last,
And think it came from them, not school:
Then we hear: 'The Master was a fool.'

BACCALAUREUS

A rascal, maybe! – What teacher ever shows us
The Truth directly, underneath our noses?
They know the way to make it seem more, or less,
Now serious, now playful, as suits the children best.

MEPHISTOPHELES

There's a moment given us for learning, truly:
But you're ready now to teach, yourself, I see.
For many moons, united with their suns,
You the riches of experience have won.

BACCALAUREUS

Experience! Mist and Foam!
And not the Spirit's equal.
Confess! What one has known,
Is not worth knowing at all.

MEPHISTOPHELES (After a pause.)

I've thought so for ages. I was a Fool,
But I think that shallow now I'm sensible.

BACCALAUREUS

That pleases me! I hear pure Reason's sound:
The first old man of sense I've ever found.

MEPHISTOPHELES

I sought for treasure, buried gold,
And brought to light frightful coals.

BACCALAUREUS

Confess now, your skull, bald and old,
Is worth no more than that empty poll.

MEPHISTOPHELES (Amiably.)

Do you know, my friend, how rude you seem to me?

BACCALAUREUS

In German, one's lying if one speaks politely.

MEPHISTOPHELES (Wheeling his chair nearer to the proscenium and the audience.)

Up here I'm dazed by light and air:
Shall I take shelter with you down there?

BACCALAUREUS

I find it arrogant that in times like these,
A man wants to be what he no longer is.
Man's life is in his arteries, and when
Are they so vibrant as in younger men?
There the fresh blood full of strength
Creates new life from its own life again.
There all works, and things get done,
The waverers fall, the capable get on.
While we've conquered half the world,
What have you done? Nodded, curled
In the sun, dreamed, weighed, plan on plan.
For sure, age is a chilling fever:
The frost of whims and need ahead.
When your thirtieth year is over,
A man's as good as dead.
It would be best to seek an early grave.

MEPHISTOPHELES
That leaves the Devil nothing more to say.

BACCALAUREUS
Unless I will it, no Devil can exist.

MEPHISTOPHELES (Aside.)
The Devil will still trip you, in a bit.

BACCALAUREUS
This is youth's noblest profession!
The world was nothing before my creation:
I drew the Sun out of the sea:
The Moon began her changeful course with me:
The daylight decked my path to greet me,
The Earth flowered, grew green, to meet me.
At my command, in primal night,
The stars in splendour swam to sight.
Who, but I, loosed from its prison
Cramped thought's philistinism?
I, quite free, as my spirit cites,
Happily following my inner light,
And speeding on, in delight,
Darkness behind: and all before me, bright.

MEPHISTOPHELES
Go forth in splendour, you primal man! –
How could insight harm you, ever:
Who can think of stupid things or clever,
That past ages didn't, long ago, understand.
Yet there's no danger from him, you see,
He'll think about it differently in time:
Even if the grape-juice acts absurdly,
In the end it changes into wine.

(To the younger members of the audience, who do not applaud.)

My words have left you cold, I gather,
May it be so for you, sweet children:
But think: the Devil's a lot older,
So you need to be old to understand him!

II

A LABORATORY

(In the fashion of the Middle Ages: lots of heavy apparatus for strange purposes.)

WAGNER (At the furnace.)
The fearful bell is sounding,
The soot-black walls shudder.
My deepest expectation
Will be unsure no longer.
Soon the dark itself will lighten:
Soon in the innermost phial,
It will glow like living fire,
Yes, like the noblest ruby's glow,
Lightning flashing in the shadow.
A clearest white light shines now!
Ah, not to lose it once more! –
Oh, God! Who's rattling at the door?

MEPHISTOPHELES (Entering.)
Greetings! And kindly meant now.

WAGNER (Anxiously.)
Welcome, to the planet of the hour!

(Whispering.)

But stifle your breath, and words' power,
A noble work is likewise being weighed.

MEPHISTOPHELES (Whispering.)
What might it be?

WAGNER (Whispering.)
A Man is being made.

MEPHISTOPHELES
A Man? And what loving couple
Have you got hidden, up the chimney?

WAGNER

God Forbid! How unfashionable!
We're free of all that idle foolery.
The tender moment from which life emerged,
The charming power with which its inner urge,
Took and gave, and clearly stamped its seal,
First in a near, and then a further field,
We now divest of all that dignity:
Though the creatures still enjoy it, we,
As Men, with all our greater gifts, begin,
To have, as we should, a nobler origin.

(He turns towards the furnace.)

It brightens! See! – Now there's a real chance,
That, if from the hundred-fold substance,
By mixing – since mixing makes it happen –
The stuff of human life's compounded,
And distilled in a flask, well-founded,
And in proper combination, grounded,
Then the silent work is done.

(He turns again to the furnace.)

It will be! The mass is clearer!
The proof comes nearer, nearer:
What man praises in deepest Nature,
Through Reason we dare to probe it,
And what she organises, here,
We're now able to crystallise it.

MEPHISTOPHELES

Who lives a while, gains much experience,
And nothing new can happen on his journey.
In years of travelling, and in my presence,
I've seen, already, crystallised humanity.

WAGNER (Up till now attending to the phial.)

It rises: flashes, there's expansion
In a moment more it will be done.
Great aims seem foolish at the outset:
But we'll laugh at Chance itself, yet,
And brains, with thoughts to celebrate,
In the future, a Thinker will create.

(He inspects the phial, rapturously.)

The glass rings with sweet power,
It darkens, clears: it must have being!
In a delicate form I see appear
A well-behaved little Man behaving.
What can the world ask more, what can we?
Now that this mystery's visible to each.
Give ear to what these sounds may be,
They make a voice: they're forming speech.

HOMUNCULUS (From the phial, to Wagner.)
Now, father! That was no joke. How are you?
Come: press me tenderly to your heart, too!
But not too hard, the glass may be too thin.
It's in the very nature of the thing:
For the natural the world has barely space:
What's artificial commands a narrow place.

(To Mephistopheles.)

But you, Rascal, my dear Cousin, are you
Here at the right moment? I thank you, too.
Good fortune's led you here to me:
Since I exist, I must be doing, you see.
I'd like to begin my work today:
You're skilful at shortening the way.

WAGNER
But first, a word! Till now I've had no direction,
When old or young teased me with a question.
For example: no one's found out, ever,
What makes body and soul fit together:
Stick tight, as if there'll be no separation,
Yet always cause each other irritation.
So then, -

MEPHISTOPHELES
Stop! I'd rather he told me,
Why married people get by so wretchedly?
You'll never discover that, my friend.
There's work to do the little Man can tend.

HOMUNCULUS
What work's to do?

MEPHISTOPHELES (Pointing to a side door.)
Employ your gifts on this!

WAGNER (Still gazing at the phial.)
Truly, you're the loveliest boy there is!

(The side-door opens: Faust is seen stretched out on a couch.)

HOMUNCULUS (Astonished.)
Interesting!

(The phial slips out of Wagner's hands, hovers over Faust, and shines on him.)

Lovely surroundings! – Clear water
In thick forest! Women there: undressing.
The loveliest of all! – It's getting clearer.
One's left, different from the rest, gleaming:
Of highest race, for sure, a heavenly name.
She places her foot in the transparent glow,
Her noble body's sweetly living flame
Cools itself in the yielding crystal flow. –
But what's that rush of beating wings for:
That thrashing, splashing, in the mirror?
The lovely girls, intimidated, flee:
Their queen, alone, looks on, composedly,
To see, with a proud feminine pleasure,
The Swan-Prince press against her knee, there,
Forward yet tame. Familiar, he seems. –
But suddenly a vapour heaves,
And covers, with the veil it weaves,
The loveliest of scenes.

MEPHISTOPHELES
All the things that you could murmur!
So little: and such a great dreamer.
I see nothing –

HOMUNCULUS
So I believe. You're Northern,
In the age of mist you're born then,
In a jumble of priest-craft and chivalry,

So how could your sight be free!
You're at home with darkness.

(He gazes around.)

Brown repulsive, mildewed walls,
Low, pointed arches, full of scrolls! –
One wakes, and gives another pain,
On the spot, dead then, he'll remain.
Wooded founts, swans, naked beauty,
That was his far-sighted dream:
How could this place do duty!
I can scarcely endure the scene.
Carry him off!

MEPHISTOPHELES
I'd be happy: a last chance.

HOMUNCULUS
Order the soldier to the fight,
Lead the maiden to the dance,
Then everything's done right.
Even now, thinks, quick as light,
It's Classical Walpurgis Night:
That's the best, if he were sent
To his own true element!

MEPHISTOPHELES
I've never heard that event named, here.

HOMUNCULUS
How could it come to your ear?
Only Romantic ghosts, for you:
A true ghost must be Classic too.

MEPHISTOPHELES
Which path do we take there? Already
Your antique colleagues quite repel me.

HOMUNCULUS
North-westward Satan, is your pleasure ground,
But this time we're South-eastward bound –
In wider space flows Peneus, the free
By bushes, groves, and damp still bays:

345

Its levels stretch to mountain ways,
And over it Pharsalus: old, yet contemporary.

MEPHISTOPHELES
Oh! Enough! And keep all the fight,
Of tyranny and slavery, out of sight.
It bores me: they're scarce done when
They start the whole thing over again:
And no one sees: they're being re-aligned,
By Asmodeus, who works them from behind.
They clash, it's said, for Freedom's right:
Seen rightly, slave with slave is all the fight.

HOMUNCULUS
Leave Mankind's wilfulness to me, then.
Each man defends himself, as best he can,
From childhood, till, at last, he is a man.
Just ask how we can get back there again.
Have you a method, then, let's see:
If you haven't, leave it all to me.

MEPHISTOPHELES
There's many a Brocken trick I could display,
But I find that Pagan bolts have barred the way.
The whole Greek race was never that much use!
They dazzle with the senses' freer play: it's true:
They lure the heart of man to happier sins:
While ours, one always finds, are gloomy things.
And now, what?

HOMUNCULUS
Once you weren't so witless:
When I spoke about Thessalian witches.
I can deliver what I said: just think a little.

MEPHISTOPHELES (Lustfully.)
Thessalian witches! Good! They're the people
I once enquired about long ago.
I don't think it would suit me, at all,
To live with them night after night, though,
Still, a visit, and a trial –

HOMUNCULUS
This mantle here,

Fold it around your knight there!
As before, the cloak can carry another,
One of you, along with the other.
I'll light the way.

WAGNER (Anxiously.)
And I?

HOMUNCULUS
Well, now, you
Stay home, there are important things to do.
Unfold all your ancient parchments,
Then, by rote, collect life's elements,
And place them together with due care,
Consider What, more deeply consider How.
Meanwhile round the world, a bit, I'll fare,
And find the last dot on the 'i', for now.
Then the great work will see its final stage:
Great effort will merit great reward, you'll see:
Gold, honour, fame, a long and ripe old age,
And science too — and virtue, possibly.
Farewell!

WAGNER (Sadly.)
Farewell! It gives me pain.
Already, I fear, I'll not see you again.

MEPHISTOPHELES
Now to Peneus, lively, on!
Sir Cousin's highly rated.

(To the audience.)

In the end we're dependent on
The creatures we've created.

III

CLASSICAL WALPURGIS NIGHT.
THE PHARSALIAN FIELDS.

(Darkness.)

ERICHTHO (The Thessalian Witch, see Lucan's Pharsalia)
This night's awesome feast, as so often in the past,
I enter now, I, Erichtho, the gloomy one:
Not so abominable as the wretched poets
Painted me, with excessive slander...they never
Cease their blame or praise...I see the valley whiten
With waves of tents that gleam greyer in the distance,
The after-image of that anxious, fearful night.
How often it's repeated! In eternity
Acted out, again, forever...No one gives the realm
To another: to the one whose power won it:
Whose strength rules. Since each, incapable of ruling
His inner self, would gladly rule his neighbour's will,
In the manner that his proud mind dictates to him...
But here a great instance was fought out, to the end,
Of how force may battle against a greater force,
Freedom's lovely thousand-blossomed garland be torn,
And stubborn laurel be wound round the ruler's brow.
Here, Pompey dreams of his youth and former greatness,
There, Caesar, listening, watches the balance tremble!
It settles, and the world knows whom it sinks towards.
The watch fires, glowing, send out their crimson flames:
The field exhales those images of squandered blood,
And lured by the strange wondrous splendour of the night,
A legion of Hellenic legends gather here.
They hover around all the fires uncertainly,
Or sit nearby, the fabled forms of ancient days....
The Moon, not full it is true, but of clearest light,
Rises, scattering mild radiance everywhere:
The ghostly tents vanish: the fires burn bluish now.
But, over my head, what sudden meteor's this?
It shines, illuminates the material globe.
I smell Life. It's not fitting for me to approach
Closer to the living, since I'm harmful to them:
It gives me a bad name, and is no benefit to me.
It sinks down already. I give way, thoughtfully!

(She Exits. The Airy Travellers speak from above.)

HOMUNCULUS

Once again float round the circle
Over flames and shuddering horror:
On the ground, and in the vale still,
It's quite ghostly, we discover.

MEPHISTOPHELES

It's the same as through my old window
In the grim and tangled north,
Really loathsome ghosts below,
I'm at home here: and there, of course.

HOMUNCULUS

See! There's a tall one striding,
With gigantic steps, before us.

MEPHISTOPHELES

As if she were afraid, now: gliding
Through the air above, she saw us.

HOMUNCULUS

Let her stride! Right away,
Set the knight down there:
He'll return to life again,
Once he breathes this mythic air.
FAUST (As he touches the ground.)

Where is she?

HOMUNCULUS

We can't say, I fear,
But you can probably enquire here.
Hurry now before it's daylight,
Go and search, from fire to fire:
Who found his way to the Mothers' side,
Won't find this harder to survive.

MEPHISTOPHELES

On my own behalf too, I'm here:
But I don't know anything better
Than each to seek, among the fires,

The adventure he desires.
Then, so that we can reunite,
Little one, shine your ringing light.

HOMUNCULUS
It shines like this, and rings.

(The glass shines and rings out powerfully.)

Now off to new and wondrous things!

FAUST (Alone.)
Where is she? – But no further answer seek...
If this is not the soil she trod,
Nor the wave that bathed her foot,
It is the air that spoke her speech.
Here! By a miracle, on Hellenic land!
I feel, the earth, too, where I stand:
A fresh power glows in me, the Sleeper,
So I am Antaeus-like in nature.
And I find the strangest things lie here,
First let me search this Labyrinth of fire.

(He moves away.)
(On the Upper Peneus)

MEPHISTOPHELES (Looking around.)
And as I wander through these fires,
I feel myself a total stranger: in the event,
They're mostly naked, a shirt here and there:
The Sphinx shameless, the Gryphon impudent:
And what's more, curly-haired and winged,
Before, behind, in eyes, reflected things...
Of course, at heart, indecency's my ideal,
But I find the Antique is a little too real.
One should control all with a modern mind,
Overlay it with fashions of assorted kinds....
Repulsive people! Yet still I have to meet them,
And, as a new guest too, correctly greet them...
Luck to you, fair ladies, and men, you wise grey ones!

A GRYPHON (Snarling. For the gold-guarding Gryphons see Herodotus'
Histories.)
Not Grey ones! Gryphons! – No one likes the name

Of something grey. Every word rings
With what conditioned it: its origins:
Grey, grievous, grumpy, gruesome, gravely, grimly,
Similarly harmonious etymologically,
Disharmonise us.

MEPHISTOPHELES
And yet, without deviation,
You like the gryp in your proud name of Gryphon.

THE GRYPHON (Snarling continuously.)
Naturally! The relationship's tried and tested:
It was often censured, but more often praised:
One grips maidens, money, gold,
To the gripper, Fortune's never cold.

GIANT ANTS
You spoke of gold: we've collected lots of it,
In rocks and caves, secretly, we've crammed it:
The Arimaspi, discovered it all, one day,
They're laughing now: they took it far away.

THE GRYPHON
We'll soon make them confess.

THE ARIMASPI (For the Scythian race of the Arimaspi and their association
with gold mining see Herodotus' Histories)
But not on this night of public festival.
By morning we'll have spent it all.
This time at least we'll achieve success.

MEPHISTOPHELES (Sitting among the Sphinxes.)
How free, and easy, I feel here,
I understand you, one and all.

SPHINX
We breathe out spirit-tones, clear,
That for you become substantial.
Now name yourself, so we can know your fame.

MEPHISTOPHELES
Men choose to saddle me with a host of names...
Are there Britons here? They travel about so much,
Looking for battlefields, and ruined walls,

The dullest classical places, waterfalls:
Here's a site that's worth all their fuss.
They spoke of me too: in their Mysteries:
And portrayed me there as Old Iniquity.

A SPHINX
How so?

MEPHISTOPHELES
I don't know why that should be.

A SPHINX
Perhaps you've knowledge of the stars?
What do you think of the present hour?

MEPHISTOPHELES (Gazing upwards.)
Star glides by star, the horned moon shines bright,
And I feel happy here, in this mournful site,
I warm myself on a lion skin: your right.
To have to take off, again: that would be hard:
Give us a riddle, or at least charades.

SPHINX
To express yourself, that would be a riddle.
Try for once tosolve your own inner muddle:
'Needed by the good man and the sinful,
To the first a breastplate in ascetic swordplay,
A wild friend for the other, to show the way,
And both amusing Zeus with their display.'

THE FIRST GRYPHON (Snarling.)
I don't like him!

THE SECOND GRYPHON (Snarling more fiercely.)
What's he after?

BOTH GRYPHONS
The nasty thing, he's not been heard of here!

MEPHISTOPHELES (Nastily)

Perhaps you think a guest's nails can't claw
Every bit as sharply as those talons of yours?

Just try it, then!

A SPHINX (Gently.)
You'll only stay until,
You leave our company, yourself, as you will:
In your own land everything worked for you,
But this if I'm not wrong's too much for you.

MEPHISTOPHELES
Looked at above, you're rather appetising,
But lower down the creature's somewhat frightening.

A SPHINX
False one, you'll do bitter penance,
These claws of ours are sound and good:
You with your withered horse's hoof,
Aren't comfortable in our presence.

(The Sirens start to sing, above them.)

What are those birds shaking
The poplar branches by the stream?

A SPHINX
Take care! The song they're making
Conquered the best there's ever been.

THE SIRENS
Ah, why should you choose to live
Amongstamazing ugliness!
Listen, we flock to you, ah yes,
With tuneful sounds, in excess,
That Sirens ought to give.

THE SPHINXES (Mocking them.)
Make them fly down here to us!
Their falcon-claws, so hideous,
They've hidden in the leaves:
They'll fall on you, cruelly, you see
If you choose to hear them sigh.

THE SIRENS
Away with hate! Away with envy!
We gather purest ecstasies,

Scattered through the sky!
On the earth, or on the sea,
With the happiest gestures, we
Greet men who wander by.

MEPHISTOPHELES
This is news of the sweetest,
Here from lyre and chest,
One note twines round another.
But this warbling's lost on me:
It crawls into my ear, you see,
Yet my heart feels nothing, here.

THE SPHINXES
Don't talk of hearts! That's idle:
A leather bag would do as well,
To match that face you wear.

FAUST (Approaching.)
Marvellous! Gazing's enough for me,
At grand repulsiveness, and solidity:
I suspect I'll find good fortune shortly:
Where will this serious gazing take me?

(He points at the Sphinxes.)

Once Oedipus stood in front of them:

(He points at the Sirens.)

Ulysses writhed in ropes for them:

(He points to the Ants.)

They gathered a mighty treasure.

(He points to the Gryphons.)

They guarded it in fullest measure.
I feel new power flowing through me:
Mighty these forms: of mighty memory.

MEPHISTOPHELES
Once you'd have run from things like these,

But now they look good to you:
When a man seeks his beloved, he's
Ready to meet monsters too.

FAUST (To the Sphinxes.)
You female forms, tell me then,
Have any of you seen Helen?

THE SPHINXES
None of us lasted till her day,
Hercules the last did slay.
You can ask Chiron, anyway:
He gallops round in this spirit night:
When he stops for you, you might.

THE SIRENS
You will not fail at all!...
How Ulysses lingered with us,
Not hurrying scornfully by us,
He'd many times recall:
All will be shown you,
If you make your journey to
Our fields, in the green sea.

A SPHINX
Don't let yourself be deceived.
Instead of Ulysses self-bonded,
We bind with good advice. On!
When you reach noble Chiron,
You'll find it's as I promised.

(Faust wanders off.)

MEPHISTOPHELES (In a temper.)
What croaks by me on beating wing,
So quick that one can't see a thing.
And one behind the other, flying?
Even a hunter would weary of these.

A SPHINX
That storm, like the winds of winter, here,
Hercule's arrows could scarce get near:
They are the swift Stymphalides,
And their croaked greetings are well-meant,

The vulture-beaked, and goose-webbed.
They'd gladly appear in our place,
As a closely-related race.

MEPHISTOPHELES (As if intimidated.)
Something else is having a hissing fit.

SPHINX
Don't be worried about those either!
They're the heads of the Lernaean Hydra,
Lopped from the trunk, but think they're it.
But, what's the matter, now then?
Why all the restless movements?
Where are you going? He's gone!...
I see that Chorus over there, that one,
Has turned your head. You'll get nowhere,
Go on: greet every sweet face there!
They're Lamiae, the lustful girls,
With smiling lips, impudent curls,
The race of Satyrs all delight in:
With them a cloven foot's the very thing.

MEPHISTOPHELES
Will you stay here? So I can find you again.

SPHINX
Yes! Mix with the flighty rabble.
In Egypt, we were accustomed, you know,
To rule for a thousand years or so.
And if you respect our location,
We'll regulate the days of Moon and Sun.
We'll sit in front of the Pyramids,
To pass judgement on the nations:
With changeless faces, there, amid
War and peace, and inundations.

(On the Lower Peneus.)

(The river-god, surrounded by nymphs and tributary streams.)

PENEUS
Stir, you reed-beds, whispering, flowing!
Sigh softly, slender rushes, bowing,
Lightly, willow-bushes, rustling,

Lisp, you poplar-branches trembling,
Through the broken dream!.....
Dreadful premonitions wake me,
Secret quivering, now, shakes me,
In my peaceful wandering stream.

FAUST (Approaching the river.)
If I heard true, as I believe:
From behind the tangled leaves
Of these shrubs and branches,
Came sounds of human voices.
Then the fount seemed to chatter,
And the breeze filled with laughter.

THE NYMPHS (To Faust.)
Just to lie here, now,
For you would be best,
Reviving your wearied
Body with coolness,
Enjoy here forever
Your fugitive rest:
Murmuring, trickling,
We'll whisper, and bless.

FAUST
I'm awake! O let them linger there
Those images without compare,
As they reached my sight.
I'm moved so marvellously!
Is it dream? Or is it memory?
Once before, I knew this delight.
The waters creep through the freshness,
The softly swaying bushes' thickness,
Without rushing, barely trickling:
A hundred founts from all sides press,
And gather to the purest brightness,
Fill the pool's shallow ring.
Glowing limbs of young girls are
Reflected by the liquid mirror,
And added to the eye's delight!
Companionably, bathing joyfully,
Swimming boldly, wading shyly,
Crying out, at last, in watery fight.
This sight's enough to renew

My eyes with gazing at the view,
But ever wider vision strains.
My glance cuts sharply through the cover,
Rich foliage, green wealth, around her,
Serves to hide the noble queen.

Marvellous! The swans approaching:
From the bays, come softly swimming,
Majestically pure their movement.
Floating calm, in sweet society,
But how proudly, self-delightedly,
Head and neck are lifted, bent......
One shines out above all others,
Boasting boldly of his favours,
Sailing swiftly in their race:
His ruffled plumage swelling,
Wave-like, on the wave he's stirring,
He hastens to the sacred place...
The others swimming here and there,
With their smooth shining feathers,
Soon meet in fine contention,
Drive away the frightened maidens,
Not thinking of their service, then
But only of their own protection.

THE NYMPHS
Sisters, bend and set you ears
To the river-banks' green turf:
If I hear rightly, coming near,
That's the sound of hooves on earth.
If I only knew who that message might
Be bringing, swiftly, to the Night!

FAUST
To me, the ground seems ringing, too
Echoing to some swift stallion's hoof.
There, gaze, my eyes!
Good luck, is nigh,
Will it come to me as well?
O, wonder without parallel!
A rider trots towards us, now,
Gifted, shines with spirit and power
Grafted to a snow-white horse...
I know him too, I can't be wrong,

It's Philyra's famous son! –
Halt, Chiron! Halt! Hear my discourse...

CHIRON (The Centaur.)
What then? What is it?

FAUST
Delay a moment!

CHIRON
I never rest.

FAUST
Well, take me with you, then!

CHIRON
Mount! And I can question you, at leisure:
Where are you going? You're by the river,
I'll carry you through the flood, with pleasure.

FAUST (Mounting his back.)
Wherever you wish. My thanks forever...
You, the great man, the noble teacher,
Famed for educating the race of heroes,
That splendid company of the Argonauts,
And all who edified the Poets' thoughts.

CHIRON
All that in its proper place!
As Mentor, even Pallas wasn't rated:
In the end they do things their own way,
As if they'd none of them been educated.

FAUST
The doctor who can name the plants,
And roots, profoundly, understands:
Who heals the sick, and soothes the wound,
Here, strong in mind and body, have I found!

CHIRON
When a hero was injured near me.
I gave the right assistance and advice:
But, at last, bequeathed my art, you see,

To priests, and herb-gathering old wives.

FAUST
You've a truly great man's ways:
He won't hear a word of praise.
He'll modestly defer to us
And act as if all were equals.

CHIRON
You seem artful at those pretences,
Which flatter common folk and princes.

FAUST
But surely you'd confess today:
You saw the greatest, of your age,
Among the noblest deeds, you trod,
And lived life as a demi-god.
Among those great heroic forms,
Who was the finest of them all?

CHIRON
Among the Argonauts, in my day,
Each was worthy, in his own way.
And with the powers he inhaled,
Knew enough when others failed.
Castor and Pollux always conquered,
When youth and beauty were honoured.
In determination, and swift help to others,
First was Calais, and Zetes his brother,
Thoughtful, clever, strong, well-advised,
Jason conquered, woman-folk's delight.
Then Orpheus: gentle, always brooding,
Sounding the lyre, quite over-powering.
Sharp-eyed Lynceus, by night and day,
Steering the sacred ship past reef and bay...
Let such dangers always be faced as brothers:
If one achieves he's praised by all the others.

FAUST
Of Hercules, you say nothing?

CHIRON
Oh! Don't rouse my yearning....
Never noting how Phoebus

Ares, or Hermes, were defined,
With my own eyes I saw before us
What all men praise as divine.
He was born a king, no other,
A splendid youth to gaze upon:
Yielding to his elder brother,
And the loveliest of women.
Gaea's never known a second,
Nor Hebe led such on to heaven's zone:
In vain for him they sing the songs,
In vain for him they carve the stone.

FAUST

The sculptors never caught his form,
However many images they made.
You've spoken of the loveliest man,
Now speak about the loveliest maid!

CHIRON

What!...I won't talk of woman's beauty,
It's so often a frozen mask to me:
I can only praise that nature, truly,
Flowing freely, and cheerfully.
Beauty's delighted with itself:
Grace makes it irresistible,
Like Helen, whom I carried.

FAUST

You carried her?

CHIRON

Yes on this very back.

FAUST

Was I not sufficiently aroused?
Such a seat, now, will bring me luck!

CHIRON

She gripped me by the mane, so,
As you are doing.

FAUST

I'm vanquished, oh,
Completely! Tell me, why here?

She is my one and only desire!
Carried her from where, to where?

CHIRON
That's easy to tell, since you enquire.
At that time, the Dioscuri, Castor and Pollux,
Freed their sister, Helen, from a nest of robbers.
The robbers then, not used to being conquered,
Regained their courage, and chased them onward.
The sister and brothers' hasty course was halted
By all the swamps that lie below Eleusis:
The brothers waded: I swam over, swiftly:
Then she sprang off, and, stroking gently
My wet mane, caressed me, thanked me,
Confident, sweetly clever were her ways.
She was so charming! Youth, delighting Age!

FAUST
Only ten years old!...

CHIRON
The philologists deceive you,
I see, while deceiving themselves too.
It's strange that with a mythological woman,
Poets use her, at will, to draw our attention,
She can never age, is never old,
Cast in the same enticing mould,
Seduced when young, in age delights:
Enough, no age restricts a poet's flights.

FAUST
Then let her be as if no age has bound her!
As Achilles on Pherae once found her,
Beyond all ages. What rare luck:
In spite of every fate, to win her love!
And shall I, by the strength of my yearning,
Not draw that unique form towards me, living,
That eternal being, equal to the divine,
Great yet tender: kind as she's sublime.
You saw her once: today I too have seen her,
Lovely in her attraction: as lovely as desired.
Now my soul and being is strongly tied:
If I can't win her, I shan't survive.

CHIRON

Ah, stranger! You're enraptured like Mankind:
Among us Spirits you seem maddened, blind.
Yet now your fate is to be met with here:
Though only for a moment, every year,
I take the time to call on Manto, there,
Aesculapius' daughter: in silent prayer
Imploring her father to add to his fame,
Enlighten, at last, each rash doctor's brain,
And persuade them never to deal death again...
I like her best of all the crowd of Sibyls,
Free of grimaces, kind and generous:
If you stay with her, she's the power too,
To heal you totally: with herbs and roots.

FAUST

I don't need healing: my mind is filled with power:
There I'd become as base as others are.

CHIRON

Don't scorn the healing of the noble fount!
We've reached the place, so, quick, dismount!

FAUST

Tell me, where, through pebbly water,
In the gloomy night, you've brought us?

CHIRON

Here Greece and Rome braved the fight,
Olympus to your left, Peneus on the right,
The greatest empire lost here to the sand:
A king flees: and citizens win the land.
Gaze around! Famous Tempe is nearby,
Eternal, there, under the moonlit sky.

MANTO (Inside, dreaming.)

Horses' hooves sound
On sacred ground,
Demi-gods are nigh us.

CHIRON

Quite right!
Just open your eyes!

MANTO (Waking.)
Welcome! I see you don't keep away.

CHIRON
And your temple's still here to stay!

MANTO
You still gallop round, untiringly?

CHIRON
And you, as ever, sit peacefully,
While I enjoy circling round.

MANTO
I wait, and Time circles me I've found.
And him?

CHIRON
The shadowy night
Has whirled him to our sight.
Helen he wants to win,
Helen's maddening him.
And he doesn't know where or how to begin:
Above all he deserves the Aesculapian healing.

MANTO
I like the ones who want impossible things.

(Chiron is already far off.)

Rash man, advance, here's joy for you!
This dark path leads to Persephone too.
Under Olympus' hollow foot, stealing,
She listens for secret, forbidden greeting.
I smuggled Orpheus down here once before:
Use your chance better! Quick! Be sure!

(They descend.)

IV

ON THE UPPER PENEUS AGAIN

THE SIRENS
Plunge now in Peneus' flood!
Here you can delight in swimming,
Song on song too, harmonising,
Does unlucky people good.
There's no healing without water!
With the shining crowd run we
Quick, to the Aegean Sea,
Where every joy's on offer.

(An Earthquake.)

The foaming wave sweeps wider,
Flowing in its bed no longer:
Earth shakes and waters roar,
Stony banks split once more.
We fly on! Come, one and all!
We'll not profit from this at all.
On! Each noble, happy guest,
To the ocean's cheerful zest,
Gleaming, where the trembling waves
Lightly heaving, wash the bays:
Where the moon's reflected light,
Wets with heaven's dew, at night.
There, a freely flowing life,
Here, an earthquake's fearful strife:
Every clever one, hasten on!
This place is a hideous one.

SEISMOS (Growling and jolting in the deep.)
Push again, with power,
With your shoulders, tower!
So the world above is ours,
Where all must yield to us.

THE SPHINXES
What a horrid shuddering,
Ugly, hideous juddering!
What a quivering and swaying,

365

Back and forwards,playing!
What an intolerable fuss!
But we'll not lose our place,
Even if all hell shakes.
Now a dome is lifted,
Wonderful. He's gifted
It to us, the ancient one,
Delos' isle was his creation,
Driven from out the wave,
To bring Latona aid.
He with striving, pushing, pressing,
Arms straight, and shoulders bending,
Like an Atlas in his action,
Lifts rock and earth, in motion,
Shingle, gravel, sand: the floors
All along our peaceful shores.
Rips our vale's quiet surface up,
Crosswise, with a single cut:
Fiercely, and unwearied,
A colossal caryatid,
Bears a fearsome weight of boulders,
Still buried, downwards to his shoulders:
But he'll come no further, now,
The Sphinxes' place is here, we vow.

SEISMOS
I myself achieved all this,
Man should admit it, finally:
If I'd not jolted and shaken it,
How could the world be so lovely? –
How could your peaks stand so high,
In the pure and splendid blue,
If I'd not pushed them to the sky,
Picturesque and charming too?
Then, thinking of my high ancestry,
Night and Chaos, I behaved badly,
And, a company of Titans, we
With Pelion and Ossa played madly,
Romping round in youthful glee,
Till, we tired of it, at last,
And set both mountains, wickedly,
On Parnassus, as a double hat....
There, now, Apollo's sweet retreat,
With the happy band of Muses.

And Jupiter, thunderbolts complete:
I even raised the high seat he uses.
So now with monstrous striving
I've pushed this upwards, from the deep,
And call, aloud, to their new being,
The joyful dwellers of the steep.

THE SPHINXES

One would think long ago,
This was lifted to the sky,
Had we not seen from down below,
How it wormed its way on high.
A bushy forest covers it,
And rock on rock is piled around:
Sphinxes don't care about it,
It won't disturb our sacred ground.

THE GRYPHONS

Gold in leaves, and gold in spangles,
Through the cracks, see, it tremble.
Don't you rob us of our treasure,
Ants, come, gather it together!

CHORUS OF ANTS

As this the giant ones
Threw to the sky,
You restless-footed ones,
Quick, climb it on high!
Rapidly in and out!
In cracks like these,
Every crumb about's
Worth you can seize.
You must uncover
Even the slightest,
In every corner
Quick as the brightest.
You must be everywhere,
Swarming around: then,
Only bring gold here!
Forget the mountain.

THE GRYPHONS

Come! Come! Heap the gold!
With our claws, we'll keep hold:

They are the best locks yet:
Great treasures they protect.

THE PYGMIES (Classical Dwarves.)
We've acquired some room,
How, it isn't clear.
Don't ask where we're from:
The main thing is we're here!
Life is cheerfully suited
To every sort of land:
Where a rock is lifted,
Dwarves are there, on hand.
Men and maids, quick and busy,
Exemplary, every pair:
In Paradise, once, maybe,
A similar race lived there.
But the best is here we find,
Thankfully our fate is blessed:
Mother Earth is always kind,
In the East as in the West.

THE DACTYLS (Little Ironworkers.)
If she can bring to light
The Little Ones in a night,
The Littlest Ones, she can make
And each will still find a mate.

THE PYGMY-ELDERS
Hurry: make space:
A convenient place!
Quickly, to work!
Strength, never shirk!
While we're in peace,
Our smithy increase,
To furnish the horde
With armour and sword.
All you ant-forms,
Moving in swarms,
Bring us the ore!
And all you Dactyls,
So many, so little,
You are commanded
To bring us the wood!
Heap it up higher,

Secretive fire,
Fetch coals as you should.

THE PYGMY GENERALISSIMO
Look lively, though,
With arrow and bow!
Shoot me the herons
Out in the ponds,
Countless they're nests,
Proud are their breasts,
Shoot them, together,
All in one blow!
So we can show
Helmets with feathers.

ANTS AND DACTYLS
Who now can save us!
We bring the iron
They forge the fetters.
It won't be soon
This thing will end,
Meanwhile we bend.

THE CRANES OF IBYCUS
Cries of murdered, calls of dying!
Fearful fluttering and flying!
Such deep moans, and such groans
Carry to our airy zones!
All already slaughtered,
Blood is reddening the water,
Misshapen dwarfish passions,
Steal the herons' noblest gems.
Now they're waving on their helmets:
Those fat-bellied bow-legged serpents.
You our armies' members,
Files of ocean-wanderers,
You we call to vengeance,
To kin-related business.
No one spare his strength or blood!
Show hatred always to that brood!

(They disperse, croaking.)

MEPHISTOPHELES (On the plain.)
Northern witches were easily controlled,
But over foreign spirits I've no hold.
The Blocksberg's a most convenient locale,
Wherever you are, you'll find yourself there still.
Dame Ilse watches for us, from her tall stone,
And Heinrich's still awake on his high throne,
At Elend, the Snorers snore away,
All's done for a thousand years and a day.
Who knows here if, where he sits, you see,
The Earth won't swell up beneath his feet?....
I wander happily through a level valley,
And in a moment there, thrown up behind me,
A mountain, true it's hardly to be called one,
But high enough to hide the Sphinxes' home –
Still, the valley breeds many a fire here,
And so illuminates this mad affair....
The magic sparks of that charming chorus.
Still enticing, vanishing, hover near us.
Gently now! All too used to nibbling,
Wherever we are, we find ourselves snatching.

THE LAMIAE (Drawing Mephistopheles after them.)
Faster, and faster!
And ever further!
Then hover again,
Chattering, staying.
It's such a pleasure,
To make the old sinner,
Pursue us, at whim,
Doing hard penance.
See, with his lame stance,
He hobbles forwards,
He stumbles onwards:
Trailing his leg, mind:
As we flee from him
He follows behind!

MEPHISTOPHELES (Standing still.)
Cursed fate! Cheated every which way!
Since Adam, seduced and led astray!
We grow old, but who grows wise?
Now, I'm tormented to the skies!
We know they're a wholly useless sex,

With laced-in bodies, and painted looks.
No healthy response at all, at bottom,
Wherever you grip, their limbs are rotten.
We know, we see, we grasp their ways,
But still we dance when woman plays!

THE LAMIAE (Pausing.)
Stop! He thinks: pauses: stays too:
Return, then, lest he should escape you!

MEPHISTOPHELES (Striding forwards.)
On, then! And let no indecision
Grip my flesh, some foolish cavil:
Since if there were no witches given,
Who the devil'd want to be a devil!

THE LAMIAE (Very graciously.)
We are circling round the hero!
Let love, in his heart, be sure to
Choose one of us for certain though.

MEPHISTOPHELES
True, in this uncertain shimmer,
You seem pretty girls together,
I'd like not to scorn you so.

EMPUSA (The demon. Pressing forward.)
Nor me! I'm the very thing,
Let me join your following.

THE LAMIAE
She's one too many in our crowd,
She'll spoil our game if she's allowed.

EMPUSA (To Mephistopheles.)
Greetings from Empusa, to you,
Your cousin, with the ass's hoof!
You've only a horse's hoof, it's true,
Yet, cousin, all the best to you!

MEPHISTOPHELES
I thought there were only strangers here,
Sadly, now, relatives appear:
It's the old story: in their dozens,

From Hartz to Hellas, always cousins!

EMPUSA

I act quickly with decision,
I can alter to your vision:
But to honour you today
My ass's head I display.

MEPHISTOPHELES

I see great things are signified,
By the relationship implied:
Be that as it may, yet I,
The ass's head will still deny.

THE LAMIAE

That ugly thing gives the frights,
To all that's lovely and delights:
The lovely and delightful before,
When she arrives, are so no more!

MEPHISTOPHELES

These cousins too, so soft and slender,
Are all suspicious, all that gender:
And beneath their cheeks, those roses,
There too, I fear, are metamorphoses.

THE LAMIAE

Try us then! We're many.
Grasp! And if you're lucky,
Secure the finest prize.
What was all that lusting for?
You're a miserable suitor,
Strutting, boasting of your size! –
Now he's mixing with our crowd:
Drop your masks: you're allowed:
And bare your being to his eyes.

MEPHISTOPHELES

I've chosen the loveliest one...

(Clasping her.)

Oh! What a skinny broom!

(Clasping another.)

And this one?…Wizened looks!

THE LAMIAE
You're worth better? Not in our books.

MEPHISTOPHELES
That little one might suit my plans…
A lizard gliding through my hands!
And snakelike are her slippery tresses.
I try the tall one to compare…
I grip a thyrsus without hair,
A pinecone, for a head, impresses!
What next?….A fat one, see,
Perhaps she'll enliven me:
Let's risk it, then! Here she is!
So puffy, flabby, in the East
There they'd prize her looks, at least…
But, oh! The puff-ball's split!

THE LAMIAE
Scatter widely, swaying, floating,
Surround him in dark flight, like lightning,
The trespassing witch's son!
Circles, terrifying, winging!
Bat-like in a silent flickering!
He'll be grateful when we've done.

MEPHISTOPHELES (Shaking himself.)
I'm no cleverer it seems, at all:
Here's absurd, and so's the north,
Here and there, the spirits tricky,
Poetry and people tacky.
Here too it's masquerade, I find:
As everywhere, the dance of mind.
I grasped a lovely masked procession,
And caught things from a horror show…
I'd gladly settle for a false impression,
If it would last a little longer, though.

(He loses his way among the rocks.)

Where am I now? Where will it wander?

There was a path, now it's a horror.
I got here by smooth and level ways,
And now the scree prevents escape.
I clamber up and down in vain,
How shall I find the Sphinx again?
I've never known anything like it, quite,
A mountain range in a single night!
I call it a lively witches' ride,
They've brought the Blocksberg, beside.

AN OREAD (A mountain nymph, from the natural rock.)
Climb up here! My range is old,
In primeval forms the peaks unfold.
Respect the steep and rocky stair,
Pindus' last slopes stretch there!
Unshakeable, once I stood, as now,
When Pompey fled across my brow.
Beside me, illusion's stones will go,
As soon as ever the cock shall crow.
I often see such fables thrown on high,
And suddenly sink back again and die.

MEPHISTOPHELES
Honour to you, you noble length,
Garlanded high with oaken strength!
The clearest moonlight never weaves
Through the darkness of your leaves –
I see a light, with parting glow,
Through the silent bushes go.
How all things come together!
Homunculus it is who's there!
Which way now, little fellow?

HOMUNCULUS
I flit about from hill to hollow
And, in the truest sense, I'd gladly 'be',
I'm so impatient, now, to smash the glass:
Only, so far, given what I can see,
I wouldn't want to do it in this pass.
But in confidence I confess I was
On the trail of two philosophers,
All I heard them say was: Nature, Nature!
I'll not part from them for anything,
They must know about earthly being:

And in the end I'll find out, too,
The cleverest place to travel to.
Mephistopheles

Well, do it on your own behalf, here.
Where the spirits all find their place,
The Philosopher can show his face.
To please you with his art and favour,
He'll make you a dozen, any flavour.
You'll have no intellect, unless you err.
If you want to 'be', make it your own affair!

HOMUNCULUS
Good advice too is not to be disdained.

MEPHISTOPHELES
Then off with you! I'll look around again.

(They part.)

ANAXAGORAS (To Thales.)
The stubborn mind will never ever bend:
What more do you need to be enlightened?

THALES
The waves will gladly bow to every wind,
Yet far from the jagged cliffs they'll end.

ANAXAGORAS
This cliff came about by fiery vapours.

THALES
By moisture living things were created.

HOMUNCULUS (Between the two.)
Let me walk beside you, please.
I myself desire to 'be'!

ANAXAGORAS
Have you, O Thales, in a single night
Brought a mount, from mud, to light?

THALES
Never has nature in her living flow,

Been bound to day, night, and hours, though.
She creates every form by rule,
At her greatest, force is never her tool.

ANAXAGORAS

Here it was! Furious Plutonic fire,
Monstrous Aeolian vapours thrown higher,
Broke through the ancient earth's smooth crust,
And raised the new mount with a swift up-thrust.

THALES

What more will come of it?
It's there, that's fine: let it sit.
One loses time in remonstrance,
And only lead the patient folk a dance.

ANAXAGORAS

The Mount quickly filled with Myrmidons,
Living in the rocky clefts and caverns:
Pygmies, ants and fingerlings,
And other active little things.

(To Homunculus.)

You've not striven hard for greatness,
Lived hermit-like, in narrowness:
If you can accustom yourself to power,
I'll crown you their king, in an hour.

HOMUNCULUS

What does Thales say?

THALES

It's not my recommendation:
With small means, you'll only do small actions:
With great means, the small achieve great ones.
Look there! A dark cloud, see, the cranes come!
So the excitable crowd will threaten,
And they would threaten the king so.
With sharpened beak, and grasping claw,
They tread the small ones to the floor:
Fate falls like lightning on those below.
It was a crime to kill the herons,
Caught on their quiet and peaceful ponds.

But that rain of arrowed slaughter,
Brings cruel and bloody vengeance after,
Summons the anger of their kin above,
To spill the Pygmies guilty blood.
What need for helmets, shields and spears?
What use the dwarves' heron-feather?
How Dactyls and Ants hide together!
The army wavers, flies, and disappears.

ANAXAGORAS (After a moment, solemnly.)
Till now I've praised the subterranean powers,
But turn, in this case, to higher ones than ours...
You! Above, always evergreen,
Triple-named, triply to be seen,
I cry to you, by my people's woe,
Diana, Luna, Hecate, so!
You, in deepest thought, the heartening,
You power profound, calmly shining,
Reveal your dark side's fearful shower,
Without spells, show your ancient power!

(A pause.)

Am I heard so swiftly?
Has my cry
To the deep sky
Stirred Nature's ranks so quickly?
Already, greater, greater, nearing,
The Goddess' orbed throne appearing,
Monstrous, fearful to the sight!
With fires that redden in the night...
No closer, threatening disc of power!
You'll straight destroy us: sea and shore!
So it was true, the Thessalian women,
Trusted with wicked magic runes,
Enchanted you from your circling path,
Wrested evil things from you, in wrath?...
The bright shield now darkens,
Suddenly splits: flashes, sparkles!
What a hissing! What a drumming!
Thunder, wind, and rain are coming! –
Humbled, on the steps of your throne! –
Forgive me! I brought this on, alone.

(He throws himself on his face.)

THALES
What has this man not heard and seen!
I'm not sure what it was that's been,
I'm not sensitive to it like him, I find.
We'd confess, these are crazy times,
The Moon is quivering quite gently,
In her place, though, just as formerly.

HOMUNCULUS
Look there, at the Pygmies seat!
The mount was round, now it's a peak.
I felt the monstrous recoil's thunder,
A rock fell from the Moon up yonder:
All alike, without asking too,
Friend and foe it squashed and slew.
I have to praise powers like those,
All creation in a single night,
Alike up there as down below,
Bringing a mountain-heap to light.

THALES
Peace! It was just an imaginary sight.
So farewell to that ugly brood!
You didn't become king, that's good.
Off now to the sea-festival, joy-blessed,
Where they'll honour a marvellous guest.

(They exit.)

MEPHISTOPHELES (Climbing up the opposite side.)
I'll have to climb through these steep rocks,
Through the roots of ancient oaks!
In my Hartz range, the smell of resin
Has a hint of pitch, almost as pleasant
As sulphur…but here, among the Greeks,
There's not a sniff, wherever one seeks:
But I'm still rather curious to know
How they make hellfire and brimstone glow.

A DRYAD (A wood nymph.)
In your own land, you're naturally adept,
Abroad, you don't know enough as yet.

You shouldn't think about home, here
With these ancient oak trees to revere.

MEPHISTOPHELES

One thinks of all one's left: besides,
What one's used to is paradise.
But tell me what's in that cave
Dimly crouching, a triple shape?

THE DRYAD

Daughters of Phorkyas! Enter the place,
And speak to them, if you're not afraid.

MEPHISTOPHELES

Why not! – I'll look, and I'm amazed!
Proud as I am, I must confess, though,
I've never seen the likes of those,
They're as foul as Ugliness any day....
How can one find deadly sin
Ugly at all when one has seen
This triple monstrosity?
We wouldn't let them cross the sill
Of the worst chamber of our hell.
But here, in the land of beauty, all things Greek,
Are famous now because they're so antique...
They seem to scent my presence: stirring,
Like vampire bats, squeaking, twittering.

THE PHORKYADS (The Three Graeae)

Give me the eye, Sisters, so I can find
Who's wandering so near our shrine.

MEPHISTOPHELES

Most Revered! Allow me near,
To receive a triple blessing here.
I come, as yet unknown it's true,
But distantly related, I think, to you.
I've already seen the elder gods,
Bowed low before Rhea and Ops:
I even saw the Fates, your sisters,
Yesterday, or the day before:
But I've never seen the likes of you.
I'm silenced now, and delighted too.

THE PHORKYADS

This spirit seems to have some sense.

MEPHISTOPHELES

I'm amazed no poet's had the intelligence
To sing of you. Tell me, how can that be?
I've never seen you properly painted:
The chisel should only try to carve you,
Not the likes of Pallas, Venus, Juno.

THE PHORKYADS

Deep in solitude and stillest night,
No one ever thought to show us three aright.

MEPHISTOPHELES

How could they? Here, concealed from view.
You can't see anyone: and they can't see you.
You need to achieve a suitable place,
Where art and splendour share the space,
Where every day, as walking, living heroes,
With giant steps, each block of marble goes.
Where –

THE PHORKYADS

Be silent, and don't tempt us to roam!
What use would it be to us, to be better known?
Born in the night, and related to the night,
To ourselves, almost: to others quite out of sight.

MEPHISTOPHELES

In that case, there's little more to say:
One can oneself to others still betray.
One eye's enough for three, one tooth as well:
Then it should be mythically possible,
To contain three beings in two,
And leave me the third form, too.
For a little while.

A PHORKYAD

What do you think? Shall we try?

THE OTHERS

Let's! – But without the tooth and eye.

MEPHISTOPHELES
Now you've denied me the best features of all:
How can I show your strict and perfect form?

A PHORKYAD
Shut one eye, that's easy to do,
Let one greedy tooth show too,
In profile you'll at once achieve
A sisterly likeness, to deceive.

MEPHISTOPHELES
Many thanks! Done!

THE PHORKYADS
Done!

MEPHISTOPHELES (As a Phorkyad, in profile.)
Already I'm one,
Of Chaos's well-beloved sons!

THE PHORKYADS
We're Chaos's daughters, of undisputed right.

MEPHISTOPHELES
O shame, now I'll be called a hermaphrodite.

THE PHORKYADS
What a beauty in our sisterly trio!
We've two eyes, and two teeth now.

MEPHISTOPHELES
I'll hide myself from every eye, as well,
And frighten devils in the lakes of Hell.

V

ROCKY COVES IN THE AEGEAN SEA

(The Moon, lingering, at the zenith.)

THE SIRENS (Lying on the cliffs round about, playing flutes and singing.)
Though the Thessalian witch-women
Wickedly, dragged you down to them,
With their horrors, long ago, in the dark,
Look quietly down, now, from the arc
Of night, on waves of glittering sparks:
Mildly flashing, bright crowds, these:
Shine now upon the swelling seas,
Which raise themselves from the deep!
We're sworn to serve you, thus,
Sweet Luna, show grace to us.

THE NEREIDS AND TRITONS (As marvels of the deep.)
Sound out loud, with clearer tones,
Ringing through the sea's wide zones:
Call the peoples of the deep!
Before the storm's ravening face,
We sank to the stillest place,
Now we're drawn, by singing, sweet.
See, how we've adorned ourselves,
In our great delight, as well,
With our crowns, so nobly gemmed,
And our belts with spangles hemmed!
These spoils, now, before you, we lay,
Treasures, shipwrecked here, and swallowed,
Your enticing songs they followed,
You the daemons of our bay.

THE SIRENS
We know well, in ocean freshness,
Fishes play in slippery smoothness,
Flickering lives, devoid of pain:
Yet you festive crowds that stray
We would rather find today,
That you're more than fish, again.

THE NEREIDS AND TRITONS

Before we came to meet you,
We were thinking of that too:
Speed away now, sisters: brothers!
It only needs the slightest journey,
For most effective proof that we,
Certainly, are more than fishes.
(They swim off.) The Sirens

They've vanished in a moment!
To Samothrace they're bent,
Gone, with a favourable breeze.
What is it they think they'll see,
In the realm of the noble Cabiri?
They're gods! But wondrously strange,
Always causing their forms to change,
Never knowing what they might be.
Stay at your clear height,
Sweet Luna, graceful light,
So we'll remain nocturnal,
Not chased by the diurnal!

THALES (On the shore, to Homunculus.)
I'd gladly lead you to old Nereus:
His home's not far away and cavernous,
But his head, it's of the very stubbornest,
He's a sour-top, and quite the nastiest.
The whole human race can't satisfy
Him, the grumbler, and needn't try.
Yet to him the future is revealed,
And so all show respect, and yield
Him honour in his high position:
He's done quite well by many a one.

HOMUNCULUS
Then let's try him, and hurry on!
My glass and flame won't fail our mission.

NEREUS (The sea-god.)
Are those human voices, in my ear?
How quickly my deepest anger stirs!
Forms, reaching for the gods, in their endeavour,
Yet condemned to be themselves, forever.
In ancient times I had heavenly rest,
Yet drove myself to act well to the best:

And then, when I'd finished what I'd done,
It was quite clear that nothing had been won.

THALES
And yet, Old Man of the Sea, we trust you:
You're the Wise: so don't drive us from you!
See this flame, he's almost human, really,
He yields himself to your advice, completely.

NEREUS
What advice! Has Mankind valued my advice?
A wise word's frozen in a stubborn ear.
No matter how often some harsh action strikes,
People remain as self-willed as before.
I warned Paris himself, in a fatherly way,
Before the foreign girl tempted him to stray.
He stood bravely on the shore of Greece,
And I told him what my Spirit could see:
The smoke-filled air, the streaming blood,
Glowing timbers, slaughter's flood,
Troy's day of judgement, caught in verse,
Its horrors known for ten thousand years.
The old man's words seemed idle to the young,
He followed his need, and Ilium was gone –
A bloody corpse, frozen with ancient pain,
For Pindus' eagles, a literary gain.
Ulysses too! Didn't I tell him about
Circe's wiles, that Cyclopean lout?
The indecision in his own shallow mind,
And all of it! What benefit did he find?
Till, late indeed, the ocean favoured him more,
And brought him, wave-tossed, to a friendly shore.

THALES
Such behaviour brings the wise man pain,
Yet the good will chance it all again.
An ounce of thanks will still please them deeply,
Outweighing tons of ingratitude completely.
And it's nothing slight we ask of you:
The boy here wants to exist, and wisely too.

NEREUS
Don't ruin such a rare mood as this!
Greater needs await me, today, than his:

I've summoned all my daughters here to me,
The Dorides, the Graces of the Sea.
Neither Olympus, nor your lands can show
Such lovely forms, with such delicate flow,
They fling themselves, with graceful actions,
From sea-horses to Neptune's stallions,
Blending so sensitively with the element,
That they seem made of foam, to all intent.
In a play of colours, on Venus' chariot shell,
Galatea, the loveliest, comes to me, as well,
Who, since Cypris turned away from us,
Rules as the new divinity of Paphos.
And so, heiress, for ages now, the sweet one,
Holds town, and temple, chariot and throne.
Away! It's time for a father's enjoyments,
Hearts without hate, lips without judgements.
Away, to Proteus! Ask that wondrous man:
How man exists, and changes, if he can.

(He vanishes into the sea.)

THALES
We'll achieve nothing by that game,
Meet Proteus: he'll vanish, just the same:
And if he stays, he'll only tell you,
What will amaze you, and confuse you.
But you've need of such advice,
Well, make tracks, then, and we'll try!

(They depart.)

THE SIRENS (On the rocks above.)
What is it we see whitening
The realms of ocean, brightening?
As when the wind prevails,
And shows the snowy sails,
So the Ocean's daughters,
Transfigured, light the waters.
Let us clamber shore-wards,
So we can hear their voices.

THE NEREIDS AND TRITONS
What in our hands we treasure,
Will give you all great pleasure.

Chelone's turtle shield
The shining form we wield:
On it gods we're bringing:
Your noblest songs, be singing.

THE SIRENS
Little in form,
Great in the storm,
Saving the shipwrecked,
Gods always respected.

THE NEREID AND TRITONS
We bring the peaceful Cabiri
To lead in your festivity,
Since in their holy presence,
Neptune's always pleasant.

THE SIRENS
We're attendant on you:
When a ship broke in two,
Their sovereign power too,
Protected the crew.

THE NEREIDS AND TRITONS
We've brought three of them along,
The fourth said he wouldn't come:
He said he was the real one,
The only thinker of the squadron.

THE SIRENS
One god will always mock
At some other god.
Honour all their courtesy,
Be fearful of their injury.

THE NEREIDS AND TRITONS
Actually, there are seven.

THE SIRENS
Where are the other three, then?

THE NEREIDS AND TRITONS
We really can't tell you that,
On Olympus one might ask:

There the eighth pines away,
No one thinks of him today!
Granted us in mercy,
But not yet completely.
These, the incomparable,
Ever wider yearning,
Hungering, are longing
For the unattainable.

THE SIRENS

We're ones who know
Where it's enthroned,
To moon and to sun,
We pray: and it's done.

THE NEREIDS AND TRITONS

See how our great glory grows,
We lead them to the feast!

THE SIRENS

The heroes of ancient story,
Are deficient now in glory,
Whatever we might be told:
Though they won the fleece of gold,

You're the cabiri.
(repeated as a full chorus.)

'though they won the fleece of gold,

We're the cabiri'.
(The Nereids and Tritons move past.)

HOMUNCULUS

I see these unformed ones,
Like pots of shoddy clay,
Against them wise men run,
And break their heads today.

THALES

That's what men ask of the dust:
The coin gains value from its rust.

PROTEUS (Unnoticed.)

It pleases me, an old connoisseur of fable!
The odder it is, the more respectable.

THALES
Where are you, Proteus?

PROTEUS (Like a ventriloquist, apparently far, and close to.)
Here! Here, too!

THALES
An old joke, which I'll forgive you:
No idle words for a friend, please!
I know you're trying to deceive.

PROTEUS (As if from the distance.)
Farewell!

THALES (Quietly to Homunculus.)
He's quite near. So, light, afresh!
He's just as curious as any fish:
And whatever form he hides in,
A flame will easily entice him.

HOMUNCULUS
I'll pour out a whole flood of light,
But soft, so the glass is still all right.

PROTEUS (In the form of a giant turtle.)
What shines with such grace and beauty?

THALES (Covering up Homunculus.)
Good! If you wish, come close to see.
It's worth a little trouble, if you can:
Show yourself two-footed like a man.
At our discretion, and by our favour.
We'll show you what we're hiding here.

PROTEUS (In a noble form.)
You still know all the worldly tricks.

THALES
Changing shape is what you still like best.

(He reveals Homunculus.)

PROTEUS (Astonished.)
A shining dwarf! That, I've never seen!

THALES
He seeks advice, and would gladly 'be'.
He is, as I've heard him say before,
Quite miraculously, only half born.
He's not lacking in mental qualities,
But short of physical capabilities:
Only the glass has given him weight at all,
He'd gladly be embodied, first of all.

PROTEUS
You are a true virgin's son,
Before you should be, you're already one!

THALES (Whispering.)
From another point of view, it's critical:
I think it makes him hermaphroditical.

PROTEUS
All the easier to achieve success:
Whatever he gets will suit him best.
No need to think about it here:
In the ocean deep you must appear!
There, first, in miniature, one snatches,
Enjoying the smallest things to swallow,
Bigger and bigger, with what one catches,
Forming the higher being to follow.

HOMUNCULUS
Here quite gentle breezes blow,
It's open: the fragrance delights me so!

PROTEUS
I think so too, loveliest of youths!
And, further on, it's more enjoyable:
On that shoreline's slender tooth,
The watery halo's indescribable.
There we'll see the crowds near to,
Drifting smoothly, to our view,
Come with me!

389

THALES
I'll keep you company.

HOMUNCULUS
A triply odd spirit-journey!

VI

THE TELCHINES OF RHODES

(The Telchines, on sea-horses and dragons, wielding Neptune's trident.)

CHORUS OF TELCHINES (The nine dog-headed Children of the Sea)
Oh, we are the ones who once forged Neptune's trident,
With which he controls the tumultuous torrent.
When the thunder erupts from the heavens, and rumbles,
Neptune will reply to those terrible grumbles:
And however the lightning zig-zags above us,
Breaker upon breaker beneath will splash upwards:
And whatever struggles between them in terror,
Long hurled all about, the deep seas will devour:
And that's why he's loaned us his sceptre today –
Now we float, calm and light, in our festive display.

THE SIRENS
You, to Helios consecrated,
You, with bright day's blessing freighted,
Greetings to this hour when
Luna's high worship rules again!

THE TELCHINES
Loveliest goddess of all in your sphere above!
To hear your brother praised, is something you love.
To blessed Rhodes lend an ear, now, from the sky,
Where an endless Paean, to him, rises on high.
He begins the day's course: he ends it again,
He eyes us all with his radiant fiery eye, then.
The mountains, the city, the sea and the strand,
Please the great god, lovely and bright is the land.
No mist drifts above us, and if one appears,
A ray, and a breeze: and the island shows clear!
There the high god's in hundreds of statues displayed,
As a youth, and a giant, the mild and the grave.
We were the first to carve forms: we began
The depiction of gods in the image of Man.

PROTEUS
Let them sing on then, and let them boast!
To the sun's sacred rays, a living host,

All their works are an empty jest.
They melt and shape untiringly:
And once, in bronze, it's plain to see,
They think they've caught the very best.
What happens at last to these proud ones?
The god's statues standing high –
An earthquake tosses to the sky:
Long since, they're all melted down.
Earth's toil, whatever else it may be,
Is nothing still, but drudgery:
The waves grant a life that's better:
I'll bear you to eternal waters,As Proteus-Dolphin. (Transforming himself.)

That's soon done!
Now you'll find your fairest luck:
I'm carrying you across my back,
To wed you with the ocean.

THALES
Yield to your praiseworthy wish,
Start at the beginning, with the fish!
Be ready for the swiftest working!
Be ruled by the eternal norms,
Move through a thousand, thousand forms,
And you'll ascend in time to Man.

PROTEUS
With spirit, join the watery plan,
Equal in size, where all began,
And move here as you wish to do:
Don't wrestle with the higher orders:
Once man, inside mankind's borders,
Then all will be over with you.

THALES
That's as may be: it's still fine,
To be a real man, in your own time.

PROTEUS (To Thales.)
As long as it's someone of your kind!
You don't just live for some brief time:
With your pale and ghostly peers,
I've watched you already for hundreds of years.

THE SIRENS (On the rocky cliffs.)
What's that ring of little clouds, set
In a circle round the moon?
They are doves, by love ignited,
Winged, white as winter noon.
All her ardent flocks of birds:
Paphos, now, has sent to us,
So our festival's completed,
Sweet and clear our happy bliss!

NEREUS (Approaching Thales.)
Though some nocturnal wanderer
Might call it only airy moonshine:
We spirits think it something other,
It's one true meaning we can find:
They are doves that accompany
My daughter in her moving shell.
Wondrous flights of artistry,
Learnt in ancient times, as well.

THALES
I too think that thing is best,
That can please the real man,
And in warm and silent nest,
Keep living Sacredness to hand.

PSYLLI AND MARSI (Peoples of Italy and North Africa. On sea-bulls, sea-heifers and sea-rams.)
In the hollow caves of Cyprus
Not yet rocked, by the sea-god,
Not yet shaken, by old Seismos,
Breathed on, by eternal breezes,
And, as in the ancient days,
Delighting in peaceful ways,
With us Venus' chariot stays,
And through nocturnal murmurs,
Through the sweet entwining waters,
We lead the loveliest of daughters,
Unseen by newer generation.
Travelling on our gentle journey
No winged lion, or eagle fear we,
Neither cross nor crescent,
Though it's throned in heaven,
Though it moves and sways,

Though it drives and slays,
Crops, towns, in ruin lays.
We, swiftly bring on
The loveliest of women.

THE SIRENS
Lightly now, and gently go,
Round the chariot, ring on ring,
Often weaving, row by row,
All in order, round it, snaking,
Approach you active Nereids
Sturdy women, sweetly wild,
Tender Dorides bring, amidst,
Galatea, Mother's child:
Most, so goddess-like her calm,
Worthy of immortality,
Yet enticing, with her charm,
As human femininity.

THE DORIDES (In Chorus, mounted on dolphins, passing Nereus.)
Lend us, Luna, light and shadow,
Clarity for flowering youth!
Charming husbands here we show:
Plead for them with our father, too.

(To Nereus.)

They are boys, whom we rescued
From the breaker's teeth, and then,
In the reeds and mosses bedded,
Warmed them back to life again,
Now with glowing kisses they
Must thank us truly here today:
Look with favour now on them!

NEREUS
Here there's a dual prize, I find, to treasure:
You show compassion, and it brings you pleasure.

THE DORIDES
Father, praise our mission, all,
And sanction our fond request,
Let us hold them fast, immortal,

On each young eternal breast.

NEREUS

Be happy with your handsome catch,
Accept the youngsters here, as men:
I can't myself grant what you ask,
Since Zeus alone can make it happen.
The waves that heave and rock you
Leave no place for love to stand,
So when this inclination leaves you,
Send them quietly back to land.

THE DORIDES

Sweet boys, you are so dear to us,
But sadly we must separate:
We asked eternal faithfulness,
But the gods forbid that fate.

THE YOUNG MEN

We're the valiant sailor lads,
If you'd refresh us further,
We've never had it quite so good
And we'll never have it better.

(Galatea approaches on her shell-chariot.)

NEREUS

It's you, my darling!

GALATEA

O father! Delight!
Linger, you dolphins, I'm gripped by the sight.

NEREUS

Past already, they're moving past,
Wheeling in circular motion:
What care they for the heart's deep emotion!
Ah, if they'd just take me with them, at last!
And yet, a single glance gives here,
Something that will last all year.

THALES

Hail! Hail! Anew!
How happy I feel, too,

Pierced by the Beautiful and True....
All things came from the watery view!
All things are sustained by water!
Ocean, grant us your realm forever.
If you didn't produce the clouds,
No flowing streams would be allowed,
The rivers wouldn't roar and shout,
The streams would never bubble out,
Where would hill, plain, and world be then?
The freshness of life's what you maintain.

AN ECHO (A chorus from the collective circles.)
The freshness of life flows back from you, again.

NEREUS
Floating, turning, they change place,
Far off, no longer face to face:
In extended linking circles,
Appropriate to the festival,
The countless company's weaving.
But Galatea's throne of shell,
I see it clearly: see it still.
It gleams like a star,
Through the throng,
A crowd, the Beloved shines among!
Though just as far,
It shimmers bright and clear,
Always true, and near.

HOMUNCULUS
In this delightful ocean
Whatever I may shine on,
Is all sweet and fair.

PROTEUS
In this living ocean,
You light's shining motion,
First rings in splendour there.

NEREUS
At the heart of the throng, what mystery
Offers itself for our eyes to see?
What shines round the shell, at Galatea's feet?
Now waxing powerful, now gentle and sweet,

As if it were fed by the pulses of Love.

THALES

Homunculus, drawn there by Proteus....
Those are the symptoms of imperious yearning,
I'd expect now the sound of an anguished ringing:
He'll shatter himself on the glittering throne:
He glitters, he flashes, already, it's done.

THE SIRENS

What fiery wonder transfigures the waves, there,
As one on another sparkles and breaks, there?
It flashes and flickers and brightens towards us:
The nocturnal tracks of the bodies shine round us,
And everything near is surrounded with flame:
So let Eros rule, now: who started the game!
Hail to the sea! Hail to the waves!
Circled, now, by the sacred blaze!
Hail to water! Hail to fire!
Hail to the rarest sweet desire!

ALL IN CHORUS

Hail, the gently flowing breeze!
Hail, hidden caverns of the seas!
Be honoured now, for evermore,
You, the Elemental four!

Act III

I

Before the Palace of Menelaus in Sparta

(Helen enters with the Chorus of Captive Trojan Women. Panthalis is leader of the Chorus.)

HELEN
I, Helen the much admired yet much reviled,
Come from the shore, where recently we landed,
Still drunk with the violent rocking of those waves
That from Phrygian heights on high-arched backs,
By Poseidon's favour, and the East Wind's power,
Carried us here to the coast of my native land.
There, below us, beside his bravest soldiers
King Menelaus, now, celebrates his return.
But you, bid me welcome, you, the lofty house
Tyndareus my father built when he returned,
Close by the slope of Pallas Athene's hill:
Here, where with Clytemnestra, in sisterhood, I
And Castor and Pollux, grew and happily played:
You, more nobly adorned than all Sparta's houses.
Be greeted by me, you honoured double doors!
Once, Menelaus the shining bridegroom came
To me, through your friendly inviting portals,
I, the one singled out from among so many.
Open to me once more, so that I might fulfil,
The King's command, truly, as a wife should.
Let me pass! And let everything be left behind,
That raged round me, till now, so full of doom.
For since, light in heart, I left this place behind,
Seeking out Venus' temple, in sacred duty,
Where instead a Trojan robber abducted me,
Many things have happened, men, far and wide,
Gladly tell of, though she's not so glad to hear them,
Round whom the story grew, and myth was spun.

CHORUS
O marvellous woman, don't disdain
Inheritance of the noblest estate!
For the highest fate's granted to you alone,

The glory of beauty that towers above all.
The Hero's name sounds his advance,
And proudly he strides:
But he bows down, most stubborn of men,
Before conquering Beauty, in mind and sense.

HELEN

Enough of that! I'm brought here by my husband,
I've been sent ahead by him, now, to his city:
But what the meaning of it is I can hardly guess.
Do I come as his wife? Do I come as the Queen?
Or a sacrifice, for a Prince's bitter pain,
And the ill fortune long endured by the Greeks?
I'm conquered: but am I a prisoner? I can't tell!
True, the Immortals appointed Fame, and Fate,
As the two ambiguous, doubtful companions
Of Beauty, to stand here at this threshold with me,
The gloomy, threatening presences by my side.
Even in the hollow ship my husband seldom
Gazed at me, or spoke an encouraging word.
He sat in front of me, as if in evil thought.
But scarcely had the foremost ship's prow greeted
Land, in that deep bay Eurotas' mouth has made,
Than he spoke to us, as the gods had urged him:
'Here my soldiers will disembark in ordered ranks,
I'll muster them, ranged along the ocean's-shore:
But you'll go on, ever on along the banks
Of sacred Eurotas, shining with bright orchards,
Guide the horses through gleaming water meadows,
Till of your lovely journey you make an end,
Where Lacedemon, once a rich spreading field,
Surrounded by austere mountains, was created.
Walk through the high-towered house of princes,
And summon the capable old Stewardess
Along with the maidservants I left behind,
Let her display the store of rich treasure to you,
That which your father left, and that I myself
Have added to, amassing it in war and peace.
You'll find it all still in the most perfect order:
It is a prince's privilege that he should find
That all is loyalty, on returning to his house,
All that he's left behind still in its proper place.
Since no slave has the power to effect a change.'

CHORUS

Let this treasure, so steadily massed,
Bring you delight, now, in eye and breast!
For the necklace bright, and the crown of gold,
Were resting, and darkening, in proud repose:
But enter now, and claim them all,
They'll quickly respond.
I love to see Beauty itself compete
Against gold and pearls and glittering gems.

HELEN

So again there came my lord's imperious speech:
'When you've examined all of it in due order,
Take as many tripods as you think you'll need,
And as many vessels as sacrifice requires,
To fulfil the customs of the sacred rites.
Take cauldrons, and basins, and circular bowls:
The purest of water from the holy fountains,
In deep urns: take care that you've dry wood too,
Such as will quickly catch fire, and hold all ready:
And finally don't forget a well-honed knife:
Everything else I'll leave for your decision.'
So he spoke, at the same time urging my going:
But he who commanded marked out nothing living
To be slain: to honour the Olympian gods.
Essential, but I'll think no more about it,
And leave all things in the hands of the gods:
They fulfil whatever is in their mind to do,
Whether or not we think it good or evil:
In either case we mortals must endure it.
Often the priest's heavy axe has been lifted,
From the bowed neck of the sacrificial victim,
So he could not slaughter it, being hindered,
By enemies near, or the gods' intervention.

CHORUS

What might happen, think not of that:
Queen, go on, now, step inside,
And be brave!
Good and evil come
Unannounced, to Mankind:
Though it's proclaimed, we'll not believe.
Troy still burned: did we not see
Death in our faces, shameful death:

And are we not here,
Your friends, happily serving,
Seeing the blinding sun in the sky
Seeing the Loveliest on Earth,
You, the kind: we the joyous?

HELEN

Let it be, as it will! Whatever awaits me,
I must go, swiftly, up to that royal house,
Long forsaken, often longed for, almost lost,
That's before my eyes once more: I know not how.
My feet don't carry me onwards so bravely, now,
Up those high steps, I skipped over as a child.

CHORUS

Sorrowful prisoners,
Oh, cast away, Sisters,
All your pain, to the winds:
Share in your mistress' joy
Share now in Helen's joy,
Who returns, truly late indeed,
To her father's hearth and home,
But with all the more firm a step,
Delightedly approaching.

Praise the sacred gods,
Creating happiness,
Bringing the wanderer home!
See the freed prisoner
Soar on uplifted wings,
Over harshness, while, all in vain,
The captives, so full of longing,
Pine away, arms still outstretched,
To the walls of their prison.

But a god snatched her up, then,
The far-exiled:
And from Ilium's fall,
Carried her back once more, home
To the old, to the newly adorned, her
Father's house,
From unspeakable
Rapture and torment,
Now, reborn, to remember

The days of her childhood.

PANTHALIS (As leader of the Chorus.)
Now leave behind the joyful path of your singing,
And turn your eyes towards the open doorway!
Sisters, what do I see! Surely the Queen returns
Waking towards us, again, with anxious steps?
What is it, great Queen? What can you have met with,
Within the halls of your house, instead of greetings,
To cause you such trembling? You can hide nothing,
Since I see your reluctance written on your brow,
And amazement competes there with noble anger.

HELEN (Who has left the doors open, in her turmoil.)
A daughter of Zeus is stirred by no common fear,
No lightly passing hand of Terror can touch her:
Only the Horror that the womb of ancient Night,
Raised from chaos, and shaped in its many forms,
In glowing clouds that shoot, upwards and outwards,
From the peak's fiery throat, to shake the hero's breast.
So here today the Stygian gods have marked
The entrance to my house with terror: and gladly
I'd take myself far away, like a guest let go,
Far from this often trodden, long yearned for threshold.
But no! I've retreated here now, into the light,
And you Powers will drive me no further, whoever
You are. Rather, I'll think of some consecration,
So the hearth-fire, cleansed, greets the wife, as the lord.

THE LEADER OF THE CHORUS
Noble lady, reveal to your maidservants here,
Who help you reverently, what has happened.

HELEN
You'll see what I saw yourselves, with your own eyes,
If ancient Night has not, straight away, swallowed it,
That shape of hers: withdrawn it to her heart's depths.
But I'll picture it to you in words, so you'll know:
As, with those recent orders in mind, I trod,
Gravely, through the palace's innermost room,
Awed by the silence of the gloomy corridors,
No sound of busy labour greeting my ears,
No sound of prompt, diligent effort meeting my eye,
No Stewardess appeared, and no maidservants,

No courtesy such as usually greets the stranger.
But as I approached closer to the hearth stone
Beside the glowing ashes that remained, I saw
A veiled woman, vast shape, seated on the floor,
Not like one who's asleep, but one deep in thought.
I summoned her to work, with words of command,
Thinking she was the Stewardess whom my husband,
Had placed there perhaps, with foresight, when he left.
But she still sat there, crouched and immoveable:
At last, stirred by my threats, she raised her arm,
As if she gestured me away from hearth and hall.
I turned aside from her, angrily, and sped,
To the steps where the Thalamos is adorned
On high, and close beside it the treasure house:
Suddenly that strange shape sprang up from the floor,
Barring my way, imperiously, showing herself,
Tall and haggard, with hollow, blood-coloured gaze:
A shape so weird that mind and eye were troubled.
But I talk to the wind: for words weary themselves
Trying to conjure forms, vainly, like some creator.
See for yourselves! She even dares the daylight!
Here am I mistress, till the King, my lord, shall come.
Phoebus, beauty's friend, drives the horrid spawn of Night
To caverns underground, or he binds them fast.

(Phorkyas appears on the threshold, between the doorposts.)

CHORUS

Much have I learned, although the locks
Curl youthfully still across my temples!
Many the terrible things I've seen,
The soldiers' misery, Ilium's night,
When it fell.

Through the clouded, and dust-filled turmoil,
The press of warriors, I heard the gods
Calling terribly, heard the ringing
Iron voice of Discord through the field,
City-wards.

Ah! They still stood there, Ilium's
Walls, but the glow of the flames
Soon ran from neighbour to neighbour,
Ever spreading, hither and thither,

With the breath of their storm,
Over the darkening city.
Fleeing, through smoke and heat, I saw
Amid the tongues of soaring fire,
The fearful angry presence of gods,
Marvellous, those striding figures,
Like giants, they were, through the gloom,
The fire-illumined vapour.

Did I see that Confusion,
Or did the fear-consumed Spirit
Create it? Never will I be able,
To say, but I'm truly certain
Of this, that here I see, Her,
Monstrous shape to my eyes:
My hand could even touch Her,
If terror did not restrain me,
Saving me from danger.

Which of the daughters
Of Phorkyas are you?
Since I liken you
To that family.

Are you perhaps one of the Graeae,
A single eye and a single tooth,
Owned alternately between you,
One born of greyness?

Monster, do you dare
Here, next to Beauty,
Show yourself to Phoebus,
And his knowing gaze?

Then step out before him regardless:
Since he'll not look at what's ugly,
Just as his holy eye,
Has never seen shadow.
Yet we mortals are compelled, ah,
By unfortunate gloomy fate,
To the unspeakably painful sight
She, reprehensible, ever ill fated,
Provokes in the lover of Beauty.

Yet hear me then, if you boldly
Encounter us: hear the curse,
Hear the threat of every abuse,
From the condemnatory mouth of the fortunate,
Whom the gods themselves have created.

PHORKYAS (The transformed Mephistopheles.)
The saying is old, with meaning noble and true,
That Beauty and Shame, together, hand in hand,
Never pursue the same path, over green Earth.
Such ancient, deep-rooted hatred lives in both,
That whenever they meet, by chance, on the way,
The one will always turn her back on her rival.
Then quickly and fiercely each goes on, again,
Shame downcast, but Beauty mocking in spirit,
Till in the end Orcus' dark void shall take her,
If age hasn't, long before then, tamed her pride.
So now I find you, impudent, come from abroad,
With overflowing arrogance, like the cranes,
Their noisily croaking ranks, high overhead,
Their long cloud, sending its creaking tones, down here,
Tempting the quiet traveller to look upwards:
Yet they pursue their way, while he follows his:
And that's the way it will be with us as well.
What then are you, wild Maenads or Bacchantes,
That dare to rage round the great royal palace?
Who are you, then, who howl at this high house's
Stewardess, like a pack of bitches, at the moon?
Do you think it's hidden from me what race you are?
You brood, begotten in battle, raised on slaughter,
Lusting for men, the seducers and the seduced,
Draining the soldiers' and the citizens' powers!
To see your crowd's like watching a vast swarm
Of locusts settle here, darkening the fields.
You the wasters of others labour! Nibbling,
Destroying, the ripening crops of prosperity!
Defeated, bartered, sold in the market, you!

HELEN
Who abuses the servants before the mistress,
Presumptuously usurping a wife's true rights?
Only to her is it given to praise whatever's
Praiseworthy: and to punish what is at fault.
I'm well content, as well, with all the services

They provided to me, when Ilium's great might,
Stood beleaguered, and fell in ruins: none the less
Just as we've endured the wretched wandering
Journey, where often one thinks only of oneself,
So here I expect it now from a happier crew:
A lord asks how slaves serve, not what they are.
So be silent, then, and no longer jeer at them.
If you've guarded the king's house well until now,
In place of the mistress, such is to your credit:
But now that she comes herself, you should draw back,
Lest you find punishment instead of fair reward.

PHORKYAS
Disciplining servants is a prerogative
That the noble wife of a king, loved by the gods,
Has duly earned by years of wise discretion.
Since you, acknowledged, take up your former place
Once more, as Queen, and mistress of the house,
Resume the slackened reins again, and rule here,
Hold the treasure in your keeping, and us with it.
But first of all defend me, who am the elder,
Against this crowd, who if they are compared
To your swanlike beauty, are only cackling geese.

THE LEADER OF THE CHORUS
How ugly ugliness looks, next to beauty.

PHORKYAS
How stupid the lack of reason, next to sense.

(From here on the Chorus answer in turn, stepping forward one by one.)

FIRST MEMBER OF THE CHORUS
Tell us of Father Erebus: tell us of Mother Night.

PHORKYAS
Speak about Scylla, sweet sister of your race.

SECOND MEMBER OF THE CHORUS
There are plenty of monsters in your family tree.

PHORKYAS
Go down to Orcus, look for your tribe down there!

THIRD MEMBER OF THE CHORUS
Those who are down there are far too young for you.

PHORKYAS
Try your arts of seduction on old Tiresias.

FOURTH MEMBER OF THE CHORUS
Orion's nurse was your great great-grandchild.

PHORKYAS
I suspect that the Harpies raised you all, on filth.

FIFTH MEMBER OF THE CHORUS
What do you feed your perfect leanness on?

PHORKYAS
Not on the blood that youall lust so much for.

SIXTH MEMBER OF THE CHORUS
You hunger for corpses, you, foul corpse yourself!

PHORKYAS
Vampire's teeth gleam there, in your shameless muzzle.

THE LEADER OF THE CHORUS
It would shut yours tight, if I called out who you are.

PHORKYAS
Well say your own name first: that'll solve the riddle.

HELEN
I intervene, not in anger but in sorrow,
To forbid this alternating discord!
A ruler meets with nothing that's more harmful
Than private disputes of his quarrelling servants.
Then his firm orders are no longer answered
With swiftly answering and harmonious action,
Instead, wilful commotion roars around him:
Self-composure lost, he abuses them in vain.
Not only that. Unacceptably, in anger,
You've summoned the wretched shapes of dreadful forms,
They surround me, so I feel I'm being whirled
To Orcus, from these familiar paternal fields.
Am I remembering? Did delusion grip me?

Was I all of that? Am I, now? And shall be still,
Symbol of dream and fear, to those who waste cities?
The maidservants shudder, but you, the eldest,
Stand there calmly: speak words of reason to me!

PHORKYAS

The favour of the gods seems only a dream
To one who recalls the troubles of long ages.
But you, blessed, beyond all aim and measure,
Quickly inflamed to every sort of daring risk,
Only found fires of love, in the realm of life,
Theseus, driven by lust, abducted you, a child,
He strong as Hercules: a man nobly formed.

HELEN

He carried me off, a slender ten-year old fawn,
And caged me in Aphidnus' tower in Attica.

PHORKYAS

But soon freed, by the hands of Castor and Pollux,
A crowd of suitors, the heroes, swarmed round you.

HELEN

Yet, I freely confess, above all, Patroclus
The image of Achilles, had my secret favour,

PHORKYAS

But your father's will bound you to Menelaus,
The brave sea rover, the defender of his house.

HELEN

He gave him his daughter, and command of the state.
Hermione came from our married existence.

PHORKYAS

But while he disputed his right to far off Crete,
To you, the lonely, came all too handsome a guest.

HELEN

Why do you recall that semi-widowhood,
And all the terrible ruin it caused around me?

PHORKYAS

To me, a free-born Cretan, his same journey

Brought captivity and years of slavery.

HELEN
He ordered you here at once, as Stewardess,
Entrusting the fortress and his treasure to you.

PHORKYAS
Which you abandoned, for Ilium's high city,
And the inexhaustible delights of love.

HELEN
Not delights, be sure! All too bitter a sorrow
Was poured endlessly over my head and breast.

PHORKYAS
Yet they say that you appeared in dual form,
Seen in Troy and, at the same time, in Egypt.

HELEN
Don't confuse my clouded, wandering mind completely.
To this moment, I don't know which of them I am.

PHORKYAS
Then they say: Achilles became your companion,
Came, burning, from the empty realm of shadows!
He'd loved you before, opposing fate's command.

HELEN
As phantom, I bound myself to a phantom.
It was a dream, as the tales themselves tell.
I fade, now, become a phantom to myself.

(She sinks into the arms of the Chorus.)

Silence! Silence!
False-seeing one, false-speaking one, you!
Out of the terrible single-toothed
Mouth, what might be breathed, so,
Out of so frightful a throat of horror!
Now the malevolent, seemingly benevolent,
Wolf's anger under the woolly fleece,
Is more terrible to me than the jaws
Of the three-headed dog.
We stand here anxiously listening:

When? How? Where, will such malice
Break out now
From this predatory monster?

Now rather than friendly words, richly laced
With trust, waters of Lethe, sweet and mild,
You stir up all from the past,
The evil more than the good,
And instantly darken
The gleam of the present
And also the future's
Sweetly glimmering, hopeful dawn.

Silence! Silence!
So the Queen's spirit, now,
Almost ready to leave her,
Can still hold, and uphold
This, the form of all forms
On which the sun ever lighted.

(Helen has recovered, and stands in the centre again.)

PHORKYAS

Shining out from fleeting vapours, comes the sunlight of our day, here,
That when veiled could so delight us, but in splendour only blinds us.
As the world is open to you, when you show your lovely face, now,
Though they scorn me so as ugly, still I know the beautiful.

HELEN

I step, trembling, from the abyss that, in fainting, closed around me,
And would gladly rest my body, tired and weary are my limbs:
But it's proper for a Queen, then, as it is for all about her,
To be calm, and courageous, whatever harm shall threaten.

PHORKYAS

In your Majesty, and Beauty, standing here, now, before us,
Your look says it commands us. What do you command? Speak out.

HELEN

Prepare yourselves to atone for what your quarrel has neglected:
Hurry with your sacrifice, now, as the king himself commanded.

PHORKYAS

All is ready in the palace, bowls, and tripods, sharpened axe-blade,

For the sprinkling, incense burning: show me now the ready victim!

HELEN
That the king has failed to tell me.

PHORKYAS
He said nothing? Words of woe!

HELEN
What's this woe that overcomes you?

PHORKYAS
Queen, it means you must be slaughtered!

HELEN
I?

PHORKYAS
And them.

CHORUS
Oh, pain and suffering!

PHORKYAS
You will fall beneath the axe.

HELEN
Presaged, though still dreadful: I, alas!

PHORKYAS
There's no escaping.

CHORUS
Oh! And us? What happens to us?

PHORKYAS
She will die a noble death, then:
But you'll hang in rows together, struggling, all along the rafters
Holding up the gabled roof there, as bird-catchers dangle thrushes.

(Helena and the Chorus stand stunned and alarmed, in striking composed groups.)

Phantoms! – Frozen images, you stand, parted
From that light you can't belong to, in your terror.
Men, and the tribe of phantoms you resemble,
Will never willingly forgo the sunlight:
But none are saved from their fate, or can defer it.
All know it's true, but only a few accept it.
Enough, you're lost! Now, quickly: start the work.

(She claps her hands: muffled dwarfish forms appear in the doorway, and
quickly carry out her orders.)

This way, you spheres, shadowy rounded forms!
Roll over here: and do what harm you wish.
Set up the gold-horned altar that you carry,
Let the gleaming axe lie there on the silver rim,
Fill the urns with water to wash away
All the hideous stains of darkened blood.
Spread the rich carpets out, here, over the dust,
So the sacrifice can kneel in royal manner,
And be wrapped around, once the head is severed,
And buried decently there, and with due honour.

THE LEADER OF THE CHORUS
The Queen stands here beside us deep in thought,
The maidservants wither away like mown grass:
I think that I, as the eldest, am bound, in sacred duty,
To barter words with you, the eldest of all by far.
You're wise, experienced, and seem well-disposed,
And though this foolish crowd baited you in error,
Speak of a way to escape this fate, if you know it.

PHORKYAS
That's easily done: it depends on the Queen alone,
To save herself, and you her followers with her.
But decision is required, and of the swiftest.

CHORUS
Most honoured of Fates, wisest of Sibyls, you,
Hold the gold shears apart: bring both aid and light:
Already, we feel ourselves swinging, struggling,
Fearful, for our limbs would rather be dancing,
And afterwards rest, soft, on our lovers' breast.

HELEN

Let them be afraid! I feel pain but no terror:
Yet if rescue's possible, I gladly accept.
To the wise, far-seeing mind, the impossible
Is often revealed as possible. Speak: say on!

CHORUS

Speak, and tell us, tell us quickly: how we might escape the terror,
Dreadful nooses that still threaten, like some kind of evil necklace
Wound around our tender necks? Already we, oh, wretched creatures,
Feel the choking, suffocating, if you, Rhea, the great mother
Of the gods, won't show us mercy.

PHORKYAS

Have you the patience to listen, to long winded
Speeches, in silence? The history's endless.

CHORUS

Patience enough! While we're listening, we're alive.

PHORKYAS

He who stays at home to guard his noble wealth
And secures the high walls of his lofty dwelling,
And maintains his roof against the driving rain,
Will prosper in all the days of his long life:
But whoever, in guilt, crosses the square-cut stones
Of the sacred threshold, swiftly, with fleeing steps,
Will, indeed find the ancient place, on their return,
But altered in every way, if not overthrown.

HELEN

Why recount these familiar sayings here?
If you'd relate things: don't provoke annoyance.

PHORKYAS

It's simple fact, in no way a criticism.
Menelaus sailed from bay to bay, looting,
Skirted the coast and islands, aggressively,
Returned with the spoils that are rusting there.
Then he spent ten long years there in front of Troy:
And I don't know how many more, on the way home.
And how are things now with this place where we stand,
Tyndareus' noble house, and the region round?

HELEN

Do you embrace all scorn so completely
You can only open your mouth to criticise?

PHORKYAS

The vales were neglected for so many years,
Those that rise behind Sparta, to the northward,
Beyond Taygetus, from where, a living stream,
Eurotas, pours downward, then along our valley,
Flows by our broad reed-beds, to feed your swans.
Up there, in the mountain vales, a bold race settled,
Pushing southward from Cimmerian darkness,
And then built an inaccessible fortress there,
From which, at will, they harass land and people.

HELEN

Have they achieved all that? It seems unlikely.

PHORKYAS

They've had time, perhaps twenty years in all.

HELENA

Is there a leader? Are they a band of robbers?

PHORKYAS

Not robbers, but one of them acts as leader.
I don't curse him, though he attacked me too.
He might have taken all, but was satisfied
With gifts, not tribute, as he called them.

HELEN

How did he look?

PHORKYAS

Less than evil! He pleased me well.
He's vigorous, daring, and sophisticated,
An intelligent man: as few among the Greeks.
They call his race Barbarians, but I'm doubtful
If they are any crueller than those heroes
Who proved such devourers of men, before Troy.
I respected his greatness, and confided in him.
His fortress! You should see with your own eyes!
It's a great deal more than the clumsy masonry
Your father rolled together, higgledy-piggledy,

Cyclopean as a Cyclops, piling raw stone,
Over raw stone: there, instead there, it's all
Plumb line and balance: it's laid out by rule.
Look from outside! It rises straight to the sky,
So firm, tightly jointed – smooth as a steel mirror
To climb – that even your thoughts slide off!
And, inside, great courts with plenty of room,
Ringed by buildings, of every use and nature.
There you'll see pillars, columns, arches, quoins,
Balconies, galleries, facing inwards and outwards,
And coats of arms.

CHORUS
What arms are those?

PHORKYAS
Ajax carried
A writhing snake on his shield: you yourself saw it.
The Seven against Thebes also bore their symbols
On each of their shields, replete with meaning.
There you saw moons, and stars in the night sky,
Heroes and Goddesses, torches, ladders, swords,
And whatever fierce weapons threaten fine cities.
Our heroic band carries such images too,
In bright colours, bestowed by our ancestors.
There you see lions, eagles with beaks and claws,
Horns of oxen, wings, roses, and peacocks' tails,
Bands too made of gold, black, silver, blue and red.
The like of these hang in their halls, row on row.
In spacious halls, as wide as the whole wide world:
You could dance there!

CHORUS
Say then, are there dancers, there?

PHORKYAS
The best! A lively crowd of golden-haired youths.
The fragrance of youth! Paris was fragrant, thus,
When he grew close to the Queen.

HELEN
You mistake your role
Completely: now speak your closing lines to me!

PHORKYAS

No, you speak the last! Grave, and distinct say: Yes!
And I'll surround you with that fortress.

CHORUS

O, speak
That one short word, and save both yourself, and us!

HELEN

What? Do I fear King Menelaus would commit
Such a cruel offence as to make me kill myself?

PHORKYAS

Have you forgotten how he wreaked mutilation,
Unheard-of, on Deiphobus, dead Paris' brother,
Because he stubbornly claimed you, the widow,
And prized you? He cropped both nose and ears,
And disfigured him, there: It was terrible to see.

HELEN

Yes he did that, and he did it for my sake.

PHORKYAS

Because of it, now, he'll do the same to you.
Beauty is indivisible: he who owns it
Destroys it, rather than share a part of it.

(Trumpets sound in the distance: the Chorus starts in terror.)

As a trumpet call pierces the ear to grip
And tear the innards: Jealousy drives her claws
Into the breast of him who can never forget
What once he had, and lost, and no longer has.

CHORUS

Don't you hear the trumpets calling? Don't you see the flash of swords?

PHORKYAS

King and master, now be welcome, gladly I'll offer my account.

CHORUS

But, what of us?

PHORKYAS

In truth, you know that her death's before your eyes,
Find your own death there within them: there's no hope left for you.
(A Pause.)

HELEN
I ponder this simple thing that I might try.
You are a hostile daemon: I feel it deeply,
I'm fearful you'll still make evil out of good.
But then, I'll follow you to that fortress, there:
I know the rest: but what the Queen might conceal
Concerning it, mysteriously, in her heart,
Be unknown to all. Now, old one, lead the way!

CHORUS
O, how gladly we're going,
On hurrying feet:
Death is behind:
Before us again,
Towering fortress
Inaccessible walls.
Though they guard us as well
As Ilium's citadel,
Still in the end, it
Fell, through the basest of ruses.

(Mists rise and spread, obscuring the background, and the nearer part of the
scene, at will.)

What is this? How?
Sisters, look round!
Wasn't it loveliest day?
Strips of vapour hover about,
Rise from Eurotas' holy stream:
Already the loveliest
Reed-wreathed shore has vanished from sight:
And the proud, free, graceful
Gentle glide of the swans
Swimming in sociable joy,
I alas see, no more!

Yet still, still
I hear them calling,
In hoarse tones, calling afar!
Proclaiming death, they are speaking.

Ah, that to us they may not,
Instead of salvation promised,
Proclaim our ruin, at last:
To us, the swanlike, long,
Lovely, white-throated, and ah!
Our Queen born of the swan.
Woe to us, woe!

All's hidden already
Vapour's swirling around.
Now we can't see one another!
What's happening? Are we moving?

We're hovering with
Straggling steps along the ground?
Can't you see? Isn't that Hermes
Soaring ahead? Doesn't his gold wand gleam,
Beckoning us, ordering us back again
To the wholly joyless, and greyly-twilit,
Intangible, phantom-filled,
Overcrowded, ever-empty Hades?

Yes, at once, now, all is darkening, dully all the vapours vanish,
Grey with gloom, and brown as walls. Walls appearing to our vision,
Blank now to our clearer vision. A court now is it? Or a deep pit?
Fearful, though, in either case, now! Sisters, oh! We are imprisoned,
Captives, as we've never been.

SCENE II

THE INNER COURT OF THE CASTLE

(Surrounded with richly ornamented buildings of the Middle Ages.)

THE LEADER OF THE CHORUS
Hasty and foolish, and typical of womankind!
They hang on the moment, sport of every breeze,
Of every chance and mischance, never knowing
How to suffer either calmly! One's always certain,
Fiercely, to contradict the others, others her:
Only, they laugh or cry alike, in joy or pain.
Now, hush! And listen to what our high-minded
Mistress may decide, here, for herself and us.

HELEN
Pythoness, where are you? However you're named:
Come out from the arches of this dark fortress.
If you come from the wondrous lord and hero
To announce me, and ready a fit reception,
Accept my thanks, and lead me there quickly:
I wish my wanderings ended. I want to rest.

THE LEADER OF THE CHORUS
Queen, in vain, you look about in all directions:
That wretched shape has vanished, stayed perhaps
There in the vapour, out of whose depths we came,
I cannot tell how, so swiftly, without a footfall.
Perhaps she wanders lost in the vast labyrinth
Of these many castles wondrously merged in one.
Seeking high and princely greeting from her lord.
But see! There a crowd moves about in readiness.
Along galleries, at windows, through the doors
Come a crowd of servants, scurrying to and fro:
It proclaims a noblest welcome for the guest.

CHORUS
My heart is eased! O, see over there,
How a company of handsome youths approach
With lingering step, in dignified order,
Marching in ranks. Who gave out the command
To marshal them, and so quickly arranged

419

All this youthful team of so handsome a race?
What shall I admire most? Is it the graceful step,
Or the curls of hair on the palest of brows,
Or the rounded cheeks with a peach's blushes,
And like it also, in their silkiest down?
I'd gladly bite, yet I'm frightened to try it:
Since in a similar case, and I shudder to say it,
The mouth was as suddenly filled, with ashes!

But the handsomest
Come to us now:
What do they carry?
Steps for the throne,
Carpets and seat,
Curtain, canopy,
Jewelled finery:
Waving above us,
Forming a garland,
Over the head of our Queen:
For she, already, invited
Ascends, to the noble seat.
Forward now,
Step by step,
Solemnly ranked.
Worthy, O worthy, triply worthy,
Let such a reception be blessed!

(What the Chorus has described takes place. After the boys and squires have
descended in long procession, Faust appears above, at the top of the staircase,
in the costume of a knight of the Middle Ages, and then descends slowly and
with dignity.)

THE LEADER OF THE CHORUS (Observing him closely.)
If indeed the gods have not, as they often do,
Only lent this man brave form, for an instant,
Exalted his dignity, and charming presence,
As a temporary act, then whatever he does
He'll succeed, whether it's warring with men,
Or in the lesser struggles with lovely ladies.
Truly I prefer him to hosts of others,
Whom my eyes have seen, the highly praised.
I see the Prince approach, with slow solemn step,
Restrained by reverence: Queen, turn towards him!

FAUST (Approaching: a man in chains at his side.)
Instead of the usual calm greeting
Instead of a reverential welcome,
Here I bring a wretch bound fast with chains,
Who failed so in his duty, I failed mine.
Kneel here, so this noble lady
May hear a prompt confession of your guilt.
This, royal Mistress, is the man selected
Because of his keen vision to gaze about
From the high tower, and to look keenly
At heaven's spaces, and the breadth of earth,
To report whatever moves here or there,
From the encircling hills, to the castle,
Whether a transit of the woolly flocks,
Or soldiers: so we can protect the first,
Attack the others. Today, negligence!
You came here: he had nothing to report:
We failed in the reception you deserved,
In honour of the guest. Now he forfeits
His guilty life, and would have shed his blood
In a merited death: but only you alone
Shall pardon him or punish, as you wish.

HELEN
Such great power you choose to grant me,
As judge, as Mistress too, though, I suspect
You intend it as a kind of test –
Yet, I'll employ a judge's first duty,
To give the accused a hearing. Speak out.

LYNCEUS, THE WARDEN OF THE TOWER
Let me kneel, and let me see her,
Let me live, or let me die,
Already I'm devoted to her
Heavenly lady from on high.

Waiting for the dawn's advances,
Gazing at her eastern house,
Suddenly the sunlight dances,
Marvellously in the south!

Drawn to see the marvel closer,
Instead of the ravine and height,
Instead of earth and heaven there,

421

I gazed at her, the sole delight.

I was granted powers of vision
Like the lynx, high in the tree:
But now I peered in indecision
As in a dark and clouded dream.

How think? Even if I'd so wished?
Wall, and tower? Bolted gate?
Mist, it rose, and cleared the mist,
Came the Goddess here in state!
I surrendered heart and eye
Drinking in the gentle light:
How that beauty blinds, and I
Was blinded wholly by the sight.

I forgot the watchman's duty,
And the promised trumpet call:
Threaten then, now, to destroy me –
Anger lies in Beauty's thrall.

HELEN
I cannot punish this evil that I brought here,
With me. Ah me! What a fierce fate it is
Pursues me, so that everywhere I possess
The hearts of men, and that they neither spare
Themselves nor anything else of worth.
They steal, seduce, fight: rushing to and fro,
Demigods, heroes, gods, even daemons
Led me in my wanderings, here and there.
Alone I've confused the world, doubly so:
Now I bring threefold, fourfold woe on woe.
Take this innocent away: let him go.
It's no shame to be deceived by the gods.

FAUST
O Queen, amazed, I see them both together:
The certain archer, and the stricken prey:
I see the bow, from which the shaft was loosed,
That wounded him. Arrow after arrow,
Now strikes me. Imagining the feathered whirr
Of arrows crossing every court and hall.
What am I now? My walls you make unsafe
My most faithful servants, you make rebels,

Already I fear my army too obeys
A victorious and unconquered lady.
What's left to do but add myself as well,
And all that I have vainly imagined mine?
Freely and loyally, before your feet,
Let me acknowledge you as Mistress,
Whose presence wins you throne and ownership.

LYNCEUS (Carrying a chest, with men bringing others.)
Queen, once more I advance!
The rich man begs a glance,
He sees you and at a glimpse,
He's a beggar, and a prince.

What am I now? What was I once?
What's to be willed? What's to be done?
What use the eye's clearest sight!
It glances from your royal might.

From the Eastwards we pressed on,
And suddenly the West were gone.
So wide and long the people massed,
The first knew nothing of the last.

The first rank fell: the next stood fast,
The third ranks' lances unsurpassed:
Each man was like a hundredfold,
Thousands died there, all untold.

We pressed forwards: we stormed on,
We were masters, then were gone:
And where I ruled as chief today,
Tomorrow robbed, and stole away.

We looked – and rapid was that look:
The loveliest women there we took,
We took the oxen from the stall,
We took the horses, took them all.

But my delight was to discover
The rarest things I could uncover:
And what other men might grasp,
To me was only withered grass.

I was on the trail of treasure,
Whatever my sharp eye could measure,
In every pocket I could see,
Every chest was glass to me.

Heaps of gold, they were mine,
And the noblest gems I'd find:
Yet now the emeralds alone
Are worthy to adorn your throne.

Sway there now 'twixt ear and lip,
You pearly spheres from oceans deep:
A place the rubies dare not seek,
So pale beside your rosy cheek.

And so the riches, every prize,
I set down here before your eyes:
Before your feet I gladly yield,
The spoils of many a bloody field.

As many chests as I've brought you,
I've many iron caskets too:
Let me follow your path still
And your treasure chambers fill.

You'd scarcely mounted to the throne,
When all bowed down, to you alone,
Wisdom, riches, worldly power,
Before your grace, that very hour.

I held it all fast: that is true
But now it's loosed, and all for you.
I thought its worth was plain to see,
But now it's nothing much, to me.

Everything I've owned will pass
From me like mown and withered grass.
O, give me just one brightening glance,
And all the value's in its dance!

FAUST
Quickly, remove the heap that boldness won,
And take no blame for it, but seek no praise.
All is hers already, that the castle

424

Hides in its lap: you offer these few things
In vain. Go and pile treasure on treasure,
In due order. Present a fine array
Of unseen splendours! Let the vaulted halls
Gleam like the clearest sky, let Paradise
Be created from their dead existence.
Quickly let flowery carpet on carpet
Be unrolled beneath her foot: she'll step
On softest ground: and let her noble gaze,
Blinding all but the Gods, fall on splendour.

LYNCEUS

What the lord commands is nothing,
For the servants, a mere plaything:
This exalted beauty rules
Over blood and treasure too.
The whole army now is tamed,
All the swords are blunt again,
Near this form of noble gold,
The sun itself is pale and cold,
Near the riches of her face
All is but an empty space.

HELEN (To Faust.)

I wish to speak to you, come here then
Beside me! For the empty place invites
Its lord, and so secures this place for me.

FAUST

First, let my loyal dedication please you,
While I kneel, noble lady: let me kiss
The gracious hand that lifts me to your side.
Confirm me as co-regent of a realm
Of unknown borders, win now for yourself
Protector, slave, worshipper all in one!

HELEN

So many wonders do I see, and hear
Amazement grips me, there's much I would know.
But teach me why that man spoke aloud
With curious speech, familiar but strange.
Each sound seeming to give way to the next,
And when a word gave pleasure to the ear,

Another came, as if to caress the first.

FAUST
If my people's speech already pleases you,
O, you'll be delighted with our singing:
It completely satisfies the heart and mind.
But to be sure of it, we'll practise too:
Alternate speech entices, calls it, forth.

HELEN
You'll tell me how to speak with lovely art?

FAUST
It's easy, it must pour forth from the heart.
And if the breast then overflows with yearning,
One looks around and asks —

HELEN
- who else is burning.

FAUST
Not backwards, forwards is the spirit's sight,
This moment now, alone, —

HELEN
- is our delight.

FAUST
She's treasure and commitment, wealth and land:
What confirmation does she give —

HELEN
— my hand.

CHORUS
Who's offended that our Princess
Grants the master of the castle
A show of friendliness?
Let's confess, that we're as fully
Prisoners, as we've been till now
Since the shameful overthrow
Of Ilium, and the anxious,
Sad, and labyrinthine voyage.

Women, used to men's desires,
Are not particular,
They are proficient.
And they award an equal right
To shepherds with their golden hair,
Dark, fauns perhaps, bristling there,
As opportunity affords,
To bodies in their vigour.
Already they sit closer, closer,
Drawn towards each other,
Shoulder to shoulder, knee to knee,
Hand in hand they sway
Across the thrones'
Soft cushioned, majesty.
Their private raptures
Revealed so boldly
To the eyes of the people.

HELEN
I feel so far away and yet so near,
And gladly say now: 'Here, I am! Here!'

FAUST
I scarcely breathe, I tremble, speech is dead:
This is a dream: time and place have fled.

HELEN
I seem exhausted, yet created new,
Enmeshed with you, the unknown and the true.

FAUST
Don't seek to analyse so rare a fate!
Our duty is to live: though but a day.

PHORKYAS (Entering suddenly.)
Spell the letters in love's primer,
Only loving, pass your time here,
Passing, let love be sublime here,
But the moment isn't right.
Don't you feel it, this dark presage?
Don't you hear the trumpet's message?
Your destruction is in sight.
Menelaus with his army
Is advancing on you quickly,

427

Arm yourself, for bitter fight!
Overwhelmed by the winners,
And defiled, like Deiphobus,
You'll all pay, for this delight.
First the lighter vessels shatter,
Then, for this one, at the altar,
The newly sharpened axe shines bright.

FAUST

Rash disturbance! Insistent, she comes pushing in here:
Senseless haste is wrong, even where there's danger.
Unlucky news makes the fairest messenger ugly:
You, ugliest of all, bring only bad news gladly.
But you'll not succeed for once: disturb the air
With your empty breath. There's no danger looming here,
Your danger's only an idle threat to me.

(Calls, and explosions from the towers, trumpets and cornets, martial music. A powerful army marches past.)

No! Now you'll see the heroes gather,
The whole wide land will here unite:
He deserves the ladies' favour,
Who, in their defence, shall fight.

(To the leaders, who step forward from the ranks, and advance.)

Rage silently, and do your duty,
Then you'll achieve the victory,
You, the prime of northern beauty,
You, the flower of the east.

Cased in steel, with steel gleaming,
The army shatters realms at will,
They appear: the earth is shaking,
They advance, it echoes still.
At Pylos, once, we came to shore,
Old Nestor is no longer living,
Our independent army saw
Us shatter all the mighty kings.

From these walls, in an instant,
Send Menelaus back to sea:
There robbing, killing, is his errand,

As is his wish and destiny.

Dukes, I greet you every one,
Commanded by the Spartan Queen:
At her feet lay vale and mountain,
Win the kingdoms in between.

Germans, with your walls and towers,
Defend Corinth and her bays!
Then Achaia's hundred gorges
I'll trust to you, the Goths, always.

Let the Franks advance on Elis,
Messene, to the Saxons brave,
Normans, hold the Argolis,
Rule the shore: and rule the wave.

When everyone has his own land,
At foreign foes, let force be aimed,
While Sparta holds the high command
Our Queen's ancestral domain.

She'll behold you each, delighting
In lands, possessed of every right:
And at her feet you'll seek her blessing,
Acknowledgement, and law and light.

(Faust descends from the throne: the Princes form a circle round him to receive
individual commands and instructions.)

CHORUS
Who wants the loveliest for himself,
First, above everything,
Would be wise to have weapons about him:
He might well gain by flattery
Whoever is noblest on Earth:
But he won't possess her in peace:
The sly, and insidious tempt her from him,
Robbers will boldly steal her from him:
He must prepare to foil them.

So I praise our Prince the while,
And think him nobler than the rest,
Since he combines wisdom and strength,

So that the powerful show obedience,
Waiting his every command.
They follow his orders faithfully,
Each as much for his own profit
As for the ruler's reward and thanks,
Winning the highest fame for both.

Who now will drag her away
From the powerful possessor?
She belongs to him: let her be his,
Doubly bestowed by us, so she
And he, are surrounded inside by thick walls,
Outside, by the greatest of armies.

FAUST

The gifts that, on those here, I bestow –
To each of them a prosperous land –
Are great and glorious, let them go!
We in the middle take our stand.

In their rivalry they'll protect you
Half-island ringed by leaping waves,
While these slender hills connect you
To Europe's last great mountain range.

This land, that outshines every land,
Be blessed for every race forever,
Delivered to my Queen's command,
That, long ago now, wondered at her,

There, by Eurotas' whispering light,
She broke radiant from the shell,
That brightness dazzling the sight
Of siblings: Leda's eyes, as well.

This land now turns to you alone,
Offering you its noblest flower:
Oh, though the whole world is your own,
Let your country hold you in its power!

And though you may endure the sun's cold arrow
Up there, on the mountain's jagged height,
See, how the rocky hillside's green below, now,
Where the goat may crop its meagre right.

The sources leap, all streams rush down as one,
Gorge, slope, and meadow are already green.
On a hundred hills, rock-folded, steep and broken,
The scattered woolly flocks are clearly seen.

Spread all around, with cautious measured stride,
The horned cattle tread the dizzy edge:
But here there's shelter that the caves provide,
Hundreds to hide them all, on the rocky ledge.

Pan guards them too: and lively nymphs live there,
In the damp fresh space of bushy clefts,
And, yearning upward to the higher air,
The crowded tree its slender branches lifts.
Primeval woods! The mighty oaks their cap:
Whose stubborn boughs stick out from them, in state:
While kindly maples, pregnant with sweet sap,
Soar cleanly upward, toying with the weight.

Pure mother's milk, in that still realm of shadows,
Flows rich, in readiness for lamb and child:
Fruit's not lacking, gift of fertile meadows,
And from the hollow trunk drips honey mild.

Here well-being's granted all the race,
Cheek and lips both to joy consent,
Each one is immortal, in their place:
And all there are healthy and content.

And thus the lovely child, of purest days,
Grows, and achieves his father's strength.
We're amazed, the question's still, always:
Are these gods, or are they truly men?

When Apollo took a shepherd's form,
The fairest of them was like the sun:
Since, where pure Nature is the norm,
Then all the worlds must move as one.

(Taking his seat beside her.)

So, this have you, and this have I achieved:
Let the past fade behind us: it is gone!

Oh, know yourself from highest gods conceived,
To the first world, alone then, you belong.

No solid fortresses shall ring you round!
In eternal youth, stands as it stood –
So our stay with all delight be crowned –
Arcadia in Sparta's neighbourhood.
Lured here to tread this blessed ground,
You fled towards a happy destiny!
Let our thrones as arbours now be found,
Our joy be Arcadian, and free!

(The scene is completely transformed. Bowers are built against a range of rocky caverns. A shadowy grove runs to the foot of the rocks that rise on all sides. Faust and Helen are not visible: the Chorus lie scattered about in sleep.)

PHORKYAS
I'm not sure how long these women have been sleeping:
Nor do I know whether they allowed themselves
To dreamwhat I saw clearly with my own eyes.
Therefore I'll wake them. The young will be amazed,
You bearded ones, too, who sit waiting there, below,
To understand the meaning of these wonders.
Wake! Wake, and shake the dew from your hair,
The slumber from your eyes! Don't blink so, but hear me!

CHORUS
Tell us, quickly, quickly, all the wonders that have happened!
If we can't believe them, we'll enjoy them with more pleasure.
For we're wholly weary sitting, staring at these empty stones.

PHORKYAS
You've hardly rubbed your eyes, yet you're already weary, children?
Well, listen: in these caverns, in these grottos, in these arbours,
Shade and shelter have been granted, to the two idyllic lovers,
Our Master and our Mistress.

CHORUS
What, within there?

PHORKYAS
Sweetly sundered,
From the world, alone they summoned me to grant them quiet service.
At their side I stood there, honoured, yet still, as one who's trusted,

Always gazed at something other, turning here and there at random.
Looked for roots and bark and mosses, being skilled in all the potions,
And so they were left alone.

CHORUS

You speak as if a whole world's space were hidden there inside, now,
Woods and fields and lakes and rivers: what a fantasy you spin!

PHORKYAS

It's true: you're inexperienced, and its depths are unexplored!
I felt, lost in contemplation, hall on hall there, court on court.
In an instant laughter echoes, through the cavernous recesses:
There I see a boy is springing, from his mother to his father,
From his father to his mother, all is dandling and caressing,
And a foolish, a fond teasing, shouts of play, and cries of joy,
Alternate, there, and I'm deaf.
A naked wingless Spirit, like a faun, and yet no creature,
Leaps across the solid floor, and the ground beneath responding,
Sends him flying through the ether, till the second leap or so, there,
He can touch the cavern roof.
Anxiously his mother's calling: 'Leap as often as you like, dear,
But all flying is forbidden, so beware of taking flight.'
And his loyal father warns him: 'In the earth's the power of swiftness,
That will quickly send you flying: touch the ground then with your toe,
And like that son of Earth's, Antaeus, you'll soon find strength again.'
So he leaps the rocky masses of the cavern, from a cornice,
To another and around then, as a ball does when it's thrown.
But suddenly he's vanished in a crevice of the cavern,
And it seems he's lost. His mother grieves for him, father comforts,
I stand there, wondering anxiously, but there again's the vision!
Do buried treasures lie there? Robes embroidered all with flowers,
He has fittingly assumed.
Tassels tremble from his shoulders, ribbons flutter round his chest,
In his hand a golden lyre, like a miniature Apollo,
He steps happily to the overhanging brink: amazing.
And the parents in delight clasp each other to their hearts,
What's that shining round his temples? It's hard to see what's gleaming,
Is it gold and gems, or flames, now, of the spirit's supreme power?
So he moves as if the stately boy's proclaimed to us already
The future Lord of Beauty, in whose members the eternal
Melodies are stirring: and so you too will also hear him,
And you too will also see him, with the rarest show of wonder.

CHORUS

Do you call this a marvel,
Crete has begotten?
Can you never have listened
To what Poetry teaches?
Have you never once heard Ionia's,
Have you never listened to Hellas'
Most ancient of legends
Of the gods and heroes?

All things that happen
In this present age,
Are mournful echoes
Of our ancestors' nobler times:
And your story can't equal
That, loveliest of lies,
Easier to believe than Truth,
That they sang of Maia's son.

That delicate and strong, yet
Scarcely born, suckling child,
Would you swaddle him in purest down,
Clothe him in costly jewelled bindings,
The crowd of chattering nurses'
Utterly senseless notion.

But strong and yet delicate,
Already the supple rascal,
Draws forth his lithe body,
Leaves behind that royal,
But timid, constraining shell,
Silent, there, in its place:

Like the finished butterfly,
From the chilly chrysalis,
Slipping, with quick unfolding wings,
Boldly into the sunlit air,
And courageously fluttering.
So did he, the liveliest,

And he quickly demonstrated
By the most skilful arts,
That he'd always be the patron
Daemon of thieves and jesters

And all seekers of profit.

From the Sea God he quickly stole
His trident, and from Ares himself,
Slyly, his sword from its scabbard:
Bow and arrows from Phoebus too,
And tongs from Hephaestus:

He even stole Father Zeus'
Lightning bolts, not scared of fire:
Then he tripped poor Eros up,
In the toils of a wrestling match:
As Venus kissed him, too, stole away,
The ribbons from her breasts.
(A pure melodious and exquisite music echoes from the cave. All listen and
appear deeply moved. There is a full musical accompaniment from this point
to the designated pause.)

PHORKYAS
Hear the loveliest of music,
Free from old mythology!
All your gods and all their antics,
Let them go, they're history.

None can understand you more,
We demand a higher art:
From the heart itself must pour,
What will influence the heart.

(She retires towards the rocks.)

Be you stirred, you awesome being,
By the sweet and flattering sound,
We, renewed to life, are feeling,
Moved to tears of joy, around.

Let the sun be lost from heaven
So it's daylight in the soul,
We'll discover in the heart, then,
What the Earth fails to hold.

(Helen. Faust. Euphorion, in costume as previously described.)

EUPHORION

Hear the song of childhood sung now,
Its delight belongs to you,
See me leap about in time, now
Let my parents' hearts leap too.

HELEN

It requires two noble hearts
For Love to bless humanity,
But to be a thing apart
They must make a precious three.

FAUST

All we sought is now discovered:
I am yours, and you are mine:
And we two are bound together,
There's no better fate to find.

CHORUS

They'll delight for many years
In this child's tender glow,
Ah, this partnership of peers,
How it's beauty moves me, so!

EUPHORION

Now let me leap, oh,
Now let me spring!
High in the air, go
Circling all things,
That's the desire
That's driving me on.

FAUST

Yet, gently! Gently!
Not into danger,
Lest a chance downfall,
Awaits the ranger,
Straight away grounds you,
Our darling son!

EUPHORION

I can't stick fast to
The ground any more:
Let go my hands and

Let go my hair,
Let go my clothes!
They are all mine.

HELEN
O think! Please think,
Whom you belong to!
How it would grieve us,
How you'd destroy too,
That sweet achievement,
Yours, his and mine.

CHORUS
I fear this unity
Soon will unwind!

HELEN AND FAUST

Calm yourself! Calm excess,
To please your parents,
Too great a liveliness,
Impulsive violence!
In rural peacefulness,
Brighten the plain.

EUPHORION
If that's what you wish, yes,
I'll stop, I'll restrain.

(He winds, dancing, through the chorus and draws them along with him.)

I'll hover here, lightly
Lively the crew.
Is this the melody,
And measure too?

HELEN
Yes that is neatly done:
Lead all the fairest on,
Through intricacy.

FAUST
Would it were over then!
Such entertainment

Won't delight me.

CHORUS (With Euphorion, dancing nimbly and singing, in interlinking ranks.)
When your arms equally
Are charmingly lifted,
Your curling hair's brightly
Loosened and shifted.

When with a foot so light
Over the earth in flight,
Thither and back again,
Step upon step, you rain,

Then your goal is in sight,
Loveliest child:
All of our hearts, beguiled,
With yours unite.

(Pause.)

EUPHORION
You're like so many
Light-footed fawns:
Now to new games we
Are quickly re-born!
I'll be the hunter,
You be the prey.

CHORUS
If you would catch us
Don't be so eager,
We too are anxious
When all is over,
To clasp the form,
You so sweetly display!

EUPHORION
Now through the vale!
Up hill and down dale!
What I gain easily
Is tedious to see,
Only what's forcibly

Won delights me.

HELEN AND FAUST
How wild he is now! And how stubborn!
There's little hope of moderation.
That's the sound of blowing horns,
Through the woods and valley ringing:
What noise, and what confusion!

CHORUS (Entering one by one, in haste.)
He is running from us swiftly:
Scorning us and always mocking,
Now he drags one from the crowd: she,
The wildest of us all.

EUPHORION (Dragging along a young girl.)
Here I'll drag the little quarry,
To enforce my wish entirely:
For my joy, and my desire,
Press her wilful heart, on fire,
Kiss her stubborn mouth at length
And proclaim my will and strength.

THE GIRL
Let me go! Since there's a strong
Resistant spirit in this body:
My will, like yours, if I'm not wrong,
Says I'm not taken easily.

You think I'm in any danger?
Force of arms is it, you claim!
Hold me fast, you foolish ranger,
And I'll scotch your little game.

(She turns to flame and flashes into the air.)

Follow me through flowing air,
Follow me through caverns bare,
Catch your fleeing prey again!

EUPHORION (Shaking off the flames.)
Rocks all around me here,
Deep in the forest view,
Make me a prisoner,

Though I'm still young and new.

Breezes are blowing fair,
Waves now are breaking there:
I hear both far away,
I'd gladly be there today.

(He leaps further up the rocks.)

HELEN, FAUST AND THE CHORUS
A chamois you'd imitate?
We're fearful of your fate.

EUPHORION
Ever higher I must climb.
Ever further I must see.

Now I know where I stand!
Amidst this semi-island,
Amidst Pelop's country,
Earth – kindred to the sea.

CHORUS
Why not live here, in peace,
Among hills and groves?
Vines then for you we'll seek,
Vines in their rows.

Vines on high ridges stand,
Figs, there, and apples gold,
Stay in this lovely land
Stay, and grow old!

EUPHORION
Do you dream of peaceful days?
Dream, then as dreamers may.
War is the watchword though.
Victory! It rings out so.

CHORUS
He who in time of peace
Wishes for war, soon
Witness's the decease,

Of hope, and fortune.

EUPHORION
Those who made this land,
With danger on every hand,
Free, and courageously,
Gave their blood lavishly:

Bring holy meaning
To that sacrifice –
See us still conquering
All whom we fight!

CHORUS
Look up there, how high he climbs!
Yet he seems to us no smaller:
In his armour, as in triumph,
How he gleams in steel and silver.

EUPHORION
Each one's no longer conscious
Of the high wall, or the rest:
Since the one enduring fortress,
Is the soldier's iron breast.

If you'd live unconquered,
Quickly arm, and fight the real foe:
Every wife an Amazon bred,
And every child a hero.

CHORUS
Sacred Poetry
Climbing, and heavenly!
Shines there, the fairest star,
Far there, and still so far!
And yet it reaches here,
Always, and still we hear,
Joy, where we are.

EUPHORION
No, not as a child do I appear,
This youth comes armed, you see:
In spirit he's already a peer,
Of the strong, the bold, and free.

Now I go!
Now, and lo,
The path to glory shines for me.

HELEN AND FAUST
You've scarcely been called to being,
Scarcely come to daylight's gleam,
And from the heights you're yearning,
For the place of pain, it seems.
Are we two
Naught to you?
Is the sweetest bond a dream?

EUPHORION
Don't you hear the thundering wave?
Through vale on vale the echoes call,
Host on host, in sand and spray,
Shock on shock, in anguished fall.
Understand
The command
Is death, now and for all.
Helen, Faust and the Chorus

What horror! What disaster!
Is then death ordained for you?

EUPHORION
Should I watch it from afar?
No! I'll share their trouble too.
Helen, Faust and the Chorus

Exuberance, danger,
Deadliest fate!

EUPHORION
Yes! – I am winged here,
I will not wait!
Onward! I must! I must!
Let me but fly!
(He hurls himself into the air: his clothes bear him a moment, his head is
illuminated and a streak of light follows.)

CHORUS
Icarus! Icarus!

No more! We sigh.

(A beautiful youth falls at the parents' feet. We imagine we see a well-known form in the dead body, but the physical part vanishes at once, while an aureole rises like a comet to heaven. The clothes, cloak and lyre remain on the ground.)

HELEN AND FAUST
At once, joy is followed,
By bitterest pain.

EUPHORION (From the depths.)

Mother, don't leave me alone,
In the shadows' domain!

(Pause) **CHORUS** (Dirge.)

Not alone! – No matter where you are,
For we believe in following you:
Oh! Though from the day you part,
Not one heart will part from you.
We scarcely wish to mourn you, even,
We sing in envy of your fate:
To you the clearest light of heaven,
Gave song and courage, true and great.

Ah! You were born for earthly fate,
High descent and supreme power:
Youth, sadly, while you went astray,
Was torn from you in its first hour!
You saw the world, with clearer vision,
You understood the yearning heart,
The glow of lovely woman's passion,
And all singing's rarest art.

Yet, irresistibly, you ran free,
In nets of indiscipline: you
Divorced yourself violently,
From custom, and from rule:
Until at last, through thinking deeper,
You gave courage greater weight,
And wished to win to splendour,
But that could not be your fate.

Whose then? – The gloomy question,
That destiny itself conceals,
While in days unblessed by fortune,
Our people's silent blood congeals.
But new songs will refresh them,
No longer bow them to the floor,
The earth shall see them once again,
As it saw them once before.

(A complete Pause. The music ends.)

HELEN (To Faust.)
Alas, the ancient word proves true for me, as well:
That joy and beauty never lastingly unite.
The thread of life, as the thread of love, is torn:
Painfully, lamenting both, I must say: farewell,
And enter your embrace, once, and then no more.
Persephone, receive me, and this child of ours!

(She embraces Faust: her body vanishes, her dress and veil remain in his hands.)

PHORKYAS (To Faust.)
Hold tight to what alone remains to you.
Don't let the garment go. Already, daemons
Pull at its hem, and wish to drag it down
Into the Underworld. Hold tight to it, now!
It no longer veils the divinity you've lost,
But it is divine. Employ then the priceless,
Noble gift for yourself, and soar on high:
It will carry you quickly from the lowest
To the highest ether, while you can endure.
We'll meet once more, far away from here.

(Helen's garments dissolve in mist, surround Faust, life him into the air, and
drift away with him.)

(Phorkyas takes Euphorion's tunic, cloak and lyre from the ground, steps
forward to the proscenium, holds them aloft and speaks.)

As always, I've discovered something good!
The flame itself has gone, that's understood,
Yet, for the world, I can't be truly sad.
Here's enough to fuel the poets' regiment,
Stir their guild to envy, make them mad,

And if I still can't lend them any talent,
At least I'll have a costume for the lad.

(She seats herself on a low column in the proscenium.)

PANTHALIS
Quick now, girls! We're all free of the magic now,
That old Thessalian woman's enthralling spell,
That jangling dizziness of confusing sound,
Troubling the ear, and more the inner sense.
Down to Hades! Since with solemn step the Queen
Descended swiftly. Let her faithful servants'
Footsteps follow her downward path without delay.
We'll find her beside the Unfathomable Throne.

CHORUS
Of course, queens are happy anywhere:
Even in Hades they're on top,
Associating proudly with their peers,
Persephone's intimate company.
But for us, then, in the background,
Of the asphodel-meadowed depths,
With their long rows of poplars,
Their fruitless crowds of willows,
What fun is there for us,
Piping like bats at twilight,
In cheerless, ghostly whispers?

PANTHALIS
Who wins no name, and wills no noble work,
Belongs to the elements: so away with you!
My own intense desire's to be with my Queen,
The individual's loyalty and not just service.

(Exits.)

ALL
We're returned to the light of day,
No longer individual, it's true,
We feel it, and we know it,
But we'll never go back to Hades.
Ever-living Nature,
Makes the most valid claim

On our spirits, and we on her.

A SECTION OF THE CHORUS
We in all the thousand branches' whispering tremors, swaying murmurs,
Sweetly rocked, will lightly draw the root-born founts of being upwards,
To the twigs: and now with leaves, and now with the exuberant blossom,
We'll adorn their floating tresses, freely thriving in the breezes.
Straight away, now, as the fruit falls, happy crowds and flocks will gather,
For the picking and the tasting, swift-arriving, busy-thronging:
Bending down, now, all around us, as before the early gods.

A SECOND SECTION OF THE CHORUS
We, against the rocky cliff face, by the smooth far-gleaming mirror,
We will nestle, softly moving, in the gentle waves that flatter:
Listening, hearing every echo, birdsong, now, or reedy fluting,
To the fearful voice of Pan, too, we'll provide a ready answer:
To the murmuring, send a murmur: to the thunder roll our thunder,
In earth-shaking repetition, in threefold, or tenfold echo.

A THIRD SECTION OF THE CHORUS
Sisters! We, of nimbler senses, hurry onwards with the waters:
For the richly covered, far-off, mountain ranges each entice us.
Ever deeper, ever downward, in meandering curves we'll water
First the meadows, then the pastures, then the house and the garden,
Where the slender tips of cypress, over banks and watery mirror,
Over all the landscape, mark it, soaring skywards in the air.

A FOURTH SECTION OF THE CHORUS
Wander where you please, you others: we will circle, we will rustle
Round the densely planted hillside, where the vine stock's growing green:
There, each day, we'll pay attention to the cultivator's passion,
Watch his diligence and care, there: watch for its uncertain outcome.
How he hoes, how he digs there, how he heaps, and prunes, and ties,
Prays to all the gods above him, most of all prays to the sun god.
The effeminate one, Bacchus, gives scant thought to faithful servants,
Rests in arbours, lolls in caverns, flirting with the youngest Faun.
Whatsoever he might need there, for his half-befuddled dreaming,
Is left for him in wineskins, stored around in jars and vessels,
Right and left, in cool recesses, gathered through the endless ages.
But when the gods, that's Helios, we mean before all others,
Cooling, wetting, warming, heating, fill the vineyard's horn of plenty,
Where the silent grower laboured, suddenly it's all enlivened,
And in every leaf there's rustling, rustling now from vine to vine.
Baskets creaking, buckets rattling, the tubs are carried groaning,

All towards enormous vats there, to the lusty treaders' dance:
So, then, all the sacred bounty, of the pure bred juicy harvest,
Fiercely trodden, spurting, foaming, mingled there, is crudely squashed.
Now the cymbals' brazen clamour's ringing boldly in our ears,
As Dionysus from his Mysteries is unveiled, and is revealed:
Here with his goat-foot Satyrs, whirling goat-foot Satyresses,
And Silenus's, unruly, long-eared ass, that brays amongst them.
Nothing's spared! The cloven feet now, trample on all decency:
All the senses whirl, bewildered: hideously, ears are stunned, there.
Drunkards fumble for their wine-cups, head and bellies over-full,
Here and there one has misgivings, but can only swell the riot,
Since to hold the latest vintage, one must drain the oldest skin!

ACT V

I

OPEN COUNTRY

THE WANDERER
Yes! Here are the dusky lindens,
Standing round, in mighty age.
And here am I, returning to them,
After so long a pilgrimage!
It still appears the same old place:
Here's the hut that sheltered me,
When the storm-uplifted wave,
Hurled me shore-wards from the sea!
My hosts are those I would bless,
A brave, a hospitable pair,
Who if I meet them, I confess,
Must already be white haired.
Ah! They were pious people!
Shall I call, or knock? – Greetings,
If, as open-hearted, you still
Enjoy good luck, in meetings!

BAUCIS (A little woman, very aged.)
Gentle stranger! Quietly, quietly!
Peace! Let my husband rest!
Long sleep lends the elderly,
Little time to work, at best.

THE WANDERER
Tell me, Mother: are you that wife
To whom thanks should be given:
Who brought a young man back to life,
When wife and husband worked as one?
Are you that Baucis who tirelessly
Restored my almost-vanished breath?

(Her husband appears.)

Are you that Philemon, who bravely
Saved my wealth from watery death?
Your swiftly burning fire,

Your silvery sounding bell,
In chance, dread and dire,
Was the outcome that befell.
And now let me walk about,
And view the boundless ocean:
Let me kneel, and be devout:
Mind troubled with emotion.

(He walks on, over the downs.)

PHILEMON (To Baucis.)
Hurry now, and lay the table,
Underneath the garden trees.
Let him go: as in the fable,
He'll not credit what he sees.

(He follows, and stands beside the Wanderer.)

Where wave on wave, foaming wildly,
Savagely mistreated you,
See a garden planted, widely,
See the Paradisial view.
I was too old to seize the day,
Unfit to work as long ago:
And while my powers ebbed away,
The tide extended its wide flow.
Clever Lords set their bold servants
Digging ditches, building dikes,
To gain the mastery of ocean,
Diminishing its natural rights.
See green meadow bordering meadow,
Field and garden, wood and town. –
But it's time to eat, so follow,
Sunset is approaching now.
See the sails, far away there,
Seeking port before the night.
The birds fly homeward through the air:
Their harbour too heaves in sight.
So gaze then, at the whole horizon,
Where the blue sea used to flow,
Right and left there, to your vision,
Densely peopled space below.

II

IN THE LITTLE GARDEN

(The three of them at table.)

BAUCIS (To the stranger.)
Are you dumb? And will you lift
Not a morsel to your mouth?

PHILEMON
He wants to comprehend the gift:
Tell him, freely then: speak out.

BAUCIS
Well! It was a marvel, really!
It troubles me to this day:
Then its whole nature, surely,
Was peculiar, in its way.

PHILEMON
Is the Emperor, then, at fault,
Who granted him the land?
Didn't a herald make his halt,
Crying out what was planned?
Not far away there, on the dunes,
The first bold step was made,
Tents, huts! – And on the downs,
A palace, quickly raised.

BAUCIS
For days, work rumbled on in vain,
Pick and shovel, blow on blow:
Where the night's fires flamed,
Next day a dam would follow.
Human blood was forced to flow,
At night, rose the sound of pain:
The seaward floating fiery glow
Was a canal, come dawn again.
He's a godless man: he'd steal
Our hut, and our few acres:
But like subjects we must kneel,

When we boast such neighbours.

PHILEMON
Yet he's offered us another
Holding, on his new-won land!

BAUCIS
Never trust what's built on water,
On the heights maintain your stand.

PHILEMON
Let's make our way to the chapel,
To watch the last glow of light,
Kneel, pray, and sound the bell,
And trust in God's ancient might!

III

THE PALACE

(Spacious pleasure-gardens: a broad straight canal. Faust in extreme old age, walking about, thoughtfully.)

LYNCEUS, THE WARDER (Through a speaking trumpet.)
The sun is fading, the last boats
Sail swiftly to the harbour here.
One large vessel gently floats,
Down the canal: and draws near.
The bright flags flutter merrily,
The masts are trimmed, in time:
The boatmen all praise you gladly,
Fortune celebrates your prime.

(The little bell on the dunes rings out.)

FAUST (Startled.)
Accursed ringing! Wounding me
With shame: a treacherous blow:
My realm's laid out there, endlessly,
But, at my back, this vexes so,
Proclaiming, with its jealous sound:
My great estate is less than fine,
The old hut, all the trees around,
The crumbling chapel, are not mine.
And even if I wished to rest there,
A strange shadow makes me shudder,
It's a thorn in my eye, and deeper:
Oh! Would I were somewhere other!

THE WARDER (From above.)
The boat is sailing, brightly dressed,
Towards us, on the evening breeze!
Heaped, with boxes, sacks and chests,
From its journey on the seas!

(A splendid boat, richly and brightly loaded with foreign goods.)

(Mephistopheles. The Three Mighty Warriors.)

CHORUS

Here we land,
Already, here.
Hail to our Lord,
Our patron dear!

(They disembark: the goods are unloaded.)

MEPHISTOPHELES

We've proven ourselves in every way,
Pleased, if we win our patron's praise.
We took two ships when we sailed before
With twenty ships we dock, once more.
What we've achieved, each fine thing,
You'll see from the cargo that we bring.
The ocean's freedom frees the mind
There all thought is left behind!
You only need a handy grip,
You catch a fish, or take a ship,
And once you're lord of all three,
The fourth one's tackled easily:
The fifth one's in an evil plight,
You have the might, and so the right.
You wonder what, and never how.
I know a little of navigation:
War, trade, and piracy, allow,
As three in one, no separation.

THE THREE MIGHTY WARRIORS

No thanks for us!
No thanks at all!
As if we've brought
A stench, that's all.
He pulls a
Nasty face again:
These royal goods
Don't please him then.

MEPHISTOPHELES

Don't expect more
Pay for it!
What you've had
Is what you get.

THE WARRIORS
That was only
To pass the time:
We want an equal
Share in crime.

MEPHISTOPHELES
Then first set out in
Hall on hall,
The costly treasures,
One and all!
And coming to
The splendid show,
He'll think it all the
More, you know,
He won't be mean,
With you, at least,
He'll give the fleet,
Feast on feast.
Tomorrow motley birds attend,
I want to take good care of them.

(The cargo is removed.)

(To Faust.)

This splendid fortune you embrace
With wrinkled brow, and gloomy face!
Your noble wisdom has been crowned,
Sea's reconciled with solid ground:
From the shore, on swifter track,
The sea wills out the ship, and back:
So speak, that here, from your spire,
Your arms might grip the world entire.
From this place the trench was cut,
Here stood the first wooden hut:
A little ditch was traced from here,
Where now vessels' wakes appear.
Your servants' toil, your thought so wise,
Have won the Earth and Ocean's prize.
From here on –

FAUST
– that accursed here!

That always brings me wretched fear,
To you who are so clever, I say it,
It gives my heart sting on sting,
It's impossible for me to bear it.
I'm ashamed to even speak the thing.
The old ones up there should yield,
I want the limes as my retreat,
The least tree in another's field,
Detracts from my whole estate.
There, to stand and look around,
I'll build a frame from bough to bough,
My gaze revealing, under the sun,
A view of everything I've done,
Overseeing, as the eye falls on it,
A masterpiece of the human spirit,
Forging with intelligence,
A wider human residence.
That's the worst suffering can bring,
Being rich, to feel we lack something.
The bell's chime, the lindens' breeze,
Like tombs in churchyards stifle me.
The exercise of my all-conquering will
Is shattered in the sand, here, and lies still.
How can I drive it from my nature!
The bell peals, and I'm an angry creature.

MEPHISTOPHELES
It's natural! Intense frustration
Drives a man to desperation.
Who doubts it! That clang I fear
Falls cruelly on a noble ear.
And that wretched bing-bang-bong,
Through the clear evening sky, that gong,
Is joined to every chance event,
From first bath to last interment.
As if between its bing and bong
Life's a dream, and then is gone.

FAUST
Such obstinacy and opposition
Diminishes the noblest position,
Until in endless pain, one must
Grow deeply weary of being just.

MEPHISTOPHELES

Why bother yourself so much about them?
Shouldn't you long ago have colonised them?

FAUST

Then go and push them aside for me! –
You know the land, with my approval,
Set aside for the old folks removal.

MEPHISTOPHELES

We'll take them up, and set them down,
They'll stand, once more: I'll be bound:
When they've survived a little force,
They'll be reconciled to it, of course.

(He whistles shrilly.)

Come: perform your Lord's command!
And tomorrow let the feast be planned.

THE THREE WARRIORS

This old Lord received us badly,
A feast now is our right: believe me.
Mephistopheles (To the audience.)
And here we see, as long ago
Naboth's vineyardstill on show. (Kings I:)

IV

DEAD OF NIGHT

LYNCEUS, THE WARDER (Singing on the watch-tower of the palace.)

For seeing, I'm born,
For watching, employed,
To the tower, I'm sworn,
While the world, I enjoy.
I gaze at the far,
I stare at the near,
The moon and the star,
The forest and deer:
The eternally lovely
Adornment, I view,
And as it delights me
I delight myself too.
You, fortunate eyes,
All you've seen, there,
Let it be as it may,
Yet it was so fair!

(Pause.)

I'm not positioned here, on high,
Just for my own enjoyment:
What horror, meant to terrify,
Threatens from the firmament!
I see sparks of fire gushing
Through the lindens' double night,
Fanned by the wind's rushing,
Ever stronger grows the light.
Ah! Within, the hut is burning,
Damp and mossy though it stand:
Swift help, in this direction turning,
Is needed, yet no aid's to hand.
Ah! The pious old couple,
So careful ever of the fire,
Made a prey to smoke, to stifle,
On this dreadful pyre!
The flame burns on: glowing red,
It's now a blackened mossy pile:

If only those good folk are rescued,
From those fires of hell, run wild!
A bright tongue of lightning heaves,
Through the branches, through the leaves:
Breaking, snapping, catching swiftly,
Withered branches flicker, glow.
Why have I such powers to see!
Why are mine the eyes that know!
The little chapel now collapses,
With the falling branches' weight.
Already with bright snakelike flashes,
The treetops, gripped, meet their fate.
Glowing crimson, to their hollow
Roots, the trunks now burn with ease. –

(A long pause. Chant.)

What used to please my eyes, below,
Has vanished with the centuries.

FAUST (On the balcony, towards the downs.)
What whining song is that, above?
Too late its word and tone reach me.
The watchman wails: yes, I'm moved:
Annoyed by this impatient deed.
But let the lime-trees be erased,
A horror now of half-burnt timber,
A watchtower can soon be raised,
To gaze around at boundless splendour.
From there I'll see my new creation,
One set aside for that old pair: at least,
They'll feel benign consideration,
Enjoying their last days in peace.

MEPHISTOPHELES AND THE THREE WARRIORS (Below.)
Here we come, and at the double:
Pardon us! We've caused you trouble.
We knocked, and knocked on the door,
But it seemed locked for evermore:
We rattled it, and shook it too,
Until the planks broke in two:
We called aloud, and threatened, then,
But there was no reply, again.
And as happens in such cases,

They heard nothing, hid their faces:
But we commenced without delay
To drive the stubborn folk away.
That pair knew scant anxiety,
They died of terror, peacefully.
A stranger, who was hiding there,
And wished to fight, we tried to scare.
But in the fast and furious bout,
From the coals that lay about,
The straw took fire. Now all three,
In that one pyre, burn merrily.

FAUST
Were you deaf to what I said?
I wanted them moved, not dead.
This mindless, and savage blow,
Earns my curse: share it, and go!

CHORUS
The ancient proverb says of course:
Yield willingly to a greater force!
While if you're bold and opt for strife,
You'll stake your house, and home – and life.

(They exit.)

FAUST (On the balcony.)
Stars hide their faces, and their glow,
The fire sinks, and flickers low:
A moist breeze fans the dying ember,
Bringing smoke and vapour closer.
Quickly said, too quickly done, I fear! –
Now, what hovers like a shadow, here?

459

V

Midnight

(Four Grey Women enter.)

THE FIRST
I am called Want.

THE SECOND
I am called Guilt.

THE THIRD
I am called Care.

THE FOURTH
Necessity, I.

THREE TOGETHER (Want, Guilt and Necessity)
The door is shut tight, and we cannot get in:
The owner is rich: he won't have us within.

WANT
I shrink to a shadow.

GUILT
To emptiest space.

NEED
The wealthy from me turn their pampered face.

CARE
Sisters, you can't enter, daren't enter there.
But, through the keyhole now, always slips, Care.

(Care disappears.)

WANT
You, my Grey Sisters, take your flight too.

GUILT
Close by your side, I come following you.

NECESSITY
Close at your heels is Necessity's breath.

THE THREE
The clouds there are moving, and cover the stars!
Behind us, behind us! From far, oh, from far,
He's coming, our Brother, he's coming, he's – Death.

FAUST (In the Palace.)
I saw four: but only three went away:
I caught no meaning from the words they say.
It sounded as if I heard – 'Necessity's breath',
And then a gloomy rhyming word, like – 'Death'.
It rang hollow, ghostly, subdued, to me.
Even now I've not won my liberty.
If I could banish Sorcery from my track,
Unlearn the magic-spells that draw me back,
And stand before you, Nature, as mere Man,
It would be worth the pain of being Human.
So was I, a seeker in the darkness,
Cursing both self and world, in wickedness.
Now the air is filled with phantom shapes,
It's hard to see how anyone escapes.
Though day may smile on us with rational gleams,
The night entwines us in a web of dreams:
We come happily from the fields of youth,
A bird croaks: what? Misfortune: is our truth.
Cloaked with superstitions, soon and late:
It's wedded to us, warns us: shows our fate.
And so, alone, intimidated, we stand.
The door creaks, yet no one is at hand.

(Anxiously.)

Is anyone there?

CARE
The answer must be, yes!

FAUST
And you, who then are you?

CARE
I am your guest.

FAUST
Be gone!

CARE
I am here, in my proper place.

FAUST (First angered, then composed, addressing himself.)
Take care: of magic spells show not a trace.

CARE
Though the ear choose not to hear,
In the heart I echo, clear:
Savage power I exercise,
Transformed I am, to mortal eyes.
On the land, and on the ocean,
Evermore the dread companion,
Always found, and never sought,
Praised, as well as cursed, in thought. –
Have you yourself not known Care?

FAUST
I sped through the World that's there:
Gripped by the hair every appetite,
And let go those that failed to delight,
Let those fly that quite escaped me.
I've desired, achieved my course,
Desired again, and so, with force,
Stormed through life: first powerfully,
But wisely now: and thoughtfully.
Earth's sphere's familiar enough to me,
The view beyond is barred eternally:
The fool who sets his sights up there,
Creates his own likeness in the air!
Let him stand, and look around him well:
This world means something to the capable.
Why does he need to roam eternity!
Let him grasp what is firm reality.
So let him wander down his earthly day:
And if ghosts haunt him, go on his way,
Find joy and suffering in striding on,

Dissatisfied with every hour that's gone.

CARE

When of man I take possession,
Then his whole world is lessened:
Endless gloom meets his eyes,
No more suns will set or rise,
Though intact, to outer sense,
He lives in the dark, intense,
Never knowing how to measure
Any portion of his treasure.
Good and ill are merely chance,
He starves, food in his hands:
Be it joy or be it sorrow
He delays it till tomorrow,
Waiting for the future, ever,
Finding his fulfilment, never.

FAUST

Be gone! And don't come near me!
Such nonsense I'll not understand.
Away, with your evil litany,
Sent to confuse the cleverest man!

CARE

Shall he come, or shall he go?
All decision is denied him:
In the middle of the road,
He staggers, feeling round him.
He's ever more deeply lost,
Seeing everything star-crossed,
Wearies himself and all the rest,
Stifles as he holds his breath:
Lifeless, but not yet gone under,
Resists despair or surrender.
So, with an incessant rolling,
A painful end, and hard going,
Now free, and now constrained,
In half sleep, poorly entertained,
Confine him in a little space:
Prepare him for Hell's other place.

FAUST

Unholy spectre! So you hand our race

To the ravages of a thousand devils:
Even transform our worthless days
To a wretched knot of entangling evils.
It's hard I know to free oneself from Demons,
The strong spirit-bonds are not lightly broken:
And yet, Care, I'll not recognise you, nor even,
That creeping power of yours, by any token.

CARE

Feel it now, as on the wind,
I, and my curse, depart, again.
Lifelong, all you men are blind,
Now, Faust, be so to the end!

(She breathes in his face, and departs.)

FAUST (Now blind.)

The night seems deeper all around me,
Only within me is there gleaming light:
I must finish what I've done, and hurry,
The master's word alone declares what's right.
Up from your beds, you slaves! Man on man!
Reveal the daring of my favoured plan.
Seize the tools: on with pick and spade!
Let the end-result be now displayed.
Strict order, and swift industry
Then the finest prize we'll see:
And so the greatest work may stand,
One mind equal to a thousand hands.

THE GREAT OUTER COURT OF THE PALACE

(Torches.)

MEPHISTOPHELES (In advance, as Overseer.)
Come on! Come on! In here, in here!
Quivering spirits of the dead,
All you patchwork semi-natures,
Sinew, bone, and tendon wed.

THE SPIRITS OF THE DEAD (Lemures, in Chorus.)
Swiftly now we are on hand
With half an impression,
That it concerns a tract of land,
Of which we'll gain possession.
Pointed stakes with us appear,
Chains to measure ground on:
But why you've called us here
Is something we've forgotten.

MEPHISTOPHELES
Artistic effort's not the prize:
Carry it out in your own manner!
Lay the longest one of you lengthwise,
Then pile the turf on him, you others.
Do as they once did for our fathers there,
Dig out a somewhat lengthened square!
Gone from a palace to a narrow place:
It's still as stupid an end for man to face.

THE SPIRITS OF THE DEAD (Digging with mocking gestures.)
When I was young and lived and loved,
I thought it was very sweet:
To happy sounds, and cheerful steps,
I lifted up my feet.

Now treacherous old age has clawed
Me with his crutch, since when
I stumble at the grave's wide door,
Why do they leave it open!

FAUST (Comes from the Palace, groping his way past the doorposts.)
How the clattering of shovels cheers me!
It's the crews still labouring on,
Till earth is reconciled to man,
The waves accept their boundaries,
And ocean's bound with iron bands.

MEPHISTOPHELES (Aside.)
And yet with all your walls and dams
You're merely dancing to our tune:
Since you prepare for our Neptune,
The Water-demon, one vast feast.
You'll be lost in every way –
The elements are ours, today,
And ruin comes on running feet.

FAUST
Overseer!

MEPHISTOPHELES
Here!

FAUST
Any way you can
Bring crowds of labourers together,
Spurred by force or hope of pleasure,
By pay, enticement or press-gang!
Report to me on progress every day,
The depth of earth and gravel dug away.

MEPHISTOPHELES (Half-aloud.)
Reporting it to me the word they gave,
Was not quite gravel, it was more like – grave.

FAUST
A swamp lies there below the hill,
Infecting everything I've done:
My last and greatest act of will
Succeeds when that foul pool is gone.
Let me make room for many a million,
Not wholly secure, but free to work on.
Green fertile fields, where men and herds
May gain swift comfort from the new-made earth.
Quickly settled in those hills' embrace,

Piled high by a brave, industrious race.
And in the centre here, a Paradise,
Whose boundaries hold back the raging tide,
And though it gnaws to enter in by force,
The common urge unites to halt its course.
Yes, I've surrendered to this thought's insistence,
The last word Wisdom ever has to say:
He only earns his Freedom and Existence,
Who's forced to win them freshly every day.
Childhood, manhood, age's vigorous years,
Surrounded by dangers, they'll spend here.
I wish to gaze again on such a land,
Free earth: where a free race, in freedom, stand.
Then, to the Moment I'd dare say:
'Stay a while! You are so lovely!'
Through aeons, then, never to fade away
This path of mine through all that's earthly. –
Anticipating, here, its deep enjoyment,
Now I savour it, that highest moment.
(Faust sinks back, the spirits of the dead take him and lay him on the ground.)

MEPHISTOPHELES
No bliss satisfied him, no enjoyment,
And so he tried to catch at shifting forms:
The last, the worst, the emptiest of moments,
He wished to hold at last in his arms.
Though against me he tried to stand,
Time is master: age lies on the sand.
The clock stands still –

CHORUS
Stands still! As midnight: silent.
The hand moves.

MEPHISTOPHELES
It falls, and all is spent.

CHORUS
It's past.

MEPHISTOPHELES
Past! A stupid word.
Then, why?
Past, and pure nothing, complete monotony!

What use is this eternal creation!
Creating, to achieve annihilation!
'There, it's past!' What's to read in it?
It's just the same as if it never lived,
Yet chases round in circles, as if it did.
I'd prefer to have the everlasting void.
Burial

A SPIRIT OF THE DEAD (Solo.)
Who's built the house so badly,
With shovel and with spade?

SPIRITS OF THE DEAD (Chorus.)
For you dull guest, in hempen dress,
It was all too carefully made.

A SPIRIT OF THE DEAD (Solo.)
Who's decked the hall so badly?
Where now the table and chairs?

SPIRITS OF THE DEAD (Chorus.)
Borrowed for a little while:
There are many creditors.

MEPHISTOPHELES
The body's here: if the spirit tries to fly,
I'll show it my blood-signed title swiftly:
Yet men have found so many methods, sadly,
To cheat the Devil of their souls, or try.
We carry on the same old way,
New ones aren't recommended:
I used to work alone: today
I have to use the help extended.
And everything goes badly too!
Ancient right, traditional use,
One can't rely on those much longer.
At the last breath, once, the soul was out,
I slipped by, and like the swiftest mouse,
Caught her! Held her fast, my claws were stronger.
Now she lingers, won't leave the gloomy place,
The foul corpse's hideous house, until
The elements force her, in hatred still,
And drive her out at last, in disgrace.
And though the hour and minute plague me,

'When', 'how' and 'where', still the tiresome query:
Old Death has lost his ancient power,
'Whether' is doubtful, never mind the hour:
Often, with lust, I saw the rigid frame
It was a sham: it stirred, and rose again.

(He makes fantastic, whirling conjuring gestures.)

Now quick! Redouble your paces, too,
You gentlemen, straight or twisted-horned,
The old Devil's grain and kernel born,
And bring Hell's jaws along with you.
True Hell has many jaws! Yes, many!
To swallow according to standing and worth:
However in this last game of all we're ready
To be a little less considerate, henceforth.

(The fearful jaws of Hell open on the left.)

The tusks yawn wide: the jaws of the abyss,
Flow with raging flames, in fury,
And in the boiling background hiss,
I see the eternal glow of the fiery city.
The crimson tide breaks against the teeth,
The damned in hope of help swim through:
But the vast hyena mangles them beneath,
And sends them to new anguish in the brew.
There are many corners to discover,
So many horrors in such little room!
You've done quite well at frightening sinners,
But still they think it dream, deceit, untrue.

(To the fat devils with short straight horns.)

Now, you fat-bellied rascals with fiery cheeks!
You've grown that way eating hellish sulphur:
Stumpy, short, with thick immoveable necks!
Watch below, for any glow of phosphor:
That's the soul, Psyche with the wings,
Pluck them off and she's a nasty worm:
I'll stamp her with my signature, first thing,
Then off with her to the whirling fiery storm!
Pass on towards the nether regions,
You barrels, since all that's your duty:

Whether she lives there, that's the notion,
None know with any accuracy.
She'll gladly lodge in the navel –
Lest she slip away from there, be careful.

(To the lean devils with long crooked horns.)

You, clowns, you giant flying creatures,
Grasp at the air: grant yourselves no rest!
Your strong arms and sharp-clawed features,
Are sure to hold the fluttering fugitive fast.
She's stuck there inside her ancient house,
And Spirit will always look for a way out.

(Glory from above, on the right.)

THE HEAVENLY HOST
Messengers follow
Heavenly kin, oh,
In leisurely flight:
Sin they forgive,
Dust they make live:
The friendship they show
To Nature below,
Floating they'll give,
As they slowly alight!

MEPHISTOPHELES
I hear discords, all that nasty jingling,
Coming from up there, with unwelcome day:
It's always that childish, girlish bungling,
That pious taste loves to hear and play.
You know how we in despicable moments,
Considered the ruin of the human race:
But the most shameful of compliments,
Is that their prayers are a worse disgrace.
These dandies come, the hypocrites:
They've snatched a heap of souls away,
Use our own weapons too to do it:
They're Devils in disguise, I'd say.
To lose this one is everlasting shame:
On to the grave, and renew your claim!

THE CHOIR OF ANGELS (Scattering roses)

Roses, you dazzling ones,
Balsam you're sending us,
Floating and trembling,
Secretly quickening,
Branches inspiring us,
Buds sweetly firing us,
Hasten to bloom!
Crimson and green, here
Springtime assume!
Carry the sleeper
To Paradise' room.

MEPHISTOPHELES (To the devils.)

Why duck and dive? Is that Hell's custom?
Stand still, and let them do their scattering.
Every gawk in place, and face them!
They think with such a flowery smattering,
To cool the heat of devils' chattering:
At your breath it melts and shrinks, again.
Now blow, you blowers! – Enough, enough!
Your bubbling's faded all that stuff. –
Not so fiercely! Close your mouths and noses!
Ah, now you've been too violent with the roses,
Where's the moderation you should have learnt?
They're not just shrivelling: they're burning, burnt!
They float about in flames, poisonous, bright:
Avoid them: close together, huddle tight! –
Your power's waning! And your courage too!
The devils sniff the strange, seductive brew.

THE CHOIR OF ANGELS

Blossoms, of joyfulness,
Flames, of true happiness,
Love, they radiate,
Bliss, they now create,
As the heart may.
Words that are truest,
Air of the clearest,
Gathering round us
Eternal day!

MEPHISTOPHELES

O, curses! O shower of shame that's shed!

Each Satan's standing on his head,
The Fatties spin like tops, in curves,
And plunge arse-upwards into Hell.
Go find the hot baths you deserve!
While at my post I'll stand here still. –

(He beats at the hovering roses.)

Will-o'-the wisps, be gone! Though you burn bright,
Snatched at, in the end, you're disgusting shite.
Why'd you keep fluttering here? Buzz off! –
They stick like tar and sulphur: filthy stuff.

THE CHOIR OF ANGELS
What is not part of you,
You need not share it:
What inwardly troubles you,
You need not bear it.
Should it close in, with force,
We will deflect its course.
Only the loving, Love
Guides to its source!

MEPHISTOPHELES
My head and heart are burnt: my liver's burnt,
By a devilish element!
Sharper than the fires of Hell! –
That's what makes you cry, so, as well,
You, the unlucky in love! Disdained,
Heads turned to the beloved, strained.
Mine, too! What's twisted it to one side?
Are they and I not sworn to eternal strife?
I, once fiercely hostile to their very sight.
Has an alien force pierced me through and through?
I gladly gaze at them, loveliest of youths:
What holds me back from cursing at the light? –
And if I let myself be seduced,
Who'll play the fool in future?
These airy fellows that I hate, too,
How lovely to me now they all appear! –
You sweet children, tell me then:
Aren't you part of Lucifer's race?
You're so nice I'd like to kiss you, and again,
It feels as if this is your proper place.

It feels as comfortable, as natural to me,
As if we'd met a thousand times before:
So surreptitiously catlike, so lustfully:
The loveliness with each glance quickens more.
Oh, come nearer: Oh, only glance at me!

THE ANGELS

We're here already, why so cautiously?
We are close, and, if you can, then stay!

(The Angels come forward and occupy the whole space.)

MEPHISTOPHELES (Crowded into the proscenium.)

You scorn us, the spirits of the damned,
Yet you're of the true Sorcerers' brand:
You lead both man and wife astray. –
What wretched luck, and dire!
Is this Love's own element?
My whole body's bathed in fire,
I scarcely feel, my head's so burnt. –
You float to and fro, sink down a while,
Move your sweet limbs with earthly guile:
True, a grave expression suits you well,
But I'd still like to see you smile a little!
That would be an eternal delight to me.
Like the lovers' mutual glance, you see:
A simper round the mouth, is how it's done,
You, the tall lad, you could make me love you,
The priest's pose doesn't really suit you,
So show a little lust, and look hereon!
You could be more modestly naked too,
That robe's long hem, so demure in its rising –
They turn away – and seen from the rear view –
Those rascals now are really appetising!

THE CHOIR OF ANGELS

You, loving fires,
Brighter, now, fanned,
Heal the damned,
With Truth, the higher!
Let them be freed
From evil indeed,
Blissfully grace,

The eternal embrace.

MEPHISTOPHELES (Collecting himself.)
What's happening to me! – Like Job, in fact
All boils, so I scare myself, and yet I've won
As well, since now my inspection's done,
And my trust in self and tribe's well placed:
The Devil's noble bits appear intact,
This love-bewitchment's only on the surface:
The wretched flames already smother,
And, as is right, I curse you all together!

THE CHOIR OF ANGELS
Pure incandescence!
Whom its flames bless,
Blissful with goodness,
Is their existence.
Gathered together,
Rise now, and praise!
Spirit can breathe here,
In purer waves!

(They rise, carrying away the immortal part of Faust.)

MEPHISTOPHELES (Looking round him.)
How then? – Where did they vanish to?
You took me by surprise, you adolescents.
Now with what they've salvaged from the tomb,
As their own prize, they've flown off to heaven:
They've stolen a great, a unique treasure:
That noble soul, mortgaged to my pleasure,
They've snatched it away, with cunning even.
But whom could I complain to, anyway?
Who'd grant me my well-earned right?
You've been swindled in your old age,
You've deserved it, this wretched slight.
At great expense, shameful! And it's gone:
I've mishandled it all disgracefully,
A common lust, an absurd passion,
Swayed the hardened devil foolishly.
And if Experience was in a mess,
With all these childish, stupid things,
It was, in truth, no trivial Foolishness,

That took possession of him in the end.

VII

MOUNTAIN GORGES, FOREST, ROCK, DESERT

(Holy Hermits, divided in ascending planes, posted among the ravines.)

CHORUS AND ECHO
Forests, they wave around,
Over them, cliffs bear down,
Roots cling to rocky ground,
Trunk upon trunk is bound,
Wave after wave sprays up,
Deep caves protecting us.
Lions prowl silently,
Round us, still friendly,
Honouring sacred space,
Love's holy hiding place.

PATER ECSTATICUS (Hovering up and down.)
Eternal, fire of bliss,
Glow of love's bond this is,
Pain in the heart, seething,
Rapture divine, foaming.
Arrows, come, piercing me,
Spears, compelling me,
Clubs, you may shatter me,
Lightning may flash through me!
So passes the nullity
Of all unreality,
And from the lasting star
Shines Love's eternal core.

PATER PROFUNDIS (At a lower level.)
As this rocky abyss at my feet,
Rests on a deeper abyss,
As a thousand glittering streams meet
In the foaming flood's downward hiss,
As with its own strong impulse, above,
The tree lifts skywards in the air:
Even so all-powerful love,
Creates all things, in its care.
Around me there's a savage roar,
As if the rocks and forests sway,

Yet full of love the waters pour,
Rushing bountifully away,
Sent to irrigate the valley here:
The lightning that flashed down,
Must purify the atmosphere,
With poisonous vapours bound –
They are love's messengers, they tell
Of what creates eternally around us.
May it inflame me inwardly, as well,
Since my spirit, cold and confounded,
Torments itself, bound in the dull senses,
As sharp-toothed fetters' agonising art.
Oh, God! Calm my thoughts, pacify us,
And bring light to my needy heart!

PATER SERAPHICUS (In the middle regions.)
What a mist of morning hovers
Through the pine-trees' swaying hair!
Can I guess what it might cover?
A crowd of spirits live there.

CHOIR OF SACRED YOUNG BOYS
Tell us, Father, where we wander,
Tell us, Kind One, who we are?
We are happy: Being's tender
To all who are, all who are.

PATER SERAPHICUS
Young boys! Born at midnight's hour,
Mind and spirit half-unveiled,
For your parents, a lost dower,
For the angels, profit gained.
You can feel that one who loves
Is near to you, so come to me:
Yet of earthly ways and moves,
You bear no traces, happily.
Rise into my eyes, those known
Organs of the earthly life,
You can use them as your own,
Gaze at all the spaces wide!

(He absorbs them into himself.)

Those are trees: those are cliffs,

A stream of water, rushing round,
With gigantic leaps it lifts,
Shortening its journey down.

THE YOUNG BOYS (From within him.)
That's indeed a mighty vision,
But it's gloomy here, you know,
With fear and dread we're all shaken.
Father, Kind one, let us go!

PATER SERAPHICUS
Rise upwards to the highest sphere,
Grow unnoticed there forever,
While in pure eternal manner,
God's presence makes you stronger.
Such is the spirit's libation,
Blending with the freest air:
Love's eternal revelation,
Bliss is unfolded there.

THE CHOIR OF YOUNG BOYS (Circling round the highest summit.)
Hands now entwining,
Joyfully circling round,
Soaring and singing
With sacred feeling's sound!
In the divinely taught,
Now you should trust:
He whom your worship sought
You'll see at last.

THE ANGELS (Soaring in the highest atmosphere, carrying the immortal part of Faust.)
He's escaped, this noble member
Of the spirit world, from evil,
Whoever strives, in his endeavour,
We can rescue from the devil.
And if he has Love within,
Granted from above,
The sacred crowd will meet him,
With welcome, and with love.

THE YOUNGER ANGELS
Every rose from the hands
Of those penitents, loving, holy,

Helped us win the victory,
The highest work, completed, stands,
The treasure of this soul we've won.
Evil bowed to petals thrown,
Devils fled the blows we threw.
Instead of Hell's hurts anew,
They felt spirits' loving pain:
Pierced with agony again
The old devil-master too was gone.
Shout with joy! All is done.

THE MORE PERFECT ANGELS

Carrying earthly remains
Is hard to endure,
Though they survive the flames,
They are still the impure.
Once a great spirit's strength
So tightly fits
All the four elements,
No angel splits
That double nature wed,
The inwardly binding:
To Eternal Love instead
Is left the unwinding.

THE YOUNGER ANGELS

Misted on rocky heights
Now we are feeling,
Nearing our clearer sight
Spiritual Being.
These clouds are vanishing
A crowd I see, moving,
Of sacred young men,
Freed from their earthly gloom,
Circling together,
Delighting again,
In the spring's brighter bloom,
In higher air.
Let them together then,
Lead him on: risen,
Perfect, and there!

THE YOUNG BOYS

Joyfully we receive

Him as a chrysalis:
So that we now achieve
A pledge of our bliss.
Let all the threads be lost
That now surround him!
He is already blessed,
Divine Love has found him.

DOCTOR MARIANUS (The transformed Faust: in the highest purest cell.)
Here is the freest view,
Of spirit borne skywards.
There women moving too
Drifting on upwards.
The splendour I see within
Garlands of stars,
There, all the Heavens' Queen
Shines from afar.

(Enraptured.)

Highest Queen of all the world!
Let me, in the blue,
With all heaven's web unfurled,
Know your mystery too.
Approve the tender, serious,
Stir of the human heart,
And in love's sacred bliss,
Raise it higher, through your art.
Our courage is unconquerable
When you command on high:
But our glow is gentler, still,
When you are satisfied.
Virgin, pure, of loveliest mind,
Mother, in all nobility,
Peer to everything divine,
Queen of our reality.
Such light cloud fragments
Wind all around her,
They are the penitents,
Women so tender,
All around her knees,
Breathing the air, free,
Desiring her mercy.
You are the Virginal Mother,

It's not surprising
Those seduced by another
Towards you are rising.
Taken in weakness now,
They are all harder to save:
Who can resist the power
Of desires that enslave?
How quickly the feet may slip
On smooth, sloping ground!
Who's un-tempted by glance and lip,
Or by flattering sounds?

(The Mater Gloriosa soars into space.)
CHOIR OF FEMALE PENITENTS
You soar, on high, now,
Towards the eternal realm,
Hear our pleading, though,
You, the peerless one,
Oh, merciful one!

MAGNA PECCATRIX (The sinful woman who anointed Christ's feet, See Luke vii:)
By the love that at the feet there
Of your son, divine, transfigured,
Let the tears like balsam flow there,
Despite the Pharisees' derision:
By the vessel, that so richly
Spread its fragrance on the ground,
By the locks of hair that softly
Dried the holy feet, shed round –

THE WOMAN OF SAMARIA (The woman at the well, See John iv)
By the well, where once before
Abraham's flocks were driven,
By the jar, that cooled the Saviour,
That to sacred lips was given:
By the pure and flowing fountain,
That poured out its clear water,
Overflowing, bright and certain,
Through all the worlds, forever.

MARY OF EGYPT (Acta Sanctorum)
By the consecrated place
Where the Lord's body lay:

By the warning arm, against my face,
That thrust me far from the doorway:
By my forty years' repentance,
Faithful, in that desert land:
By the blissful final sentence
That I wrote there on the sand —

ALL THREE
Since you offer your presence
To the worst sinner,
The prize of penitence
Soars upwards forever,
Begrudge not this true soul,
Who, this once, transgressed,
Not knowing she might fall,
Commensurate forgiveness!

A PENITENT, FORMERLY NAMED GRETCHEN (Stealing closer.)
Oh, bow down,
You peerless one,
You radiant one,
Your face, in mercy, towards my bane!
My true beloved,
No longer clouded,
Returns to me again.

THE SACRED YOUNG BOYS (Nearing, hovering in circles.)
With mighty limbs, already
He is beyond us there,
Returning to us, so richly,
The rewards of our care.
We were taken early
Out of life's chorus:
Yet he's learned, so he
Will gently teach us.

THE PENITENT, FORMERLY NAMED GRETCHEN
Changed to himself, he's scarce aware
Of the spirits' noble choir all around,
He hardly knows his new life, there,
Already he's so like the sacred crowd.
See, how he's thrown off every bond
Of his old earthbound integument,
And his first youth now's re-found,

It shines through his ethereal garment.
Allow me to teach him, here,
The new light still blinds him so.

THE MATER GLORIOSA

Come! Rise towards the higher spheres!
Gaining awareness of you, he will follow.

DOCTOR MARIANUS (Bowing, in adoration.)

Gaze towards that saving gaze,
All you, the penitent and tender,
To all those blissful ways,
Give thanks, and follow after.
Let every finer sense, unseen,
Be offered to her service,
Virgin, Mother now, and Queen,
Goddess, grant your mercies!

THE MYSTIC CHOIR

All of the transient,
Is parable, only:
The insufficient,
Here, grows to reality:
The indescribable,
Here, is done:
Woman, eternal,
Beckons us on.

The Faust Book
the
Wolfenbüttel Manuscript

HISTORIA & TALE OF

DOCTOR JOHANNES FAUSTUS

The sorcerer, wherein is described specifically and veraciously:

His entire life and death,

How he did oblige himself for a certain time unto the Devil,

And what happened to him,

And how he at last got his well-deserved reward

Rare revelations are also included, for these examples are most useful and efficacious as a highly essential Christian warning and admonition, that the laity, in order to protect themselves from similar maculations of the most shameful sort, have especial cause to heed and to avoid such a desperate fate.

Of His Parentage and Youth

I

Doctor Faustus, the son of a husbandman, was born in Roda in the Province of Weimar. His parents were godfearing and Christian people with many connections in Wittemberg. A kinsman who dwelt there was a citizen and possessed of considerable wealth. He reared Faustus for the parents and kept him as his own child, for, being himself without issue, he adopted this Faustus, made him his heir, and sent him to school to study theology. Faustus, however, strayed from this godly purpose and used God's Word vainly.

Therefore we shall blame neither his parents nor his patrons, who desired only the best (as do all pious parents), nor shall we mix them into this *Historia*. For they neither witnessed nor experienced the abominations of their godless child. One thing is certain: that these parents, as was generally known in Wittemberg, were quite heartily delighted that their kinsman adopted him. When they later perceived in Faustus his excellent *ingenium* and *memoria*, it did most assuredly trouble them, just as Job in the first chapter of that Book was concerned for his children, lest they sin against the Lord. Therefore pious parents do sometimes have godless, naughty children, and I point this out because there have been many who imputed great guilt and calumny to these parents whom I would herewith pardon. Such distortions are not merely abusive. If they imply that Faustus had been taught such things by his parents, they are also slanderous. Indeed, certain charges are alleged--to wit: that his parents had permitted wantonness in his youth, and that they had not diligently held him to his studies. It is charged that, so soon as his cleverness-- together with his lack of inclination to theology--was perceived, it being further public hue and cry that he was practicing magic, his family should have prevented it betimes. All such rumors are *somnia*, for the parents, being without guilt, should not be slandered. But now *ad propositum*.

Faustus was a most percipient and adroit fellow, qualified and inclined toward study, and he performed so well at his examination that the rectors also examined him for the *Magister* Degree. There were sixteen other candidates, to whom he proved in address, composition, and competence so superior that it was immediately concluded he had studied sufficiently, and he became *Doctor Theologiæ*. For the rest, he was also a stupid, unreasonable and vain fellow, whom, after all, his companions always called the *speculator*. He came into the worst company, for a time laid the Holy Scriptures behindst the door and under the bench, did not revere God's Word but lived crassly and godlessly in gluttony and lust (as the progress of this *Historia* will sufficiently manifest). Surely the proverb is true: what is inclined to the Devil will go to the Devil.

Furthermore, Doctor Faustus found his ilk, who dealt in Chaldean, Persian, Arabian and Greek words, *figuræ, characteres, coniurationes, incantationes*; and these things recounted were pure *Dardaniæ artes, Nigromantiæ, carmina, veneficii, vaticini, incantationes*, and whatever you care to call such books, words and names for conjuring and sorcery. They well pleased Doctor Faustus, he speculated and studied night and day in them. Soon he refused to be called a *Theologus*, but waxed a worldly man, called himself a *Doctor Medicinæ*, became an *Astrologus* and *Mathematicus*--and, for respectability, a physician. At first he helped many people with medicaments, herbs, roots, waters, receipts, and clisters. He became learned besides, well versed in the Holy Scriptures, and he knew quite accurately the Laws of Christ: he who knoweth the will of the Lord and doeth it not, he is doubly smitten. Likewise, thou shalt not tempt the Lord thy God. All this he threw in the wind and put his soul away for a time above the door sill, wherefore there shall for him be no pardon.

How Doctor Faustus Did Achieve
and Acquire Sorcery

II

As was reported above, Doctor Faustus' complexion was such that he loved what ought not be loved, and to the which his spirit did devote itself day and night, taking on eagle's wings and seeking out the very foundations of Heaven and Earth. For his prurience, insolence and folly so pricked and incited him that he at last resolved to utilize and to prove certain magical *vocabula, figuræ, characteres* and *coniurationes* in the hope of compelling the Devil to appear before him. Hence (as others also report and as indeed Doctor Faustus himself later made known) he went into a great dense forest which is called the **Spesser Wald** and is situated near Wittemberg. Toward evening, at a crossroad in these woods, he described certain circles with his staff, so that, beside twain, the two which stood above intersected a large circle. Thus in the night between nine and ten o'clock he did conjure the Devil.

Now the Devil feigned he would not willingly appear at the spot designated, and he caused such a tumult in the forest that everything seemed about to be destroyed. He blew up such a wind that the trees were bent to the very ground. Then it seemed as were the wood with devils filled, who rode along past Doctor Faustus' circle; now only their coaches were to be seen; then from the four corners of the forest something like lightning bolts converged on Doctor Faustus' circle, and a loud explosion ensued. When all this was past, it became light in the midst of the forest, and many sweet instruments, music and song could be heard. There were various dances, too, and tourneys with spears and swords. Faustus, who thought he might have tarried long enough now, considered fleeing from his circle, but finally he regained his godless and reckless resolve and persisted in his former intention, come whatever God might send. He continued to conjure the Devil as before, and the Devil did mystify him with the following hoax. He appeared like a griffon or a dragon hovering and flattering above the circle, and when Doctor Faustus then applied his spell the beast shrieked piteously. Soon thereafter a fiery star fell right down from three or four fathoms above his head and was transformed into a glowing ball. This greatly alarmed Faustus, too. But his purpose liked him so well, and he so admired having the Devil subservient to him that he took courage and did conjure the star once, twice, and a third time, whereupon a gush of fire from the sphere shot up as high as a man, settled again, and six little lights became visible upon it. Now one little light would leap upward, now a second downward until the form of a burning man finally emerged. He walked round about the circle for a full seven or eight minutes. The entire spectacle, however, had lasted until twelve o'clock in the night. Now a devil, or a spirit, appeared in the figure of a gray friar, greeted Doctor Faustus, and asked what his desire and intent might be. Hereupon Doctor Faustus commanded that he should appear at his house and lodging at a certain hour the next morning, the which the devil for a while refused to do. Doctor Faustus conjured him by his master, however, compelling him to fulfill his desire, so that the spirit at last consented and agreed.

Here Followeth the *Disputatio* Held

by Faustus and the Spirit

III

Doctor Faustus returned home and later the same morning commanded the spirit into his chamber, who indeed appeared to hear what Doctor Faustus might desire of him (and it is most astounding that a spirit, when God withdraws his hand, can so deceive mankind). Doctor Faustus again commenced his machinations, conjured him anew, and laid before the spirit these several articles, to wit:

Firstly, that the spirit should be subservient and obedient to him in all that he might request, inquire, or expect of him, throughout Faustus' life and death.

Secondly, that the spirit would withhold no information which Faustus, in his studies, might require.

Thirdly, that the spirit would respond nothing untruthful to any of his *interrogationes*.

The spirit immediately rejected the articles, refused Faustus, and explained his reason: that he had not complete authority except in so far as he could obtain it from his lord who ruled over him. He spake: Sweet Fauste, it standeth neither within my election nor authority to fulfill thy desires, but is left to the Hellish god.

Faustus replied: What? How am I to understand thee? Art thou not thine own master?

The spirit answered: Nay.

Faustus then said to him: Sweet spirit, explain it to me then.

Now thou shalt know, Fauste, said the spirit, that among us there is a government and sovereignty, just as on earth, for we have our rulers and governors and servants--of whom I am one--and we call our kingdom Legion. For although the banished devil Lucifer brought about his own fall through vanity and insolence, he raised up a Legion, nevertheless, and a government of devils, and we call him the Oriental Prince, for he had his sovereignty in Ascension. It is thus a sovereignty *in Meridie, Septentrione* and *Occidente* as well. Therefore, inasmuch as Lucifer the fallen angel now hath his sovereignty and principality beneath the Heavens, we must, on account of this transformation, betake ourselves unto mankind and serve them. But with all his power and arts man could not make Lucifer subservient, except that a spirit be sent, as I am sent. Certainly we have never revealed to men the real fundament of our dwelling place, nor our rule and sovereignty. No one knoweth what doth occur after the death of the damned human--who learneth and experienceth it.

Doctor Faustus became alarmed at this and said: Then I will not be damned for thy sake.

The spirit answered: **Wilt not agree? For thee no plea. If there be no plea, thou must come with me. Thou wost it not when we hold thee. Yet come thou must with me, nor helpeth any plea: an insolent heart hath damned thee.**

Then Doctor Faustus said: A pox take thee! Hence! Begone !

Even in the moment when the spirit was about to withdraw, Doctor Faustus did change his vacillating mind. He conjured the spirit to appear at the same place at vespers to hear what else he would require. The spirit granted this and disappeared from before him.

The Second *Disputatio* with the Spirit

IV

At Vespers, or at four 0' clock in the evening, the flying spirit again appeared unto Faustus and proffered his obedience and subservience in all things, if so be that Faustus would tender certain articles to him in return. Would he do that, then his desires would know no want. These following were the several articles required by the spirit:

Firstly, that he, Faustus, would agree to a certain number of years, at the expiration of which he would promise and swear to be his, the spirit's, own property.

Secondly, that he would, to the further confirmation thereof, give himself over with a writ to this effect authenticated in his own blood.

Thirdly, that he would renounce the Christian Faith and defy all believers.

Should he observe all such points, every lust of his heart would be fulfilled, And (spake the spirit) thou shalt immediately be possessed of a spirit's form and powers. Puffed up with pride and arrogance, Doctor Faustus (although he did consider for a space) had got so proud and reckless that he did not want to give thought to the weal of his soul, but came to terms with the evil spirit, promised to observe all his articles, and to obey them. He supposed that the Devil might not be so black as they use to paint him, nor Hell so hot as the people say.

Doctor Faustus' Third *Colloquium* with the Spirit,

Which Was Called Mephostophiles--

Concerning Also the Pact Which

These Two Made

V

Now as for the Pact, it came about on this wise. Doctor Faustus required the spirit to come before him on the next morning, commanding him to appear, so often as he might be called, in the figure, form and raiment of a Franciscan Monk,and always with a little bell to give certain signals withal, in order that by the sound it might be known when he was approaching. Then he asked the spirit his name, and the spirit answered: Mephostophiles. --Even in this hour did the godless man cut himself off from his God and Creator to become a liege of the abominable Devil, whereto pride, arrogance and transgression did bring and seduce him.

Afterwards, in audacity and trangression, Doctor Faustus executed a written instrument and document to the evil spirit. This was a blasphemous and horrible thing, which was found in his lodging after he had lost his life. I will include it as a warning to all pious Christians, lest they yield to the Devil and be cheated of body and soul (as afterward his poor famulus was by Doctor Faustus to this devilish work seduced).

When these two wicked parties contracted with one another , Doctor Faustus took a penknife, pricked open a vein in his left hand (and it is the veritable truth that upon this hand were seen graven and bloody the words: *o homo fuge--id est:* o mortal fly from him and do what is right), drained his blood into a crucible, set it on some hot coals and wrote as here followeth.

Doctor Faustus' *Instrumentum,*

or Devilish and Godless Writ

Obligatio

VI

I, JOHANN FAUSTUS, Dr.,

Do publicly declare with mine own hand in covenant & by power of these presents:

Whereas, mine own spiritual faculties having been exhaustively explored (including the gifts dispensed from above and graciously imparted to me), I still cannot comprehend;

And whereas, it being my wish to probe further into the matter, I do propose to speculate upon the *Elementa;*

And whereas mankind doth not teach such things;

Now therefore have I summoned the spirit who calleth himself Mephostophiles, a servant of the Hellish Prince in Orient, charged with informing and instructing me, and agreeing against a promissory instrument hereby transferred unto him to be subservient and obedient to me in all things.

I do promise him in return that, when I be fully sated of that which I desire of him, twenty-four years also being past, ended and expired, he may at such a time and in whatever manner or wise pleaseth him order, ordain, reign, rule and possess all that may be mine: body, property, flesh, blood, etc., herewith duly bound over in eternity and surrendered by covenant in mine own hand by authority and power of these presents, as well as of my mind, brain, intent, blood and will.

I do now defy all living beings, all the Heavenly Host and all mankind, and this must be.

In confirmation and contract whereof I have drawn out mine own blood for certification in lieu of a seal.

Doctor Faustus, Adept

in the *Elementa* and in Church Doctrine.

Concerning the Service that Mephostophiles

Used Toward Faustus

VII

Doctor Faustus having with his own blood and in his own hand committed such an abomination unto the spirit, it is certainly to be assumed that God and the whole Heavenly Host did turn away from him. He dwelt in the house of his good Wittemberg kinsman, who had died and in his testament bequeathed it to Doctor Faustus. With him he had a young schoolboy as famulus, a reckless lout named Christoph Wagner. Doctor Faustus' game well pleased Wagner, and his lord also flattered him by saying he would make a learned and worthy man of him. A tune like that appealed to him (youth being always more inclined toward wickedness than toward goodness).

Now Doctor Faustus, as I said, had no one in his house save his famulus and his spirit Mephostophiles, who, in his presence, always went about in the form of a friar, and whom Doctor Faustus conjured in his study, a room which he kept locked at all times. Faustus had a superfluity of victuals and provisions, for when he desired a good wine the spirit brought it to him from whatever cellars he liked (the Doctor himself was once heard to remark that he made great inroads on the cellar of his Lord Elector of Saxony as well as those of the Duke of Bavaria and the Bishop of Saltzburg). He likewise enjoyed cooked fare every day, for he was so cunning in sorcery that when he opened a window and named some fowl he desired, it came flying right in through the window. His spirit also brought him cooked meat of a most princely sort from the courts of the nobility in all territories round about. The fabrics for his apparel and that of his boy (he went sumptuously attired) the spirit also had to buy or steal by night in Nuremberg, Augsburg or Frankfurt. A similar injury was done the tanners and cobblers. In sum, it was stolen, wickedly borrowed goods, so that Doctor Faustus' meat and clothing was very respectable, but godless. Indeed Christ our Lord doth through John call the Devil a thief and a murderer, and that is what he is.

The devil also promised to give Faustus twenty-five Crowns a week, which amounts to 1,300 Crowns a year, and that was his year's emolument.

Concerning Doctor Faustus' Intended

Marriage

VIII

While he lived thus day in and day out like an Epicure--or like a sow--
with faith neither in God, Hell nor the Devil, Doctor Faustus' *aphrodisia* did
day and night so prick him that he desired to enter matrimony and take a wife.
He questioned his spirit in this regard, who was to be sure an enemy of the
matrimonial estate as created and ordained by God.

The spirit answered: Well, what is thy purpose with thyself? *Viz.*, had
Faustus forgot his commitment, and would he not hold to the promise wherein
he had vowed enmity to God and mankind ? If so, then neither by chance nor
by intent dare he enter matrimony.

For a man cannot serve two masters (spake the devil), God and us, too.
Matrimony is a work of the Lord God. We, who take our profit from all that
pertains to and derives from adultery and fornication, are opposed to it.
Wherefore, Fauste, look thou to it: shouldst thou promise to wed, thou shalt
then most assuredly be torn into little pieces by us. Sweet Fauste, judge for
thyself what unquiet, antipathy, anger and strife result from matrimony.

Doctor Faustus considered various sides of the matter, his monk
constantly presenting objections. At last he said: Well, I will wed, let come of
it what may!

When Faustus had uttered this resolve, a storm wind did fall upon his
house and seemed about to destroy it. All the doors leapt from their hooks,
and at the same instant his house was quite filled with heat, just as if it were
about to burn away into pure ashes. Doctor Faustus took to his heels down the
stair, but a man caught him up and cast him back into the parlor with such a
force that he could move neither hand nor foot. Round about him everywhere
sprang up fire. He thought he would be burned alive, and he screamed to his
spirit for help, promising to live in accordance with every wish, counsel and
precept. Then the Devil himself appeared unto him, so horrible and malformed
that Faustus could not look upon him.

Satan said: Now tell me, of what purpose art thou?

Doctor Faustus gave him short answer, admitting that he had not
fulfilled his promise in that he had not deemed it to extend so far, and he did
request Grace.

Satan answered him equally curtly: Then be henceforth steadfast. I tell
thee, be steadfast

After this, the spirit Mephostophiles came to him and said unto him: If
thou are henceforth steadfast in thy commitment, then will I tickle thy lust

otherwise, so that in thy days thou wilt wish naught else than this--namely: if thou canst not live chastely, then will I lead to thy bed any day or night whatever woman thou seest in this city or elsewhere. Whosoever might pleasethy lust, and whomever thou might desire in lechery, she shall abide with thee in such a figure and form.

Doctor Faustus was so intrigued by this that his heart trembled with joys and his original proposal rued him. And he did then come into such libidinousness and debauchery that he yearned day and night after the figure of the beautiful women in such excellent forms, dissipating today with one devil and having another on his mind tomorrow.

Doctor Faustus' *Questio*

of his Spirit Mephostophiles

IX

Now after Doctor Faustus had for a time carried on such a very fine matrimony with the Devil (as was reported above), his spirit committed unto him a great book containing all manner of sorcery and *nigromantia*, wherein he indulged himself in addition to his devilish wedlock (these *dardaniæ artes* later being found with his famulus and son Christoph Wagner). Soon his curiosity did prick him and he summoned his spirit Mephostophiles, with whom he desired to converse and to whom he said : Tell me, my servant, what manner of spirit art thou?

The spirit answered and spake: This disputatio and question, if I am to elucidate it for thee, my Lord Fauste, will move thee somewhat to discontent and to contemplation. Moreover, thou ought not have asked such of me, for it toucheth on our arcana. But I must obey thee.

Thou shalt know therefore that the Banished Angel at the time of his fall was still graciously and kindly disposed toward man, who had just been created. But soon the leaf did turn and Lucifer, become enemy to God and all mankind, presumed to work all manner of tyranny upon men--as is every day manifest when someone falleth to his death; another hangeth, drowneth or stabbeth himself; a third is stabbed, driven mad, and the like other cases which thou might have observed. Because the first man was created so perfect by God, the Devil begrudged it him. He beset Adam and Eve and brought them with all their seed into sin, and out of the Grace of God. Such, sweet Fauste, is the onslaught and tyranny of Satan. Likewise did he unto Cain: He caused the people of Israel to worship him, to sacrifice unto strange gods and to go lustfully in unto the heathen women. It was one of our spirits who pursued Saul and drave him into madness, pricking him on til he took his own life. Another spirit is amongst us, Asmodeus, who slew seven men in lechery. Then there is the spirit Dagon, who caused 30,000 men to fall way from God, so that they were slain and the Ark of God was captured. And Belial, who did so prick David's heart that he began to number the people, and 60,000 perished. It was one of us who sent Solomon awhoring after false gods. Without number are our spirits that do insinuate themselves among men and bring them to fall. To this very day we still distribute ourselves over all the world, using every sort of guile and rascality, driving men away from the Faith and urging them on to sin and wickedness, that we may strengthen ourselves as best we can against Jesus by plaguing his followers unto death. We possess of course the hearts of all kings and rulers of this world, hardening them against the teachings of Jesus and of his apostles and followers.

Doctor Faustus answered and spake: So hast thou possessed me also? Sweet fellow, tell me the truth.

The spirit answered: Well why not? As soon as we looked upon thy heart and saw with what manner of thoughts thou didst consort, how thou couldst neither use nor get another than the Devil for such an intent and purpose, lo, we then made those thoughts and strivings yet more impious and bold, and so prurient that thou hadst no rest by day nor by night, all thine aspirations and endeavors being directed toward the accomplishment of sorcery. Even while thou didst conjure us, we were at making thee so wicked and so audacious that thou hadst let the very Devil fetch thee before thou hadst forsaken thy purpose. Afterward, we encouraged thee yet further until we had planted it into thy heart not to falter in thy cause until thou hadst a spirit subservient unto thee. In the end, we persuaded thee to yield thyself to us finally and with body and soul. All this, Lord Fauste, thou canst confirm in thine own heart.

It is true, quoth Doctor Faustus, there is no turning from my way now. I have ensnared myself. Had I kept god-fearing thoughts, and held to God in prayer, not allowing the Devil so to strike root within me, then had I not suffered such injury in body and soul. Ay, what have I done, etc.

The spirit made answer: Look thou to it.

Thus did Doctor Faustus take his despondent leave.

A *Disputatio* Concerning the Prior State

of the Banished Angels

X

Doctor Faustus again undertook a discourse with his spirit, asking: How, then, did thy master, Lucifer, come to fall?

This time, Mephostophiles asked of him a three-day prorogation, but on the third day the spirit gave him this answer: My Lord Lucifer (who is so called on account of his banishment from the clear light of Heaven) was in Heaven an angel of God and a cherub. He beheld all works and creations of God in Heaven and was himself with such honor, title, pomp, dignity and prominence as to be the exemplary creature before God, in great perfection of wisdom, yea in such brilliance that he outshone all other creatures and was an ornament beyond all other works of God, gold and precious stones, even the sun and stars. For so soon as God created him He placed him upon the Mount of God as a sovereign prince, and he was perfect in all his ways.

But so soon as he rose up in insolence and vanity and would exalt himself above Orient he was driven out from the House of Heaven, thrust down into fiery brimstone which is eternally unextinguished and tormenteth him forever. He had been honored with the crown of all Heavenly pomp. But since he sat in spiteful council against God, God sat upon His Throne of Judgement and condemned him to Hell, whence he can never more rise up.

Doctor Faustus, having heard the spirit concerning these things, did now speculate upon many different tenets and justifications. He went in silence from the spirit into his chamber, laid himself upon his bed and began bitterly to weep and to sigh, and to cry out in his heart. For the account by the spirit caused him this time to consider how the Devil and Banished Angel had been so excellently honored of God, and how, if he had not been so rebellious and arrogant against God, he would have had an eternal Heavenly essence and residence, but was now by God eternally banished.

Faustus spake: O woe is me and ever woe! Even so will it come to pass with me also, nor will my fate be the more bearable, for I am likewise God's creature, and my insolent flesh and blood have set me body and soul into perdition, enticed me with my reason and mind so that I as a creature of God am strayed from Him and have let the Devil seduce me to bind myself unto him with body and soul, wherefore I can hope no more for Grace, but must needs be, like Lucifer, banished into perpetual damnation and lamentation. Ah woe and ever woe! To what perils I am exposing myself! What is my purpose with myself? 0, that I were never born!

Thus did Doctor Faustus complain, but he would not take faith, nor hope that he might be through penitence brought back to the Grace of God. For if he had thought: The Devil doth now take on such a color that I must look up to Heaven. Lo, I will turn about again and call upon God for Grace and Forgiveness, for to sin no more is a great penance. Then Faustus would have betaken himself to church and followed Holy Doctrine, thereby offering the Devil resistance. Even if he had been compelled to yield up his body here on earth, his soul would nevertheless have been saved. But he became doubtful in all his tenets and opinions, having no faith and little hope.

A *Disputatio* Concerning Hell,

How It Was Created and Fashioned;

Concerning Also the Torments in Hell

XI

Doctor Faustus felt, no doubt, contrition in his heart at all times. It was a concern for how he had endangered his own salvation when he plighted himself to the Devil for the sake of temporal things. But his contrition was the contrition and penance of Cain and Judas. Indeed there was contrition in his heart, but he despaired of the Grace of God, it seeming to him an impossibility to gain God's favor: like unto Cain, who also despaired, saying his sins were greater than could be forgiven him. It was the same with Judas.

And it was the same with Doctor Faustus. I suppose he looked up to Heaven, but his eyes discerned naught therein. They say that he dreamt of the Devil and of Hell. That means that when he recalled his transgressions he could not help thinking that frequent and much disputation, inquiry, and discourse with the spirit would bring him to such a fear of the consequences of sin that he would be able to mend his ways, repent his sins, and sin no more.

Thus Doctor Faustus again decided to hold discourse and a colloquium with the spirit, asking him: What is Hell ; further, how Hell.was created and constituted; thirdly, about the manner of wailing and lamentation of the damned in Hell; and fourthly, whether the damned could come again into the favor of God and be released from Hell.

The spirit gave answer to none of these questions or articles, but spake: As concerns thy purpose, Lord Fauste, thy *disputatio* on Hell and Hell's effects on man, thy desire for elucidation--I say to thee: what is thy purpose with thyself?

If thou couldst ascend directly into Heaven, yet would I fling thee down into Hell again, for thou art mine, walking my path toward Hell even in thy many questions about Hell. Sweet Fauste, desist. Inquire of other matters. Believe me, my account will bring thee into such remorse, despondency, pensiveness, and anxiety that thou wilt wish thou hadst never posed this question. My judgement and advice remains: desist from this purpose.

Doctor Faustus spake: And I will know it or I will not live, and thou must tell it me.

Very well, quoth the spirit, I will tell thee. It costeth me little grief.

Thou wouldst know what Hell is, but the mortal soul is such that all thy speculations can never comprehend Hell, nor canst thou conceive the manner of place where the Wrath of God is stored. The origin and structure is God's

Wrath, and it hath many titles and designations, as: House of Shame, Abyss, Gullet, Pit, also *Dissensio*. For the souls of the damned are so shamed, scorned and mocked by God and His Blessed Ones as to be confined in the House of the Abyss and Gullet. For Hell is an insatiate Pit and Gullet which ever gapeth after the souls which shall not be damned, desiring that they, too, might be seduced and damned. This is what thou must understand, good Doctor.

So soon as my master was fallen, and even in that moment, Hell was ready for him and received him. It is a Darkness where Lucifer is all banished and bound with chains of darkness, here committed that he may be held for Judgement. Naught may be found there but fumes, fire and the stench of sulphur. --But we devils really cannot know in what form and wise Hell is created, either, nor how it be founded and constructed by God, for it hath neither end nor bottom.

That is my first and second report, which thou hast required of me. For the third, thou didst conjure me and demand of me a report as to what manner of wailing and lamentation the damned will find in Hell. Perchance, my Lord Fauste, thou shouldst consult the Scriptures (they being withheld from me). But now even as the aspect and description of Hell is terrible, so to be in it is an unbearable, acute agony. Inasmuch as I have already given account of the former, thy hellish speculations on the latter will I also satisfy with a report. The damned will encounter all the circumstances which I recounted afore, for what I say is true:

The pit of Hell, like woman's womb and earth's belly, is never sated. Nevermore will an end or cessation occur. They will cry out and lament their sin and wickedness, the damned and hellish hideousness of the stench of their own afflictions. There will then be at last a calling out, a screaming and a wailing up unto God, with woe, trembling, whimpering, yelping, screaming and pain and affliction, with howling and weeping. Well, should they not scream woe and tremble and whimper, being outcast, with all Creation and all the children of God against them, bearing perpetual ignominy while the blessed enjoy eternal honor? And the woe and trembling of some will be greater than that of others, for, as sins are not equal, neither are the torments and agonies the same.

We spirits shall be freed. We have hope of being saved. But the damned will lament the insufferable cold, the unquenchable fire, the unbearable darkness, stench, the aspect of the devils, and the eternal loss of anything good. Oh, they will lament with weeping of eyes, gnashing of teeth, stench in their noses, moaning in their throats, terror in their ears, trembling in their hands and feet. They will devour their tongues for great pain. They will wish for death, would gladly die, but cannot, for death will flee from them. Their torment and agony will wax hourly greater and acuter.

There, my Lord Fauste, thou hast thy third answer, which is consonant with the first and second. Thy fourth question pertaineth to God: whether He will receive the damned into His Grace again. Thanks to thine other, related inquiries, and mine own views concerning Hell and its nature, how it was created of God's Wrath, we have been able to clarify certain fundamentals in advance. Thou shalt now receive one further, specific account (notwithstanding that it will be in direct violation of thy contract and vow).

Thy last question is whether the damned in Hell can ever come again into the favor and Grace of God, and mine answer is: No. For all who are in Hell are there because God banished them there, and they must therefore burn perpetually in God's Wrath and severity, must remain and abide in a place where no hope can be believed. Yea, if they could eventually gain the Grace of God (as we spirits, who always have hope and are in constant expectancy) they would take cheer, and sigh in anticipation. But the damned have even as little hope as have the devils in Hell of transcending their banishment and disgrace. They can have no more hope of salvation than can they hope for a twinkling of light in Hell's darkness, for refreshment with a drink of water in hellfire's heat and anguish, or for warmth in Hell's cold. Neither their pleading, nor their prayer, their crying nor their sighing will be heard, and their conscience will not let them forget.

Emperors, kings, princes, counts and other such regents will lament: had they but not lived all in violence and lust, then they might come into the favor of God. A rich man: had he but not been a miser. A frivolous man: had he but not been vainglorious. An adulterer and philanderer: had he but not indulged in lechery, adultery and fornication. A drunkard, glutton, gambler, blasphemer, perjurer, thief, highwayman, murderer, and their ilk: had I but not filled my belly daily with sumptuousness, pleasure and superfluity of drink and victual, had I but not cheated, blasphemed God in my heart, had I but not scolded wickedly and wantonly against God at every opportunity, had I but not borne false witness, stolen, sacked, murdered, robbed, then perhaps I could still hope for Grace. But my sins are too great and cannot be forgiven me, wherefore I must suffer this hellish torment. Hence may I, damned man, be sure that there is no Grace for me.

Let it be understood then, my Lord Fauste, that the damned man--or the soul, if you will--can no more attain Grace than can he hope for an end to his sufferings or a tide wherein he might perchance be removed from such anguish. Why, if they could be given the hope of dipping water day by day from the sea at the sea shore until the sea were dry, then that would be a redemption. Or if there were a sandheap as high as Heaven from which a bird coming every other year might bear away but one little grain at a time, and they would be saved after the whole heap were consumed, then that would be a hope. But God will never take any thought of them. They will lie in Hell like unto the bones of the dead. Death and their conscience will gnaw on them. Their firm belief and faith in God--oh they will at last acquire it--will go unheeded, and no thought will be taken of them. Thou thinkest perhaps that the damned soul might cover itself over and conceal itself in Hell until God's Wrath might at last subside, and thou hast the hope that there might come a release if thou but persist in the aim of hope that God might still take thought of thee--even then there will be no salvation. There will come a time when the mountains collapse, and when all the stones at the bottom of the sea are dry, and all the raindrops have washed the earth away. It is possible to conceive of an elephant or a camel entering into a needle's eye, or of counting all the raindrops. But there is no conceiving of a time for hope in Hell.

Thus, in short, my Lord Fauste, hast thou my fourth and last report. And thou shalt know that if thou ask me more of such things another time thou shalt get no audience from me, for I am not obligated to tell thee such things. Therefore leave me in peace with further such probings and *disputationes.*

Again Doctor Faustus departed from the spirit all melancholy, confused and full of doubt, thinking now this way now that, and pondering on these things day and night. But there was no constancy in him, for the Devil had hardened his heart and blinded him. And indeed when he did succeed in being alone to contemplate the Word of God, the Devil would dizen himself in the form of a beautiful woman, embrace him, debauching with him, so that he soon forgot the Divine Word and threw it to the wind.

His Almanacs and Horoscopes

XII

Doctor Faustus, being no longer able to obtain answers from his spirit concerning godly matters, now had to rest content and desist from this purpose. It was in those days that he set about making almanacs and became a good *astronomus* and *astrologus*. He gained so much learning and experience from the spirit concerning horoscopes that all which he did contrive and write won the highest praise among all the *mathematici* of that day (as is, after all, common knowledge by now) .His horoscopes, which he sent to great lords and princes, always were correct, for he contrived them according to the advice of his spirit as to what would come to pass in the future, all such matters falling duly out even as he had presaged them.

His tables and almanacs were praised above others because he set down naught in them but what did indeed come to pass. When he forecast fogs, wind, snow, precipitation, etc., these things were all quite certain. His almanacs were not as those of some unskilled *astrologi* who know of course that it gets cold in the winter, and hence forecast freezes, or that it will be hot in the summer, and predict thunderstorms. Doctor Faustus always calculated his tables in the manner described above, setting what should come to pass, specifying the day and the hour and especially warning the particular districts-- this one with famine, that one with war, another with pestilence, and so forth.

A Disputatio, or Inquiry Concerning

the Art of Astronomia, or Astrologia

XIII

One time after Doctor Faustus had been contriving and producing such horoscopes and almanacs for about two years he did ask his spirit about the nature of *astronomia* or *astrologia* as practiced by the *mathematici*.

The spirit gave answer, saying: My Lord Fauste, it is so ordained that the ancient haruspices and modern stargazers are unable to forecast anything particularly certain, for these are deep mysteries of God which mortals cannot plumb as we spirits can, who hover in the air beneath Heaven where we can see and mark what God bath predestined. Yes, we are ancient spirits, experienced in the Heavenly movements. Why, Lord Fauste, I could make thee a perpetual calendar for the setting of horoscopes and almanacs or for nativity investigations one year after the other. --Thou bast seen that I have never lied to thee. Now it is true that the Patriarchs, who lived for five and six hundred years, did comprehend the fundamentals of this art and became very adept. For when such a great number of years elapse a lunisolar period is completed, and the older generation can apprise the younger of it. Except for that, all green, inexperienced *astrologi* have to set up their horoscopes arbitrarily according to conjecture.

A Disputatio and False Answer

Which the Spirit Gave to Doctor Faustus

XIV

The spirit, finding Doctor Faustus all sorrowful and melancholy, did ask him what his grievance might be, and what was on his mind. When he saw that Doctor Faustus would give him no answer, he became importunate and pressing, demanding to know the exact nature of Faustus' thoughts, so that he might be of some aid to him if at all possible.

Doctor Faustus answered, saying: Well, I have taken thee unto me as a servant, and thy service doth cost me dear enough. Yet I cannot have my will of thee, as would be proper of a servant.

The spirit spake: My Lord, thou knowest that I have never opposed thee, but have ever humored thee. Except on one occasion, when I withheld information on one specific subject and under certain express terms, I have ever been submissive unto thee. Now why wilt thou not reveal thy desires? What is in thy mind?

With such talk the spirit stole away the heart of Faustus, and he confessed that he had been wondering how God created the world, and about the original birth of mankind. The spirit now gave Faustus a godless, unchristian and childish account and report on this subject, saying:

The world, my Lord Fauste, hath never experienced birth and will never know death, and the human race has always existed. There is not any origin or beginning of things. The earth subsists, as always, of itself. The sea arose from the earth, and the two got along so very well that one would think they had carried on a conversation in which the land had required his realm from the sea, the fields, meadows, woods, grass and trees; and that the sea had likewise demanded his own realm of water with the fish and all else therein. Now they did concede to God the creation of mankind and of Heaven, and this is the way they finally became subservient to God. Thou wilt observe that I have explained how from one realm there finally arose four: air, fire, water, and earth. I know none other, nor briefer, way of instructing thee.

Doctor Faustus speculated on these things but could not comprehend them, for in the first chapter of Genesis he had read how Moses had told it otherwise. For this reason, he made no further comment.

How Doctor Faustus Traveled

Down to Hell

XV

With each passing day, Doctor Faustus' end drew closer, and he was now come into his eighth year, having been for the most part of the time engaged in inquiry, study, questioning and *disputationes*. In these days he again did dream of Hell, and it caused him again to summon his servant, the spirit Mephostophiles, demanding that he call his own lord, Belial, unto him. The spirit agreed to do this, but instead of Belial a devil was sent who called himself Beelzebub, a flying spirit reigning beneath Heaven. When he asked what Doctor Faustus desired of him, Faustus asked whether it could not be arranged for a spirit to conduct him into Hell and out again, so that he might see and mark the nature, fundament, quality and substance of Hell.

Yes, answered Beelzebub, I will come at midnight and fetch thee.

Well, when it got pitch dark Beelzebub appeared unto him, bearing upon his back a bone chair which was quite enclosed round about. Here Doctor Faustus took a seat, and they flew away. Now hear how the Devil did mystify and gull him, so that he had no other notion than that he really had been in Hell.

He bare him into the air, where Doctor Faustus fell asleep just as if he were lying in a bath of warm water. Soon afterward he came upon a mountain of a great island, high above which sulphur, pitch and flashes of fire blew and crashed with such a tumult that Doctor Faustus awoke just as his devilish dragon swooped down into the abyss. Although all was violently burning round about him, he sensed neither heat nor fire, but rather little spring breezes as in May. Then he heard many different instruments whose music was exceeding sweet, but, as bright as shone the fire, he could see no one playing, nor durst he ask, questions having been strictly forbidden him.

Meanwhile, three more devilish dragons had flown up alongside Beelzebub. They were just like him and they went flying along ahead of him as he penetrated further into the chasm. Now a great flying stag with mighty antlers and many points came at Doctor Faustus and would have dashed him off his chair and down into the pit. It frightened him greatly, but the three dragons flying ahead repulsed the hart. When he was better come down into the *spelunca*, he could see hovering about him a great multitude of serpents and snakes, the latter being unspeakably big. Flying lions came to his aid this time. They wrestled and struggled with the great snakes until they conquered them, so that he passed through safely and well.

When Doctor Faustus had attained a greater depth, he saw a huge, flying, angry bull come forth out of a hole which might have been an old gate.

Bellowing and raging, he charged Faustus, goring his sedan chair with such a force as to overturn pavilion, dragon and Faustus, who now did fall off from his chair into the abyss, down and down, screaming woe and waily and thinking : All is over now. He could no longer see his spirit, but at last an old wrinkled ape caught him up as he fell, held him and saved him. But then a thick dark fog fell upon Hell, so that he could not see anything at all until presently a cloud opened up, out of which climbed two big dragons pulling a coach along after them. The old ape was setting Faustus upon it when there arose such a storm wind with terrible thunder claps and stench of sulphur and quaking of the mountain or abyss that Faustus thought he must faint away and die.

He was indeed enveloped in a deep darkness for about a quarter of an hour, during which time he had no perception of the dragons or of the coach, but he did have a sensation of movement. Again the thick dark fog disappeared, and he could see his steeds and coach. Down the cavern shot such multitude of lightning and flames upon his head that the boldest man--not to mention Faustus--would have trembled for fear. The next thing he perceived was a great turbid body of water. His dragons entered it and submerged. Yet Faustus felt no water at all, but great heat and radiance instead. The current and waves beat upon him until he again lost both steeds and coach and went falling deeper and deeper into the terror of the depths. At last he found himself upon a high, pointed crag and here he sat, feeling half dead.

He looked about, but as he was able to see and hear no one, he began contemplating the bottomless pit. A little breeze arose. All around him was naught but water. He thought to himself: What shalt thou do now, being forsaken even by the spirits in Hell? Why thou must hurl thyself either into the water or into the pit. At this thought he fell into a rage, and in a mad, crazy despair he leapt into the fiery hole, calling out as he cast himself in: Now, spirits, accept my offering. I have earned it. My soul hath caused it.

Well, just at the moment when he hurled himself head over heels and went tumbling down, such a frightful loud tumult and banging assailed his ears, and the mountainpeak shook so furiously that he thought many big cannons must have been set off, but it was only that he had come to the bottom of Hell. Here were many worthy personages in a fire: emperors, kings, princes and lords, many thousand knights and men-at-arms. A cool stream ran along at the edge of the fire, and here some were drinking, refreshing themselves, and bathing, but some were fleeing from its cold, back into the fire. Doctor Faustus stepped up, thinking he might seize one of the damned souls, but even when he thought he had one in his hand it would vanish. On account of the intense heat, he knew he could not stay in this vicinity, and was seeking some way out when his spirit Beelzebub came with the sedan chair. Doctor Faustus took a seat and away they soared, for he could not long have endured the thunderclaps, fog, fumes, sulphur, water, cold and heat, particularly since it was compounded with wailing, weeping and moaning of woe, anguish and pain.

Now Doctor Faustus had not been at home for a long while. His famulus felt sure that, if he had achieved his desire of seeing Hell, he must have seen more than he had bargained for and would never come back. But even while he was thinking thus, Doctor Faustus, asleep in his pavilion, came flying home in the night and was cast, still asleep, into his bed. When he awoke early the next morning and beheld the light of dawn, he felt exactly as if he had been imprisoned for some time in a dark tower. At a later date, of course, he became acquainted only with the fire of Hell, and with the effects of those flames, but now he lay in bed trying to recollect what he had seen in Hell. At first he was firmly convinced that he had been there and had seen it, but then he began to doubt himself, and assumed that the Devil had charmed a vision before his eyes. --And this is true, for he had not seen Hell, else he would not have spent the rest of his life trying to get there. This history and account of what he saw in Hell--or in a vision--was written down by Doctor Faustus himself and afterwards found in his own handwriting upon a piece of paper in a locked book.

How Doctor Faustus Journeyed Up

into the Stars

XVI

This record was also found among his possessions, having been composed and indited in his own hand and addressed to one of his close companions, a physic in Leipzig named Jonas Victor. The contents were as followeth :

Most dear Lord, and Brother ,

I yet remember, as ye no doubt do, too, our school days in Wittemberg, where ye at first devoted yourself to *medicina, astronomia, astrologia, geometria*, so that ye are now a *mathematicus* and *physicus*. But I was not like unto you. I, as well ye know, did study *theologia*–although I nevertheless became your equal in the arts ye studied, too.

Now, as to your request that I report some few matters unto you and give you my advice: I, neither being accustomed to denying you aught, nor having ever refused to report aught to you, am still your servant, whom ye shall ever find and know to be such. I do express my gratitude for the honor and praise which ye accord me. In your epistle ye make mention of mine Ascension unto Heaven, among the stars, for ye have heard about it, and ye write requesting that I might inform you whether it be so or not, sithence such a thing doth seem to you quite impossible. Ye remark in addition that it must have occurred with the aid of the Devil or of sorcery. As quoth the clown to the Emperor when asked if he had sullied his breeches, "Ay, how wilt thou bet, Fritz!" --Well, whatever means might have been used, it hath finally been accomplished, and of this *figura, actus* and event I can make you the following report:

One night I could not go to sleep, but lay thinking about my almanacs and horoscopes and about the properties and arrangements in the Heavens, how man--or some of the physics--hath measured those ornaments and would interpret them, even though he cannot really visualize such things and hence must base his interpretations and calculations quite arbitrarily on books and the tenets in them. While in such thoughts, I heard a loud blast of wind go against my house. It threw open my shutters, my chamber door and all else, so that I was not a little astonished. Right afterward I heard a roaring voice saying:

Get thee up! Thy heart's desire, intent and lust shalt thou see.

I made answer: If it be possible for me to see that which hath just been the object of my thoughts and wishes, then I am well content.

He did answer again, saying: Then look out at thy window where thou canst see our carriage.

That I did, and I saw a coach with two dragons come flying down. The coach was illuminated with the flames of Hell, and inasmuch as the moon shone in the sky that night I could see my steeds as well. These creatures had mottled brown and white wings and the same color back; their bellies, however, were of a greenish hue with yellow and white flecks.

The voice spake again: Well get thee in and be off!

I answered: I will follow thee, but only on condition that I may ask any question I like.

Good, he answered, be it then in this instance permitted thee. So I climbed up onto my casement, jumped down into my carriage, and off I went, the flying dragons drawing me ever upward; and it did seem a miracle that the coach really had four wheels that crunched right along as if I were journeying over land. --To be sure, the wheels did gush forth streams of fire as they whirled around.

The higher I ascended, the darker did the world become, and when I would look down into the world from the Heavens above, it was exactly as if I were gazing into a dark hole from bright daylight. In the midst of such upward shooting and soaring, my servant and spirit came whirring along and took a seat beside me in the coach.

I said to him: My Mephostophiles, what is to become of me now?

Let such thoughts neither confuse thee nor impede thee, spake he and drave on higher upward.

Now Will I Tell You What I Did See

XVII

Departing on a Tuesday, and returning on a Tuesday, I was out one week, during which time I neither slept nor did feel any sleep in me. Incidentally, I remained quite invisible throughout the journey. On the first morning, at break of day, I said to my Mephostophiles:

I suppose thou dost know how far we are come (now as long as I was up there I knew neither hunger nor thirst, but I could well observe only by looking back at the world that I was come a good piece this night).

Mephostophiles said: In faith, my Fauste, thou art now come forty-seven mile up into the sky.

During the remainder of the day I discovered that I could look down upon the world and make out many kingdoms, principalities and seas. I could discern the worlds of Asia, Africa and Europe, and while at this altitude I said unto my servant:

Now point out to me and instruct me as to the names of these various lands and realms.

This he did, saying: This over here on the left is Hungary. Lo, there is Prussia. Across there is Sicily--Poland--Denmark--Italy -Germany. Now tomorrow shalt thou inspect Asia and Africa and canst see Persia, Tartary, India and Arabia. --But just look, right now the wind is changing and we can observe Pommerania, Muscovy and Prussia. See, there is Poland--and Germany again--Hungary--and Austria.

On the third day I did look down into Major and Minor Turkey, Persia, India and Africa. I saw Constantinople before me, and in the Persian and Constantinopolitan Sea many ships with war troops shuttling busily back and forth. Constantinople looked so small that there appeared to be no more than three houses there, with people not a span long.

Now I departed in July when it was very hot, and, as I looked now this way and now that, toward the East, South and North, I observed how it was raining at one place, thundering at another, how the hail did fall here while at another place the weather was fair. In fine, I saw all things in the world as they do usually come to pass.

After I had been up there for a week, I began to observe what was above me, watching from a distance how the Heavens did move and roll around so fast that they seemed about to fly asunder into many thousand pieces, the cloud sphere cracking so violently as if it were about to burst and break the world open. The Heavens were so bright that I could not perceive anything any higher up, and it was so hot that I should have burned to a crisp had my servant not charmed a breeze up for me. The cloud sphere which we see down there in the world is as solid and thick as a masonry wall, but it is of one piece and as clear as crystal. The rain, which originates there and then falls upon the earth, is so clear that we could see ourselves reflected in it.

Now this cloud sphere moveth in the Heavens with such a force that it runneth from East to West despite the fact that sun, moon and stars strive against it, so that the momentum of the cloud sphere doth indeed drive sun, moon and stars along with it. Thus we see how and why these bodies needs must proceed from East to West. Down in our world it doth appear --and I myself thought so, too--that the sun is no bigger than the head of a barrel. But it is in fact much bigger than the whole world: for I could discover no end to it at all. At night, when the sun goeth down, the moon must take on the sun's light, this being why the moon shineth so bright at night. And directly beneath Heaven there is so much light that even at night it is daytime in Heaven--this even though the earth remaineth quite dark. Thus I saw more than I had desired. One of the stars, for example, was larger than half the world. A planet is as large as the world. And, in the aery sphere, there I beheld the spirits which dwell beneath Heaven.

While descending, I did look down upon the world again, and it was no bigger than the yolk of an egg. Why, to me the world seemed scarcely a span long, but the oceans looked to be twice that size. Thus, on the evening of the seventh day did I arrive home again, and I slept for three days on a row. I have disposed my almanacs and horoscopes in accordance with my observations, and I did not wish to withhold this fact from you. Now inspect your books and see whether the matter is not in accordance with my vision.

And accept my cordial greetings,

Dr. Faustus

Astroseer.

Doctor Faustus' Third Journey

XVIII

It was in his sixteenth year that Doctor Faustus undertook a tour or a pilgrimage, instructing his servant that he should conduct and convey him whithersoever he would go. He journeyed invisible down to Rome, where he went unseen into the Pope's Palace and beheld all the servants and courtiers and the many sorts of dishes and fine foods that were being served.

For shame! he remarked to his spirit. Why did not the Devil make a Pope of me?

Yes, Doctor Faustus found all there to be his ilk in arrogance, pride, much insolence, transgression, gluttony, drunkenness, whoring, adultery and other fine blessings of the Pope and his rabble. This caused Doctor Faustus to observe:

Methought I were the Devil's own swine, but he will let me fatten for a long while yet. These hogs in Rome are already fatted and ready to roast and boil.

Since he had heard much of Rome, he remained for three days and nights in the Pope's Palace, using his sorcery to render himself invisible. Now hear ye the adventures and the art which he used in the Pope's Palace.

The good Lord Faustus, having had little good meat and drink for some time, came and stood invisible before the Pope's board, even as he was about to eat. The Pope crossed himself before taking meat, and at that moment Doctor Faustus did blow hard into his face. Every time the Pope crossed himself, Faustus would blow into his face again. Once he laughed aloud, so that it was audible in the whole hall; again, he did weep most convincingly. The servants knew not what this might portend, but the Pope told his people it was a damned soul of which he had exacted penance and which was now begging for absolution. Doctor Faustus enjoyed this very much, for such mystifications well pleased him, too.

When the last course finally arrived and was set before the Pope, Doctor Faustus, feeling his own hunger, raised up his hands, and instantly all the courses and fine dishes together with their platters flew right into them. Together with his spirit he then rushed away to a mountain in Rome called the Capitolium, there to dine with great relish. Later he sent his spirit back with an order to fetch the daintiest wines from the Pope's table together with the finest goblets and flaggons.

When the Pope found out how many things had been stolen from him, he caused all the bells to be rung throughout the entire night and had mass and petition held for the departed souls. In anger toward one particular departed soul, however, he formally condemned it to purgatory with bell, book and candle. As for Doctor Faustus, he accepted the Pope's meat and drink as an especial dispensation. The silver was found in his house after his death.

At midnight, when he was sated with the victuals, he bestrode a horse and flew off to Constantinople. Here Doctor Faustus viewed the Turkish Emperor's might, power, brilliance and court entourage for a few days. One evening when the Emperor sat at table Doctor Faustus performed for him an apish play and spectacle. Great tongues of fire burst up in the hall, and when everyone was hastening to quench them, it commenced to thunder and lighten. Such a spell was cast upon the Turkish Emperor that he could not arise, nor could he be carried out of there. The hall became as bright as the very homeland of the sun, and Faustus's spirit, in the figure, ornaments and trappings of a Pope, stepped before the Emperor, saying:

Hail Emperor, so full of grace that I, thy Mahomet do appear unto thee!

Saying nothing more, he disappeared. This hoax caused the Emperor to fall down upon his knees, calling out unto Mahomet and praising him that he had been so gracious as to appear before him.

The next morning, Doctor Faustus went into the Emperor's castle, where the Turk has his wives or whores, and where no one is permitted except gelded boys who wait upon the women. He charmed this castle with such a thick fog that naught could be seen. Now Doctor Faustus transformed himself as had his spirit before, but posed as Mahomet himself, and he did reside for a while in this castle, the mist remaining throughout his stay, and the Turk during this same period admonishing his people to perform many rites. But Doctor Faustus drank and was full of good cheer, taking his pleasure and dalliance there. When he was through he used the same art as before and ascended into the sky in papish raiment and ornament.

Now when Faustus was gone and the fog disappeared, the Turk came to his castle, summoned his wives and asked who had been there while the castle was for so long surrounded with fog. They informed him how it was the god Mahomet who at night had called this one and that one to him, lain with them and said that from his seed would rise up a great nation and valiant heroes. The Turk accepted it as a great benefit that Mahomet had lain with his wives, but he wondered if it had been accomplished according to the manner of mortals. Oh yes, they answered, that was the way it had been done. He had called them, embraced them, and was well fitted out--they would fain be served in such sort every day. He had lain with them naked and was certainly a man in all parts, except that they had not been able to understand his tongue. The priests instructed the Turk that he ought not believe it had been Mahomet, but rather a phantom. The wives on the other hand said, be it ghost or man, he had been very kind to them and had served them masterfully, once or six times-- nay, even more often--in a night; all of which caused the Turk much contemplation, and he remained doubtful in the matter.

Concerning the Stars

XIX

A prominent scholar in Halberstadt, Doctor N. V. W., invited Doctor Faustus to his table. Before supper was ready, Faustus stood for a while gazing out the window at the Heavens, it being Harvest time and the sky filled with stars. Now his host, being also a Doctor of Physic and a good *astrologus*, had brought Doctor Faustus here for the purpose of learning from him divers transformations in the planets and stars. Therefore he now leaned upon the window beside Doctor Faustus and looked also upon the brilliance of the Heavens, the multitude of stars, some of which were shooting through the sky and falling to the earth. In all humility he made request that Doctor Faustus might tell him the condition and quality of this thing.

Doctor Faustus began on this wise: My most dear Lord and Brother, this condition doth presuppose certain other matters which ye must understand first. The smallest star in Heaven, although when beheld from below it seems to our thinking scarcely so big as our large wax candles, is really larger than a principality. Oh yes, this is certain. I have seen that the length and breadth of the Heavens is many times greater than the surface of the earth. From Heaven, ye cannot even see earth. Many a star is broader than this land, and most are at least as large as this city. --See, over there is one fully as large as the dominion of the Roman Empire. This one right up here is as large as Turkey. And up higher there, where the planets are, ye may find one as big as the world.

A Question on This Topic

XX

I know that to be true, saith this doctor. But my Lord Faustus, how is it with the spirits who vex men and thwart their works (as some people say) by day and by night as well?

Doctor Faustus answered: We ought not to begin with this topic, but with the ordinances and creation of God, it being in accordance with these that the sun doth at break of day turn again toward the world with his radiance (it being also nearer in summer than in winter), and that the spirits then move beneath the cloud sphere where God hath committed them that they may discover all his portents. As the day progresses, they rise upward beneath the cloud sphere, for they are granted no affinity with the sun: the brighter it shines, the higher they do seek to dwell. In this context we might speak of forbidden days, for God hath not granted them light nor allowed them such a property.

But by night, when it is pitch dark, then they are among us, for the brightness of the sun--even though it is not shining here--is in the first Heaven so intense that it is as daylight there (this being why in the blackness of night, even when no stars shine, men still perceive Heaven) .It followeth therefore that the spirits, not being able to endure or to suffer the aspect of the sun, which hath now ascended upwards, must come near unto us on earth and dwell with men, frightening them with nightmares, howling and spooks. Now what will ye wager and bet: when ye go abroad in the dark without a light--if ye dare do such a thing--a great fear will seize you. Furthermore, if ye are alone by night ye are possessed by strange phantasies, although the day bringeth no such things. At night some will start up in their sleep, another thinks there be a spirit near him, or that one be groping out for him, or that another will walk round in the house, or in his sleep, etc. There are many such trials, all because the spirits are at that hour near to vex and plague men with multitudinous delusions.

The Second Question

XXI

I thank you very much, spake the doctor, my dear Lord Faustus, for your brief account. I shall remember it and ponder upon it my life long. But, if I may trouble you further, would ye not instruct me once more as concerns the brilliance of the stars and their appearance by night.

Yea, very briefly, answered Doctor Faustus. Now it is certain, so soon as the sun doth ascend into the Third Heaven (if it should move down into the First Heaven, it would ignite the earth--but the time for that is not yet come, and the earth must still proceed along her God-ordained course), when the sun doth so far withdraw itself, I say, then doth it become the right of the stars to shine for as long as God hath ordained. The First and Second Heavens, which contain these stars, are then brighter than two of our summer days, and offer an excellent refuge for the birds by night.

Night, therefore, observed from Heaven, is nothing else than day, or, as one might also aver, the day is half the night. For ye must understand that when the sun ascends, leaving us here in night, the day is just beginning in such places as India and Africa. And when our sun shineth, their day waneth, and they have night.

The Third Question

XXII

But I still do not understand, spake the Doctor from Halberstadt, the action of the stars, how they glitter, and how they fall down to earth.

Doctor Faustus answered: This is nothing out of the ordinary, but an everyday happening. It is indeed true that the stars, like the Firmament and other *Elementa*, were created and disposed in the Heavens in such a fashion that they are immutable. But they do undergo certain changes in color and in other external qualities. The stars manifest superficial changes of this sort when they give off sparks or little flames, for these are bits of match falling from the stars--or, as we call them, shooting stars. They are hard, black, and greenish.

But that a star itself might fall--why this is nothing more than a fancy of mankind. When by night a great streak of fire is seen to shoot downward, these are not falling stars, although we do call them that, but only slaggy pieces from the stars. They are big things, to be sure, and, as is true of the stars themselves, some are much bigger than others. But it is my opinion that no star itself falleth except as a scourge of God. Then such falling stars bring a murkiness of the Heavens with them and cause great floods and devastation of lives and land.

A History of the Emperor Charles V

and Doctor Faustus

XXIII

Our Emperor Charles the Fifth of that name was come with his court entourage to Innsbruck, whither Doctor Faustus had also resorted. Well acquainted with his arts and skill were divers knights and counts, particularly those whom he had relieved of sundry pains and diseases, so that he was invited, summonsed and accompanied to meat at court. Here the Emperor espied him and wondered who he might be. When someone remarked that it was Doctor Faustus, the Emperor noted it well but held his peace until after meat (this being in the summer and after St. Philip and St. James) .Then the Emperor beckoned Faustus into his Privy Chamber and, disclosing to him that he deemed him adept in *nigromantia*, did therefore desire to be shown a proof in something which he would like to know. He vowed unto Faustus by his Imperial Crown that no ill should befall him, and Doctor Faustus did obediently acquiesce to oblige his Imperial Majesty.

Now hear me then, quoth the Emperor. In my camp I once did stand pondering on my ancestors who before me had risen to such high degree and sovereignty as would scarcely be attainable for me and my successors, especially how Alexander the Great, of all monarchs the most mighty, was a light and an ornament among all Emperors. Ah, it is well known what great riches, how many kingdoms and territories he did possess and acquire, the which to conquer and to organize again will fall most difficult for me and my succession, such territories being now divided into many separate kingdoms. It is my constant wish that I had been acquainted with this man and had been able to behold him and his spouse in the person, figure, form, mien and bearing of life. I understand that thou be an adept master in thine art, able to realize all things according to matter and complexion, and my most gracious desire is that thou give me some answer now in this regard.

Most gracious Lord, quoth Faustus, I will, in so far as I with my spirit am able, comply with Your Imperial Majesty's desire as concerns the personages of Alexander and his spouse, their aspect and figure, and cause them to appear here. But Your Majesty shall know that their mortal bodies cannot be present, risen up from the dead, for such is impossible. Rather, it will be after this wise: the spirits are experienced, most wise and ancient spirits, able to assume the bodies of such people, so transforming themselves that Your Imperial Majesty will in this manner behold the veritable Alexander.

Faustus then left the Emperor's chamber to take counsel with his spirit. Being afterward come in again to the Emperor's chamber, he indicated to him that he was about to be obliged, but upon the one condition that he would pose no questions, nor speak at all, the which the Emperor agreed unto. Doctor Faustus opened the door. Presently Emperor Alexander entered in the very form which he had borne in life--namely: a well-proportioned, stout little man with a red or red-blond, thick beard, ruddy cheeks and a countenance as austere as had he the eyes of the Basilisk. He stepped forward in full harness and, going up to Emperor Charles, made a low and reverent curtesy before him. Doctor Faustus restrained the Emperor of Christendom lest Charles rise up to receive him. Shortly thereafter, Alexander having again bowed and being gone out at the door, his spouse now approached the Emperor, she, too, making a curtesy. She was clothed all in blue velvet, embroidered with gold pieces and pearls. She, too, was excellent fair and rosy-cheeked, like unto milk and blood mixed, tall and slender, and with a round face.

Emperor Charles was thinking the while: Now I have seen the two personages whom I have long desired to know, and certainly it cannot be otherwise but that the spirit hath indeed changed into these forms, and he doth not deceive me, it being even as with the woman who raised the prophet Samuel for Saul.

But the Emperor,desiring to be the more certain of the matter, thought to himself: I have often heard tell that she had a great wen on her back. If it is to be found upon this image also, then I would believe it all the better.

So, stepping up to her, he did lift her skirt, and he found the wen. For she stood stock still for him, disappearing again afterwards. Thus the Emperor's desire was granted withal, and he was sufficiently content.

Concerning the Antlers of a Hart

XXIV

Upon a time soon after Doctor Faustus had accomplished the Emperor's will as was reported above he, hearing the signal for meat in the evening, did lean over the battlements to watch the domestics go out and in. There he espied one who was fallen asleep while lying in the window of the great Knights' Hall across the court (it being very hot) .I would not name the person, for it was a knight and a gentleman by birth.

Now with the aid of his spirit Mephostophiles, Faustus did charm a pair of hart's horns upon the knight's head. This good lord's head nodded upon the window sill, he awoke, and perceived the prank. Who could have been more distressed! For , the windows being closed, he could go neither forward nor backward with his antlers, nor could he force the horns from off his head. The Emperor, observing his plight, laughed and was well pleased withal until Doctor Faustus at last released the poor knight from the spell again.

Concerning Three Lords Who Were

Rapidly Transported to the Royal

Wedding in Munich

XXV

Three sons of noble lords (whom I dare not call by name) were students in Wittemberg. They met together on a time and, talking of the magnificent pomp which would attend the wedding of the son of the Duke of Bavaria in Munich, did heartily wish that they might go there, if only for a half an hour. Such talk caused the one of them to take thought of Doctor Faustus, and he said to the other two lords:

Cousins, if ye will follow me, hush and keep it to yourselves, then will I give you good counsel, how we can see the wedding and then be back to Wittemberg again in the self-same night. Here is what I have in mind: if we send for Doctor Faustus, tell him what we desire, and explain our plans to him, giving him a bit of money besides, then he surely will not deny us his aid.

Having deliberated and agreed upon the matter, they called on Doctor Faustus, who, touched by their present and also being well pleased with a banquet which they were clever enough to give in his honor, did consent to grant them his services.

The day arrived when the wedding of the Bavarian Duke's son was to be celebrated, and Doctor Faustus sent word to the young lords that they should come to his house arrayed in the very finest clothing they possessed. He then took a broad cloak, spread it out in his garden (which lay right beside his house), seated the lords upon it, himself in their midst, and at last gave strict command that none should speak a word so long as they be abroad--even though they be in the Bavarian Duke's Palace and someone should speak to them, they should give no answer--the which they all did pledge to obey. This matter being settled, Doctor Faustus sat down and commenced his *coniurationes*. Presently there arose a great wind which lifted the cloak and transported them through the air with such speed that they arrived betimes at the Duke's court in Munich.

They had travelled invisible, so that no one noticed them until they entered the Bavarian Palace and came into the hall, where the Marshall, espying them, indicated to the Duke of Bavaria how, although the princes, lords and gentlemen were already seated at table, there were still standing three more gentlemen without who had just arrived with a servant, and who also ought to be received. The old Duke of Bavaria arose to do this, but when he approached and spake to them, none would utter a word.

This occurred in the evening just before meat, they having hitherto observed all day the pomp of the wedding without any hindrance, for Faustus' art had kept them invisible. As was reported above, Doctor Faustus had sternly forbidden them to speak this day. He had further instructed them that so soon as he should call out: Up and away! all were to seize upon the cloak at once, and they would fly away again in the twinkling of an eye.

Now when the Duke of Bavaria spake to them and they gave no answer, handwater was proffered them anyhow. It was then that Doctor Faustus, hearing one of the lords forget himself and violate his command, did cry aloud: Up and away! Faustus and the two lords who held to the cloak were instantly flown away but the third, who had been negligent, was taken captive and cast into a cell. The other two lords did upon arrival at midnight in Wittemberg behave so glumly on account of their kinsman that Doctor Faustus sought to console them, and he promised that the young man would be released by morning.

The captive lord, being thus forsaken, in locked custody besides, and constrained by guards, was sore afraid. To make matters worse, he was questioned as to what manner of vision he been a part of, and as to the other three who were now vanished away.

He thought: If I betray them, then the ending will be bad.

He therefore gave answer to none who were sent to him, and when they saw that nothing was to be got out of him this day they finally informed him that on the morrow he would be brought down to the dungeon, tortured, and compelled to speak. The lord thought to himself:

So my ordeal is appointed for the morrow. If Doctor Faustus should not release me today, should I be tortured and racked, then I needs must speak.

But he still had the consolation that his friends would entreat Doctor Faustus for his release, and that is indeed the way it fell out. Before day break Doctor Faustus was in the cell, having cast such a spell on the watch that they fell into a heavy sleep. Faustus used his art to open all doors and locks, and he brought the lord punctually to Wittemberg, where a sumptuous honorarium was presented him as a reward.

Concerning an Adventure with a Jew

XXVI

It is said that the fiend and the sorcerer will not wax three penny richer in a year, and even so did it come to pass with Doctor Faustus. Much had been promised by his spirit, but much had been lies, for the Devil is the spirit of lies. Mephostophiles had once reproached Doctor Faustus, saying:

With the skill wherewith I have endowed thee thou shouldst acquire thine own wealth. Such arts as mine and thine can scarcely lose thee money. Thy years are not yet over. Only four years are past since my promise to thee that thou wouldst want neither for gold nor for goods. Why, thy meat and drink hath been brought thee from the courts of all the great potentates, all by mine art (what the spirit here states, we did already report above).

Doctor Faustus, who did not know how to disagree with these things, began to take thought and to wonder just how apt he might be in obtaining money. Not long after the spirit had told him those things, Faustus went banqueting with some good fellows and, finding himself without money, went and raised some in the Jewish quarter, accepting sixty Talers for a month's time. The money-lender, when the loan fell due, was ready to take his capital together with the usury, but Doctor Faustus was not at all of the opinion that he ought to pay anything. The fellow appeared at Faustus' house with his demand and received this answer:

Jew, I have no money. I can raise no money. But this I will do. From my body I will amputate a member, be it arm or leg, and give it thee in pawn--but it must be returned so soon as I am in money again.

The Jew (for Jews are enemies to us Christians, anyhow) pondered the matter and concluded that it must be a right reckless man who would place his limbs in pawn. "But still he accepted it. Doctor Faustus took a saw and, cutting off his leg withal, committed it unto the Jew (but it was only a hoax) upon the condition that it must be returned so soon as he be in money again and would pay his debt, for he would fain put the member back on. The Jew went away with the leg, well satisfied at first with his contract and agreement. But very soon he became vexed and tired of the leg, for he thought:

What good to me is a knave's leg? If I carry it home it will begin to stink. I doubt that he will be able to put it on again whole, and, besides, this pledge is a parlous thing for me, for no higher pawn can a man give than his own limb. But what profit will I have of it?

Thinking these and such like things as he crossed over a bridge, the Jew did cast the leg into the water. Doctor Faustus knew all about this of course, and three days later he summoned the Jew in order to pay and settle his account. The Jew appeared and explained his deliberations, saying he had thrown the leg away because it was of no use to anyone. Doctor Faustus immediately demanded that his pledge be returned or that some other settlement be made. The Jew was eager to be free of Faustus, and he finally had to pay him sixty Guilders more (Doctor Faustus still having his leg as before).

An Adventure at the Court

of the Count of Anhalt

XXVII

Faustus came upon a time to the Count of Anhalt, where he was received with all kindness and graciousness. Now this was in January , and at table he perceived that the Countess was great with child. When the evening meat had been carried away and the collation of sweets was being served, Doctor Faustus said to the Countess:

Lady, I have always heard that the greatbellied women long for diverse things to eat. I beg your Grace not to withhold from me what you would please to have.

She answered him: Truly my Lord, I will not conceal from you my present wish that it were Harvest time, and I were able to eat my fill of fresh grapes and of other fruit.

Doctor Faustus said: Gracious Lady, this is easy for me to provide. In an hour your Grace's will shall be accomplished.

Faustus now took two silver bowls and set them out before the window. When the hour was expired he reached out the window and drew in one bowl with white and red grapes which were fresh from the vine, and the other bowl full of green apples and pears, but all of a strange and exotic sort. Placing them before the Countess, he said to her:

Your Grace need have no fear to eat, for I tell you truly that they are from a foreign nation where summer is about to end, although our year is, to be sure, just beginning here.

While the Countess did eat of all the fruit with pleasure and great wonderment, the Count of Anhalt could not withhold to ask for particulars concerning the grapes and other fruit.

Doctor Faustus answered: Gracious Lord, may it please your Grace to know that the year is divided into two circles in the world, so that it is summer in Orient and Occident when it is winter here, for the Heavens are round. Now, from where we dwell the sun hath at this season withdrawn to the highest point, so that we are having short days and winter here, but at the same time it is descending upon Orient and Occident--as in Sheba, India and in the East proper. The meaning of this is that they are having summer now. They enjoy vegetables and fruit twice a year in those parts. Furthermore, gracious Lord, when it is night here, day is just dawning there. The sun hath even now betaken himself beneath the earth, and it is night; but in this very instant the sun doth run above the earth down there, and they shall have day (in likeness thereof, the sea runneth higher than the world, and if it were not obedient to

God, it could inundate the world in a moment) .In consideration of such knowledge, gracious Lord, I sent my spirit to that nation upon the circumference of the sea where the sun now riseth, although it setteth here. He is a flying spirit and swift, able to transform himself in the twinkling of an eye. He hath procured these grapes and fruit for us.

The Count did attend these revelations with great wonderment.

The Manner in Which Doctor Faustus

as *Bacchus* Kept Shrovetide

XXVIII

The greatest effort, skill and art produced by Doctor Faustus was that which he demonstrated to the Count of Anhalt, for with the aid of his spirit he accomplished not merely the things I have told about, but he created all sorts of four-footed beasts as well as winged and feathered fowl, too. Now after he had taken leave of the Count and was returned back to Wittemberg, Shrovetide approached. Doctor Faustus himself played the role of *Bacchus*, entertaining several learned students, whom he persuaded, after they had been well fed and sated by Faustus, had crowned him *Bacchus* and were in the act of celebrating him) to go into a cellar with him and to try the magnificent drinks which he would there offer and provide them, a thing to which they readily assented. Doctor Faustus then laid out a ladder in his garden, seated a man on each rung, and away he whisked, coming by night into the cellar of the Bishop of Saltzburg

Here they tasted all sorts of wine, for this bishop hath a glorious grape culture, but when the good gentlemen were just in a fine temper, the Bishop's butler by chance did come downstairs and seeing them (for Doctor Faustus had brought along a flint so that they might better inspect all the casks), did charge them as thieves who had broken in. This offended Doctor Faustus, who, warning his fellows to prepare to leave, seized the butler by the hair and rode away with him until he saw a great high fir tree, in the top of which he deposited the frightened man. Being returned home again, he and his Shrovetide guests celebrated a *valete* with the wine which he had brought along in a big bottle from the Bishop's cellar . The poor butler had to hold fast all night to the tree, lest he fall out, and he almost froze to death. When day brake and he perceived the great height of the fir as well as the impossibility of climbing down (for it had no branches except in the very top), he had to call out to some peasants whom he saw drive by, and tell them what had happened to him. The peasants did marvel at all this and, coming into Saltzburg, reported it at court. This brought out a great crowd, who with much exertion and effort with ropes did bring the butler down. But he never knew who those were whom he had found in the cellar, nor who he was who had put him into the tree top.

Concerning Helen, Charmed Out of Greece

XXIX

On Whitsunday the students came unannounced to Doctor Faustus' residence for dinner, but, as they brought ample meat and drink along, they were welcome guests. The wine was soon going round at table, and they fell to talking of beautiful women, one of the students asserting that there were no woman whom he would rather see than fair Helen from Greece, for whose sake the worthy city of Troy had perished. She must have been beautiful, he said, for she had been stolen away from her husband, and a great deal of strife had arisen on her account.

Doctor Faustus said: Inasmuch as ye are so eager to behold the beautiful figure of Queen Helen, I have provided for her wakening and will now conduct her hither so that ye may see her spirit for yourselves, just as she appeared in life (in the same way, after all, that I granted Emperor Charles V his wish to see the person of Emperor Alexander the Great and his spouse).

Forbidding that any should speak or arise from table to receive her, Faustus went out of the parlor and, coming in again, was followed at the heel by Queen Helen, who was so wondrously beautiful that the students did not know whether they were still in their right minds, so confused and impassioned were they become. For she appeared in a precious deep purple robe, her hair, which shone golden and quite beautifully glorious, hanging down to her knees. She had coal black eyes, a sweet countenance on a round little head. Her lips were red as the red cherries, her mouth small, and her neck like a white swan's. She had cheeks pink like a rose, an exceeding fair and smooth complexion and a. rather slim, tall and erect bearing. *In summa*, there was not a flaw about her to be criticized. Helen looked all around in the parlor with a right wanton mien, so that the students were violently inflamed with love for her, but since they took her to be a spirit they controlled their passion without difficulty, and she left the room again with Doctor Faustus.

After the vision had passed away, the young .men begged Faustus to be so good as to have the image appear just once more, for they would fain send a painter to his house the next day to make a counterfeit of her. This Doctor Faustus refused to do, saying that he could not make her spirit appear at just any time, but that he would procure such a portrait for them. Later, he did indeed produce one, and all the students had it copied by sending painters to his house (for it was a fair and glorious figure of a Woman). Now it is unknown to this day who got this painting away from Doctor Faustus. As concerns the students, when they came to bed they could not sleep for thinking of the figure and form which had appeared visibly before them, and from this we may learn how the Devil doth blind men with love--oh it doth often happen that a man awhoring for so long that at last he can no longer be saved from it.

Concerning a Gesticulation

Involving Four Wheels

XXX

Doctor Faustus was summoned and commanded to come to the town of Brunswick to cure a marshall there who had consumption. Now he was used to ride neither horseback nor by coach, but was of a mind to walk wherever he was invited as guest or summoned as physician. When he was about a half a quarter from Brunswick and could see the town before him, a peasant with four horses and an empty wagon came clattering along. Doctor Faustus addressed the clown in all kindness, requesting that he be allowed to climb on and be driven the rest of the way up to the town gate, but the bumpkin refused to do this and turned Faustus away, saying he would have enough to haul on his return trip. Doctor Faustus had not been serious in his request, wanting only to prove the peasant, whether there were any love to be found in him, but now he repaid the clown's churlishness (such as is, after all, commonly found among peasants) in like coin, speaking to him thus:

Thou bumpkin and worthless ass, since thou hast demonstrated such churlishness unto me, and since thou wilt certainly use others the same and probably already hast done so, thou shalt this time be paid for thy trouble. Thy four wheels shalt thou find one at each gate of Brunswick town. Immediately the wagon wheels sprang away, floating along in the air so that each one came to a different gate, without being noticed by anyone there. The peasant's horses also fell down as if they had suddenly died and lay there quite still. At this was the poor clown sore affright, measuring it as a special scourge of God for his misanthropy. All troubled and weeping, with outstretched hands and upon his knees, he did beg Faustus for forgiveness, confessing himself indeed well worthy of such punishment, but vowing that the next time this would serve as a remembrance to him, so that he would never use such misanthropy again.

Doctor Faustus took pity upon the clown's humility and answered him, saying that he must treat no one else in this hard manner, there being nothing more shameful than the qualities of churlishness and misanthropy--and the wicked pride which accompanieth them. Now the man should but take up some earth and throw it upon the team, which would then rise up and live out its days. So it came to pass, Faustus saying as he departed from the peasant:

Thy churlishness cannot go altogether unpunished, but must be repaid in equal measure, inasmuch as thou hast deemed it such a great effort to take a tired man onto an empty wagon. Lo, thy wheels are without the town at four different gates. There wilt thou find all four of them.

The peasant went along and found them as Doctor Faustus had said, but with great effort, travail and neglect of the trade and business which he had intended to accomplish. And thus will churlishness ever punish its owner.

Concerning Four Sorcerers Who Cut Off

One Another's Heads and Put Them

On Again. Wherein Doctor Faustus

Attending Their Performance,

Doth Play the Major Role

XXXI

Doctor Faustus came to the Carnival in Frankfurt, where his spirit
Mephostophiles did inform him that there were four sorcerers at an inn in Jews
Alley who were attracting a great audience by chopping off one another's heads
and sending them to the barber to be trimmed. Now that vexed Faustus, who
liked think that he were the only cock in the Devil's basket. When he went to
behold the thing, he found the sorcerers just getting ready to chop off their
heads, and with them was a barber who was going to trim and wash them.
Upon a table they had a glass cruse with distilled water in it. One among them,
the chief sorcerer and also their executioner, laid his hands upon the first of his
fellows and charmed a lily into this cruse. It waxed green, and he called it the
Root of Life. Now he beheaded that first fellow and let the barber dress the
head, then set it upon the man's shoulders again. In one and the same instant,
the lily disappeared and the man was whole again. This was done with the
second and the third sorcerer in like manner. A lily was charmed for each in
the water, they were executed, their heads were then dressed and put back on
them again.

At last it was the turn of the chief sorcerer and executioner . His Root of
Life was blooming. away in the water and waxing green, now his head was
smitten off also, and they set to washing it and dressing it in Faustus' presence,
which sorcery did sorely vex him: the arrogance of this *magicus princeps,* how
he let his head be chopped off so insolently, with blasphemy and laughter in
his mouth. Doctor Faustus went up to the table where the cruse and the
flowering lily stood, took out his knife, and snipped the flower, severing the
stem. No one was aware of this at the time, but when the sorcerers sought to
set the head on again their medium was gone, and the evil fellow had to perish
with his sins upon his severed head.

Afterwards they did find the stem cut, but they were not able to discover
how this came to pass. This is the way the Devil at last rewards all his servants,
absolving them thus, the manner in which Doctor Faustus dealt with this man

being entirely consonant with the shameful absolution which he did himself receive when he was repaid for his own sins.

Concerning an Old Man Who Would

Have Converted Doctor Faustus

from His Godless Life

XXXII

A Christian, pious, godfearing physician, a person zealous of the honor of God, was also a neighbor of Doctor Faustus, and, seeing that many students frequented Faustus' house, he considered such a den as bad as a brothel, for he did compare Faustus to all the Jews, who, so soon as they fell away from God also became His declared enemies, dedicating themselves unto sorcery for the sake of prophecy and deceit, seeking not only the bodily harm of many a pious child whose parents have devoted much effort to his Christian rearing, but also causing him to forget the Lord's Prayer. This old neighbor of Doctor Faustus had observed his rascality in such a light for long years and no longer doubted the devilish nature of his mischief, but he also knew that the time was not yet ripe for the civil authorities to establish these facts.

Considering thus above all the weal of the young men he did in Christian zeal summon Faustus as a guest into his own lodging. Faustus came, and at table his old godfearing patron addressed him thus:

M y sweet Lord, as a friend and as a Christian I ask you not to receive my discourse in rancor or ill will, nor to despise these small victuals, but charitably to take and to be content with what our sweet Lord provideth us.

Doctor Faustus requested him to declare his purpose, saying he would, attend him obediently. His patron then commenced:

My sweet Lord and Neighbor, ye know your own actions, that ye have defied God and all the Saints, that ye have given yourself up unto the Devil, whereby ye are now come into God's greatest wrath and are changed from a Christian into a very heretic and devil. O why do ye deprave your soul! Ye must not heed the body, but your sweet soul, lest ye reside in the eternal punishment and displeasure of God. Look ye to it, my Lord, ye are not yet lost if ye will but turn from your evil way, beseech God for Grace and pardon, as ye may see in the example in *Acts* viii concerning Simon in Samaria, who had also traduced many. They thought him to be a god, calling him the Power of God and *Simon Deus Sanctus*. But he was converted when he heard a sermon of St. Philip, was baptized and did believe on our Lord Jesus Christ. It is particularly noted and praised in *Acts* how he did afterward much consort with Philip. Thus, my Lord, allow my sermon also to appeal to you. O, let it be a heartfelt Christian admonition! To sin no more is the penance wherewith ye must seek Grace and pardon, as ye may learn from the fine examples of the thief on the cross, as well as from St. Peter, St. Matthew and Magdalena. Yea, Christ our Lord speaketh unto all sinners: Come unto me, all ye that labor and are heavy laden, and I will give you rest. Or, in the Prophet Ezekiel: I have no pleasure in the death of the wicked; but that the wicked should turn from his way and live, for his hand is not withered, that he were no longer useful. I beg you my Lord, take my plea to your heart, ask God for pardon for Christ's sake, and abjure at the same time your evil practices, for sorcery is against God and His Commandment, inasmuch as He doth sorely forbid it in both the Old and the New Testaments. He speaketh: Ye shall not allow them to live, ye shall not seek after them nor hold counsel with them, for it is an abomination unto God. Thus St. Paul called Bar-Jesus, or Elymas the Sorcerer, a child of the Devil and an enemy of all righteousness, saying that such should have no share in the Kingdom of God.

Faustus attended him diligently and said that the speech had well pleased him. He expressed his gratitude to the Old Man for his good will and took his leave, promising to comply in so far as he was able.

When he arrived home he took the Old Man's counsel to heart, considering how he had indeed depraved his soul by yielding himself up to the accursed Devil, and at last Faustus felt a desire to do penance and to revoke his promise to the Devil.

While he was occupied in such thoughts, his spirit appeared him, groping after him as if to twist his head off his shoulders. The spirit then spake, rebuking him: What is thy purpose with thyself?

He reminded him of his motives in first consigning himself to the Devil. Having promised enmity toward God and all mankind, he was not now fulfilling that pledge but was following after this old reprobate, feeling charity toward a man and hence toward God--now, when it was already too late and when he was clearly the property of the Devil.

The Devil hath the power (he spake) to fetch thee away. I am in fact now come with the command to dispose of thee--or to obtain thy promise that thou wilt never more allow thyself to be seduced, and that thou wilt consign thyself anew with thy blood. Thou must declare immediately what thou wouldst do, or I am to slay thee.

Sore affright, Doctor Faustus consented, sat down and with his blood did write as followeth (this document being found after his death):

Pact

XXXIII

I Doctor Johann Faustus,

Do declare in this mine own hand and blood:

Whereas I have truly and strictly observed my first *instrumentum* and pact for these nineteen years, in defiance of God and all mankind;

And Whereas, pledging body and soul, I therein did empower the mighty God Lucifer with full authority over me so soon as five more years be past;

And Whereas he hath further promised me to increase my days in death, thereby shortening my days in Hell, also not to allow me to suffer any pain;

Now Therefore do I further promise him that I will never more heed the admonitions, teachings, scoldings, instructions or threats of mankind, neither as concerneth the Word of God nor in any temporal or spiritual matters whatsoever; but particularly do I promise to heed no man of the cloth nor to follow his teachings.

In good faith and resolve contracted by these presents and in mine own blood, etc.

Now just as soon as Faustus had executed this godless, damned pact, he began to hate the good Old Man so intensely that he sought some means to kill him, but the Old Man's Christian prayers and Christian ways did such great offense to the Evil Fiend that he could not even approach him.

Two days after the events just recounted, when the Old Man was retiring, he heard a mighty rumbling in his house, the like of which he was never wont to hear. It came right into his chamber, grunting like a sow and continuing for a long time. Lying abed, the Old Man began to mock the spirit, saying:

Ah, what a fine bawdy music! Now what a beautiful hymn sung by a ghoul! Really a pretty anthem sung by a beautiful angel--who could not tarry in Paradise for two full days. This wretched fellow must now go avisiting in other folks' houses, for he is banished from his own home.

With such mockery he drave the spirit away. When Doctor Faustus asked him how he had fared with the Old Man, Mephostophiles answered that he had not been able to lay hold on him, for he had worn armor (referring to the prayers of the Old Man) and had mocked him besides.

Now the spirits and devils cannot suffer a good humor, particularly when they are reminded of their fall. Thus doth God protect all good Christians who seek in Him succor against the Evil One.

How Doctor Faustus Brought About

the Marriage of Two Lovers

XXXIV

A student in Wittemberg, a gallant gentleman of the nobility named N. Reuckauer, was with heart and eyes far gone in love with an equally noble and exceedingly beautiful gentlewoman. Of the many suitors (among them even a young knight) whom she turned down, this Reuckauer was privileged to occupy the least place of all. But he was a good friend of Doctor Faustus, having often sat with him at meat and at drink, so that when the acute affects of his love for the gentlewoman caused him to pine away and fall ill, Faustus soon learned of it. He asked his spirit Mephostophiles about the cause of this serious condition and, being told that it was the love affair, soon paid a visit to the nobleman, who was greatly astonished to learn the true nature of his illness. Doctor Faustus bade him be of good cheer and not to despair so, for he intended to help him win the affections of this lady so completely that she should never love another. And so it did indeed come to pass, for Doctor Faustus so disturbed the heart of the maiden with his sorcery that she would look upon no other man, nor heed any other suitor, although many gallant, wealthy noblemen were courting her.

Soon after his conversation with Reuckauer, Faustus commanded the young man to clothe himself sumptuously and prepare to accompany him to the maiden's house, for she was now in her garden with many other guests who were about to begin a dance, and there Reuckauer was to dance with her . Doctor Faustus gave him a ring, telling him to wear it on his finger during the dance with this lady, for just as soon as he might touch her with his ring finger she would fall in love with him and with no other. Faustus forbade Reuckauer to ask her hand in marriage, explaining that she would have to entreat him.

Now he took some distilled water and washed Reuckauer with it, so that his face presently became exceeding handsome. Reuckauer followed Faustus' instructions carefully, danced with the lady and, while dancing, touched her with his ring finger. Instantly, her whole heart and love were his, for the good maiden was pierced through with Cupid's arrow.

That night in her bed she found no rest, so often did her thoughts turn to Reuckauer. Early the next morning she sent for him, laid her heart and her love before him, and begged him to wed her. He gave his consent, for he loved her ardently. Their wedding was celebrated anon, and Doctor Faustus received a handsome honorarium.

Concerning Divers Flora

in Doctor Faustus' Garden

on Christmas Day

XXXV

In the midst of winter at the Christmas season, several gentlewomen came to Wittemberg to visit their brothers and cousins, all young gentlemen students there who were well-acquainted with Doctor Faustus. He had been invited to their table on more than one occasion, and, desirous now of repaying such social debts, he did invite these lords to bring their ladies to his domicile for an evening draught of wine. To come to his house, they had to trudge through a deep snow which lay over the town, but Doctor Faustus had used his peculiar sorcery to prepare a splendid marvel in his garden for them, and when they arrived there they beheld no snow at all, but a lovely summer day with all manner of flora. The grass was covered all over with many blossoms. Beautiful vines were growing there, all hung with divers sorts of grapes. There were roses, too, white, red and pink, as well as many other sweet smelling flowers, and it was all a great delight to behold.

Concerning an Army Raised Against

My Lord of Hardeck

XXXVI

Doctor Faustus, being on a journey to Eisleben and about halfway there, did see seven horse riding in the distance. He recognized their leader, for it was that Lord of Hardeck upon whose forehead (as we have reported) he had charmed a set of hart's horns while at the Emperor's court. The lord, who knew Faustus quite as well as Faustus knew him, called his men to a halt. When Faustus noticed this action he immediately retired toward a little hill.

The knight ordered a lively charge to intercept him, and also commanded the firing of a musket volley, but although they spurred their mounts hard to overtake Faustus, he achieved the higher ground first, and by the time the horses had topped the rise he was vanished from their sight. Here the knight again called a halt. They were looking about, trying to catch sight of Faustus, when they heard in the copse below a loud noise of horns, trumpets and military drums, all tooting and beating. Some hundred horse came charging in upon them, and the knight with his men took to their heels.

They at first sought to slip around the side of the hill home, but here they encountered a second great armed band all poised for the charge and barring their way. They turned about to dash away--and beheld a third troop of horsemen. They tried still another route, but again found themselves faced with men ready for battle. The same thing happened five times, just as often as they turned in a fresh direction. When the knight saw that he could nowhere escape but was threatened with a charge from every direction, he rode alone right into the main host, ignoring the danger to himself, and asked what might be the cause for his being surrounded and menaced on all quarters.

None would speak to him or say a word until at last Doctor Faustus came riding up to the knight (who was now restrained on all sides) and proposed that he surrender himself as a prisoner or taste the edge of the sword. The knight was convinced that he had encountered a natural army prepared for battle, and when Faustus now demanded their muskets and swords, then took their horses as well, it did not occur to him that it might be naught but sorcery. Presently, Doctor Faustus brought the men fresh, enchanted horses and new muskets and swords, saying to the knight (who no longer even knew him to be Faustus):

My Lord, the commander of this army hath bid me let you go this time-- but upon a condition and probation. Will ye confess that ye did pursue a man who hath sought and received, and is henceforth shielded by, our commander's protection?

The knight had to accept this condition. When they came back to his castle again, his men rode the horses out to drink, but once in the water the horses disappeared. The good fellows almost drowned, and had to ride back home afoot. When the knight beheld his men coming in all muddy and wet, and when he learned the cause of it all, he knew right away that it was Doctor Faustus' sorcery, even of the same sort as had been used to shame and mock him before. But since he had this time given Faustus his pledge, he would not break it. As for Faustus, he hitched the horses together, sold them and got some money in his pockets again. Thus did he heap coals upon the wrath of his enemy.

Concerning the Beautiful Helen

from Greece, How She Lived for a Time

With Doctor Faustus

XXXVII

Doctor Faustus would fain omit or neglect naught pleasant and good unto the flesh. One midnight towards the end of the twenty-second year of his pact, while lying awake, he took thought again of Helen of Greece, whom he had awakened for the students on Whitsunday in Shrovetide (which we reported). Therefore, when morning came, he informed his spirit that he must present Helen to him, so that she might be his concubine.

This was done, and Helen was of the following description (Doctor Faustus had a portrait made of her): Her body was fine and erect, well-proportioned, tall, snow-white and crystalline. She had a complexion which seemed tinted with rose, a laughing demeanor, gold-yellow hair which reached almost to the calves of her legs, and brilliant laughing eyes with a sweet, loving gaze. Her nose was somewhat long, her teeth white as alabaster. *In summa*, there was not a single flaw about her body. Doctor Faustus beheld her and she captured his heart. He fell to frolicking with her, she became his bedfellow, and he came to love her so well that he could scarcely bear a moment apart from her.

While fond Faustus was living with Helen, she swelled up as were she with child. Doctor Faustus was rapturously happy, for, in the twenty-third year of his pact, she bare him a son whom he called Justus Faustus. This child told him many I things out of the future history of numerous lands. Later, When Faustus lost his life, there was none who knew whither wife and child were gone.

Concerning One Whose Wife Married

While He Was Captive in Turkey,

and How Doctor Faustus Informed

And Aided Him

XXXVIII

A fine gentleman of the nobility, Johann Werner of Reuttpueffel from Bennlingen, who had gone to school with Faustus and was a learned man, had been married for six years to an extremely beautiful woman, Sabina of Kettheim, when he was one evening through guile and drink brought to take an oath to go along to Turkey and the Holy Land. He kept his pledge and promise, saw many things, endured much, and had been gone almost five years when there came to his wife certain report that he was dead. The lady mourned for three years, during which time she had many suitors, among them an excellent person of the nobility whose name we dare not mention, but whom she now accepted.

When the time was approaching for their marriage celebration, Doctor Faustus discovered it, and he asked his Mephostophiles whether this Lord of Reuttpueffel were still alive. The spirit answered yes, he be alive and in Egypt in the city of Lylopolts, where he lay captive, having attempted to visit the city of Al-Cairo. This grieved Doctor Faustus, for he loved his friend and had not been pleased that the lady was remarrying so soon. He knew her husband had loved her well. The time for the marriage consummation and the subsequent ceremony being at hand, Doctor Faustus gazed into a mirror wherein he could see all things and by which means he was also able to inform the Lord of Reuttpueflel that his wife was about to be wed, at which the latter was much astonished.

The hour of consummation arrived. The nobleman disrobed and went out to cast his water. It was then that Mephostophiles did use his art, for when the man came in and leapt into Sabina's bed to enjoy the fruits of love, when they hoisted their shirts and squeezed close together, it was all to no avail. The good lady, seeing that he did not want on and was hesitating, did reach out herself for the tool, wishing to help him, but she could achieve naught, and the night wore on in mere grasping, wiggling, and squeezing. This did cause the lady to grieve and to think on her previous husband whom she thought to be dead, for he had rightly known how to tousle her.

On the very same night, Faustus had freed the nobleman and had brought him asleep back to his castle. Now when the good lady beheld her young lord she fell at his feet and begged his forgiveness, indicating at the same time that the other had had naught and had been able to accomplish naught. My Lord of Reuttpueffel, noting that her account corresponded with what Doctor Faustus had reported, did accept her back again. The other good fellow, who finally recovered his potency, rode hastily away, not wishing to be seen again because of what had happened to him. Later, he lost his life in a war. The husband, however, is still jealous; and the good lady must hear from him, even though he did not witness it, how she did after all lie with another, who felt her and grasped her and, had he been able to cover her, would have done that, too.

Concerning the Testament:

What Doctor Faustus Bequeathed

His Servant Christoph Wagner

XXXIX

Now during this whole time, right into the twenty-fourth year of his pact, Doctor Faustus had been keeping a young apprentice, who studied there at the University in Wittemberg and who became acquainted with all the tricks, sorcery and arts of his master. The two were cut from the same piece of cloth. Wagner was a wicked, dissipated knave who had gone about begging in Wittemberg but had found no kindness with anyone until he had met Faustus, who took the stripling in as his famulus and even called him his son, letting him enjoy his ill-gotten gains. Neither troubled himself with the price of them.

When his twenty-four years were all but run out, Faustus called unto himself a notary together with several magisters who were his friends. In their presence he bequeathed his famulus his house and garden, which were located on the Ring-Wall in Scherr Alley, not far from the Iron Gate and indeed right beside the houses of Ganser and of Veitt Rottinger (since that time, it has been rebuilt, for it was so uncanny that none could dwell therein). He also left him 1,600 guilders lent out on usury, a farm worth 800 guilders, 600 guilders in ready money, a gold chain worth 300 crowns, some silver plate given him by a man named Kraffter, as well as such other things as he had taken away from various courts--those of the Pope and of the Turk, for example. All these items together were worth many hundred guilders. There was not really much household stuff on hand, for he had not lived much at home, but at inns and with students, in gluttony and drunkenness.

The Discourse Which Doctor Faustus Held

With His Son Concerning the Testament

XL

The testament being drawn up, Faustus summoned his famulus, explained to him how he had made that person beneficiary of his estate who had been a trusty servant throughout his life and had never revealed any of his secrets, and how he would, in addition, like to grant this person one further request, if he would but name it. Wagner asked for Faust's cunning, but this fine father reminded his pretty son (who should have been named Christ**less** Wagner) that he would, after all, inherit all his books, and that he must diligently guard them, not letting them become common knowledge, but taking his own profit from them by studying them well (this route to Hell).

As to my cunning (spake Faustus), thou canst win it if thou wilt but love my books, heed no man else, and follow in my footsteps. Hast thou none other request?--That thou be served by my spirit? This cannot be, for Mephostophiles oweth me no further debt, nor doth he bear affinity to any other man. But if thou art fain to have a spirit as servant I will help thee to another.

Three days later, Faustus again called his famulus unto him, asking whether he were still of a mind to possess a spirit, and, if so, in what form he would have him.

My Lord and Father, answered Wagner, in the form of an ape let him appear, for even in such a manner and form would I have him.

A spirit immediately came bounding into the parlor in the figure of an ape, and Doctor Faustus said:

Lo, now seest thou him, but he will not obey thee until I be dead. At that time my Mephostophiles will vanish forever, and thou shalt never see him more. Then, if thou wilt perform what is necessary--this being thine own decision--then canst thou summon thy spirit unto thee by calling upon Urian, for this is his name. In return, I do beg of thee not to publish my deeds, arts and adventures before the time of my death, but then to write all these matters down, organizing and transferring them into a *Historia* and compelling Urian to help thee by recalling unto thee whatever thou canst not remember, for men will expect these things of thee.

What Doctor Faustus Did

in the Final Month of His Pact

XLI

His days ran out like the sand in an hourglass, and when only one month remained of the twenty-four years which he had contracted of the Devil (as ye have read) Doctor Faustus became fainthearted, depressed, deeply melancholic, like unto an imprisoned murderer and highwayman over whose head the sentence hath been pronounced and who now in the dungeon awaiteth punishment and death. Filled with fear, he sobbed and held conversations with himself, accompanying such speeches with many gestures of his hands. He did moan and sigh and fall away from flesh. He kept himself close and could not abide to have the spirit about him.

Doctor Faustus His Lamentation,

that He Must Die at a Young

and a Lusty Age

XLII

Sorrow moved Doctor Faustus to set his grief in words, lest he forget it. Here followeth one such written complaint:

Alas, thou reckless, worthless heart! Thou hast seduced the flesh round about thee, and my fate is fire. The blessedness which once thou didst know is lost.

Alas, Reason and Free Will! What a heavy charge ye do level at these limbs, which may expect naught else than rape of their life!

Alas ye limbs, and thou yet whole body! It was ye who let Reason indict Soul, for I might have chosen succor for my soul by sacrificing thee, my body.

Alas, Love and Hate! Why abide ye both at once in my breast? Your company hath occasioned all mine anguish.

Alas, Mercy and Vengeance ! Ye have caused me to strive after glory and rewarded me with infamy.

Alas, Malice and Compassion! Was I created a man that I might suffer those torments which now I see before me?

Alas, alas, is there aught in the wide world that doth not conspire against this wretch?

Alas, of what help is this complaint?

Doctor Faustus Lamenteth Yet Further

XLIII

Alas, alas, wretched man, o thou poor accursed Faustus, now in the number of the damned! I must await the inestimable pains of a death far more miserable than any tortured creature hath yet endured.

Alas, alas, Reason, Willfulness, Recklessness, Free Will! O, what a cursed and inconstant life hast thou led! How unseeing, how careless wast thou! Now become thy parts, soul and body, unseeing and ever more unseen.

Alas, Worldly Pleasure! Into what wretchedness hast thou led me, darkening and blinding mine eyes!

Alas, my timid heart! Where were thine eyes?

And thou my poor soul! Where was thy knowledge?

All ye senses! Where were ye hid?

O, miserable travail! O sorrow and desperation forgotten of God!

Alas, grief over grief, and torment upon woe and affliction! Who will release me? Where am I to hide? Whither must I creep? Whither flee? Wherever I may be, there am I a prisoner.

The heart of Doctor Faustus was so troubled that he could speak no more.

Doctor Faustus His Hideous End

and *Spectaculum*

XLIV

His twenty-four years were run out. As he lay awake in the night, his spirit came unto him to deliver up his writ, or contract, thus giving him due notice that the Devil would fetch his body in the following night, and allowing him to make any necessary preparations for that event. This occasioned such a renewed moaning and sobbing into the night that the spirit returned, consoling him and saying:

My Fauste, be not so faint of heart. Thou dost indeed lose thy body, but thy time of judgement is yet far distant. Why surely thou must die--even shouldst thou live for many hundreds of years. The Jews and the Turks must also die expecting the same perdition as thou--even emperors die thus, if they be not Christian. After all, thou knowest not yet what it be that awaiteth thee. Take courage, and despair not so utterly. Dost not remember how the Devil did promise thee a body and soul all of steel, insensitive to the pain which the others will feel in Hell?

This and such like comfort and consolation he gave him, but it was false and not in accord with the Holy Scriptures. Doctor Faustus, having none other expectation than that he must absolve his debt and contract with his skin, did on this same day (in which the spirit had announced that the Devil was about to fetch him) betake himself unto the trusted friends with whom he had spent many an hour, the magisters, baccalaureates and other students, entreating them now to go out to the little village of Rimlich with him, about a half mile removed from the town of Wittemberg, there to take a repast with him. They would not turn him away, but went along and ate a morning meal with many costly courses both of meat and of drink, served by the host at an inn.

Doctor Faustus joined in their merriment, but he was not merry in his heart. Afterward, he entreated all his guests to do him the great kindness of remaining to eat supper with him, too, and to stay the night here as well, for he had something important to tell them. Again they agreed, and they took the evening meal with him also.

It was finished, and a last cup had been passed. Doctor Faustus paid the host, and addressed the students, saying that he wished to inform them of some things. They gave him their attention, and Doctor Faustus said unto them:

M y dear, trusted, and very gracious Lords: I have called you unto me for this good and sufficient cause. For many years now, ye have known what manner of man I be, the arts and the sorcery I have used. All these things come from none other than from the Devil. I fell into such devilish desires through none other cause than these: bad company, mine own worthless flesh and blood, my stiff-necked, godless will, and all the soaring, devilish thoughts I allowed in my head. I gave myself up unto the Devil and contracted with him for a term of twenty-four years, setting my body and soul in forfeit. Now are these twenty-four years run out. I have only this night left. An hourglass standeth before mine eyes, and I watch for it to finish.

I know that the Devil will have his due. As I have consigned my body and soul unto him with my blood in return for certain other costly considerations, I have no doubt that he will this night fetch me. This is why, dear and well-beloved, gracious Lords, I have summoned you here just before the end to take one last cup with me, not concealing from you the manner of my departure. I entreat you now, my dear gracious Brothers and Lords, to bring my cordial and brotherly greetings to my friends and to those who do honor my memory, to bear no ill will toward me but, if ever I have offended you, to forgive me in your hearts. As regardeth my *Historia* and what I have wrought in those twenty-four years, all these things have been written down for you.

Now let this my hideous end be an example unto you so long as ye may live, and a remembrance to love God and to entreat Him to protect you from the guile and the deceit of the Devil, praying that the Dear Lord will not lead you into temptation. Cling ye unto Him, falling not away from Him as I damned godless mortal have done, despising and denying Baptism (Christ's own Sacrament), God, all the Heavenly Host and mankind--such a sweet God, who desireth not that one shall be lost. Shun bad company, which would lead you astray as it hath me, go earnestly and often to church, war and strive constantly against the Devil with a steadfast faith in Christ and always walking a godly path.

Finally, my last request is that ye go to bed and let nothing trouble you, but sleep on and take your rest even if a crashing and tumult be heard in this house. Be not afraid. No injury shall befall you. Arise not out of your beds. Should ye find my corpse, convey it unto the earth, for I die both as a bad and as a good Christian. Contrition is in my heart, and my mind doth constantly beg for Grace and for the salvation of my soul. O I know that the Devil will have this body--and welcome he is to it, would he but leave my soul in peace. Now I entreat you: betake yourselves to bed. A good night to you--unto me, an evil, wretched and a frightful one.

Faustus needed great resolve and courage to make this confession and to tell his tale without weakening, and becoming fearful and faint. As for the students, they were cast into great wonderment that a man could be so reckless as thus to imperil body and soul for no more profit than knavery, knowledge and sorcery. But, as they loved him well, they sought to console him thus: Alas dear Fauste, how have ye imperiled yourself! Why remained ye so long silent, revealing none of these things to us? Why, we should have brought learned

Theologi who would have torn you out of the Devil's nets and saved you. But now it is too late and surely injurious to body and soul.

Doctor Faustus answered, saying: Such was not permitted me. Often was I amind to seek counsel and succor of godfearing men. Indeed, once an Old Man did charge me to follow his teachings, leave my sorcery and be converted. Then came the Devil, ready to put an end to me (even as he will this night do), saying that in the moment of my conversion--nay, even in the instant of such an intent on my part--all would be over with me.

Upon hearing these words, and understanding that the Devil would surely dispatch Faustus this night, the students urged him to call upon God, begging Him for forgiveness for Jesus Christ's sake, saying:

O God, be merciful unto me poor sinner, and enter not into judgement with me, for I cannot stand before Thee. Although I must forfeit my body unto the Devil, wilt Thou preserve my soul!

Faustus agreed to do this. He tried to pray, but he could not. As it was with Cain, who said his sins were greater than could be forgiven him, so was it with Faustus also, who was convinced that in making his written contract with the Devil he had gone too far. But the students and good lords prayed and wept for Faustus. They embraced one another and, leaving Faustus in his chambers, retired to bed, where none could rightly sleep, for they lay there awake, awaiting the end.

And it came to pass between twelve and one O' clock in the night that a great blast of wind stormed against the house, blustering on all sides as if the inn and indeed the entire neighborhood would be torn down. The students fell into a great fear, got out of their beds and came together to comfort one another, but they did not stir out of their chamber. The innkeeper went running out of the house, however, and he found that there was no disturbance at all in any other place than his own. The students were lodged in a chamber close by the rooms of Doctor Faustus, and over the raging of the wind they heard a hideous music, as if snakes, adders and other serpents were in the house. Doctor Faustus' door creaked open. There then arose a crying out of Murther! and Help! but the voice was weak and hollow, soon dying out entirely.

When it was day the students, who had not slept this entire night, went into the chamber where Doctor Faustus had lain, but they found no Faustus there. The parlor was full of blood. Brain clave unto the walls where the Fiend had dashed him from one to the other. Here lay his eyes, here a few teeth. O it was a hideous *spectaculum*. Then began the students to bewail and beweep him, seeking him in many places. When they came out to the dung heap, here they found his corpse. It was monstrous to behold, for head and limbs were still twitching.

These students and magisters who were present at Faustus' death gained permission afterwards to bury him in the village. Subsequently, they retired to his domicile where they found the famulus Wagner already mourning his master. This little book, *Doctor Faustus His Historia*, was already all written out. Now as to what his famulus wrote, that will be a different, new book. On this same day the enchanted Helen and her son Justus Faustus were also gone.

So uncanny did it become in Faustus' house that none could dwell there. Doctor Faustus himself walked about at night, making revelations unto Wagner as regardeth many secret matters. Passers-by reported seeing his face peering out at the windows. Now this is the end of his quite veritable deeds, tale, *Historia* and sorcery. From it the students and clerks in particular should learn to fear God, to flee sorcery, conjuration of spirits, and other works of the Devil, not to invite the Devil into their houses, nor to yield unto him in any other way, as Doctor Faustus did, for we have before us here the frightful and horrible example of his pact and death to help us shun such acts and pray to God alone in all matters, love Him with all our heart and with all our soul and with all our strength, defying the Devil with all his following, that we may through Christ be eternally blessed. These things we ask in the name of Christ Jesus our only Lord and Savior. Amen. Amen.

www.ingramcontent.com/pod-product-compliance
Lightning Source LLC
Chambersburg PA
CBHW052346020726
47503CB00001B/124